AF352290

Economic Development in Latin America

Economic Development in Latin America

Essay in Honor of Werner Baer

Edited by

Hadi Salehi Esfahani, Giovanni Facchini,
and Geoffrey J.D. Hewings

First published 2010 by
PALGRAVE MACMILLAN

Palgrave Macmillan in the UK is an imprint of Macmillan Publishers Limited, registered in England, company number 785998, of Houndmills, Basingstoke, Hampshire RG21 6XS.

Palgrave Macmillan in the US is a division of St Martin's Press LLC, 175 Fifth Avenue, New York, NY 10010.

Palgrave Macmillan is the global academic imprint of the above companies and has companies and representatives throughout the world.

Palgrave® and Macmillan® are registered trademarks in the United States, the United Kingdom, Europe and other countries.

ISBN: 978–0–230–22381–3 hardback

This book is printed on paper suitable for recycling and made from fully managed and sustained forest sources. Logging, pulping and manufacturing processes are expected to conform to the environmental regulations of the country of origin.

A catalogue record for this book is available from the British Library.

A catalog record for this book is available from the Library of Congress.

10 9 8 7 6 5 4 3 2 1
19 18 17 16 15 14 13 12 11 10

Printed and bound in Great Britain by
CPI Antony Rowe, Chippenham and Eastbourne

Contents

Tables

Figures

Preface: A Tribute to Werner Baer

Larry Neal

This volume was assembled from contributions by colleagues who are colleagues, friends, collaborators, or former students of Professor Werner Baer, the *Jorge Paulo Lemann Professor of Economics* at the University of Illinois at Urbana-Champaign. Before presenting the contributions, a tribute to Werner Baer offered at the conference held in December 2006 by his long-time colleague Larry Neal is presented here.

It is both an honor and a privilege to be able to express in public the admiration and affection that I hold for Professor Werner Baer, my colleague for now 32 years here at Illinois.

His continued energy and productivity makes it hard for any of us to realize that this year marks his 75th birthday as well. Now it is my professional obligation as an economic historian to tell you that the year of his birth, 1931, was in general a very bad year for the world economy. Werner may be one of the few good things to have come out of it. It was an especially bad year in the country of his birth, Germany, where eventually it became very bad indeed to be identified as Jewish. This aspect of Werner's background may come as a surprise to many of you – I was not aware of it myself until a few years ago when I met a childhood friend of Werner's, Hugo Kaufmann, the Director of the EU Center at CUNY, at a conference of other Team Europe members and EU Center Directors. Hugo is Swiss Jewish and he told me that his father helped Werner's father, a medical doctor, get out of Nazi Germany with his family through Switzerland. I have tried to get more of this aspect of Werner's background out of him since, but have generally come up dry – it's not something he wishes to revisit, being at heart an optimistic soul always looking forward to the next project rather than dwelling on the past.

Safe eventually in New York City at the end of World War II, Werner did his undergraduate work in Economics at Queens College there, went on to get his master's and Ph.D. in Economics at Harvard. More or less by chance, he tells me, he decided to take an interest in Brazil just as an exotic example of a country then underdeveloped, but with vast natural resources. Brazil enchanted him and has remained the guiding focus of his professional life since. The extent of his commitment is no surprise to participants in this conference, but it always surprises his colleagues here at Illinois, even myself at times. Years ago, well before Werner's heart attack, when I was still playing pickup basketball with Lenny Mirman, Lenny and I were sitting on the sidelines of a gym at the IMPE Center resting between games.

Looking up, we saw Werner doing his noontime laps jogging around the indoor track that was on the balcony of the gym. We both waved at him and shouted, "Werner!" No response – he just kept doggedly jogging on. Second time around, we stood up and shouted more loudly; still no response. By the third time, we were sitting back down, so this time I just called up, "Brazil!" Werner stopped, looked around, shrugged, and then kept jogging. Of course he couldn't see us because we were both rolling on the floor with laughter.

Of course, Werner's enthusiasm for life in general is not confined to Brazil. The most vivid example of that for me came after he had recovered from his heart attack, thanks to quadruple bypass surgery. Werner was so pleased with his recovery that one time he told me, "Larry, you should get bypass surgery too, it's great!" Not being an enthusiast in general myself, I told Werner that I would wait until I had my heart attack.

Werner is best known to his colleagues, of course, for the number and quality of graduate students that he attracts to the University of Illinois, mainly from Brazil, but also from the rest of Latin America and indeed from Europe as well. A number of my own graduate students who have gone on to productive careers in Economic History, in fact, were first recruited to the University of Illinois by Werner, starting with Eugene White who encountered Werner at a seminar at Oxford University when Werner had first come to Illinois. After that, I made it a regular habit to pick off any of Werner's students who decided that there was too much competition in Latin American topics from his other students and were looking for a topic in another part of the world.

The reason Werner attracts so many students is because he really cares for them and their welfare while here in the Midwest, terra incognita to most foreigners (how many TV programs or movies are set in downstate Illinois? And how many foreigners find *The Blues Brothers* to be a great American film?). Werner also cares for their intellectual progress here as well as their professional progress when they have graduated. And their gratitude keeps coming back, most obviously to his colleagues in the form of each new generation of students who find it attractive to come to Illinois, and less obviously in the honorary degrees and national awards that he receives regularly in Brazil. I have tried to emulate Werner as best I can in my own specialty within Economics, but I still look to him as the role model for all of us in that regard.

If you wonder why Werner continues to give of himself so generously to his students and his colleagues, I think one explanation has to come from living up to the example of his father, who did manage to get his family out of war-torn Europe alive. I learned recently from Werner, when asking him about his relationship with Hugo Kaufman when they were both children in Switzerland during World War II, that his father in fact did not escape the Nazis because he continued to practice medicine. Eventually he was in a prison camp in the south of France. A serious epidemic of typhus broke out there, medical supplies were not available, and people were dying. Taking advantage of the resulting confusion, Werner's father escaped from the camp, but instead of fleeing to the French underground, he went to the local Gestapo office, explained the need for medical supplies, and returned with the necessary medicine to the camp, saving many lives. Perhaps Werner is still trying to top that! Regardless, we all hope that he continues his academic efforts for many more years, given the benefits he continues to give the rest of us.

The publication of this book would not have been possible without the financial support of the following units at the University of Illinois at Urbana-Champaign: College of Liberal Arts and Sciences, Department of Economics, Illinois Center for International Business Education and Research (CIBER), Center for Latin American Studies, Center for Global Studies, and Department of History. Many colleagues and Ph.D. students at the Department of Economics and elsewhere at the University of Illinois contributed to the organization of the conference and provided good comments on the presentations. Among the students, special thanks should go Bin Lin, Emilie Teresa Bagby, Marcelo Aarestrup Arbex, Michael T. Dorsch, Odilon Roberto Vilar D. Camara, and Seryoung Park who served on the local organizing committee. Finally, as expected, the endeavor benefited from the enthusiastic encouragement of Werner's numerous students around world.

Contributors

Edmund Amann is Reader in Development Economics at the University of Manchester, Adjunct Associate Research Professor at the Regional Economics Applications Laboratory (REAL) at the University of Illinois, Urbana-Champaign, and Professorial Lecturer at the Paul H. Nitze School for Advanced International Studies, Johns Hopkins University. His research interests center on the economies of Latin America. He is especially interested in how issues of technological change, income distribution, and growth impact the region. Dr. Amann's recent publications include Regulating Development: Evidence from Africa and Latin America (ed.), Edward Elgar (2007).

Márcio Guerra Amorim is the manager of *The Observatory of Occupational Trends and Forecasting*, a unit at the National Office of *SENAI* (*Brazil's National Service for Industrial Apprenticeship*). His main research is directed to the forecast of changes in labor markets and productive structure, with results at the industrial and occupational levels. These results are used to measure the changes and trends in the labor market and their impacts on the vocational educational training.

Carlos R. Azzoni is currently Dean of the School of Economics, Administration, and Accounting of the University of São Paulo. He is full Professor of Economics at USP (from 1973), with an M.S. and a Ph.D. from that university. He was Visiting Professor at Cornell University (1979), Ohio State University (1984/85), and the University of Illinois (2002).

His area of research is economic inequality in general, with a focus on regional inequality. He has worked for seven years at the State of Sao Paulo Secretariat of Planning, chairing the regional planning division of that agency.

He has published nine books (in Portuguese) and over 70 scientific papers, both in Brazilian and international refereed academic journals. He has participated in more than 120 international conferences in Economics.

He has worked as consultant for many Brazilian organizations, in both the private and public sectors. He has also worked as consultant for the World Bank, the Interamerican Development Bank and OECD – the Organization for Economic Cooperation and Development.

Ricardo Bebczuk is Professor of Economics and Finance and Senior Researcher at CEDLAS, Universidad Nacional de La Plata, Argentina. He holds a Ph.D. in Economics from the University of Illinois at Urbana-Champaign. He specializes in financial markets and corporate finance. His work on financial development, access to credit, and corporate finance and governance has been published in international journals, and he has received three Ibero-American research awards. He is the author of three books, among them *Asymmetric Information in Financial Markets: Introduction and Applications*, Cambridge University Press, is used as a reference in undergraduate and graduate courses in more than 20 countries. In addition, he has written chapters for other five books published in the United States. He has taught in Argentina at the universities of La Plata, San Andres, CEMA, and Di Tella and gives graduate courses and seminars in several foreign institutions. He regularly provides consulting and research services for WB, IDB, IMF, UN, ECLAC, and OECD. At present he is also a senior Visiting Researcher for the Central Bank of Argentina.

Carlos Alberto Primo Braga is currently Director of the Economic Policy and Debt Department, at the World Bank. He has written extensively on topics such as the multilateral trade system, regional trade agreements, intellectual property rights, information technology and development, and services liberalization. From 2003 to 2006, he was the Senior Adviser of the World Bank's International Trade Department. Based in Geneva, he was responsible for covering international trade issues vis-à-vis European-based institutions, including the WTO. He is a graduate ofthe Instituto Tecnológico de Aeronáutica (Mechanical Engineering) and the University of São Paulo (MA, Economics), Brazil, and holds a Ph.D. in Economics from the University of Illinois at Urbana-Champaign.

Mauricio Bugarin received a B.A. and a M.A. in Mathematics at the University of Brasilia and an M.S. and a Ph.D. in Economics at the University of Illinois at Urbana/Champaign. He was co-organizer of the First Brazilian Workshop of the Game Theory Society and co-founder of the Masters Program in Public Policy at the University of Brasilia. He is now Professor of Economics at Ibmec São Paulo where he is also the Director of Undergraduate Studies in Economics. Prof. Bugarin's main interests are the interaction between economics and politics and he publishes on such topics as voting behavior, electoral campaign financing, fiscal federalism and political business cycles, monetary policy, and health economics. His research has been awarded several prizes, including six Brazilian Treasury Secretariat Research Prizes as well as the 2002 Haralambos Simeonidis Prize for the best paper by a Brazilian author. Additional information can be found in his homepage at: http://bugarin.ibmecsp.edu.br/.

Mirta N.S. Bugarin is currently serving as a senior researcher at FUCAPE Business School, Espíritu Santo, Brazil, after retiring from the University of Brasília, D.F., Brazil, in 2006. She obtained her Ph.D. in Economics at the University of Illinois at Urbana-Champaign and her research interests include areas of economic growth and public policies.

Tiago Vanderlei de Vasconcelos Cavalcanti, who was born in Recife, Brazil, holds a Ph.D. in Economics from University of Illinois at Urbana-Champaign. He is a Lecturer in Economics at the University of Cambridge and is a fellow of Churchill College, Cambridge. He taught at Universidade Nova de Lisboa from 2001 to 2003, Universidade Federal de Pernambuco from 2003 to 2007, and was a Visiting Assistant Professor at Purdue University from 2005 to 2006. He was invited for academic visits at University of Illinois, Banco de Portugal, and Banco Central de la Republica Argentina. Dr. Tiago Cavalcanti's teaching and research focus on macroeconomics, economic development, and inequality. His research has appeared in scientific journals such as *Review of Economics and Statistics, Journal of Monetary Economics, Economic Theory, European Economic Review, Journal of Mathematical Economics, Macroeconomic Dynamics*, and *Economics Letters*.

Donald V. Coes is Professor of Economics at the University of New Mexico. Since receiving his Ph.D. from Princeton University in 1978, much of his work has focused on Brazil. He has taught there as a Fulbright Visiting Professor and as a Visiting Researcher of Brazil's National Research Council (CNPq). From 1976 to 1990 he was a faculty member of the Department of Economics at the University of Illinois at Urbana-Champaign. At UNM he has been Professor of International Management and Associate Director of the Latin American and Iberian Institute.

Wendy Cunningham is the manager of the Bank's Child and Youth Development Unit at the World Bank. She is responsible for coordinating the Bank's efforts to provide evidence-based program and policy advice on a range of child and youth development issues in developing countries, with a particular focus on youth employment. Before joining her current Unit, she was a Senior Economist in the Human Development Department for Latin America and the Caribbean, where she led studies and projects in social protection, labor markets, and youth development. Wendy has a Ph.D. in Labor Economics from the University of Illinois and has published on labor markets, informal sector employment, gender, and youth development.

Hadi Salehi Esfahani is a Professor of Economics at the University of Illinois at Urbana-Champaign. In addition, he currently serves as the Editor of the *Quarterly Review of Economics and Finance*, the President of Middle East Economic Association, and the Director of the Global Studies Initiative at the University of Illinois. He has also worked for the World Bank as a Visiting Staff Economist and a Consultant. He has received his B.S. in engineering from Tehran University and a Ph.D. in Economics from the University of California at Berkeley. His theoretical and empirical research is in the field of the political economy of development. He has published numerous articles on the role of politics and governance in fiscal, trade, and regulatory policy formation. His articles have appeared in many journals including *The Economic Journal, Review of Economics and Statistics, Journal of Development Economics, International Economic Review, Oxford Economic Review, and World Development.*

Giovanni Facchini holds a Ph.D. from Stanford University and a Laurea in Economics from the University of Trento. He is a Professor of Economics at Erasmus University in Rotterdam and at the University of Milan, a Research Affiliate of the Center for Economic Policy Research (CEPR) in London, and of the CES-Ifo Institute in Munich, and the coordinator of the International Migration Program at the Centro Studi Luca d'Agliano in Turin. He is also a Faculty Affiliate of the Institute for Government and Public Affairs at the University of Illinois. Giovanni has been on the economics faculty at the University of Illinois and at the University of Essex, and has taught at Stanford, ECARES (Universite' Libre de Bruxelles, Belgium), Hong Kong University of Science and Technology, and the University of Sao Paolo (Brazil) among others. His research focuses on international trade and international factor mobility. His papers have been published extensively in journals like the *Journal of the European Economic Association*, the *Review of Economics and Statistics*, the *Journal of International Economics*, the *Journal of Public Economics*, the *Canadian Journal of Economics*, and *Economic Policy.*

Arturo José Galindo is Senior Research Economist in the Research Department of the Inter-American Development Bank. He holds an M.A. and a Ph.D. in Economics from the University of Illinois at Urbana Champaign, and a B.A. and M.S. in Economics from Universidad de los Andes in Bogotá Colombia. Previously, he was the Chief Economic Advisor of the Banking Association of Colombia, the Colombian Government Advisor on Coffee Affairs, advisor to the Ministry of Finance, and worked at the Central Bank of Colombia. He has been a consultant to the World Bank and Professor at Universidad de los Andes and Universidad del Rosario in Colombia. His works has been published extensively in Journals like the *Journal of International Economics*, the *Journal of Development Economics*, *Emerging Markets Review, Economic Development and Cultural Change*, and the *Quarterly Review of Economics and Statistics*, among others, in fields including banking, capital markets, and international finance. He has edited books on similar topics.

Andrés Gallo is Associate Professor and Richard deRaismes Kip fellow at the Department of Economics and Geography and Co-Director of the Flagship program in International Business at the Coggin College of Business, University of North Florida. Andrés received his Ph.D. in Economics at the University of Illinois at Urbana-Champaign. He received his Licentiate degree in Economics from the Universidad Nacional de La Plata, La Plata, Argentina. He also received a graduate Diploma in Economics from the Instituto Torcuato Di Tella, Buenos Aires, Argentina, and a Master of Science from the University of Illinois at Urbana-Champaign. His research interests include institutions and economic development, property rights, political economy, technology, and international economics.

Patricio Aroca Gonzalez is Professor and Head of IDEAR at the Universidad Católica del Norte, Antofagasta, Chile, and Affiliated Research Professor at REAL, University of Illinois. He earned a B.S. in Business (1983) from the Austral University (Chile), an M.A. in Economics (1987) from the University of Chile, an M.S. in Policy Economics (1994), and a Ph.D. in Economics (1995) from the University of Illinois at Urbana-Champaign. He specializes in econometrics, natural resources, and regional economics, and more specifically works with Input-Output analysis, Spatial Econometrics, Regional Growth, and Labor Interregional Migration. From 1997 to 2000 was Dean of the Faculty of Economics and Business of the Universidad Católica del Norte and a consultant for the World Bank, IADB, UNCTAD, the Chilean Government, and CELADE-ECLAC. paroca@ucn.cl

Joaquim J.M. Guilhoto is Professor of Economics at the University of São Paulo (USP), and Adjunct Professor in the Regional Economics Applications Laboratory (REAL) at the University of Illinois. For more than 20 years he has been working as a researcher and professor, specializing in structural analysis of national and regional economies; lately he has been working with environmental models and economic modeling for projecting future economic trends. His main sphere of work concerns input-output models and applied general equilibrium models. He has more than 200 works published nationally and internationally in his field of research, including books, papers, and chapters in books. Professor Guilhoto has supervised, submitted more than 25 Masters and Ph.D. dissertations.

Juliana Guimarães, who was born in Recife, Brazil, holds a Ph.D. in Economics from University of Illinois at Urbana-Champaign. She is a Teaching Associate in Economics at the University of Cambridge and is a fellow of Newnham College, Cambridge. She was a Pos-Doc at Universidade Nova de Lisboa from 2001 to 2003 and is currently on leave from the Universidade Federal de Pernambuco. Dr. Juliana Guimarães's teaching and research interests focus on Labor Economics, Economics of Education, and Applied Econometrics. Her research has appeared or is forthcoming in scientific journals such as *Empirical Economics* and the *Brazilian Review of Econometrics*.

Eduardo Haddad holds a B.A. in Economics from the Federal University of Minas Gerais, Brazil (1993). In January 1995 he received an M.A. in Economics from the University of Illinois at Urbana-Champaign; he defended his Ph.D. dissertation, at the same institution, in December 1997. In 1998, he was engaged in post-doctoral research at the University of Oxford Centre for Brazilian Studies, in the UK. In January 1999,

Prof. Haddad joined the faculty at the University of Sao Paulo, Brazil. He is currently full Professor at the Department of Economics at that university, where he teaches courses on Regional and Urban Economics and General Equilibrium Modeling. He is the Director of Research of the Institute of Economic Research Foundation – FIPE – and also holds a position as Adjunct Associate Professor at the Regional Economics Applications Laboratory – REAL – at the University of Illinois at Urbana-Champaign. Prof. Haddad is the author of the book *Regional Inequality and Structural Changes: Lessons from the Brazilian Experience* (Ashgate, 1999), and has published on regional and interregional input-output analysis, general equilibrium modeling, and various aspects of regional economic development in developing countries, especially in Brazil, in both national and international journals; he has also contributed chapters to international books in the fields of regional science and economic development. Prof. Haddad has acted as a consultant for the World Bank, the Inter-American Development Bank, United Nations – UNDP – the Joint Africa Institute, and many other public and private organizations, both national and international. Since October 2006, he has acted as the elected President of the Brazilian Regional Science Association. He has also served as President of the Regional Science of Americas since November 2008.

Geoffrey J.D. Hewings is Director of the Regional Economics Applications Laboratory at the University of Illinois. He has overseen the development of regional and interregional models in Chile, Colombia, and Brazil and continues to work on a diverse set of applications ranging from trade liberalization to convergence and transportation infrastructure.

Silvio Massaru Ichihara is head of the planning department of the Sao Paulo State Secretariat of Transportation. Currently, his research provides elements for government decisions, emphasizing the analysis of project finance and the impacts of investments in regions, industries, and logistic chains. He specializes in structural analysis of regional economies, engineering of transportation, and quantitative geography tools. In 2008, his doctoral thesis was defended combining models of input-output with transport systems and GIS.

Joseph L. Love is interested in the history of economic ideas, policy, and performance in Brazil and in Latin America as a whole. He now directs the Lemann Institute of Brazilian Studies at the University of Illinois, where he was formerly director of the Center for Latin American and Caribbean Studies. He is the author of *Rio Grande do Sul and Brazilian Regionalism, Sao Paulo in the Brazilian Federation*, and *Crafting the Third World: Theorizing Underdevelopment in Romania and Brazil* (all with Stanford University Press). In addition, he has authored some 70 scholarly articles and essays and has co-edited several books, including *Brazil under Lula* (2009), with Werner Baer.

William F. Maloney is lead economist in the World Bank's Development Economics Research Group. He has published on issues related to international trade and finance, developing country labor markets, and innovation. Before joining the Bank permanently, Mr. Maloney was Assistant Professor of International and Development Economics at the University of Illinois, Urbana-Champaign (1990–1997). He also consulted for the World Bank on Mexico (1994–1995) and Nigeria (1986) and the Harvard Kennedy School of Government (1982). Mr. Maloney received a B.A. degree from Harvard University (1981), where he studied economics and political science. He then studied at the University of the Andes in Bogota, Colombia (1982–1983) before attending the University of California Berkeley for his Ph.D. in Economics (1990).

Bernardo Mueller is Associate Professor of Economics at the University of Brasília. He graduated from the University of Illinois in 1995. His research has focused on property rights to land and its effect on investment and rural conflict in Brazil. In addition, he has done research on executive-legislative relations and political institutions in general. His research has appeared in numerous journals including *Journal of Law, Economics and Organization, Journal of Economic and Environmental Management, Environment and Development Economics, Land Economics, Comparative Political Studies, Journal of Legislative Studies and Comparative, Labor Law & Policy Journal*. Since 1999 he has been Associate Editor at Environment and Development Economics. Current projects include analyzing the low incidence of rental contracts in Latin America, political institutions at state level in Brazil, and the political role of public prosecutors in Brazil.

Charles Mueller has a Ph.D. (1974) and Masters (1971) from Vanderbilt University and is currently Emeritus Professor at the Department of Economics at the University of Brasília, where he is also Associate Researcher. From 1988 to 1989 he was President of IBGE the Brazilian Census Bureau. He specializes in Agricultural Economics and Environmental Economics having authored one of the first textbooks on environmental economics in Brazil. Much of his recent work focuses on the expansion of the agricultural frontier in Brazil and its impact on the environment.

Larry Neal is Professor Emeritus of Economics at the University of Illinois at Urbana-Champaign and a Research Associate of the NBER. He was the Founding Director of the European Union Center at Illinois. Currently, he is Visiting Professor at the London School of Economics. He is past president of the Economic History Association and the Business History Conference. From 1981 through 1998, he was editor of *Explorations in Economic History*. He is author of *The Rise of Financial Capitalism: International Capital Markets in the Age of Reason*, Cambridge University Press, 1990, *The Economics of the European Union and the Economies of Europe,* Oxford University Press, 1998, co-author (with Rondo Cameron) of *A Concise Economic History of the World*, 4th ed., Oxford University Press, 2002, *The European Union and the European Economies*, Cambridge University Press, 2008, and co-editor (with Jeremy Atack) of *The Origins and Development of Financial Markets and Institutions*, Cambridge University Press, 2009, as well as numerous articles in American and European economic and financial history. He was a Guggenheim Fellow and a Fulbright Research Scholar during 1996–1997 and an Alexander von Humboldt Fellow in 1982. His current research deals with development of microstructure in securities markets and risk management in the first emerging markets in modern Europe.

José Ricardo Nogueira holds a Ph.D. in Economics from University College London and is currently on the faculty of the department of economics, Universidade Federal de Pernambuco, Brazil, where he heads the Public Sector Economics Research Group. His main area of research interest is the development and application of tax-benefit microsimulation models.

Veridiana de Andrade Nogueira holds a B.S. in Economics from the University of São Paulo. She finished her undergraduate program in 2003. Her Graduation Thesis title is "The calculus of consent: an alternative to the Theory of Welfare". In 2004, she was admitted to the graduate program in Economics of the University of São Paulo. Since 2007 she works in the private financial sector in São Paulo.

Ugo Panizza is the Chief of the Debt and Finance Analysis Unit in the Division on Globalization and Development Strategies of UNCTAD. He is also a Lecturer at the Graduate Institute of International and Development Studies of the University of Geneva, where he teaches econometrics and development economics. Prior to joining UNCTAD, Ugo was a Senior Economist in the Research Department of the Inter-American Development Bank (1998–2006). He also worked in the Africa Region of the World Bank and was an Assistant Professor in the Department of Economics of the University of Torino and the Department of Economics of the American University of Beirut. Ugo has published more than 50 papers in professional journals and edited volumes and two books on the Latin American debt and bond markets. His research interests include international finance, sovereign debt, banking, political economy, and public sector labor markets. Ugo holds an undergraduate degree from the University of Torino and a Ph.D. in Economics from the Johns Hopkins University (Baltimore). Ugo's papers and publications can be downloaded at http://upanizza.googlepages.com/

Henrique Pires completed his M.A. in Economics at the University of Brasilia in 2000. He worked for several years at the Brazilian National Treasury Secretariat, where he contributed to the Brazilian States' debt renegotiation process, which led to the Brazilian Fiscal Responsibility Law. Pires was a

Ph.D. student at the University of Brasilia at the time of his premature death in December 2004.

Jaime Reis is a senior research fellow at the Instituto de Ciências Sociais of the University of Lisbon. He holds a D. Phil in History from the University of Oxford and has taught at the Universities of Vanderbilt, Leicester, Glasgow, Nova de Lisboa, and the European University Institute. He is a former president of the European Historical Economics Society and is currently a co-editor of the *European Review of Economic History*. He is a member of the Lisbon Academy of Sciences. He has published extensively on the history of money and banking, labor markets, human capital, and agriculture in Europe and Latin America.

Larry Samuelson obtained all three of his degrees from Illinois, completing his PhD in 1978. He moved to Yale University in 2007 after serving on the faculties of Florida, Syracuse, Penn State, and Wisconsin. He has broad theoretical interests, currently centered on game theory. In addition to his many publications in the leading journals in economics, he has published two important books, *Evolutionary Games and Equilibrium Selection*, (MIT Press, 1997) and with George J. Mailath *Repeated Games and Reputations: Long-Run Relationships* (Oxford University Press, 2006). In 1994, he was elected as a Fellow of the Econometric Society.

André Portela de Souza holds a B.S. in Economics from the Federal University of Bahia, an M.S. in Economics from the University of São Paulo, and a Ph.D. from Cornell University. He was Visiting Professor at Vanderbilt and Cornell Universities. After teaching at the Department of Economics of the University of São Paulo, he moved to the São Paulo School of Economics, Fundação Getúlio Vargas. His research interests include issues related to labor market, social security, inequality, poverty, education, infant labor, and public policy evaluation.

Paul Streeten is a Professor Emeritus at Boston University. He has been a distinguished academic, working on Development Economics since the 1950s. He has been an editor of the journal *World Development* since its foundation in 1972. In the 1960s he worked at the new Ministry of Overseas Development in the UK and acted as the Director of the Institute of Development Studies (IDS) before he became Warden of Queen Elizabeth House, Oxford. During the periods 1976–1980 and 1984–1985, he worked at the World Bank and helped to formulate the basic needs approach to development. Since 1990, he has been involved with both the UNDP's Human Development Report and UNESCO's World Culture Reports.

1
Introduction

Hadi Salehi Esfahani, Giovanni Facchini,
and Geoffrey J.D. Hewings

The economies of Latin America have presented fascinating challenges for development economists. At times, these economies appeared to be textbook case studies of successful development experiences; at other times, they almost defied interpretation. In this volume, a sample of some of these challenges is presented; the contributions range from broad concerns with development to more familiar themes of the role of agriculture and income inequality, as well as to more recent concerns with investment in human capital, regional problems (within countries), and the important role that external institutions have played and continued to play in the continent. While some of the analyses examine all of Latin America, most are focused on one country and in particular on Brazil. Werner Baer is one of the world's leading authorities on the economy of the Latin American giant, and thus it should not be surprising that many of the contributions in this volume reflect this particular interest.

The role of institutions

In the first chapter of this volume, Streeten explores the philosophical considerations that arise from the international interdependence associated with increased trade liberalization. He suggests that international cooperation is desirable and that the prevention of international wars is a public good. After discussing several options and alternatives, he raises the issue of the creation of a genuine transnational secretariat whose loyalty would be to only the global community, and which would be trusted by both donors and recipients. He notes that there is a need, stemming from the fact that the staff of the present multilateral agencies do not quite achieve this, partly because the system of country quotas in recruiting emphasizes national origin rather than merit, partly because the organizations are intergovernmental institutions, and partly because the recruitment, training, location, etc. of their staff to some extent conflict with the ethos of a staff serving only the global community.

Love takes a historical perspective on the role of institutions and in particular on how UNCTAD affected the development of the post World War II trading system. He highlights the role of Prebisch, and by extension, the Latin American governments who backed his initiatives in the 1960s in the mobilization of third world governments to take common action on commodity and trade issues of mutual concern. This has been a common theme at recent WTO meetings and Love's interpretive commentary traces the degree to which these concerns were identified and common bonds across countries realized.

Braga addresses the effects of a policy that has long been associated with Latin American economies, namely import substitutions industrialization. He reviews the history and expectations associated with the introduction of this policy, with a particular focus on Brazil. In the latter part of his chapter, he explores the role of trade in general, and its liberalization in particular, on income distribution and poverty. While Braga agrees that trade liberalization can be a force for poverty reduction, the outcomes are very much dependent upon factors such as the initial conditions of the country undergoing reform, the nature of the reform, who the poor are, and how they sustain themselves.

International organizations, and in particular the IMF, take center stage also in Gallo's contribution. His is a tale of two countries, Argentina and Brazil. After the devaluation of 1999 Brazil pursued an economic policy closely monitored and supported by the IMF, while Argentina, after the crisis of 2001–2002 pursued a more independent policy that, in many cases, opposed the IMF's recommendations. This chapter compares the performance of the two countries and analyzes the benefits of pursuing, or not, an IMF recipe to get out of a balance of payments crisis. What is revealed is that following the IMF recipe is not a guarantee for either success or failure.

Aroca Gonzalez et al. focus instead on the working of institutions within countries, and in particular they examine the role of the informal sector in the labor markets of developing economies, focusing on the experiences in Brazil and Mexico. The results they find are consistent with workers viewing informal self-employment as a desirable sector, but one that, in the presence of binding credit constraints, requires the accumulation of resources over time to enter. The policy issue is whether entry into the informal self-employment sector is voluntary and whether it is seen as an intermediate step in view of possible entry into the formal sector.

Reis provides a historical perspective on the development of what he refers to as the Atlantic Periphery, examining the role of institutions, especially those created by the Portuguese in the latter part of the nineteenth century and the earlier twentieth. The analysis is based on the behavior of economic agents in small-scale mortgage credit markets, with data derived from six counties in provincial Portugal, between the 1870s and the 1910s.

Based on nearly 1800 mortgage contracts, three tests were devised to determine whether lenders found that judicial institutions were good at enforcing contracts and property rights. The conclusions from this analysis can arguably be extended to the overall performance of the judiciary as a whole in Portugal, and the method seems robust enough that it can serve for comparative, international purposes as well.

Bebczuk et al. contribute to the debate on the role of exchange rate manipulation by offering new empirical macro-level evidence on the impact of real exchange rate devaluations on growth for a large sample of countries during the 1976–2003 period, using newly constructed measures of dollarization and various interaction effects. Their study confirms that investment is the main channel through which the macroeconomic adjustment is achieved following a real exchange rate devaluation. Microeconomic research has shown that firms with dollarized liabilities adjust capital expenditure negatively when faced with devaluations while other firms respond positively. This chapter shows that at the macro level, the adjustment also comes through investment rather than consumption.

Income distribution and economic development

If the role of institutions in Latin America has been the subject of much research, the effects of development on income distribution have been studied almost as frequently. Coes examines the recent evolution of income distribution in Brazil; however, he explores the use of stochastic dominance to compare alternative income distributions. He also raises the interesting question of whether consumption inequality might be a better measure than income inequality, especially because data on consumption are often collected in more detail and more regularly. Agriculture and agricultural policy have occupied a great deal of the policy space in developing economies and continue to do so at meetings of the WTO.

Mueller and Mueller examine the role of agriculture and land reform in Brazil over a period of more than four decades. They begin their analysis considering an era of difficulty for agriculture – the 1950s and 1960s – and come to consider the modern and dynamic sector of the Brazilian economy that agriculture has become today. They note, though, that it has only been in the relatively recent past that land reform has taken place. Interestingly, they point out that land reform was promoted not as a major tool for the expansion of agricultural production or to achieve greater productivity, but as a tool to redistribute assets among different social groups.

Mirta Bugarin develops instead a recursive general equilibrium model to analyze the effects of heterogeneity in educational attainments in explaining income inequality. The model is calibrated to the Brazilian economy and is used to suggest policy interventions that can contribute to reducing, in the long run, the observed levels of inequality.

Regional aspects of economic development

The analysis of regional inequality in Brazil has been the subject of much recent research. The role of structural change and its impact on employment is analyzed in the chapter by Guilhoto et al. Comparing employment generation per R$1 million, they found that employment in agriculture declined faster than in other sectors. Indeed, by 2002 the number of jobs was only two-thirds of that in 1996. In contrast, the footwear industry recorded an increase of 12 jobs for every R$1 million of expanded production. All told, 30 of the 42 sectors identified showed decreased values of direct employment between 1996 and 2002 while only five sectors had this value increased by more than two jobs per R$1 million. Clearly, labor productivity increases were the dominant characteristic of structural changes over this period.

Complementing this analysis of structural change, Haddad examines the role of trade liberalization and regional economic development where regions are taken to be subnational spatial units, in this case within Brazil. The issue is timely given the current propositions that a region's competitive position is closely aligned with its ability to compete in external markets. Interestingly, the analysis of the Brazilian experience reveals that this is not uniform across the country's regions (states). Market forces seems to favor the center and south of Brazil in terms of their response to trade liberalization – a problem further exacerbated by the concentration and asymmetries in interstate trade.

Guilhoto et al. explored employment changes in Brazil and noted the downward pressure on employment generation presented by technological change. In a similar fashion Souza et al. examine the role of labor mobility in assessing the degree to which markets are able to move to equilibrium across the geographic spaces of countries as large as Brazil. This discussion returns to the issue of regional inequality and whether this may result from differences in mobile, nongeographic characteristics, such as education, family size, etc. or if, even after controlling for these variables, a "regional" residual would still be present. The decomposition of income differences between urban and rural areas indicates that education variables are the most important factor, followed by demographic characteristics, but that geographic differences also play a role.

New challenges

Looking ahead, what are the new challenges facing the region in an era of globalization? Amman begins the discussion with an evaluation of neoliberal policies posing the question about the implications of the current turn to the left in many countries in Latin America. Drawing on the experiences of Brazil, Argentina, Venezuela, and Bolivia, Amman attempts to explore the degree to which neoliberal policies have been abandoned in favor of alternatives. As he notes, if there has been a change, it is still work in progress, characterized by an uncertain abandonment of neoliberal policies in favor of a more pragmatic approach in which fiscal constraints are employed and markets are encouraged to work, but with an emphasis on those parts of society that were formerly marginalized by "pure" market policies.

Bugarin et al. address one aspect of macroeconomic policy, deficit reduction, within a fiscal federalism framework, essentially amplifying Amman's comment about the way some policy levers associated with neoliberalism are being tweaked to address more traditional development concerns with equity. The tension that they explore is how decentralization can be managed in such a way that macroeconomic policy is not compromised – especially policy related to government spending. They show that the usual revenue-sharing rules between federal and local levels of government are powerful instruments that can be used by the central authority in order to induce the local decisionmakers to reduce their deficit levels. The sharing rules that implement such a responsible fiscal policy at the state level were called deficit targeting rules, because of their resemblance to the traditional inflation targeting rules in the monetary policy literature. However, the real challenge here is negotiating these targets with subnational governments rather than imposing them, so the latter have an incentive to cooperate.

Cavalcanti et al. focus instead on human capital accumulation, and compare the well-being of American and Brazilian students. Happiness studies have become increasingly popular, as many analysts find fault with the restrictive view of utility as being entirely based on monetary measurements. The results reveal that a higher fraction (about two times higher) of students at Purdue University in the United States than at the Federal University of Pernambuco report themselves to be very happy when one controls for variables such as age, gender, family income, and working status. Women report themselves to be happier than men at Purdue, but men tend to be somewhat happier than women at UFPE. They also show that family wealth does seem to buy extra happiness in Brazil, but not in the United States.

A retrospective on Werner Baer

The final two chapters provide, in the case of Samuelson, the perspective of a former student who, while influenced by Werner Baer, managed not to become a development economist! Azzoni traces Werner Baer's published contributions to enhancing the understanding of Brazil – both within the country and outside.

The contributions provide a diversity of perspectives and issues that reflect well the economies about which the chapters are written. It is clear that the challenges facing Latin America, and Brazil in particular, have been daunting; however, it is also becoming evident that a new generation of scholars – while adopting the paradigms and practices of modern economics – has also been able to bring a more critical perspective to the analysis of Latin American economies. The pace of change is likely to quicken as greater data availability, complemented by even more imaginative forms of analysis, generates the bases for even more creative insights into a part of the world that never fails to offer so many opportunities for testing received theory and wisdom.

Part I
The Role of Institutions

2
International Cooperation and Global Justice

Paul Streeten

Introduction

Werner Baer's work has been concerned with real, practical problems, mainly in Latin America. He has made great contributions to their solutions. He has, on the whole, avoided the more speculative reaches of our subject. Yet, I think, or at least hope, that the following more philosophical than economic reflections will meet with his approval.

Many of the problems in the international relations of interdependence arise from a combination of the free rider problem, Olson's problem,[1] and the prisoners' dilemma. Indeed, the free rider problem or the contributor's dilemma is a special case of the prisoners' dilemma. The free rider problem in international relations exists because some of the solutions of international difficulties consist in the provision of public goods.[2] A public good is one from whose supply all those who value it can benefit, irrespective of whether they have contributed to its costs. The concept can readily be extended to cover common goals or common interests, the achievement of which benefits all, irrespective of whether they have contributed to achieving those goals or interests. The enjoyment of the good or service by one person does not detract from its enjoyment by others. In this sense, international cooperation toward a desirable aim and the prevention of international wars are public goods. So are markets and a working international monetary order with an international central bank as a lender of last resort and as a provider of liquidity. Scientific research that is freely promulgated is of this kind. A global income tax and the coordination of international fixed investment decisions fall under the same heading. But these public goods will be systematically undersupplied, because any one country will not find it worth its while taking the appropriate action, relying on others to do so, even though the benefits would exceed the costs were all to contribute. Moreover, each country, knowing that others will act this way, will have no incentive to be the only one that contributes to something that also benefits others. As a result, international cooperation, peace, research, international monetary stability, and world development will be undersupplied. No one contributes and everyone is worse off. The invisible hand that, according to Adam Smith, coordinates the independent decisions of a multitude of individuals can also be applied to the unintended coordination of the actions of nation states. But this invisible hand that is supposed to guide the self-interest of each agent, whether individual or country, to the common good, is nowhere to be seen.[3]

It is true that free rider problems are not ubiquitous. Individuals may be afraid of the sanctions to such behavior. Or they may avoid free riding because they believe that their contributions will make others contribute. Individuals sometimes do behave according to Kant's categorical imperative, in a manner that can be universalized. Otherwise, why should anybody applaud after a theater performance (assuming you don't get intrinsic pleasure from clapping) or go to the trouble of voting in a democratic election? But Kant's categorical imperative, or the notion that we should behave in the way we should want others to behave, applies less to the actions of nation states than to those of individuals. Just as hypocrisy is said to be the compliment that vice pays to virtue, so an excessive emphasis on the priority of narrow national self-interest announced by heads of states is the compliment that virtue pays to vice. Yet leadership and even hegemony, particularly by a strong superpower, and enlightened self-interest can contribute to Kantian behavior by nation-states.

The prisoners' dilemma arises because each country, in promoting its own national interest, contributes to a situation in which all countries are worse off. Just as public goods are undersupplied, public bads are oversupplied. No single actor has an adequate incentive to remove them. This applies to competitive protectionism, beggar-my-neighbor devaluations and deflations, the spread of inflation, investment wars, the arms race, global pollution of the air and the sea, overfishing and excessive exploitation of exhaustible resources to which no property rights are attached, and similar situations. The situation can be likened to that of a crowd in which each member, wishing to see better a passing parade, rises to his or her tiptoes, with the result that no one sees better but everyone is more uncomfortable. What is needed is either coordination and cooperation or supranational sanctions that force all countries to act in what will turn out to be their self-interest. Without such coordinated or enforced action, the outcome of nationally rational actions will be irrational damage and mutual impoverishment. For the damaging action is the best, whether other nations act similarly or not.

On the other hand, according to Coase's theorem, if, in the absence of transaction costs and in the presence of a legal framework and full information, one country inflicts damages on another which are greater than the benefits to the first country, the injured country can enter into a contract and compensate the injuring country for not inflicting the injury and be better off, or the injuring country can compensate the injured country for the damage and still be better off. Such international compensations or bribes are in fact not common, but they point in principle to the other extreme from that of the prisoners' dilemma. In such a world, Pareto optimal allocations would be achieved, for any deviation would give rise to joint gains out of which losers could be compensated for accepting them.

The difficulties of reaching Coase-type agreements and the dangers of ending in prisoners' dilemma situations are aggravated by four factors. First, although the United States of America is a hegemonous power, she is not prepared to carry a large part of the cost of the public goods and to exercise leadership to make others contribute. Second, the proliferation of independent states to a total of 192 makes reaching agreement more difficult than it was in an age when fewer governments could establish a system of mutual trust or enforcement (Olson's problem). It is true, however, that most states are quite small and that coordination by a few large ones is what matters. Third, the rapid pace of social and technical change makes it more difficult to evolve the stability on which trust can be built. It has been shown that repeated games of the prisoners' dilemma in similar situations tend to lead to cooperative solutions. Rapid change of the conditions on which cooperation is based prevents the basis for this to be formed.[4] Fourth, the absence of warlord governments and world courts makes it impossible to establish property rights, enforce contracts, and set sanctions against breaking agreements.

If all outcomes were noncooperative prisoners' dilemmas, no government would be possible. If all were according to Coase's theorem, no government would be needed (except for income redistribution).[5] The actual world is between the two extremes, but the relations between states are nearer the prisoners' dilemma end of the spectrum for the four reasons given.

Three systems

In order to set up a framework for a more constructive response to the call of the South for a better world order Kenneth Boulding's distinction between the exchange system, the threat system, and the integrative system is useful. The exchange system is based on the principle "I do something good for you if you do something good for me." It covers the area of mutual interests. The threat system is based on the principle "unless you do something good for me I shall do something horrid to you." In the integrative or love system, the principles of love and duty applied to ourselves and our family and friends are extended to other members of a wider community. We do good neither in the expectation of receiving good in return nor under the threat of harm, but from a sense of unity or solidarity or duty. This sense can derive from a common ideology or from a sense of community and obligation. These not only reduce the danger of too many free riders, so that each contributes voluntarily to the common good that also benefits him or her, but also lead to some sacrifices for the benefit of others: genuine altruism. The three systems correspond roughly to positive-sum games, in which all participants benefit, avoiding negative-sum games in which all would lose in the absence of coordinated action, and zero-sum games, in which one side has to make concessions for the benefit of others.

Systems can, of course, be mixed. What appears to be a genuine sacrifice in the short run may turn out to be beneficial to the party making the sacrifice in the long run, the removal of a benefit (such as access to markets) can constitute a threat, or the division of joint gains can give rise to conflicts. This, in practice, is a particularly important obstacle to the pursuit of positive-sum games. The gains come to be accepted and only the wrangles over their division remain.

It is important to distinguish between doing what is right and wishing to be seen to be doing right because this is in the nation's self-interest. The United States is dedicated to a value system, what Gunnar Myrdal called the American Creed. It adds cohesion to American society and strength to its foreign policy. But it is an entirely different thing to say, as a paragraph in the Kissinger Commission Report on Central America does, that it is in the American self-interest *to be seen* to be acting right. "To preserve the moral authority of the United States. To be perceived by others as a nation that does what is right because it is right is one of the country's principal assets."[6] There is all the difference in the world between doing what is right because it is right, and doing it because the United States must be seen to do what is right because it is right. It is in the U.S. national interest to be seen to act in a moral way. The first action is moral, disinterested; the second self-interested.

The distinction between the three systems is useful for a clear analysis but not for negotiations. There we have an interest in pretending that what is truly a benefit to us is a sacrifice, so that we may get concessions on other fronts.

The exchange system of mutual interests has been much promoted by think tanks and international organizations. Trade liberalization is the most frequently advocated policy. "Man was born free, yet everywhere he is in chains." Similarly, almost all economists recommend free(r) trade, yet everywhere there is protection.

It might be thought that, by and large, people, groups, and nations are very good at detecting and pursuing their self-interest and that not much exhortation is needed. But, as we have seen, there can be important divergences between reaching for and achieving what is in one's interest. In some cases the self-interested action leads to damage to oneself. We have already discussed the prisoners' dilemma and the free rider problem. The first leads to the infliction of mutual harm, the second to the undersupply of pubic goods and the oversupply of public bads. In addition, the national interest may be damaged for several reasons. There can be conflict between groups with different levels of power, articulateness, and influence, so that the more powerful influence policy more strongly, even if their gains are smaller than the losses of the less powerful, less articulate, and less influential. There may be conflict between dispersed larger and concentrated smaller gains, between uncertain larger and certain smaller gains, between larger future and smaller present gains, or between perceived larger but really smaller gains. The last may be one of the reasons why the general public and policymakers are not prepared to surrender national sovereignty, even though its surrender would lead to a more effective achievement of self-interested objectives than the adherence to full sovereignty, autonomy, and control, in the same way in which the acceptance of traffic regulations enlarges our freedom to drive accident-free, while restricting our freedom of choice. Finally, the gains to some may be much larger than the gains to others who, though gaining a little, resent this. In any case, the distribution of gains presents quite different problems at the international level from those at the national. For any national community a central government can tax and redistribute gains if this is deemed desirable. But in the absence of a world government, this cannot be done at the international level.

In all these cases selfish action may not lead to the achievement of the self-interest, and the achievement of self-interested objectives may involve some sacrifice in unconstrained and uncoordinated selfishness. Moreover, it would be only by a fluke of coincidence if the actions dictated by national self-interest were to coincide with our development objectives, whether these are accelerated growth, growth with equity, redistribution with growth, or basic needs. In particular, the poorest groups and the poorest countries will tend to be left out in a strategy based on national self-interest.

Removal of dangers of the threat system, the avoidance of negative-sum games, should have a high priority for this system can lead to mutual impoverishment and even destruction: disarmament, removal of the threat of protection, an end to beggar-my-neighbor deflation and devaluation or inflation, and of "voluntary" export restraints are clearly lines worth pursuing. They call for international coordination and institutional responses of the kind discussed above and below.

It may be thought that all agreements entered into voluntarily between states must amount to positive-sum games in which each side is better off, but this is not so. Some alliances may be formed with the specific purpose, or with the unintended result, of inflicting costs on outsiders. In this case alliances or pacts can lead to negative-sum games.

One of the reasons why agreements on avoiding negative-sum games, on reducing bads and creating antibads, are so difficult, is to be found in the logic of collective action, well analyzed by Olson.[7] The larger the group, the weaker is the incentive for any one member to contribute to the action that benefits all. We have now 192 countries in the world. As a result, public goods are not produced, or are underproduced, even though their value is greater than their costs to the group of countries as a whole. It is true that some smaller subset of countries, the Group of 7 or 8, may take responsibility for the rest, but may also act in a way that imposes costs on others.

We can build on areas of common national interests, emphasizing mutual benefits to be derived from, for example, resumption of orderly and equitable growth in the world economy, forswearing self-defeating protectionism, exploring ways of increasing the resources in globally scarce supply, etc. But while there is considerable scope for positive-sum games in exploring areas of mutual and common interests, and of avoiding self-defeating, mutually destructive policies of the prisoners' dilemma type, there is also a "higher" interest in a world order that both is, and is seen to be, equitable, that is acceptable and therefore accepted, and that reduces conflict and confrontation.

All societies need for their self-regulation and for social control a basis of moral principles. Individuals are ready to make sacrifices for the communities they live in. This forms the basis for the integrative system. Can this principle stop at the nation state? A belief in the harmony between self-interest and altruism is deep-seated in Anglo-Saxon thought and action. One is reminded of the eighteenth-century Bishop Joseph Butler: "When we sit down in a cool hour, we can neither justify to ourselves this or any other pursuit, till we are convinced that it will be for our happiness ..."[8] The only question is why it appears to be easier to identify, or at least harmonize, individual happiness with the national interest than with that of the world community. It is odd that a moral, disinterested concern by members of rich countries with the development of the poor is hardly ever conceded. As hypocrisy is the tribute vice pays to virtue, so professions of national self-interest in the development of poor countries may be the tribute that virtue has to pay to vice.

In the present fashion of stressing common and mutual interests we run the danger of underestimating the power of moral or humanitarian appeals. The Netherlands, Sweden, and Norway, which have put international cooperation squarely on a moral basis, have hit the 0.7 percent aid target. It is the countries in which aid has been sold to the public as being in the national self-interest where the effort is lagging.

The common interest must also be defined in terms of different time horizons: the next year, the next five years, the next 20 years. There may be conflicts and trade-offs between these different time spans. For example, concessionary aid to the poorest may involve sacrifices in the near future, but by laying the foundations for a world in which all human beings can fully develop their potential it contributes to the long-term interest of all humanity.

One difficulty is that in democracies adults have votes, but children and the unborn have none. The fight is not only against powerfully organized vested interests, but also against our own short-term interests that neglect those of future generations.

Any attempt to build cooperation for development on moral principles has to answer three questions. First, do the rich in a community have an obligation of social justice (not only in charity) to the poor and do the poor have a just claim on the rich? Second, does humankind constitute a community in the relevant sense or do communities stop at national boundaries? Third, does the existence of national governments not interfere with the discharge of the obligations of the rich, if such obligations exist, to the poor in the world community, if there is such a community?

The first question cannot be answered without an analysis of various theories of moral philosophy, but both utilitarianism and various types of entitlement theory would provide a basis for an obligation of the rich to contribute to improving the lot of the poor in a community. Perhaps more difficult is the case for saying that mankind does constitute a community in the relevant sense. Social contract theories might say that we need not do anything for the world community because the world community does not do anything for us, whereas the state provides protection, security, and certain other services. However, even if the first two questions were answered in the affirmative, the third presents the difficulty that the discharge of the obligation may take the form of what opponents of aid-giving have called a redistribution of resources from the poor in rich countries to the rich in poor countries. To meet this difficulty, we have to exercise our institutional imagination in finding procedures and institutions that avoid, or at least minimize, this possibility.

The "higher" interest in an acceptable world order can be defined either in moral terms or in terms of the desire to avoid negative-sum games, to avoid breakdown and wars. Whatever the definition and justification, its aim is to transform adversary relationships into cooperation. When interests diverge or conflict, the task of statesmanship is to reconcile them. This is a task quite different to, and more important than, that of exploring areas of common or mutual interest. It is in this light that cooperative action to eradicate world poverty and restructure the international economic order has to be seen.

What, then, are the requirements for a sensible international order? It will consist of negative rules of what governments must not do, and agreements on certain positive cooperative actions. The rules of abstention will be intended to prevent negative-sum games, and the rules of action to create some public goods and avoid public bads. Ralph Bryant has called these rules "supranational traffic regulations."[9] Some critics have accused developing countries of wishing exemption from some general rules (such as reciprocity in tariff reductions or the banning of preferential trade agreements) to which the developed countries should adhere. The discussion about appropriate rules for international economic relations has suffered from a long-standing confusion. It is the confusion between *uniform* (sometimes also called *general*) principles or rules (the opposite of specific ones and therefore necessarily simple) and *universal* principles or rules (which may be highly specific and complicated, provided that they contain no uneliminable reference to individual cases). Further confusion is caused if a third characteristic of rules is added, namely *inflexibility* over time, and confused with either uniformity or universality. A rule is capable of being *altered*, though it remains either uniform, that is, simple, or universal, that is, may have a lot of exceptions written into it. The equal treatment of unequals is not a principle of justice, and a general rule commanding it is an unjust rule. In order to prevent partiality and partisanship, rules have to be universal, that is, they should not contain references to individual cases. They may not, and indeed should not, be uniform. They should pay attention to the varying characteristics and circumstances of different countries.

Those who charge developing countries with asking for exemptions from rules that ought to apply to them are guilty of this confusion between *uniform* and *universal* rules. Thus a differentiated system of multitier preferences according to the level of development of the exporting countries may be best and most just for a group of trading countries at different stages of development. A fair system of rules also points to the differentiation in responsibilities and rights according to circumstances. Middle income countries would not have responsibility to give aid, but neither would they receive it. They would not have to give trade preferences, but neither would they receive them. Even finer differentiation would be possible. A country with a large balance of payments surplus might be asked to contribute loans because of its foreign exchange earnings and, if its citizens enjoy high incomes, to aid because of its income per head, but might receive trade preferences if its level of industrialization is low. The uniform 0.7 percent aid target would be replaced by a system in which those below a certain income per head would be exempted, and the percentage target would rise with income per head.

There is, of course, a practical and tactical case for *simple* rules, which might overrule the case for fairness for universal, though complex, rules: they are less open to abuse and easier to police. There may also be a tactical case for uniform rules; they may be easier to negotiate. It is for such pragmatic reasons, rather than on theoretical grounds, that one may advocate that rules should not be too complex and should not be changed too often.[10]

Any specific proposals such as nonreciprocity in trade concessions or trade preferences would, of course, have to be examined on their merits. But the distinction between "exemption from rules" and "drawing up new rules" is logically untenable to the extent to which the call for exemption is really a call for a set of universal rules that pays attention to the different characteristics and circumstances of different countries, just as income tax allowances for dependents or lower rates on earned income than on unearned are not "exceptions" but reflect our notions of fairness.

Those who are concerned with changing the rules of international relations are aiming partly at removing biases in the present rules, partly at the exercise of countervailing power where at present the distribution of power is thought to be unequal, and partly at counteracting biases that arise not from rules but from the nature of economic processes such as the cumulative nature of gains accruing to those who already have more resources and the cumulative damage inflicted on those who have initially relatively little.

Insofar as the call for new rules is about strictly economic relations, there is scope for positive-sum games. But insofar as it is about national power relations between sovereign states with different and conflicting aims, power is by its very nature a *relative* concept, and what is at stake are zero-sum games. The demand by developing countries for greater participation in the councils of the world and for corrections in the biases of the international power distribution is bound to diminish the power of the industrialized countries in conditions of conflict.

Institutional reform

In addition to rules, there is a need for institutions. Let me give six illustrations of the kind of institutional reform I have in mind. First, there is the creation of a global central bank that would be able to create and withdraw international liquidity, both for transactions and for precautionary reasons. A panic run on the banks would cause an international financial breakdown unless an institutional arrangement existed that provided the required liquidity.

The global central bank would also be responsible for the growth of global reserves at a pace that gives neither an inflationary nor a deflationary bias to the world economy. In the absence of such a global authority, the competitive actions of states will tend to be either too restrictive, transmitting unemployment and with unused industrial capacity, as each country scrambles to accumulate scarce reserves, or too expansionary, transmitting inflation throughout the world, as the reserve currency incurs large current account deficits to pay for economic or military ventures abroad.

Second, there is the institution of a global income tax, levied progressively on Gross National Product (GNP) per head, or, better, consumption per head in order to encourage saving, with a lower exemption limit, collected automatically but disbursed to developing countries according to agreed criteria. The monitoring of the fulfillment of the criteria should be done by groups of developing countries themselves or by a mutually accepted global council.

Third, there is a case for a global body to provide information on decisions for fixed, durable investment with long construction periods, so that we avoid the lurches between scarcity and excess capacity in steel, shipbuilding, and fertilizers that we suffer from now. It should obviously not be a supercartel that goes in for market-sharing agreements but a method of coordinating investment decisions.

Fourth, there is an international investment trust that channels the surpluses of the current account surplus countries in a multilaterally guaranteed scheme to developing countries. It would have guarantees against inflation and exchange rate losses for the lenders and the loans would be on commercial terms to middle income countries. Japan has for some time been the largest lending country with a large and long-standing surplus in its current account, followed by Germany. More recently, the oil-exporting countries have registered even higher surpluses which may last for some time. These surpluses are in search of good and safe investment opportunities. This calls for the creation of appropriate institutions to convert these surpluses into long-term loans to capital-hungry developing countries. This would be in the interests of Japan and Germany, which could continue their export-led growth without having either to reduce their rate of savings or find domestic, lower yielding alternatives; it would be in the interest of other OECD (Organization for Economic Cooperation and Development) countries on whose exports some of the loans would be spent; it would be in the interest of the capital-hungry developing countries whose resources are waiting to be mobilized by such capital flows; and it would be in the interest of the world economy which could maintain its expansionary momentum. An interest-subsidy scheme could be grafted onto this for the low income countries.

If this argument is accepted, the call for Japan to raise its level of consumption or to divert investment to the domestic market is seen to be misplaced. Higher consumption by the rich should not be applauded in a world that is short of savings and in need of capital. Further, higher domestic Japanese investment is not desirable if it is subject to declining returns. Instead of calling on Japan to reflate, we should mobilize its excess savings and channel them on acceptable terms, by long-term lending or equity capital, through either the private or the public capital markets to developing countries.

Fifth, there should be a better way of dealing with the oil price problem than the erratic zigzag movements that we have experienced since 1973. Oil producing and oil consuming countries would get together and agree on a small, annual increase in the real price of oil, say 2 percent. This assumes agreement on the best guess as to the real price of oil in 20 years. The balance of payments surpluses generated by such an increase could be channeled into the investment trust proposed above. The incentives to explore more oil, alternatives to oil, and conservation would be gradual and steady. The incentives for the oil exporting countries to use their revenue for investment in alternative productive assets would also be gradual and steady. Incentives to consumers of oil would permit a foreseeable and gradual adaptation. There would be neither debt crises nor the sloshing around of large funds in search of remunerative and safe returns. In addition, the world economy would be spared at least one major source of shocks and instability. Both inflation and unemployment would be reduced.

Sixth, there is a case for a global migration agency. The free movement of people across national frontiers has not kept pace with the movement of goods, services, and capital. Differential permission to migrate, favoring skilled and highly educated people while barring the entry of unskilled workers has damaged developing countries in two ways: first, by depriving them of many of the trained and skilled people on whom they have spent large resources; and second, by making an egalitarian incomes policy impossible if they want to stem too heavy a brain drain. International action to reduce some of these undesirable effects and a move toward a system of global taxation of migrants should be on our global agenda.

There is also a need for reforming the institutions charged with North-South cooperation. There are lessons to be learned from the Marshall Plan. It is now generally agreed that the Marshall Plan loans to Europe were given on too soft terms, perhaps in too large amounts, but that they achieved their objective of rapid European reconstruction. It has also become a platitude to say that the lessons are not applicable to developing countries today because in Europe the human capital existed, and to reconstruct with a skilled and highly motivated labor force is much easier than developing an underdeveloped society. However, one important lesson can still be learned from the Marshall Plan. Critics from both the Left and Right have pointed to the numerous faults of aid and in particular that it has not achieved its intended objectives, whether these are poverty alleviation, redistribution, or economic growth. They conclude that we should get rid of aid. A better conclusion would be to get rid of the faults and to evolve mechanisms to ensure that the objectives of the aid donors are achieved. The intervention of donor governments for the purpose of applying performance criteria to development aid has been regarded as inconsistent with national sovereignty, has been dismissed as intrusive, and has bred acrimony. It has also been difficult to separate objectives of accelerating development from objectives in the narrow national interest such as export promotion, gaining votes in the UN, forming political alliances, or getting strategic support. Performance criteria imposed in bilateral relations by donor governments have therefore been suspect and counterproductive.

The task is then to evolve institutions that achieve the objectives of the donors and the recipients and are trusted by both sides. It is to resolve the dilemma between avoiding intrusiveness and paying respect to national sovereignty on the one hand and responsible accounting for taxpayers' money on the other. Here the Marshall Plan has still something to teach. It is not about the speed of development which, for European reconstruction was much faster than for the structural changes needed for development; nor is it about the terms of the aid, which were too soft compared with today's terms of development aid, but about monitoring procedures. The European powers were encouraged to monitor one another's performance and the heavy hand of the U.S. government was kept out of it. Each government submitted a plan that was inspected, vetted, and monitored by other European governments in the Organisation for European Economic Cooperation (OEEC). Control by peers rather than supervisors is also a principle advocated in business management. A similar procedure could be adopted for groups of developing countries.

Final thoughts

There are at least two other options. It would be desirable to create a genuine transnational secretariat whose loyalty would be to only the global community and who would be trusted by both donors and recipients. The staff of the present multilateral agencies do not quite achieve this, partly because the system of country quotas in recruiting emphasizes national origin rather than merit, partly because the organizations are intergovernmental institutions, and partly because the recruitment, training, location, etc. of the staff of these organizations to some extent conflicts with the ethos of a staff serving only the global community. In addition to acquiring technical competence, the staff would be trained to be sensitive to social and political factors.

Finally, we might consider setting up a council of wise men and women whose task it would be to monitor the performance of both donors and recipients, and whom again both sides would trust. The existence of national governments that insist on the exercise of their full sovereignty interferes at present with the moral and enlightened self-interest objectives of development cooperation. Not until this obstacle is overcome can we make progress.

Notes

1. See below.
2. See Kindleberger (1978, p. 15; 1986).
3. Related problems have also been discussed under the concepts of "tragedy of the commons" (each agent, acting in his or her self-interest, contributes to social losses such as overgrazing on a common pasture or overpopulating the Earth) and "social traps" (no driver has an incentive to install a gadget that reduces pollution). These, as well as the prisoners' dilemma, "collective action", and Olson's problem are special instances of "market failure."
4. See Axelrod (1984).
5. See Lipton (1985).
6. See Ash (1984).
7. See Olson (1971).
8. Joseph Butler, *Sermons*, Sermon 11, paragraph 20.
9. See Bryant (1980, p. 470).
10. Of this long-standing confusion between universal and uniform, or general, rules even such a clear-headed thinker as David Hume is guilty. Hume contrasts the highly specific reactions when we are seeking our own self-interest with the

"universal and perfectly inflexible" laws of justice. He seems, like many others (including the WTO) not to make a necessary distinction between general principles (the opposite of specific ones and therefore necessarily simple) and universal principles (which may be highly specific and highly complicated, provided that they contain no unelimininable reference to individual cases). Thus Hume says in one place "universal and perfectly inflexible" but lower down "general and inflexible." And the use of the word "inflexible" conceals a confusion between a principle being able to be altered (which has nothing to do with its universality and generality) and its having a lot of exceptions written into it (which is consistent with universality but not with generality). Hume evidently thinks that the rules of justice have to be simple, general ones. He argues that unless the rules are general, people will be partial in their application of them and "would take into consideration the characters and circumstances of the persons, as well as the general nature of the question ... the avidity and partiality of men would quickly bring disorder into the world, if not restrained by some general and inflexible principles." However, this is fallacious. In order to prevent people from being partial, the principles have to be universal, that is, not contain references to individuals; they may, and indeed should, not be general; surely our judgments based on them ought to "take into consideration the characters and circumstances of the persons, as well as the general nature of the question."

References

Ash, T. (1984) "Back Yards," *New York Review of Books*, November 22, 1984.

Axelrod, R. (1984) *The Evolution of Cooperation*, New York: Basic Books.

Bryant, R. (1980) *Money and Monetary Policy in Interdependent Nations*, Washington D.C.: The Brookings Institution.

Kindleberger, C. (1978) *Government and International Trade*, Essays in International Finance, 129, Princeton, NJ: Princeton University.

Kindleberger, C. (1986) "International Public Goods without International Government," *American Economic Review*, 76, 1–13.

Lipton, M. (1985) "Prisoners' Dilemma and Coase's Theorem: A Case for Democracy in Less Developed Countries?" in R. Matthews (ed.) *Economy and Democracy*, London: Macmillan.

Olson, M. (1971) *The Logic of Collective Action*, 2nd edition, Cambridge: Harvard University Press.

3
Latin America, UNCTAD, and the Postwar Trading System

Joseph L. Love

Introduction

The generation of Latin Americans who made policy in the 1930s had learned the bitter lesson of overdependence on commodity prices, and their representatives took the lead at Bretton Woods Conference of the United Nations to call for a trading system that would support prices at stable and remunerative levels. At the 1944 meeting, delegates from Chile, Cuba, Bolivia, Brazil, and Peru all presented resolutions to that effect (U.S. Department of State, 1948). Brazil even proposed a special conference on price stability in commodities. Chile and Iraq sponsored a declaration to "bring about orderly marketing of staple commodities at prices fair to producer and consumer." (U.S. Department of State, 1948, p. 941) Yet Bretton Woods created a liberal international monetary and trading system, establishing the International Monetary Fund and the World Bank,[1] and paying little heed to the Latin American concern about commodities.

Latin American delegations took a similar position on commodities at the United Nations' Conference on Trade and Employment at Havana, Cuba, in March, 1948. The delegates met to consider a "third leg" for the tripod of the international trading system – an International Trade Organization (ITO), which would complement the World Bank and IMF. The General Agreement on Tariffs and Trade (GATT) had been established at Geneva in 1947, but its "most-favored-nation" provision was seen as inadequate for the needs of the developing countries, eager both to industrialize and to defend their commodity exports. GATT was the club of the rich nations, and Latin American delegates at Havana strongly attacked it while they "sought freedom to set up new preferential systems, impose import quotas, and employ other restrictive devices without prior approval" [from GATT] (see Wilcox, 1949, p. 49).

At that meeting Latin Americans also favored industrialization and commodity stabilization agreements (Wilcox, 1949, pp. 26, 120). They wanted the ITO to have been an organization more favorable to the poorer agriculture- and mineral-trading nations than the U.S.-sponsored draft proposed, especially if the ITO were able to regulate and support commodity prices. In the end, however, the original free-trade-inspired project prevailed (U.S. Department of State, n.d.). It, in turn, was rendered null when, after the outbreak of the Korean War in 1950, the Truman administration abandoned the idea of getting the recalcitrant U.S. Congress to approve the ITO.

UNCTAD: The beginnings

The French economist François Perroux has somewhere remarked that to get what you want, it is far more important to set the rules than to play the game well. Such was the case with GATT as far as the incipient third world was concerned. Therefore, the creation in 1964 of the United Nations Conference on Trade and Development (with its clumsy acronym UNCTAD) seemed to fulfill the long-standing Latin American aspiration for an international trading agency devoted to commodity protection and development through trade.

UNCTAD's initial program did promise the realization of those hopes. The organization was established at the highest level of UN agencies, and its director held the title of Secretary-General. The first person to hold that post was Raúl Prebisch, who had shaped UN policy for Latin America at the Economic Commission for Latin America (usually known by its Spanish acronym, CEPAL).[2] The Argentine economist, who had organized and directed his country's central bank during the years 1935–1943, had raised his UN agency out of the realm of technical assistance to a dynamic research institution and policy formulator; CEPAL had developed a set of theories and a program based on them, announced in Prebisch's 1949 manifesto, *Latin America and its Principal Problems*.[3] In the 1950s and early 1960s, the halcyon years of CEPAL, Prebisch had directly influenced government policy in a number of countries – notably Brazil, Chile, and Mexico, and he had recruited leading young economists to his organization from across Latin America (see Love, 1994). Along the way, Prebisch had earned a reputation as one of the few renowned authorities on development issues who hailed from a third world venue.[4]

Prebisch was chosen to direct the agency by the (overall) UN Secretary-General, U Thant, from among several other contenders. In 1961 Prebisch had welcomed John F. Kennedy's Alliance for Progress, and he was the coordinator of the "Nine Wise Men" who oversaw the ambitious program to deliver $20 billion in public and private investment to Latin America over a ten-year period. The Alliance's "clock" coincided with the Development Decade declared by the United Nations.

As early as 1961, Prebisch had begun to doubt the validity of the original formulation of his development program, in the wake of widespread abuses of CEPAL's recommendations for import-substitution-industrialization (ISI), and the rising import bill associated with industrialization. Therefore, he now recognized the necessity of stimulating (remunerative) exports in the development process.

The number of third world nations represented at the UN was expanding rapidly in the 1960s, as nations on the African continent gained their independence. Together, and working with the Economic and Social Council of the UN (ECOSOC), the nations of the "South" successfully promoted the creation of UNCTAD in the General Assembly in 1962. The first UNCTAD meeting took place in Geneva, the seat of the new Secretariat, from March to June, 1964. According to one account, this meeting had 4000 official delegates from 119 countries, along with representatives of numerous international organizations, and was the "largest international event ever held on any subject to that time." A permanent structure to deal with trade issues was approved, and the link between trade and development was recognized. This organization, in Prebisch's view, was to be "activist, not policy-neutral" (see Dosman and Pollock, 1998).

Prebisch, CEPAL, and UNCTAD

The original UNCTAD program was that of CEPAL, mutatis mutandis, extended to the global level. Prebisch's *Reports* to the organization, if not *cepalismo* whole cloth, were definitely international adaptations of the regional agency's program as it had evolved by the early 1960s. Prebisch, in an unpublished interview in 1985, did not take credit for establishing the organization – rather he saw as its chief architect the UN economist, Wladyslaw Malinowski, a Polish citizen who had previously been instrumental in the establishment of the UN's regional economic organizations (ECE, ECAFE, and CEPAL) and had headed ECOSOC in the early 1960s. Together, Prebisch and Malinowski were chiefly responsible for establishing UNCTAD as a permanent UN organization, rather than a one-off conference.[5]

Prebisch's *Reports* on the two UNCTAD conferences that he organized, those of 1964 and 1968, contained some of the theses familiar to all those acquainted with CEPAL structuralism. First of all, the world was divided into "Centers" and "Peripheries" (see Prebisch, 1964; 1968). Second, the secular deterioration of the terms of trade of agriculture and mineral exporters was affirmed as a fact, presumably to the displeasure of first world representatives, who doubted or denied the existence of secular deterioration (Prebisch, 1964, pp. 14–17; on the long debate about the validity of the deterioration thesis, for an extensive review of the literature generally supporting the idea in more sophisticated form than Prebisch's original version, see Diakosavvas and Scandizzo, 1991).

Prebisch's views on trade – beginning with the terms-of-trade thesis – and his experience in CEPAL had taught him that commodity policy, such as buffer stocking, however necessary, was not sufficient to advance the growth and development of the world's agrarian nations. Industrialization was necessary, and third world countries needed as part of their intermediate and long-term industrialization policies to move from exporting raw materials to exporting manufactures.

As noted, Prebisch had learned to emphasize the expansion of trade for underdeveloped countries in the latter 1950s, because of the need to pay for imports of capital, inputs, and fuels, as ISI proceeded in Latin America. He recognized the limits of ISI in his 1964 report to UNCTAD. But in addition he now insisted on *ESI* – *export*-substitution industrialization replacing traditional commodity exports with manufactures or semimanufactures (Prebisch, 1964). Prebisch clearly saw the direction in which world trade was moving, because by 1975 one-third of exports of less-developed countries (LDCs) by value, excluding petroleum, consisted of manufactures (Lewis, 1978). Thus commodity price supports were a basic concern of UNCTAD, but they could not be the exclusive concern.

Prebisch (1964, pp. 11–14) emphasized the "trade gap," a rather vague term which he introduced with the remark that the demand for primary products grew slowly as an element in world demand, compared to the demand for industrial products. The deterioration argument was implicit in that very observation, along with an even older conviction of Prebisch's that the "external imbalance" of poor nations was a sustained and structural feature of underdevelopment (Prebisch, 1964, pp. 107–108). By 1964 he was already concerned about income concentration in third world countries, with an eye perhaps to disquieting studies based on the Latin American national censuses of 1960. Partly as a solution, Prebisch called for land reform at UNCTAD I, an idea put forth in the Charter of the Alliance for Progress (1961) and in Prebisch's *Towards a Dynamic Development Policy for Latin America* (1963); in fact, however, the problem was more acute in Latin America than in other world regions (see Prebisch, 1964, pp. 112–117).

What was *not* part of previous CEPAL policy in the UNCTAD program was an appeal for a Generalized System of Preferences (GSP) whereby the industrialized countries would make tariff and other trade concessions to low-income countries for their new industrial products, without requiring reciprocity (Prebisch, 1964, pp. 117–122).

Elaborating UNCTAD: Geneva and New Delhi

In his confidential report to U Thant on the UNCTAD's first conference in 1964, Prebisch was optimistic about the prospects of the new organization, reiterating his view that the underdeveloped countries could close the "trade gap" through future industrial exports. Yet he also noted the conference's insistence in its resolutions on "stable, equitable and remunerative" prices for staple commodities produced by low-income countries, coupled with the need for greater access to the markets of developed countries (e.g. the lifting of quantitative restrictions on imports) and, in the LDCs, export diversification, facilitated by state planning of industrialization.[6] The conference established three permanent committees – one on commodities, another on manufactures, and a third on invisibles and financing.

As a practical politician, Prebisch realized that resolutions could be effective only if they were translatable into meaningful agreements. Crucial, of course, was the support of the United States and other rich countries, which could exercise a veto over the programs of all three committees; invisibles and financing were almost totally under the control of the high-income nations. Advancing the Secretary-General's agenda within UNCTAD meant the development of "conciliation machinery," and inside and outside the organization, it meant long and hard bargaining.

Perhaps the greatest reason for optimism, thought Prebisch, was the constitution of a new force within the third world contingent in UNCTAD, namely, the "Group of 75," which by the end of the meeting at Geneva had become the "Group of 77."[7]

This political alliance, he believed, could exercise real pressure in pursuit of its members' interests in the years to come. In fact, the G77 soon became a permanent entity, and over time organized chapters in other international organizations (see below).

Encouraged by initial third world victories in principle – and there had been few concessions to third world interests, even in principle, at Bretton Woods and Havana – Prebisch became an itinerant preacher to spread the UNCTAD evangel. He took his message on unequal exchange, the Trade Gap, concessionary financing, and export-substitution industrialization to Africa and Asia, as well as to Latin America. Between 1964 and 1969 he logged 600,000 miles giving speeches and meeting heads of government and their ministers (Dosman and Pollock, 1998, p. 584). On the force of his ideas and personality, Prebisch attempted to strengthen and expand the G77 as an effective voice on trade and development. In this he succeeded, and the considerable majority of the G77 nations supported Prebisch's Generalized System of Preferences, whereby the industrialized nations would suspend the most-favored-nation provisions of GATT to lower tariffs on new industrial exports from the countries of the South.

In the meantime, he recruited first-rank economists to carry out commodity agreement studies, notably Alfred Maizels of Britain and Jan Tinbergen, the future Nobel Prize winner, of the Netherlands. The former became a permanent UNCTAD employee, while Tinbergen was contracted to work with Maizels on the details for a model commodity agreement. They decided to elaborate a buffer stock scheme for cocoa. This commodity was chosen because it was widely produced in Africa and Latin America, but not in developed countries, and therefore competition in production between rich and poor countries would be absent. The study would be used as a model for UNCTAD II negotiations in 1968. The cocoa scheme was an exemplar for Prebisch's Integrated Commodity Program. But political factors intervened: buffer stocks would have to be paid for, and Prebisch wanted a tax for that purpose on cocoa importers. Another relevant political factor, Prebisch and his staff learned, was that U.S. cocoa traders made considerable sums on arbitrage actions that would be lost if there were a stabilization of cocoa prices. Not surprisingly, the U.S. delegation rejected the project.[8] An additional motive, thought David Pollock, Prebisch's assistant at UNCTAD, was that the United States thought a model agreement on cocoa would help consolidate the G77 as a political force at UNCTAD II (Dosman and Pollock, 1998, p. 592).

In a statement at that meeting in New Delhi in February, 1968, Secretary-General Prebisch reiterated his message of persistent external disequilibrium;[9] he pointed to the "savings gap" – the difference between mounting investment requirements and the domestic savings of the developing nations; and he referred to developing countries' "external vulnerability" to sudden changes in the Centers' economic performance and signals, such as interest rates. The "vulnerability" term dates back to his characterization of Latin American economies at the Banco de México in 1944. In his final report on UNCTAD's Second Conference, Prebisch criticized the industrialized countries for dallying on meaningful agreements for the GSP, for not agreeing to finance export shortfalls (supplementary financing), and for raising nontariff barriers against Third World manufactures.[10]

Secretary-General Prebisch further criticized the machinery of UNCTAD as far too complex. In the 1985 interview Prebisch said, "New Delhi was unmanageable. I could not see what was going on, notwithstanding that every sector had a responsible man."[11] In fact, 137 countries were represented at the Conference, along with 44 international organizations. There were 965 separate working meetings, occurring over the eight weeks of the meeting (Dosman and Pollock, 1998, p. 596).

Although unwieldy, the huge and sprawling organization did have the merit of being relatively transparent, while its bureaucratic rival GATT was shrouded from public view (see Krishnamurti, 1985). GATT officials liked to think of UNCTAD as the "General Assembly" of UN trade-related agencies, where rhetoric was produced, while GATT was the "Security Council," where all the consequential decisions were made. GATT tried to woo away members of the G77 from loyalty to UNCTAD by setting up a Committee on Trade and Development in 1965 (Dosman and Pollock, 1998, p. 594). Meanwhile, the IMF, another nontransparent organization, would not provide UNCTAD with sufficient data to study if and how the former entity's policies harmed developing countries' interests (Haji, 1985).

Conflicts, achievements, and third world mobilization

The most basic cleavage in UNCTAD, of course, was the rich against the poor, obfuscated in part by the lip service that the former were willing to render to the aspirations of the poor. Still another problem was the divisions among the commodity-exporting countries, of which the most obvious was that of the OPEC countries against the petroleum-poor members of the G77 after the quadrupling of oil prices in the wake of the Arab-Israeli war of 1973 (Williams, 1991, pp. 148–151). Another example was a resistance to the GSP by African countries that had special trading privileges from the European Economic Community; according to one researcher, Prebisch played a critical role in defending the GSP against regional schemes to benefit former colonial areas (Williams, 1991, p. 121). Finally, there was the problem of cleavages *within* third world countries' bureaucratic elites: the minister of development would tend to favor UNCTAD recommendations, while the minister of finance would tend to favor those of the IMF (Dosman and Pollock, 1998). It was an unequal match. One harsh judgment on the organization was that UNCTAD stood for "Under No Circumstances, Take Any Decisions,"[12] In fact, it took many decisions: the problem was their implementation in the face of opposition from the rich nations.

Nonetheless, getting UNCTAD II to approve the GSP was a victory (Dosman and Pollock, 1998, p. 595). The most economically advanced Latin American counties stood to gain most from the GSP in the short run, while the large majority of African countries would not, as they had few immediate prospects of exporting manufactures. Later the Africans received some compensatory considerations at the ministerial meeting of the G77 in Algiers in 1967. In a separate and more direct effort to sell the GSP, Prebisch deployed Latin American diplomats and trade experts to try to reverse the United States' initially negative attitude toward the GSP, and they succeeded in the same year, 1967, one year ahead of UNCTAD II (Williams, 1991, p. 121). Lyndon B. Johnson's government may have reversed its position in part to repair its image in Latin America after the bad feelings engendered by the invasion of the Dominican Republic two years earlier.

But the GSP could not yet be implemented, and the world was changing rapidly in the 1960s, while Prebisch's own views on the problem of development were also quickly evolving; he was moving toward a dependency perspective, and at UNCTAD he was criticizing the role of third world elites – African politicians, he thought were abusing the "trade gap" concept to cover up their own corruption. In fact, by the late 1960s Prebisch already favored "conditionality" for third world regimes, that is, that international lending agencies should make their loans to such governments conditional on the achievement of certain fiscal, financial, and commercial reforms (Dosman and Pollock, 1998, pp. 599–601). For all these reasons – and the fact that Prebisch did not want to preside over a "forum," as he now considered UNCTAD to be – he announced his resignation from the organization in November, 1968, effective the following March. He returned to regional Latin American agencies, doing a special study for the Inter-American Development Bank and later returning to CEPAL.

No new international economic order, but modest gains

However effective UNCTAD was, Prebisch played the leading role not only in founding the G77, but in initiating the process that would result in the "Declaration on the Establishment of a New International Economic Order" (NIEO) by the UN General Assembly in 1974.[13] The declaration consisted of 20 broadly stated demands, mostly derived from previous UNCTAD programs, but often radicalized. These included "sustained improvement in the terms of trade for primary products"; favorable terms for obtaining financial transfers for third world nations; a reform of the international monetary system; preferential treatment for LDCs in trade agreements; and regulation of multinational corporations by all states which claimed "sovereign equality" (Arndt, 1987, p. 142).

The complex process culminating in the 1974 demand for an NIEO occurred largely through the interaction of the G77 and the Non-Aligned Movement, an association founded in 1961 and which could claim 102 members by 1992. Early in the second decade of its existence, the turbulent 1960s, the NAM moved beyond political issues to take an interest in third world trade matters. Although the membership of the NAM and that of the G 77 largely overlapped, the somewhat smaller NAM – in which Latin America was significantly underrepresented, because of the region's close association with the United States – pressed for more radical policies within the G77. The dramatic success of OPEC in 1973–1974 was a stimulus to demand a broad range of price hikes for commodities producers. The result was a call for an NIEO in the General Assembly in May, 1974 (Sauvant, 1981). While the charge of "politicization" circulated in GATT and IMF circles, such an epithet almost inevitably arises when the prevailing rules of the game are challenged (see Bergsten et al., 1975, pp. 5–6).

The oil crisis of the 1970s and the debt crisis of the 1980s severely weakened third world unity, and the unwillingness of the first world nations to accede to NIEO demands left its agenda largely unfulfilled. However, the G77 did push the Prebisch program beyond the GSP in further bending the GATT rules. The Ministerial Meeting of the G77 at Arusha, Tanzania, in 1979, in preparation of UNCTAD V, produced the "Arusha Program for Collective Self-Reliance." After its adoption by UNCTAD at the Manila meeting the same year, this manifesto, contrary to many others, had a positive outcome. Its backers secured the permission of developed countries during the Tokyo Round of GATT negotiations to permit third world nations to offer tariff concessions to one another, thereby obviating the most-favored-nation provisions of GATT. The Arusha Program thus initiated the process of creating what was confusingly termed a "Global System of Trade Preferences" along with the GSP, which referred to concessions to low income countries by developed countries.

Although less important, UNCTAD also established a "Common Fund" in 1980. The G77 wanted indexation of prices across a range of commodities supported by a Common Fund, but the developed countries, led by the United States, Germany, and Japan, rejected the idea, and were likewise cool to the basic idea of buffer stocking to protect prices. The rich countries would not supply significant financing for the Common Fund, and in the end, the developing countries at UNCTAD V established little more than the principle that the Common Fund was a legitimate device to serve the interests of primary commodity producers. The G77 settled for what it could get, "dependent as it was on the magnanimity of the developed world." The Common Fund finally began to operate in 1988 (Williams, 1991, p. 155).

Conclusion

Latin Americans had led the way in the effort to cut a larger wedge of the international economic pie for commodity-dependent countries at Bretton Woods, at Havana, and within CEPAL. When Raúl Prebisch became the first Secretary-General of UNCTAD, he represented a regional aspiration to defend the commodity-exporting countries' interests. Prebisch projected the program he had developed at CEPAL onto the world scene with UNCTAD. In a judgment that has the force of crudity, Heinz Arndt (1987, p. 141) has written that UNCTAD was "a trade union of LDCs, with a program of demands on the developed countries ready-made by Raúl Prebisch." Although Prebisch left UNCTAD shortly after UNCTAD II at New Delhi, the Portuguese economist Eduardo de Sousa Ferreira believes that Prebisch's ideas dominated the first four meetings of UNCTAD – corresponding to the first decade and a half of the organization's existence – during which UNCTAD sought to change the structure of world trade. At UNCTAD V, the effort turned more to changing structures *within* the blocs of the rich and poor nations (Sousa Ferreira, 1981, p. 157).

Prebisch lived long enough to see the implementation of an International Cocoa Agreement (1981), and it was the first to use buffer stocks. It was not notably successful, however, in raising world prices (see Meerheaghe, 1991, p. 147). The GSP was a more obvious success, in that $70 billions' worth of LDC exports annually were receiving preferential treatment by 1994. More modest gains had been scored by an agreement on a Global System of Trade Preferences among third world countries, finally achieved in 1989. In addition, by the mid-1990s, a half-dozen international commodity agreements were in effect, and the Common Fund had begun to support buffer stocks in 1988 (UNCTAD, 1994, p. 5).

Yet in 1985, the year before his death, Prebisch still held that very little had been achieved concretely, other than the GSP. In retrospect, he was surprised that rich Arab states benefiting from OPEC's windfall gains of 1973–1974 did nothing to support buffer stocks at the Manila meeting of UNCTAD in 1979. He had hoped for $500 million from Arab governments to start the Common Fund. But they gave nothing; India alone among the low income countries pledged $30 million.[14] But Prebisch (1985, pp. 3–9) principally faulted the developed countries for the ineffectiveness of international development policies – and not so much for preventing the implementation of UNCTAD-negotiated agreements, but for increasingly posing trade barriers to third world manufactures in the form of nontariff restrictions.

Blocking the path of "reform," from the third world perspective, was the policy of the United States, which, as a general principle, has consistently preferred liberalization of trade from Bretton Woods to the present.[15] True, there was a diminution of, if not a hiatus in, neoliberal rules from the Kennedy government through the first half of the Johnson administration, when UNCTAD was formed, but the moment was relatively brief.

Perhaps the chief achievement of Prebisch – and by extension, the Latin American governments who backed his initiatives in the 1960s – was the mobilization of third world governments to take common action on commodity and trade issues of mutual concern. A total of 160 nations attended the tenth UNCTAD conference in Bangkok in the year 2000, at which occasion LDCs were still demanding better access to rich countries' markets while they charged that the WTO (formed in 1995 to replace GATT) was as much a rich man's club as GATT had been.[16] At the twelfth conference in Sao Paulo in 2004, third world countries complained bitterly at their shrinking "policy space" in the face of rising numbers of binding rules about world trade set by the WTO and the IMF. But UNCTAD retained its popularity among LDC governments, and in 2006, according to its website, UNCTAD had 192 member states. Within UNCTAD, the G77 now includes 131 member states, and is apparently alive and well as a bureaucratic structure. In 2000 the G77 held its first meeting of heads of state; that is, countries were represented at the highest political level. By the late 1960s, the G77 had developed a continuing institutional structure, which in turn developed chapters of the G77 in the Food and Agricultural Organization (FAO) in Rome, the United Nations Industrial Development Organization (UNIDO) in Vienna, UNESCO in Paris, the United Nations Environment Program (UNEP) in Nairobi, and the Group of 24 in the IMF and World Bank.

Given the growth of the GSP, the existence of the Common Fund, several commodity agreements, and the continued mobilization of the G77, Prebisch today might evaluate UNCTAD's experience differently than he did in 1985. One can imagine his pronouncing the same judgment he did for Latin American regional integration in the 1980s: "It was not a failure. It was not a success. It was a mediocrity. A typical Latin American mediocrity."[17]

Notes

1. Known also as the International Bank for Reconstruction and Development.
2. Comisión Económica para América Latina.
3. English ed., 1950.

4. The other two in this period were Hla Myint of Burma and Arthur Lewis of the British West Indies. Of course, Prebisch's ideas were controversial, but that was also the case of all the other first-generation economists represented in the World Bank-sponsored Meier and Seers (1984) book *Pioneers in Development*. Prebisch's essay was called "Five Stages in My Thinking on Development," 173–204.
5. Raúl Prebisch, interview by David Pollock, Washington, D.C., May 21–23, 1985, MS (courtesy of David Pollock). Zenon Carnapas credits Prebisch and Malinowski jointly with making UNCTAD a permanent entity of the UN. See Carnapas (1985).
6. [Raúl Prebisch] "Report on First UNCTAD to U Thant." Dag-1/5.2.1.7/3; Office of the Secretary-General; Records of U Thant – 1961–1971; UN Commissions, Committees and Conferences; Folder title: UNCTAD, Raúl Prebisch, Confidential Report to U Thant, 3, 10. (Located at UN Archives, New York)
7. Ibid, 15.
8. Prebisch interview MS, 101–102.
9. Raúl Prebisch, "Statement by Dr. Raúl Prebisch, Secretary-General, UNCTAD, at the Thirty-Ninth Plenary Meeting of the Conference (February 2, 1968)," in United Nations Conference on Trade and Development, *Report on 2nd Conference Held at New Delhi (February 1 to March 29, 1968)*, 70–76.
10. Ibid, 70–76.
11. Prebisch, interview with David Pollock, Washington, D.C., May 21–23, 1985, MS, 107.
12. On the politics of UNCTAD, see Nye (1973, p. 334). But UNCTAD was not the only UN agency criticized for its inaction; the glacial pace of GATT negotiations has prompted critics to suggest the organization's acronym stands for "General Agreement to Talk and Talk." (see Babai, 1993, pp. 342–348).
13. That the NIEO movement began with Prebisch's efforts at UNCTAD is confirmed in standard economics textbooks on development and in a history of development theory, for example, Todaro (1985, p. 560) and Arndt (1987, p. 141).
14. Prebisch, interview with David Pollock, Washington, D.C., May 21–23, 1985, MS, 110.
15. Of course the United States does not necessarily practice what it preaches, as George W. Bush's actions to protect American steel showed in 2002.
16. *New York Times*, February 20, 2000.
17. Prebisch, interview with David Pollock, Washington, D.C., May 21–23, 1985, MS, 79.

References

Arndt, H.W. (1987) *Economic Development: The History of an Idea*, Chicago, IL: University of Chicago Press.
Babai, D. (1993) "General Agreement on Tariffs and Trade," in J. Krieger (ed.) *Oxford Companion to Politics of the World*, New York: Oxford University Press, 342–348.
Bergsten, C.F., R.O. Keohane, and J.S. Nye (1975) "International Economics and International Politics: A Framework for Analysis," in C.F. Bergsten and L.B. Krause (eds.) *World Politics and International Economics*, Washington, D.C.: Brookings Institution.
Carnapas, Z. (1985) "Wladyslaw R. Malinowski (1909–1975)," in M.Z. Cutajar (ed.) *UNCTAD and the South-North Dialogue: The First Twenty Years*, Oxford: Pergamon.

Diakosavvas, D., and P.L. Scandizzo (1991) "Trends in the Terms of Trade of Primary Commodities, 1900–1982: The Controversy and Its Origins," *Economic Development and Cultural Change*, 39, 231–264.

Dosman, E.J., and D.H. Pollock (1998) "Hasta la UNCTAD y de regreso: divulgando el evangelio. 1964–1968," *Estudios Sociologicos del Colegio de Mexico*, 14, 573–603.

Haji, I. (1985) "Finance, Money, Developing countries and UNCTAD," in M.Z. Cutajar (ed.) *UNCTAD and the South-North Dialogue: The First Twenty Years*, Oxford: Pergamon.

Krishnamurti, R. (1985) "UNCTAD as a negotiating instrument on trade policy: The UNCTAD-GATT relationship," in M.Z. Cutajar (ed.) *UNCTAD and the South-North Dialogue: The First Twenty Years*, Oxford: Pergamon.

Lewis, W.A. (1978) *The Evolution of the International Economic Order*, Princeton, N.J.: Princeton University Press.

Love, J. (1994) "Economic Ideas and Ideologies in Latin America since 1930i," in L. Bethell (ed.) *Cambridge History of Latin America*, Cambridge: Cambridge University Press, vol. 6, part 1, 393–460.

Meier, G.M., and D. Seers (eds.) (1984) *Pioneers in Development*, New York: Oxford University Press.

Nye, J.S. (1973) "UNCTAD: Poor Nations' Pressure Group," in R.W. Cox and H. Jacobson (eds.) *The Anatomy of Influence: Decision Making in International Organizations*, New Haven, CT: Yale University Press.

Prebisch, R. (1964) *Toward a New Trade Policy for Development*, Report by the Secretary General of the United Nations Conference on Trade and Development, New York: United Nations.

Prebisch, R. (1968) "Statement by Dr. Raúl Prebisch, Secretary-General, UNCTAD, at the Thirty-Ninth Plenary Meeting of the Conference (February 2, 1968)," in United Nations Conference on Trade and Development, *Report on 2nd Conference Held at New Delhi (February 1 to March 29, 1968)*, 70–76.

Prebisch, R. (1985) "Two decades after," in M.Z. Cutajar (ed.) *UNCTAD and the South-North Dialogue: The First Twenty Years*, Oxford: Pergamon.

Sauvant, K.P. (1981) *The Group of 77: Evolution, Structure and Organization*, New York: Oceana.

Sousa Ferreira, E. (1981) "UNCTAD V: O carácter neoclássico da Nova Ordem Econômica Internacional," *Estudos de Economia: Revista do Instituto Superior de Economia*, 1, 157–170.

Todaro, M.P. (1985) *Economic Development in the Third World*, 3rd ed. New York: Longman.

U.S. Department of State (1948) *Proceedings and Documents of the United Nations Monetary and Financial Conference*, Bretton Woods, New Hampshire, July 1–22, 1944, 2 vol., Washington: United States Government Printing Office.

U.S. Department of State (n.d.) *Havana Charter for an International Trade Organization and Final Act and Related Documents*, Dept. of State, pub. 3117, Washington, D.C., n.d.

UNCTAD (1994) *Securing Growth and Development: A Guide to UNCTAD. 30 Years and Beyond*, Geneva: United Nations.

Van Meerhaeghe, M.A.G. (1991) *International Economic Institutions*, Boston, MA: Kluwer.

Wilcox, C. (1949) *A Charter for World Trade*, New York: Macmillan.

Williams, M. (1991) *Third World Cooperation. The Group of 77 in UNCTAD*, London: Printer.

4
Import Substitution Industrialization in Latin America: Experience and Lessons for the Future

Carlos A. Primo Braga

Introduction

Werner Baer's contributions to the analysis of Latin American economic development occupy a well deserved place in the economic literature dedicated to the region. But Werner is an unusual scholar. He has been not only an influential thinker and researcher, but also he has "engineered" one of the largest informal networks of scholars interested in Latin American Economics – encompassing generations of his students (including myself) and collaborators at Vanderbilt University, the University of Illinois at Urbana-Champaign, the University of São Paulo, the Catholic Universities in Rio and Lima, etc. Accordingly, his impact on the debate of Latin America's economic experience goes well beyond his writings.

In this paper, I discuss his analyses of the pros and cons of import substitution industrialization (ISI) in Latin America, focusing mainly on the case of Brazil. I review a selected number of his many contributions to this literature and, in particular, I ask to what extent some of the questions posed by his earlier papers on ISI remain relevant to the contemporary debate on trade and development.

The next section reviews the main insights and questions that can be extracted from some of his contributions to the literature, while the following one revisits some of these questions from the perspective of the ongoing debate on trade and development.

ISI: Experiences and interpretations

This section borrows its name from one of Werner's seminal papers (Baer, 1972) which analyzed the process of Latin American industrialization in the 1950s and 1960s. In that paper, the nature of ISI, the results of the industrialization process, and the prospects for future development policies in the region were reviewed.

Stiglitz (1987, p. 141) points out that there are two "conflicting paradigms for development strategies." One emphasizes the importance of the principle of comparative advantage, preaching free market and export-oriented policies. The other highlights that "there is a natural path of development … and that path, for most part, involved heavy industrialization." This development strategy has been typically associated with interventionist trade policies and focus on fostering a domestic market via ISI.

In his evaluation of the ISI experience in Latin America, Werner Baer adopts an analytical approach that borrows from both paradigms. He presents ISI as "destiny" while criticizing the excessive attention to "efficient allocation of resources" that could perpetuate a focus on "myopic" comparative advantage (i.e. a static rather than a dynamic perspective). At the same time, he recognizes that "one-size does not fit all" in evaluating ISI experiences in Latin America. Accordingly, he underscores the relevance of some of the criticism coming from adepts of the "market-oriented" paradigm, while pointing out that some of this criticism applies much better to small economies (e.g. Chile) than to the larger Latin American economies (e.g. Brazil).

The point of departure of his evaluation is the proposition that "all countries which industrialized after Great Britain, went through a stage of ISI; that is, all passed through a stage where the larger part of investment in industries was undertaken to replace imports" and that "in this early ISI process [in Europe and the United States in the nineteenth century] governments played an active role in encouraging and protecting the development of infant industries" (Baer, 1972, pp. 95–96). He goes on to attribute the delay with which Latin American countries embarked in this process to socioeconomic considerations: an elite focused on the high profitability of primary exports, supply-side bottlenecks (weak entrepreneurial classes, poor endowment of skilled labor, and inadequate infrastructure), as well as limited market size and pressures from external powers interested in the maintenance of liberal trade policies.

His analysis of the historical path towards ISI in Latin America differentiates between ISI spurts induced from abroad (associated with external shocks such as the two world wars and the Great Depression) and ISI as a deliberate policy tool for economic development in the 1950s and 1960s. He points out that after World War II, most "of the larger countries of Latin America implicitly or explicitly accepted the ECLA analysis of the hopelessness of gearing their economies towards the traditional world division of labor" (Baer, 1972, p. 97). In most countries, the mix of trade and macroeconomic policies adopted in this phase typically involved trade barriers and exchange rate controls, taxing export activities and fostering import substitution. In many countries this was complemented by a complex mechanism of preferences for strategic imports (e.g. capital goods and industrial raw materials), the direct participation of the state in the economy (via state-owned enterprises), and cheap credit for "strategic" sectors. It is worth noting, however, that foreign capital was often an important partner in this process "by transferring know-how and organizational capabilities" while benefiting from the rents associated with protected markets.

ISI led to significant structural changes in the Latin American economies in the post-World War II era, with the manufacturing sector expanding its share of GDP between 1950 (19.6 percent) and 1967 (24.1 percent). Structural change was particularly significant in the case of Brazil where industry increased its share in the economy from 19.8 percent in 1947 to 28 percent by 1968. Industrial growth became the main driver of Latin American economies over these two decades.

By the 1970s, however, the ISI model was already reaching its limits. Not only the size of Latin American domestic markets constrained the opportunities for further industrialization, but also the accumulation of distortions associated with the panoply of government interventions imposed a growing "drag" on the growth prospects of these economies. Moreover, monetary and fiscal profligacy often became the macroeconomic companions of ISI, as governments tried to stimulate economies amid growing signs that the growth dividend of the "easy" ISI phase was gone. These actions paved the way to the growing external debt and balance of payments crises experienced by Latin American countries in the 1980s.

In a paper coauthored with Don Coes (Baer and Coes, 2002, p. 862), which focuses on Brazil, Werner points out that macroeconomic "pressures, especially external ones, were the major forces in bringing this phase [ISI] of Brazilian economic history to an end. Over the last two decades, especially in the 1990s, the pendulum began to swing back to a much more open economic model, in which barriers to foreign trade and capital flows were substantially eased." This characterization can be extended to other Latin American economies. At the same time, the inevitable question is to *what extent can the pendulum once again swing back towards a more interventionist and closed model of development?* After all, as pointed out in Zagha et al. (2006, p. 9), "although nearly every country in Latin America and the Caribbean has pursued economic reform," growth over the last two decades has remained elusive. Against this background, the fact that "reform fatigue" has become a common denominator in the region is not surprising.

An answer to the chances of recidivism (particularly with respect to protectionist trade policies) has to address not only economic considerations, but also the evolving political environment in Latin American countries. In this paper, I will limit myself to the economic aspects that Baer identified as major challenges for policymakers dealing with the implications of ISI in the 1970s. It can be argued that these issues (Baer, 1972; 1984) provide a useful reference to judge the extent to which policy options adopted in the

1980s and 1990s have paved the way for a sustainable model of economic integration for Latin American economies.

Revisiting the trade and development nexus

One possible characterization of Baer's extensive review of the key challenges faced by Latin American policymakers in the aftermath of the ISI phase can be summarized by the following three questions: (1) can trade policy be an effective instrument for a proactive industrial policy? (2) Could Latin American countries adopt the Asian model (of manufactured-based outward orientation)? (3) Can the trade regime be reformed in a way that helps poverty alleviation and fosters a more equitable distribution of income? The answers to these questions are explored below.

The revival of interest in industrial policy

By the late 1990s, some analysts felt confident enough to argue that "It is generally believed that import substitution at a minimum outlived its usefulness and liberalization of trade is crucial both for industrialization and economic development." (Krueger, 1997, p. 1). But the "eternal" debate about the pros and cons of industrial policy (and trade protectionism) has taken a new format in the last few years, reflecting the contributions of authors such as Rodrik and Hausmann and reviews of the lessons from the 1990s.[1]

At the core of this debate is the proposition – see Baer (1972, p. 110) – that there is no easy economic method to evaluate if the costs of ISI-related "inefficiencies" dominated "the modernization or development" brought by ISI. In other words, to what extent the costs of resource misallocation and rent-seeking behavior surpassed the benefits of diffuse externalities associated with technological progress and learning-by-doing.

The answer to this question remains controversial. Some (e.g. Rodrik, 2006) argue that the focus on static efficiency gains does not amount to a growth strategy. From this perspective, the dismantling of trade interventions will not necessarily pave the way to a new model of export-driven development. According to this perspective, the reduction of the antiexport bias brought by comprehensive trade liberalization in Latin America did not generate enough incentives for steering these countries into an export-driven growth path. These critics emphasize, for example, the importance of "self-discovery" – that is, the knowledge generated by firms that invest in "experiments" to identify what they are good at producing and exporting – arguing that unless there is a proactive governmental policy to stimulate these "experiments" this type of entrepreneurship tends to be undersupplied, inhibiting the process of economic diversification and growth.

In sum, although the debate on the Latin American experience with respect to ISI has converged to the recognition that "wholesale" trade protection is not conducive to sustained economic growth, many of the questions posed by Werner Baer in the 1970s remain relevant to the debate about how best to implement trade policy as a lever to a growth-oriented strategy. The revival of interest in policy activism illustrates the currency of many of the points raised in his earlier contributions.

Export pessimism?

Baer (1984, p. 133) poses the question "[could] the world have accommodated a situation where many Latin American countries would have emulated the East Asian superexporters?" He goes on to quote Cline (1982), suggesting that if most developing countries were to follow this model this "would have resulted in untenable market penetration into industrial countries."

Export pessimism in its different formats (secular decline of terms of trade for commodity exporters, the political economy of market access in industrialized countries, etc.) has often been at the very core of inward-oriented strategies of development. The Cline experiment focus on the implications of generalizing the manufactured-exports intensity achieved (1976) by the "Gang of Four" (Hong Kong, China; South Korea; Singapore; and Chinese Taipei) to all developing countries and argues that the "fallacy of composition" holds, that is, if all developing countries were to adopt an export-oriented strategy the results would be quite different from the experience of the superexporters.

The reality of the expansion of China's exports in the last two decades, however, underscores that the scope for expansion of manufactured exports from developing countries was much bigger than "export pessimists" believed. The absorptive capacity of import markets is often underestimated, in particular, with respect to opportunities for intra-industry trade. Moreover, the main implication of implementing trade reforms that eliminate the antiexport bias of ISI practices is to allow private actors to explore unforeseen export opportunities, contesting new markets that are impossible to predict ex ante.

Mexico and Chile, for example, have significantly expanded their export volumes (and value-added) in the last decade, illustrating that an outward-oriented strategy can be successfully pursued by Latin American countries. It remains true, however, that Latin American and Caribbean (LAC) countries have lagged behind East Asia and Pacific (EAP) countries in terms of their integration into the world economy. In the mid-1980s, both regions had similar trade to GDP ratios. By 2004, LAC's trade to GDP ratio was 40 percent below that of EAP. In short, the region as whole has remained an underperformer in terms of trade expansion in spite of significant trade reforms in the last two decades. But as EAP countries' performance illustrates, the reason for this has less to do with the absorptive capacity of industrialized countries than with macroeconomic variables (e.g. frequent reliance on overvalued exchange rates as monetary anchors) and institutional factors (e.g. government effectiveness, control of corruption), not to mention a distorted structure of production inherited from reliance on extreme ISI.

Trade and poverty

Another theme often addressed in Werner Baer's work is the interaction between trade regimes, poverty, and income distribution. He highlights (Baer 1972, p. 178), for example, the difficulties in pursuing redistributive efforts in the post-ISI era to the extent that the "profile of the productive structure which resulted from the ISI process reflects the demand profile [often based on quite unequal income distribution] which existed at the time when the process was started." Baer (2002) contrasts neoliberal policies followed by most Latin American countries in the 1990s with the ISI era. He points out that although "ISI helped diversify the economies of the region and neo-liberalism increased efficiency by opening the economies to more trade and foreign investments none of the regimes effectively solved the region's distributional problems" (Baer, 2002, p. 309).

Werner Baer's skepticism about the impact of trade liberalization – a usual backbone of neoliberal reforms – on poverty and inequality is warranted. After all, it is important to recognize that trade liberalization can be a force for poverty reduction, but the ultimate outcome will depend on many other factors, including initial conditions of the country undergoing reform, the nature of the reform, who the poor are, and how they sustain themselves.[2]

Analyses of the linkages between trade and growth, both cross-country analyses and country-specific studies, tend to confirm a positive association, even though the magnitude of such a relationship is controversial. After all, there are no examples of countries sustaining long-term growth without being open to trade. Sustained economic growth, in turn, is typically associated with improvements in the minimum standard of living and poverty reduction over time.

Trade liberalization can contribute to this process not only by promoting growth, but also by changing the relative prices of the products that are relevant to the poor. In developing countries, protection is often higher on relatively skill-intensive goods.[3] Thus trade liberalization can benefit the poor over the better-off via its impact on prices.

It is well known, however, that trade liberalization generates both winners and losers. Households with little access to credit or located in remote areas where subsistence farming is prevalent may not benefit from the process. Moreover, imperfections in the price transmission mechanism are often present in developing countries where markets are characterized by high transaction costs and are poorly integrated into the international economy. In Mexico, for example, world prices have been differentially transmitted on a regional basis, depending on distance from the border and nature of the traded good (Nicita, 2005). As a consequence, northern states can expect more reduction of poverty associated with trade liberalization than southern ones. In other words, trade liberalization can increase income inequality and this underscores the importance of complementary governmental policies to deal with its side effects.

It is also important to recognize that income effects of trade reforms are relatively more important for the poor than are consumption effects. If the price of one commodity increases significantly, it is often possible to consume less of it. But it is much more difficult to shift from being an unskilled worker to being a skilled worker or to become an entrepreneur. The wage rate of unskilled labor remains the key variable in determining if the poor gain more or less than the average in the process of trade reform. In modeling trade liberalization in the case of Brazil, for example, Filho et al. (2005) show that multilateral trade liberalization could improve income distribution in Brazil, reflecting its potential impact on agriculture and related industries in the poorest parts of the country.

As pointed out in World Bank (2005, p. 151), however, "the evidence on trade liberalization and wage inequality remains inconclusive. In Argentina, Brazil, Costa Rica, the Dominican Republic, and Mexico, the industries that are most exposed to international competition pay the highest wages." To the extent that adoption of new technologies could be fostered by trade openness, this can lead to a relative increase in the demand for skilled labor, leading to more inequality. Actually, Perry and Olarreaga (2006) argue that in the case of Latin America relative factor endowments (relative richness in natural resources), dynamic effects of trade (leading to skill-biased technical change), and a prereform structure of protection biased toward unskilled-labor-intensive sectors explain increases in the overall income inequality in LAC in contrast with the experience of other developing regions.

Summing up, it is clear that trade liberalization is not a "silver bullet" to deal with poverty and income distribution problems. In this context, Werner Baer's concerns remain valid and underscore the complexity of addressing these issues in the post-ISI era. Measures to facilitate trade and market integration, as well as labor market reforms, education policies, and social "safety nets" are important complements to trade reform as far as the final distributive impacts of trade liberalization are concerned.

Concluding remarks

As illustrated by this brief review of some of Werner Baer's contributions to the literature on economic development in Latin America, many of the questions raised in his seminal work remain relevant to the modern debate on trade liberalization and models of development. For those like me, who have benefited from Werner's intellectual leadership and friendship, this is both a reminder of the relevance of his contributions to the economic literature and a reassurance that North-South academic collaboration can make a difference.

Notes

The views expressed here are personal and should not be attributed to the World Bank Group, its Executive Directors, or the countries they represent.

1. See Rodrik (2006); Hausmann and Rodrik (2003), and World Bank (2005).
2. For a detailed analysis of the evidence on the links between trade liberalization and poverty see Winters, McCulloch, and McKay (2004).
3. Note that this is not necessarily the case in LAC as pointed out by Perry and Olarreaga (2006).

References

Baer, Werner (1972) "Import Substitution and Industrialization in Latin America: Experiences and Interpretations," *Latin American Research Review*, 7, 95–122.

Baer, Werner (1984) "Industrialization in Latin America: Successes and Failures," *Journal of Economic Education*, 15, 124–135.

Baer, Werner (2002) "Neo-Liberalism in Latin America – a Return to the Past?" *Financial Markets and Portfolio Management*, 16, 309–315.

Baer, Werner, and Donald V. Coes (2002) "National Sovereignty and Consumer Sovereignty: Some Consequences of Brazil's Economic Opening," *The Quarterly Review of Economics and Finance*, 42, 853–863.

Cline, William R. (1982) "Can the East Asian Model of Development Be Generalized?" *World Development*, 10, 81–90.

Ferreira Filho, Joaquim Bento de Souza, and Mark Horridge (2005) "The Doha Round, Poverty, and Regional Inequality in Brazil," in Thomas W. Hertel and L. Alan Winters (eds.) *Poverty & the WTO: Impacts of the Doha Development Agenda*, Washington, D.C.: World Bank and Palgrave McMillan.

Hausmann, Ricardo, and Dani Rodrik (2003) "Economic Development as Self-Discovery," *Journal of Development Economics*, 72, 603–633.

Krueger, Anne (1997) "Trade Policy and Economic Development: How We Learn," *American Economic Review*, 87, 1–22.

Nicita, Alessandro (2005) "Mexican Households: The Effect of the Doha Development Agenda," in Thomas W. Hertel and L. Alan Winters, (eds.) *Poverty & the WTO: Impacts of the Doha Development Agenda*, Washington, D.C.: World Bank and Palgrave McMillan.

Perry, Guillermo, and Marcelo Olarreaga (2006) "Trade Liberalization, Inequality and Poverty Reduction in Latin America," Paper presented at ABCDE Conference, Saint Petersburg: mimeo.

Rodrik, Dani (2006) "Goodbye Washington Consensus, Hello Washington Confusion?" *Journal of Economic Literature*, 44, 973–987.

Stiglitz, Joseph (1987) "Learning to Learn, Localized Learning and Technological Progress," in P. Dasgupta and P. Stoneman, (eds.) *Economic Policy and Technological Performance*, Cambridge: Cambridge University Press.

Winters, L. Alan, Neil McCulloch, and Andrew McKay (2004) "Trade liberalization and Poverty: The Evidence So Far," *Journal of Economic Literature*, 42, 72–115.

World Bank (2005) *Economic Growth in the 1990s: Learning from a Decade of Reform*, Washington, D.C.: The World Bank.

Zagha, Roberto, Gobind Nankani, and Indermit Gill (2006) "Rethinking Growth," *Finance and Development*, 43, 7–11.

5
With or without the IMF? Economic Recovery after Devaluation in Argentina and Brazil

Andres Gallo

Introduction

The recent experience of the IMF in Latin America is far from promising. The failure of Argentina's economic program in 2001 represented a hard blow to the effectiveness of the IMF's (2003) rescue policies and diminished the institution's support among both developing and developed countries. In many instances, Dr. Baer analyzed the relationship of Brazil and other Latin American countries with the IMF and other international institutions (Amann and Baer, 2002; 2005; Baer, 2001; Baer et al., 2002). One of his main concerns is how countries deal with the IMF's proposed policies and what degree of freedom governments have. This paper is an attempt to evaluate how much a country needs the IMF. The recent experience of devaluation and recovery of Argentina and Brazil offers an interesting case for analysis. After devaluation in 1999, Brazil pursued an economic policy closely monitored and supported by the IMF, while Argentina, after the crisis of 2001–2002, pursued a more independent policy that, in many cases, went against the IMF's recommendations. This chapter compares the performance of both countries and the benefits of whether or not to pursue an IMF recipe for getting out of a balance of payments crisis. As it shows, following the IMF recipe is not a guarantee for either success or failure.

Crisis and recovery in Argentina and Brazil

In the late 1990s and early 2000s Brazil and Argentina went through economic crises and devaluation. Both countries came from fixed exchange-rate regimes, although the Convertibility Program implied a higher degree of economic, and political, compromise to the fixed exchange rate (Baer et al., 2002). In the end, the inconsistencies of these regimes, the outfall from the Russian and Korean crises, and the inability to generate economic growth forced devaluation and abandonment of such policies. Even though the economic crisis was severe in both countries, the Brazilian economy was able to react in a better fashion to devaluation, while the Argentine economy underwent the most serious economic depression of its history (see Tables 5.1a and b). In Brazil the economy ground to a halt in 1998 and 1999 (close to zero GDP growth) but quickly recovered after devaluation (Amann and Baer, 2002). On the other hand, Argentina went through a deep recession from 1999 to 2001, but devaluation could not stop the economic debacle. As a result, the economy dropped by 18.4 percent between 1999 and 2002 (Gallo et al., 2006). Brazil transitioned to a floating exchange rate without major shocks on the economy, but Argentina went through rough times, which involved the default on government debt, the *pesification* of all contracts in the economy, bankruptcy of the banking system, and borderline maxidevaluation-cum-hyperinflation before the government was able to restore some macroeconomic stability (Gallo et al., 2006). As the data show, the impact of the economic crisis and devaluation was stronger in Argentina than Brazil.

Many studies have addressed the reasons for the economic crisis and weaknesses of the economic models in each country (Alvarez-Plata and Schrooten,

Table 5.1a   Economic indicators (Brazil)

	GDP real growth	GDP per capita (ppp 2000 US$)	Inflation rate	Exchange rate	Investment (% GDP)	Debt (% GDP)	Exports (% GDP)	Imports (% GDP)	Trade (% GDP)
1990	−4.2	6497.2	2947.7	–	20.1	25.9	8.2	6.9	15.2
1991	1	6447.2	432.7	–	19.7	29.7	8.7	7.9	16.6
1992	−0.5	6292.5	951.6	–	18.9	33.0	10.9	8.3	19.2
1993	4.9	6537.9	1927.9	0.03	20.8	32.8	10.5	9.1	19.6
1994	5.9	6767.5	2075.8	0.64	22.1	27.9	9.5	9.2	18.7
1995	4.2	6940.1	66.0	0.92	22.2	22.8	7.7	9.5	17.2
1996	2.7	7021.1	15.7	1.01	20.9	23.4	7.1	9.2	16.3
1997	3.3	7176.1	6.9	1.08	21.4	24.5	7.5	10.1	17.7
1998	0.1	7099.7	3.2	1.16	21.1	30.7	7.3	9.9	17.2
1999	0.8	7137.2	4.9	1.81	20.1	45.7	10.3	11.8	22.1
2000	4.4	7300.8	7.0	1.83	21.5	40.4	10.7	12.2	22.8
2001	1.3	7350.6	6.8	2.36	21.2	45.4	13.2	14.2	27.4
2002	1.9	7393.9	8.4	2.92	19.7	50.6	15.5	13.4	28.9
2003	0.5	7305.5	14.7	3.08	19.7	46.8	16.4	12.8	29.1
2004	4.9	7531.3	6.6	2.93	21.3	36.8	18.0	13.4	31.4
2005	2.3	–	6.9	2.43	–	–	–	–	–
2006	3.5	–	4.6	2.18	–	–	–	–	–

Source: World Development Indicators (WDI), World Bank, at www.worldbank.org and Euromonitor, 2006.

Table 5.1b   Economic indicators (Argentina)

	GDP real Growth	GDP per capita(ppp 2000 US$)	Inflation rate	Exchange rate	Investment (% GDP)	Debt (% GDP)	Exports (% GDP)	Imports (% GDP)	Trade (% GDP)
1990	−1.3	8998.5	2313.9	0.49	14.0	44.0	10.4	4.6	15.0
1991	10.5	9864.3	171.6	0.95	14.6	34.5	7.7	6.1	13.7
1992	10.3	10,755.3	24.9	0.99	16.7	29.9	6.6	8.1	14.7
1993	6.3	11,174.3	10.6	1	19.1	27.2	6.9	9.3	16.2
1994	5.8	11,682.7	4.1	1	19.9	29.1	7.5	10.6	18.1
1995	−2.8	11,254.4	3.3	1	17.9	38.2	9.6	10.1	19.7
1996	5.5	11,756.6	0.2	1	18.1	40.8	10.4	11.1	21.5
1997	8.1	12,571.2	0.5	1	19.4	43.8	10.5	12.8	23.3
1998	3.9	12,955.8	0.9	1	19.9	47.3	10.4	12.9	23.3
1999	−3.4	12,400.2	−1.1	1	18.0	51.4	9.8	11.5	21.3
2000	−0.8	12,173.6	−0.9	1	16.2	51.9	10.9	11.5	22.4
2001	−4.4	11,523.2	−1.1	1	14.2	57.3	11.5	10.2	21.7
2002	−10.9	10,676.7	25.8	3.06	12.0	146.9	27.7	12.8	40.5
2003	8.8	11,363.9	13.4	2.9	15.1	128.2	25.0	14.2	39.2
2004	9	12,221.6	4.4	2.92	19.1	110.6	25.3	18.1	43.4
2005	9.2	–	9.6	2.9	–	–	–	–	–
2006	7.3	–	10.1	3	–	–	–	–	–

Source: World Development Indicators (WDI), World Bank, at www.worldbank.org and Euromonitor, 2006.

2004; Amann and Baer, 2002; Boinet et al., 2005; Buscaglia, 2004; Calvo and Talvi, 2005; Corrales, 2002; Dominguez and Tesar, 2005; Fraga, 2000; Goretti, 2002; Manzetti, 2002). Even though the debate is far from closed, this chapter concentrates on the aftermath of the crisis and which strategies each country followed to be able to restart economic growth.

Postcrisis economic model in Brazil

In the aftermath of the crisis, the Brazilian economy faced an economic policy dilemma (Amann and Baer, 2002; Goretti, 2002). Many commentators believed that the government was going to revert to old policies of irresponsible monetary emission to finance budget deficits.[1] However, the management of the devaluation allowed the economy to show a quick economic recovery with a low inflation rate and a smooth transition to a flexible exchange rate (Amann and Baer, 2002). The monetary and fiscal restraint helped the economy to make the transition and stabilize just a year after devaluation.[2] Nonetheless, the Argentine crisis and the upcoming presidential election in 2002, with the growing possibility of Lula being elected president, increased uncertainty over economic performance (Boschi, 2005;

Goretti, 2002).[3] While Cardozo's party offered a continuation of a policy of open markets and orthodox policies, Lula's candidacy rode on the back of a political coalition with deep roots in social and welfare policies. Lula's campaign tried to emphasize that his government would not promote a strong departure from orthodox policies. Financial markets reflected this nervousness through their performance and lack of interest in Brazilian assets.[4] Nonetheless, Lula's victory did not bring chaos but a continuation of the policies that gave the economy an ordered way out of the crisis.[5] The government pursued a policy of dialog and collaboration with the IMF, while at the same time trying to adjust to the social demands from its constituencies. Economic policy followed an orthodox pattern of a floating exchange rate and consistent monetary and fiscal policies, which quickly restored confidence about the path of the economy.[6] The result was economic growth and a higher degree of predictability of government policy (see Tables 5.1a and b). Investors changed their preelection view of Lula, and realized that his government was not going to change the economic model of the Brazilian economy.

Social policies were more difficult to implement, since the orthodox economic model limited the ability to pursue dramatic changes on social resources or income distribution[7] (see Figure 5.1). Total expenditure as percentage of GDP did not change from the levels reached by the previous government. There was no significant change in the percentage of total government expenditure devoted to social welfare programs. As a result, the government focused on the redesign of social programs within the budget limits. Nonetheless, corruption scandals and lack of speed in implementing

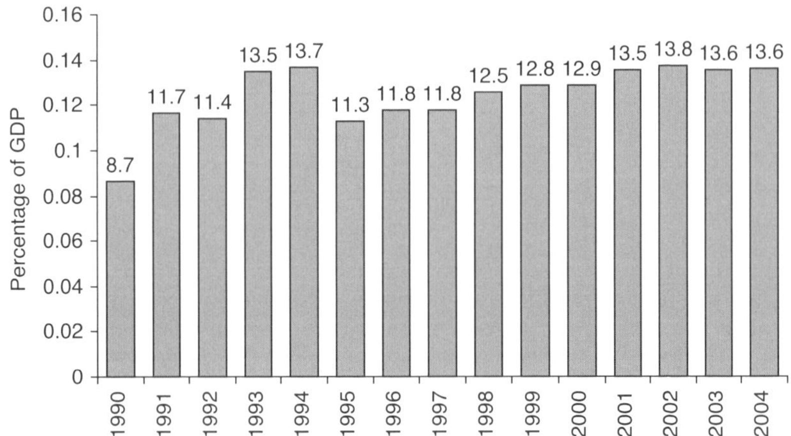

Figure 5.1   Welfare expenditure in Brazil

Source: Own elaboration based on Euromonitor 2006.

reform undermined the success of such policies and hurt Lula's support at its political base.

This year (2006), the government faces the challenge of a new presidential election and the need for Lula to improve his chances of being reelected.[8] The flexible exchange rate led to an appreciation of the real with respect to the U.S. dollar, which reduced the competitiveness of Brazilian exports. The economy has slowed down and the uncertainty of the election has created some uneasiness among investors. On the political front, Lula's government tried to boost popularity by canceling all debt with the IMF, a decision that Argentina quickly followed.[9]

Poscrisis economic model in Argentina

Argentina's recession was much more severe than Brazil's (see Tables 5.1a and b). The collapse of the financial and banking system in late 2001 led to a political crisis without precedent, in which five presidents were named and resigned in a span of ten days (Corrales, 2002; Manzetti, 2002). In early 2002, the provisional government declared it would default on all foreign debt, the devaluation of the peso and the modification of all contracts in the economy according to the new reality of the country (Gallo et al., 2006). The management of the crisis was far from ordered and in many cases represented desperate attempts to maintain some kind of stability amid the general economic chaos (Corrales, 2002). Economic activity came to a halt and GDP plunged in a recession that seemed unending (Tables 5.1 and b). The government's attempt to control fiscal and monetary policies led the economy very close to hyperinflation, and the IMF decided not to help the country in the solution of the crisis.[10] After one year of effort the economy stabilized and economic activity started to show signs of recovery. The deep devaluation promoted import substitution industries and the favorable international prices fostered agricultural exports – the only bright spot during the years of recession.[11] A new government was elected in early 2003 to deal with a difficult economic situation.[12] The government was in default on its debt, the banking system was bankrupt, contracts with privatized companies were suspended, and the economy was just showing some signs of recovery (Gallo et al., 2006). The government followed a monetary policy focused on sustaining the exchange rate at three pesos per U.S. dollar, in order to maintain the competitiveness of domestic industry and agricultural exports (Tables 5.1a and b). Income from exports was quickly monetized by the Central Bank, leading to an increase in domestic demand.[13] As a result, the economy started to recover and quickly showed signs of improvement (Tables 5.1a and b). Inflationary pressures were too low, given the low level of utilization of industrial capacity and high unemployment rates.[14] On the fiscal side, economic activity increased resources and the default allowed the government to save resources and run fiscal surpluses.[15] This economic model continued in place throughout 2005 and 2006, while the IMF recommended a more flexible exchange rate and an immediate agreement with debt holders. Because of the opposed points of view, the government decided to close all channels of communication with the IMF and pursue a more independent economic policy.[16]

In early 2005 the government gave debtors a "take it or leave it" offer for the defaulted debt, leading to the highest cut on sovereign debt in history.[17] The IMF did not support this program, but debtors, faced with no other choice, accepted the deal (Sturzenegger and Zettelmeyer, 2005). The restructuring of the debt allowed the government to go back to the financial markets, although the initial premium was high (see Figure 5.2). The fiscal situation remained under control and favorable international conditions, high prices for exports, and low interest rates allowed for a sustained economic growth (Tables 5.1a and b).

By late 2005 the economic expansion was straining the available industrial capacity and employment had dropped dramatically.[18] As a result, inflationary pressures appeared.[19] The government resorted to exerting political pressure on different industries and later to control prices directly, set prohibitions on exporting meat and increased taxes on exports.[20] To minimize criticism and opposition from the IMF, the government followed Brazil's example and canceled its debt with the IMF using Central Bank reserves. The Central Bank continued to sterilize the inflow of U.S. dollars in the economy, allowing the country to maintain an exchange rate close to three pesos per U.S. dollar and containing the domestic demand. Nonetheless, the interest rate on short-term notes has increased, as a result of both the volume of the debt and the increase in U.S. interest rates. This policy is generating a cost in terms of the short-term bonds the Central Bank has to issue to pursue this policy.[21] Investment has remained the Achilles' heel for this economic model, as price controls, contract and judiciary uncertainty, and heterodox policies do not promote much investment beyond the real estate boom and public works. Nonetheless, the policy of confrontation with the IMF has given political and economic payoffs to the government, despite the challenges ahead.

Comparing economic performance in the aftermath of the crisis

In order to assess the benefits of counting on the support of the IMF, while undergoing an economic crisis, this section compares the performance of the main economic indicators for Argentina and Brazil. According to the policies described above, Brazil followed an IMF-friendly policy pattern, with a floating exchange rate, fulfillment of its debt payments, adequate fiscal and monetary policies while Argentina followed policies in direct opposition to the IMF and the international financial community, that is, defaulting on its debt, controlling the exchange rate through monetary emission and market controls, sterilizing the inflow of foreign exchange, using controls to stop inflation, but maintaining a surplus on fiscal accounts. The IMF's preferred set of policies was well established in the Memorandum of Economic Policies and Letters of Intent both countries signed after devaluation (see Table 5.2). As we can see, the set of policies agreed with the IMF were very similar, with some adjustments depending on the particular situation in each country.

International markets reacted to the differences in the economic crises in both countries (see Figure 5.2). While the high jump in country risk in Brazil, resulting from the devaluation of 1999 led to a jump of more than 500 basis points, it seems small compared with the jump of more than 6000 basis points in Argentina between June 2001 and June 2002. The Brazilian economy followed with a high jump in risk in 2002 fueled by the fear of spread from Argentina and the possible election of Lula. Nonetheless, the country risk strongly declined by the end of 2002 and beginning of 2003 as markets realized that Lula's policies were consistent with the sustainability of the economy and the Argentine crisis was limited to its domestic market. Finally, in 2005, Argentina returned to the international markets and the country risk dropped substantially, as the government moved out of default and started to pay interest on the new bonds.

In terms of economic growth, the performances have been quite different. The effect of devaluation on the Brazilian economy meant a slowdown for the economy, while the Argentine crisis produced a decline in real GDP of 18.4 percent (from 1998 to 2002). However, the recovery in Argentina has been strong, with a growth of 38.9 percent from 2002 to 2006, while Brazil grew by 11.6 percent in the same period. As a whole, the Brazilian economy grew 21.2 percent from 1997 to 2006, while the Argentine economy reached a growth rate of 13.4 percent. As a result, part of the explanation for the amazing performance of the Argentine economy in the last few years can be explained by the strong negative effect of the crisis on the economy. This negative effect is seen on the loss of per capita GDP measured against U.S. dollars. In Argentina, per capita GDP fell by 2.8 percent from 1997 to 2004, while in Brazil it increased by 4.9 percent during the same period (Figure 5.3).

Devaluation produced an adjustment of the nominal exchange rate in Brazil, while it drastically changed relative prices in Argentina (Figure 5.4). This difference in the effects of devaluation is reflected on the abrupt change of the trade balance in Argentina (Figure 5.5). The devaluation cum recession increased the trade surplus from 1.3 percent of GDP in 2001 to 14.9 in 2002. This has surplus declined in the last few years because of the economic growth, but it is still higher than in Brazil,

Table 5.2   Policies agreed with the IMF

	Brazil	**Argentina**
Fiscal policies	Fiscal adjustment increasing primary surplus from 0.6 % to 2.3% of GDP Other fiscal measures: Increase public tariffs and energy prices Suspend tax rebates to exporters Increase interest rates on consumer loans Increase social security contributions for military personnel Reduction in federal budget expenditures for wages and salaries States need to adjust their fiscal accounts	Restructure public debt held by private creditors Keep fiscal deficit under control (primary surplus need to reach 2.1 % of GDP up from 1.9 %) Set a ceiling on expenditures Limit transfers from the Central Bank to the government Provincial governments should adjust their fiscal accounts
Monetary policy	Focus on inflation Strength independence of Central Bank by legislation Strength supervision of banks and other financial institutions Reduce role of public banks in the economy (restructure banks) Central Bank should stop intervention in exchange-rate markets Allow foreign banks participation in local market	Focus should change to inflation Full flexibility of exchange rates without Central Bank intervention Increase Central Bank Independence through legislation Strength bank and financial regulation authority from the Central Bank Reform public banks
Structural reforms	Constitutional amendment on social security Tax reform to simplify and eliminate certain taxes Fiscal responsibility law Continue with privatization program	Tax reform to simplify and eliminate certain taxes Reform of fiscal relationship with provinces Mechanism to deal with liquidation of low performing banks Legal reform to protect investors' rights

Source: Memorandum of Policies, Brazil March 1999 and Letter of Intent and Memorandum of Economic Policies, Argentina, January 2003. IMF, at www.imf.org.

resulting in part to the differences in exchange-rate policies applied by each country.

In Argentina there was a similar effect on total debt as a percentage of GDP, which abruptly increased to 147 percent in 2002 and declined in 2005,

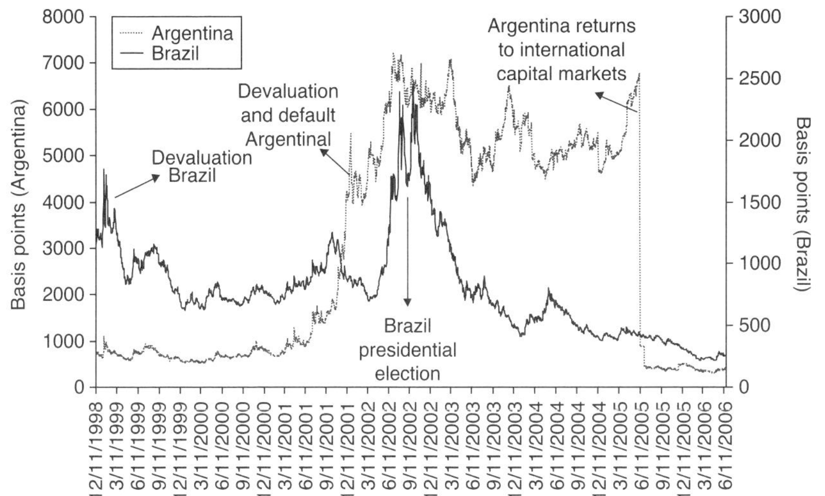

Figure 5.2   Country risks: Brazil and Argentina

Source: Own elaboration from the Ministry of the Economy, Argentina, www.mecon.gov.ar.

as a consequence of the default. In Brazil the debt burden increased in 1999, as a result of devaluation, but it did not get out of control, fluctuating with the changes in the exchange rate.

In the case of investment, Argentina suffered a strong setback, with low levels of investment from 2000 to 2003. This deficit in real investment has not been complemented by flows of foreign direct investment, which drained in 2001. While Argentina had a higher inflow of capital as percentage of GDP during the 1990s, the same was the case in Brazil from 2000 to 2004 (Figure 5.6). Moreover, the decline in the inflow of capital to Argentina is more noticeable when we take into account the value of investment in US dollars (Figure 5.7).

Inflation and exchange rates have been under control in both countries, although Argentina is having problems because its monetary policy is devoted to the control of the latter. Total inflation after devaluation, from 1999 to 2006 was 78 percent for Brazil, and 59 in Argentina. Nonetheless, Argentina had an inflation rate of 63 percent from 2002 to 2006, which increased in the last quarter of 2006. As a consequence, the government introduced price controls and other measures in order to sustain prices at low levels. In the short run price controls proved useful in countering inflation, but the results in the medium term, once controls are lifted, are uncertain (Figure 5.8).

The situation with regard to budget surpluses changed drastically after devaluation. Both countries switched from deficit to surplus, improving their fiscal situation. In the case of Argentina, the debt default, which

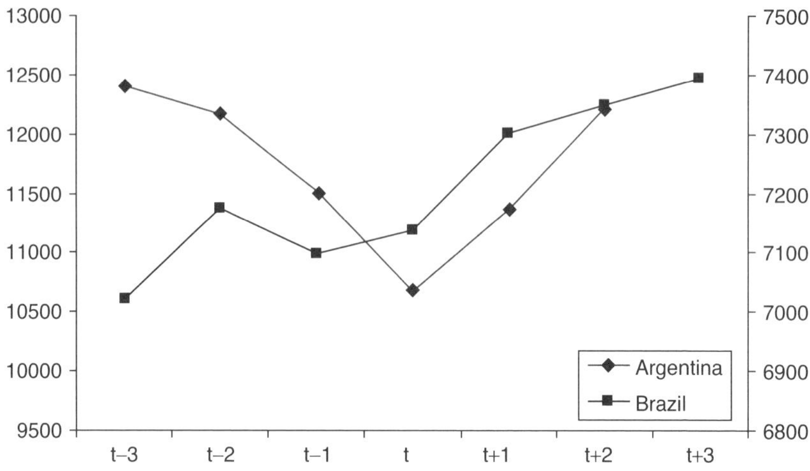

Figure 5.3   GDP per capita (PPP 2000 US dollars)

Note: *t* is the year of the devaluation, which is 1999 for Brazil and 2002 for Argentina.

Source: Own elaboration from World Development Indicators (WDI), World Bank, at www. worldbank.org.

Figure 5.4   Nominal exchange rate (per US dollar)

Source: Own elaboration from IMF Financial and Monetary Statistics, at www.imf.org.

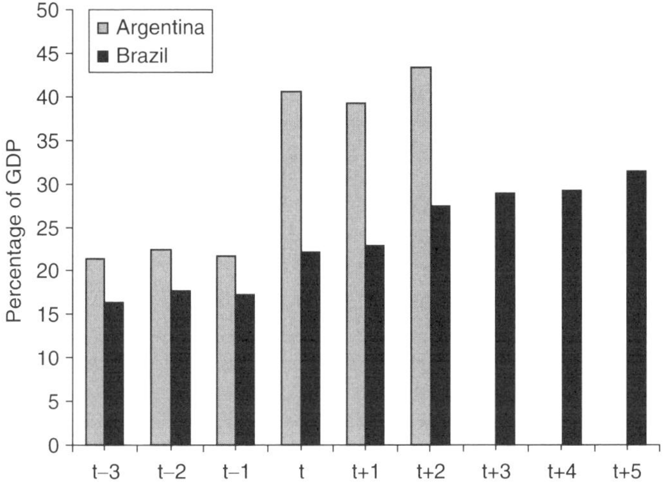

Figure 5.5   Trade surplus

Source: Own elaboration from World Development Indicators (WDI), World Bank, at www.worldbank.org.

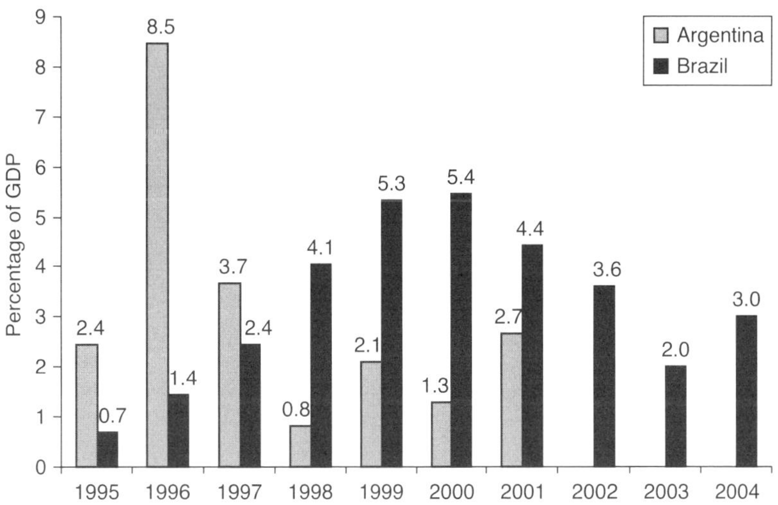

Figure 5.6   Foreign direct investment (net inflows as a percentage of GDP)

Source: Own elaboration from World Development Indicators (WDI), World Bank, at www.worldbank.org.

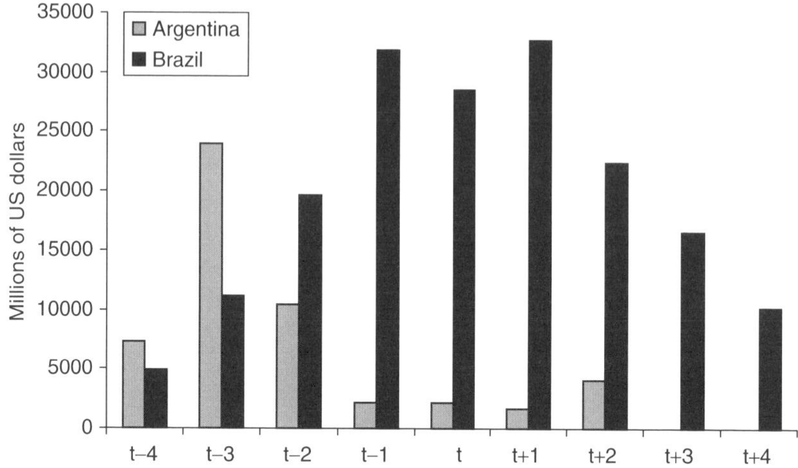

Figure 5.7   Foreign direct investment

Source: Own elaboration from World Development Indicators (WDI), World Bank, at www. worldbank.org.

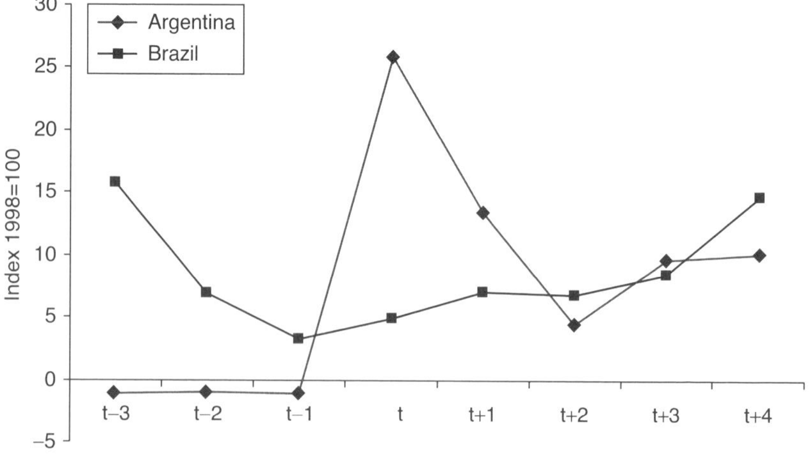

Figure 5.8   Inflation rate

Source: Own elaboration from IMF Financial and Monetary Statistics, at www.imf.org.

allowed the government to avoid payment of interest for more than three years, helped to sustain a budget surplus (Figure 5.9).

With respect to unemployment, there was no change in Brazil, while in Argentina the crisis sharply increased the unemployment rate (Figure 5.10).

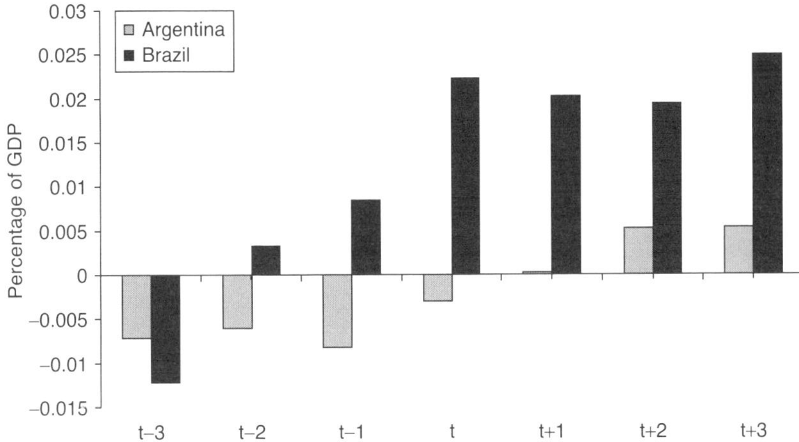

Figure 5.9   Budget surplus as a percentage of GDP

Source: Own elaboration from IMF Financial and Monetary Statistics, at www.imf.org.

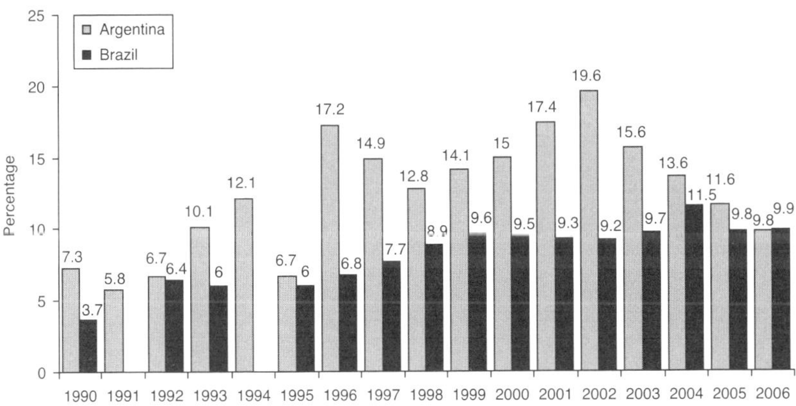

Figure 5.10   Unemployment rates

Source: Own elaboration from IMF Financial and Monetary Statistics, at www.imf.org.

Nonetheless, the rapid economic recovery helped to reduce unemployment rates to levels similar to those in Brazil.

Looking ahead, challenges and opportunities

As this paper has shown, both countries faced challenges to their fixed exchange policies and devaluation was the path used to change the situation. Nonetheless, their economic programs after devaluation were different. While Brazil moved to a flexible exchange-rate policy and focused monetary policy on inflation, with a fiscal policy consistent with macroeconomic equilibrium, Argentina chose a higher exchange-rate level and designed a monetary policy to sustain it. As demand increased, and the economy reached higher levels of production, the Central Bank started to sterilize incoming reserves, as a way of stopping excessive inflationary pressures. Nonetheless, the government is attempting to control inflation by using strict price controls, limits on exports, and taxes. The fiscal policy and the debt default helped to sustain the macroeconomic situation, and the booming economy is pushing down the unemployment rate. The situation in Argentina, however, looks weaker than in Brazil.

Despite the perceived weaknesses in the Argentine economic program, the aftermath of the crisis has not produced much difference in the current performance of both countries. Economic growth resumed, inflation and exchange rates are under control, and the level of debt seems to be between manageable ranges. Nonetheless, the IMF supported Brazilian policies, while at the same time opposing many of those of Argentina. Did following the IMF's advice make a difference? The answer seems to be no.

One of the main objectives of the IMF is to help countries to get through economic crises and to help them grow. From the comparison drawn in this paper, economic recovery has been equally successful in Brazil and Argentina. It is also true that positive conditions in international markets, high prices for agricultural exports, and low interest rates eased the situation. As a result, the question that remains is whether the economic model can be sustained in each country and what the rate of success will be in the medium run.

Notes

1. "Brazil's tradition of inflation and indexation will make it difficult for the government to keep inflationary expectations in check in the wake of the devaluation, despite the relatively closed nature of the economy (in 1998 imports accounted for 7.9 percent of GDP) and despite the depressed state of domestic demand and deflationary forces in the world economy. Producers and retailers alike have been quick to raise prices in the wake of the devaluation. But the government has clamped down on abusive pricing, and it will be helped by a reluctance on the part of the public, particularly the poor, to accept a return to inflation after past four years of price stability. The EIU expects the devaluation to have a greater pass-through impact on prices than is likely to be assumed in the redrafted IMF agreement. But we expect inflation to be contained to around 25 percent. Under these assumptions, a return to widespread indexation of prices and salaries will not occur, and the conditions would be created for a slow reduction in inflation in 2000." *The Economist* Intelligence Unit, Brazil Country Report, 1st Quarter 1999, 10.
2. "Having consolidated the fiscal adjustment in recent months with the approval of the DRU, the LRF, a minimum wage of R151, and a fiscally conservative budget, the government will wait until after the October municipal elections to seek

approval for reform of the tax system and social security, which are crucial for competitiveness and the long-term health of the public finances respectively. The government is on course to meet its target of a primary surplus of 3.25 percent of GDP. Monetary policy will remain cautious and dependent on the degree of US monetary loosening. The economy is set to recover in 2000–2001. The inflation target will be achieved. The trade balance will swing into surplus but the overall external financing requirement will remain large." *The Economist* Intelligence Unit, Brazil Country Report, June 2000, 3.

3. "Financial markets have become volatile at the prospect of a Lula victory, adding to interest charges on the public debt. The termination of all cooperation by the Partido da Frente Liberal (PFL) with the government has also hampered the passage of legislation needed to meet primary fiscal targets and to move ahead with reform. Investors remain nervous of the Partido dos Trabalhadores (PT), despite the moderation of its stance on economic policy." *The Economist* Intelligence Unit, Brazil Country Report, June 2002, 16.

4. "... the PT has been keen to emphasize its commitment to the responsible management of the economy and has abandoned its radical stance on fiscal spending and relation with the IMF. Lula has also made significant efforts to improve his own image as a statesman, by engaging in high profile international visits. Drawing on the lessons of previous campaigns, the PT's television spots have been crafted carefully to underline the message of responsible government. But despite these efforts, Lula's strong showing in the polls has generated a degree of anxiety among investors that has already been reflected in currency jitters and the widening of spreads on Brazilian debt, adding to the burden of public debt servicing. This development has underlined the urgency of Lula's efforts to win over sections of the business community." *The Economist* Intelligence Unit, Brazil Country Report, June 2002, 12.

5. "The government is maintaining the orthodox macroeconomic framework inherited from the previous administration, of Fernando Henrique Cardoso in 1995–2002, which encompasses fiscal discipline, a floating exchange-rate and inflation targeting." *The Economist* Intelligence Unit, Brazil Country Report, September 2003, 8.

6. "Since coming to power in January, the Partido dos Trabalhadores (PT, the Workers Party) government has been remarkably successful at building consensus and maintaining the confidence of the markets. As a result, it has been congratulated by the IMF while managing to retain a relatively high level of public support despite very tight economic management." *The Economist* Intelligence Unit, Brazil Country Report, September 2003, 12.

7. "Tight fiscal restraint has limited the government's scope for initiation or expansion of social welfare programmes, but a series of announcements have been made in an attempt to demonstrate its commitment to social reform. These include the approval of a targeted employment programme for those who have never worked before; the imposition on banks of a requirement to increase the volume of small loans (see Economic policy); affirmation that the government is preparing legislation criminalising "illicit enrichment, citing diversion of resources from social programmes; and a literacy programme which aims to harness voluntary effort." *The Economist* Intelligence Unit, Brazil Country Report, September 2003, 17.

8. "Corruption investigations that erupted in mid-2005 drag on, but the political environment is increasingly dominated by the October 2006 presidential and legislative elections. The president, Luiz Inácio Lula da Silva of the leftist Partido dos Trabalhadores (PT), is expected to seek re-election. Following a steep decline in his

approval ratings in the second half of 2005, Mr da Silva's popularity has rebounded in 2006. Provided that no new corruption scandals emerge, an improved public relations campaign, higher public investment spending, the impact of social assistance programmes and an increase in the minimum wage will help consolidate the recovery of his support among the poor majority of the population." *The Economist* Intelligence Unit, Brazil Country Report, June 2006, 7.

9. Whatever the economics involved, wriggling free from the tutelage of the IMF is always good politics, in Latin America in particular. That is why Brazil's finance ministry announced on December 13th that it would repay early its entire debt of $15.5 billion falling due to the IMF over the next two years. The immediate effect was to rush Néstor Kirchner, Argentina's president, into an identical declaration just two days later. He said his government would repay $9.8 billion to the Fund, before the end of this month. In both cases, the motivations were similar. More telling was the difference in market reaction and policy implications.

    "Both governments claimed they would make financial gains from the move – a saving of over $900m in interest payments for Brazil and of $842m for Argentina. In both cases, the more powerful motive was political. Brazil's president, Luiz Inácio Lula da Silva, is burdened with a corruption scandal and a below-par economy as he prepares for a tough fight to win a second term in an election next October. Paying off the IMF will please his left-wing supporters without ruffling financial markets. Mr Kirchner runs the risk that by the time he seeks a second term at an election in April 2007, Argentina's economic recovery may have run out of steam. Paying off the Fund will 'generate freedom for national decisions', he said. Even *La Nación*, a habitually Kirchner-sceptic newspaper, hailed this as an 'historic' move." *The Economist*, December 20, 2005, at http://www.economist.com/World/la/displayStory.cfm?story_id=5327790.

10. "Our growth forecast for Argentina is based on the assumption that the current situation will not develop into a spiral of high inflation or hyperinflation and, eventually, dollarisation. However, if the current programme fails or if negotiations with the IMF do not move forward sufficiently rapidly, this risk will increase. The economy will remain depressed during 2002, but should start to stabilise in 2003."

    "After three years of deflation, the devaluation of the peso has fuelled price increases. Although inflation will accelerate in the near future, our primary forecast is that hyperinflation will be avoided. The ability of the authorities to control the growing pressures for indexation will be crucial – Argentina has a deep-rooted tradition of indexation to the U.S. dollar. In our view, indexation is unlikely in the current context of a severely depressed economy. However, popular demands for the reinstatement of real purchasing power through wage increases are likely to re-emerge before mid-year." *The Economist* Intelligence Unit, Argentina Country Report, April 2002, 6–7.

11. "During the first half of 2002 real agricultural output increased by 1 percent, while the production of fisheries rose by 1.4 percent. These were the only two sectors that recorded positive output growth rates during the period. The record soybean harvest was the main factor behind growth in agriculture." The *Economist Intelligence* Unit, Argentina Country Report, December 2002, 26.

12. "The new president, Nestor Kirchner, who was sworn on May 25th, was elected with a relatively weak mandate and lacks a strong base within the ruling but divided Partido Justicialista." *The Economist* Intelligence Unit, Argentina Country Report, June 2003, 3.

13. "After pursuing an expansionary monetary policy during the second quarter of the year, the authorities subsequently adopted a more conservative stance. While during the second quarter of the year the monetary base increased at a monthly rate of 7.1 percent, during the third quarter the rate of expansion slowed to 2.4 percent per month. This was facilitated by a fall in the supply of dollars, which reduced pressures for the authorities to intervene in the foreign-exchange market to maintain the competitiveness of the peso. The smaller dollar surplus in the third quarter stemmed from a lower trade surplus and higher capital outflows. However, this pattern was reversed in October, and official intervention in the foreign-exchange market increased again, causing the expansion of the monetary base to accelerate as the Central Bank sought to prevent the price of the dollar from falling below Ps2.8: US$1. To partly sterilise the resulting monetary expansion, the authorities issued new Letras del Banco Central (Lebacs, Central Bank paper), the stock of which reached Ps8.7bn at the end of October (compared with Ps3.4bn at the beginning of the year)." *The Economist* Intelligence Unit, Argentina Country Report, December 2003, 24.
14. Utilization of industrial capacity was at 55.5 percent on June 2002, while unemployment was close to 20 percent. Source, National Ministry of Economy of Argentina, at www.mecon.gov.ar.
15. "During the third quarter of 2004 the public-sector finances recorded a strong surplus, continuing the trend established in the first half. Primary government spending rose – pushed up by higher transfers to the provinces, the increase in public-sector wages and higher infrastructure spending – but at a lower rate than revenue. The overall non-financial public sector surplus (NFPS) for the third quarter (on a cash basis, and including transfers to the provinces) was Ps5.0bn. The cumulative primary surplus for the first nine months was Ps16.8bn, equivalent to 5 percent of GDP." *The Economist* Intelligence Unit, Argentina Country Report, December 2004, 16.
16. "The government repaid the SDR6.7bn (US$9.5bn) it owed to the IMF at the beginning of January from Central Bank reserves. We do not expect it to seek another deal with the Fund to replace the stand-by arrangement it suspended in the third quarter of 2004. The government will make use of heterodox measures (including price controls and export taxes) to meet its macroeconomic and fiscal targets, an approach it regards as vindicated by three years of strong economic growth and increased stability, but it will try to dodge the politically costly structural reforms advocated by the Fund. These reforms include a comprehensive overhaul of fiscal relations between the federal government and the provinces, one of the causes of the unmanageable build-up of debt in the 1990s." *The Economist* Intelligence Unit, Argentina Country Report, February 2006, 2.
17. "In recent statements, the Fund has indicated that it wants to see a 'realistic strategy' to deal with holders of the 24 percent of the defaulted external debt (US$19.5bn) who refused to enter the debt swap. Argentina has agreed in principle to address the issue of holdouts at some time in the future, although what kind of deal they will be offered is as yet unclear. So far, the Argentinean government has insisted that those bondholders who failed to enter the swap would receive nothing."*The Economist* Intelligence Unit, Argentina Country Report, April 2005, 2.
18. "Rapid output growth has taken the level of capacity utilisation in industry to 75.1 percent, close to its 1998 peak. Capacity utilisation rose by 2 percentage points in September, the largest monthly rise since February. The industrial sectors where capacity is most stretched are petroleum refining, where it is running

at 94.3 percent, basic metal industries (87.3 percent) and textiles (88.2 percent)." *The Economist* Intelligence Unit, Argentina Country Report, December 2005, 32.
19. "During the third quarter of 2005 the consumer price index (CPI) increased by 2.6 percent quarter on quarter, picking up compared with the 2 percent rise in the second quarter, but lower than the 4 percent experienced in the first three months of the year. On a monthly basis, the CPI rose by 1 percent in July, by 0.4 percent in August and by 1.2 percent in September, the highest monthly rise in prices since March." *The Economist* Intelligence Unit, Argentina Country Report, December 2005, 25.
20. "The government will concentrate on maintaining large fiscal surpluses, keeping the economy growing strongly, and combating resurgent inflation. It will also try to redistribute income to poor households following the recovery from a severe economic crisis in 2001–2002. Keeping the economy growing without generating higher inflation hinges on increasing investment, which has now exceeded the pre-crisis peak of 1998 in real terms. Investment will be encouraged by targeted incentives, with the aim of removing bottlenecks in sectors, such as energy and industrial inputs, which have arisen as a result of strong domestic and export demand. The government will use so-called price agreements (under which moral persuasion will be applied to leading producers and retailers to lower prices in the expectation that competitors will follow suit) and export taxes to stem price rises on the domestic market." *The Economist* Intelligence Unit, Argentina Country Report, June 2006, 8.
21. "The Central Bank will target a level of monetary aggregates consistent with a gradual lowering of inflation, which rose sharply in 2005. But it will also be guided by the conflicting goal of maintaining exchange-rate competitiveness. The Central Bank will continue to intervene in the currency market, accumulating foreign-exchange reserves while issuing Central Bank paper to sterilise the impact on the money supply. The government will also combat inflation directly by seeking price agreements. There was little effective tightening of monetary policy in 2005, with real interest rates still negative, but interest rates have risen in 2006 and we expect this trend to continue if the Central Bank is to adhere to money supply targets and roll over its increasing stock of paper. Greater government borrowing on the domestic market to repay debt issued in the wake of the crisis in 2001–2002, and higher US interest rates, will add to upward pressure on local interest rates." *The Economist* Intelligence Unit, Argentina Country Report, June 2006, 9.

References

Alvarez-Plata, P., and M. Schrooten (2004) "Misleading Indicators? The Argentinean Currency Crisis," *Journal of Policy Modeling*, 26, 587–603.

Amann, E., and W. Baer (2002) "Anchors Away: The Cost and Benefits of Brazil's Devaluation," *World Development*, 31, 1033–1046.

Amann, E. and W. Baer (2005) "From the Developmental to the Regulatory State: The Transformation of the Government's Impact on the Brazilian Economy," *The Quarterly Review of Economics and Finance*, 45, 421–431.

Baer, W. (2001) *The Brazilian Economy: Growth and Development*, 5th ed., Westport, CT: Praeger.

Baer, W., P. Elosegui and A. Gallo (2002) "The Achievements And Failures of Argentina's Neo-liberal Economic Policies," *Oxford Development Studies*, 30, 63–85.

Boinet, V., O. Napolitano, and N. Spagnalo (2005) "Was the Currency Crisis in Argentina Self-fulfiling?" *Review of World Economics/Weltwirtschaftliches Archiv*, 141, 357–368.

Boschi, M. (2005) "International Financial Contagion: Evidence from the Argentine Crisis of 2001–2002," *Applied Financial Economics*, 15, 153–163.

Buscaglia, M. (2004) "The Political Economy of Argentina's Debacle," *Policy Reform*, 71, 43–65.

Calvo, G., and E. Talvi. (2005) "Sudden Stop, Financial Factors And Economic Collapse In Latin America: Learning From Argentina And Chile," NBER Working Paper 11153.

Corrales, J. (2002) "The Politics of Argentina's Meltdown," *World Policy Journal*, 19, 29–42.

Dominguez, K., and L. Tesar (2005) "International Borrowing And Macroeconomic Performance In Argentina," NBER Working Paper 11353.

Fraga, A. (2000) "Monetary Policy During the Transition to a Floating Exchange Rate: Brazil's Recent Experience," *Finance & Development*, 37, 16–18.

Gallo, A., J. Stegmann, and J. Steagall (2006) "The Role of Political Institutions in the Resolution of Economic Crises: The Case of Argentina 2001–2005," *Oxford Development Studies*, 34, 193–217.

Goretti, M. (2002) "The Brazilian Currency Turmoil of 2002: A Nonlinear Analysis," *International Journal of Finance and Economics*, 10, 289–306.

IMF (2003) *Lessons from the Crisis in Argentina*, Prepared by the Policy Development and Review Department In Consultation with the Other Departments, Approved by Timothy Geithner, October 8, 2003.

Manzetti, L. (2002) "The Argentine Implosion," *The North South Agenda Paper Fifty Nine*, Florida: University of Miami.

Sturzenegger, F., and J. Zettelmeyer (2005) "Haircuts: Estimating Investor Losses in Sovereign Debt Restructurings, 1998–2005," IMF Working Paper 05/137, Washington, D.C.

6
The Decision to Become Informal Self-Employed in Latin America

Patricio Aroca Gonzalez, Wendy Cunningham, and William F. Maloney

Introduction

Much of the literature on the informal self-employed sector in LDCs, with roots in Harris and Todaro (1970), has assumed a dualistic labor market where self-employed workers who are unprotected by labor legislation are rationed out of protected or "formal" salaried sector jobs by above-market clearing remuneration in the protected sector. In this view, the sector is generally an involuntary holding pattern for young workers entering the labor force or older workers dismissed from formal jobs. In economic upturns, transitions should be largely unidirectional, from informal microenterprises to the formal sector.

In the next section, a review of the relevant literature will be provided prior to an examination of the determination of the entry into self-employment in the following section. This will set up the presentation of the model, data, and estimation. Some concluding remarks will complete the chapter.

Literature review

There is little reason to suppose that the expanding literature on self-employment in the industrialized world, that views self-employment as a desirable and more flexible alternative to waged work (see Blanchflower and Oswald, 1998), may not also be relevant in LDCs. In fact, sociologists have been advancing this hypothesis for decades by actually asking workers about their motivations to be informal self-employed. In *Men in a Developing Society, Geographic and Social Mobility in Monterrey Mexico*, Balan (1973) conducted extensive retrospective interviews with workers and found that being one's own boss is well regarded and that workers often considered movement into self-employment from salaried positions an improvement in job status. Of the moves from formal positions into self-employment, the study found that 57 percent were moves upward in job quality, 30 percent were horizontal (which the authors argue improves welfare because of the greater independence), and only 11 percent were downward. Tables 6.1 and 6.2 confirm this from motivational responses from microenterprise surveys in Mexico and Brazil. Among Mexican self-employed men, roughly 60 percent reported leaving their previous job and entering self-employment for higher pay or greater independence.[1] These findings are broadly confirmed in the mammoth Brazilian Annual National Household Survey (*Pesquisa Nacional por Amostra de Domicílios* – PNAD), in which more than 62 percent of self-employed men stated that they did not want a formal sector job, primarily because they were happy with their current job.

The large presence of women in the sector similarly does not seem to be driven by the inability to find a formal sector job but rather due to balancing family responsibilities. Cunningham (1999a; 2001a; 2001b) shows, strikingly, that while women are "overrepresented" in the informal sector, this is not the case for single women who are, in fact, overrepresented in the *formal* sector (see Figure 6.1). However, among the many possible adverse consequences of marriage, a relocation to the informal sector is common. Tables 6.1 and 6.2 again confirm that being married was the primary reason for women to leave a previous job and enter self-employment in Mexico and in Brazil; competing household chores emerges as a key reason for women to choose not to be formal salaried workers. Consistent with these findings, Bosch and Maloney (2004), using labor transition data, show that there is a corridor of extraordinarily high mobility between absence from the labor force and informal self-employment for women that does not appear for men. This suggests, again, relatively low labor force attachment and that the border between the state of being self-employed, perhaps selling products at the market for a day or week, and being out of the labor force and focusing on household responsibilities is relatively porous and transient (Geldstein, 2000). Because, in this aspect too, the behavior of men and women is so different, this paper will focus primarily on the former.

Table 6.1   Mexico: Interviews with informal self-employed workers

Reasons for leaving last job	Men %	Women %
Fired, firm closed, contract ended	20.4	11.46
Low pay	21.68	10.93
To be independent	36.89	10.23
Retired	2.31	0.53
Moved	4.1	5.11
Married	0.35	46.03
Illness	4.29	7.05
Other	9.98	7.05
Observations	5923	567

Source: Mexican National Survey of Microenterprises (1992).

Table 6.2   Brazil: Interviews with self-employed workers

	Men %	Women %
1) *Would not like to be a formal sector employee*	62.00	51.20
2) *Reason for not wanting to be formal*		
Earn more in current job	17.20	9.10
Competing household chores	0.20	31.40
Need time for other activities	3.00	7.30
Happy with current job	65.20	41.10
Did not want to undertake requirements to be formal	11.00	7.40
Other	3.40	3.40

Source: Brazil Annual National Household Survey (PNAD, 1989).

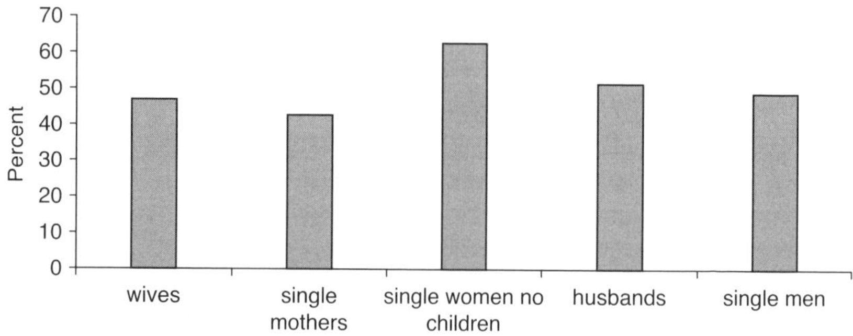

Figure 6.1   Participation in the formal sector by gender and marital status
Source: Cunningham (2001a).

Finally, studying labor market transitions in Mexico and Brazil, Maloney (2003) and Bosch and Maloney (2005) show that transitions between formal salaried work and informal self-employment are largely inconsistent with the standard queuing theory. Figure 6.2 suggests that these flows are highly correlated over the business cycle. The rise in transitions in both directions during the boom of 1988–1991 is suggestive of accelerated rematching across sectors, similar to what has been observed in the U.S. within the "formal" sector. Were the market sharply segmented, we would expect to see reduced flows into informal self-employment as flows into formality rose disproportionately. This is not the case and, in fact, net flows into self-employment increased during this boom, along with an increase in relative earnings.

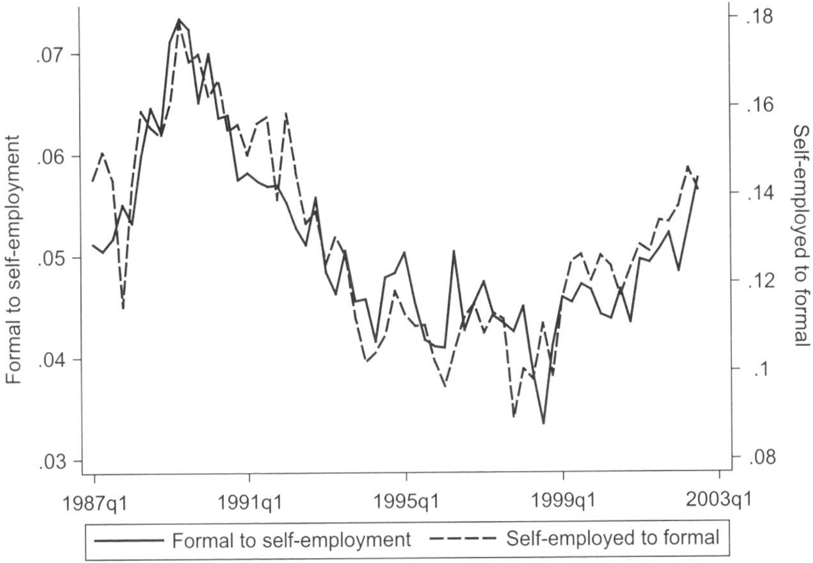

Figure 6.2 Labor flows between the formal salaried and informal self-employed sectors

Source: Bosch and Maloney (2004).

What determines the timing of entry into self-employment?

The dynamics underlying patterns of male worker transitions into self-employment further challenge the traditional Harris-Todaro (1970) model. Were informal self-employment an "easy entry" sector where workers queued for formal sector jobs, we would expect them to be younger. However, as Figure 6.3 suggests, entry increases with age. This means that Latin American countries share the same puzzle identified in the U.S. literature: Johnson (1978), Jovanovic (1979), and Miller (1984) argue that younger individuals are better able to bear the risk involved and hence should be heavily represented among entrants into self-employment. However, as Evans and Jovanovic (1989) note, this is inconsistent with Evans and Leighton's (1989) finding that the rate at which individuals exit the employed sector and enter self-employment (hazard rate) is constant across ages. They attribute this finding to liquidity constraints that dictate that workers require time to accumulate the financial capital needed to start a business.

This phenomenon may be exacerbated in the developing world where credit markets are poorly developed. Balan (1973, p. 217) find corroborating evidence in their interviews with workers: "First, the man must accumulate capital. This is no easy matter when he has a manual job and must provide

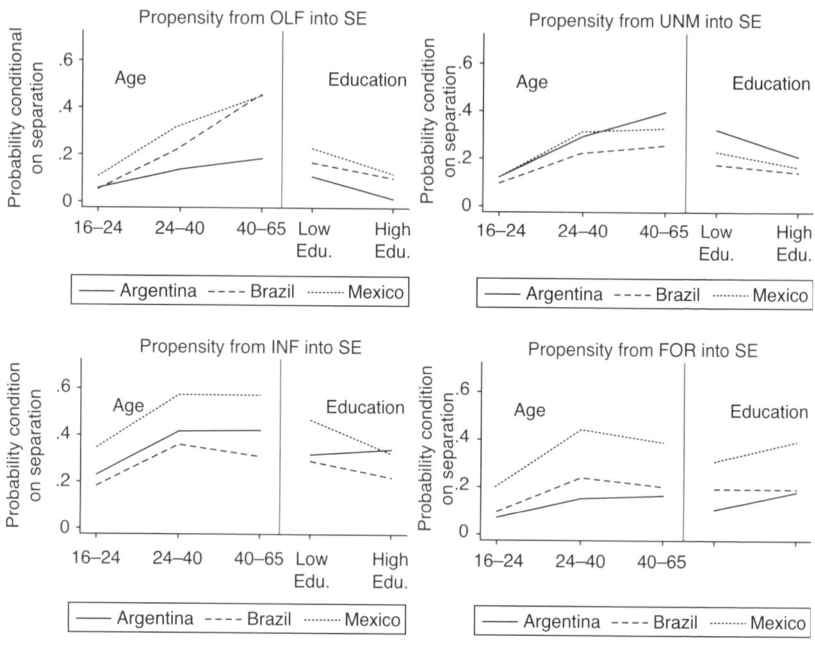

Figure 6.3　Entry into informal self-employment by age and education
Source: Bosch and Maloney (2005).

for a large family, so it generally takes years to accumulate enough capital. There must be sufficient funds not only to set up the business, but also to keep it going during the months or years while it runs at a deficit…these kinds of capital requirements are modest enough, but the capital is not easy to come by for the working classes of Monterrey or elsewhere in Mexico." Our sociologists suggest that the potential Mexican entrepreneur is rational, forward looking, and subject to the same types of constraints faced by his counterparts in advanced. This is also suggested by the Brazilian case where a relaxing of credit constraints effected by an increase in the value of unemployment insurance, had a significant positive impact on exits from unemployment into self-employment (Cunningham, 1999). In the next section, we will formalize this intuition and in the following one we provide supportive econometric evidence.

Modeling entry into self-employment

The sociologists' intuition can be rephrased as a Stopped Markovian Decision Process (SMDP)[2] where individuals faced with uncertainty about future streams of income as salaried and self-employed workers must decide their optimal savings and switching strategies. Their behavior can be seen as similar to that of workers who, perhaps with the idea of opening a business upon their return, migrate to a country that offers the possibility of accumulating wealth more quickly, and return home only when they reach their target level of savings (see Piore, 1979). This problem has been analyzed in detail by Berninghaus and Seifert-Vogt (1993) and we adapt their framework to our problem as a way of generating predictions to be tested in the empirical analysis.

We assume that the worker will open his own business at time τ and plans to operate it for T-τ years where T is the end of his planning horizon. He has subjective expectations π on the return to his accumulated real wealth x_τ that he has invested in the business. Upon starting his business, the worker will choose a sequence of consumption bundles, c_t to maximize:

$$\sum_{t=\tau}^{T} u(c_t)$$

$$\text{(6.1)}$$

$$\text{s.t. } 0 < c_t < x_t, \dots x_{t+1} = \pi\left(x_t - c_t\right), \dots t = \tau, \dots, T$$

where $u(.)$ represents the continuous per period utility function. We abstract from the discount factor since it will be the same in both sectors and we assume it unchanged. This reduces to a standard dynamic programming problem where $V\tau\,(x)$ is the value function at switch time τ, that is, the maximal value of the sum of per period utility from being an entrepreneur from τ to T.

While in the salaried sector from $t = 1, \dots, (\tau-1)$ the worker earns y_t where $\{Y_t\}$ is a stochastic process whose probability law is known to the worker. In each period, the worker chooses a consumption bundle c_t subject to the condition $c_t \le (x_t + y_t)$. Any surplus can be saved at a real interest rate, $it_{+1,}$ which is the realized value of a stochastic process $\{I_t\}$ governing the behavior of real interest rates. In each period, the worker must decide whether to work in the salaried sector for another period or to start his business and receive $V_t(x_t)$.

The optimal policy for this problem is a sequence of consumption strategies $(c(.))$ and the stopping (switching) time τ such that the total expected reward E

$$E_{(x_0, i_0, y_0)}\left(\sum_{t=0}^{\tau-1} u(c_t(.)) + V_\tau(x_\tau)\right)$$

$$\text{(6.2)}$$

is maximized given the initial state (x_0, i_0, y_0). The optimal stopping time is associated with each "state history" (x_t, i_t, y_t) and because these are realizations of a stochastic process, the τ, too is a random variable.

From the framework, several predictions emerge. First, there exists a critical level of target savings below which the worker will prefer to continue to stay salaried. For the case of a two-period model with logarithmic utility, Berninghaus and Seifert-Vogt show that the target level of savings falls with a rise in the subjective return to self-employment, π, rises with an increase in the opportunity cost of savings, i, and rises if a higher wage in the salaried sector raises the required comparable stream of income resulting from self-employment, and hence the start up capital required. The first two also have a predictable effect on the switch time, τ. In the last case, however, the overall impact of current income on τ is ambiguous since higher incomes both increase the level of target savings as well as increasing the possible rate of savings accumulation. Given two workers with identical savings, the one with higher income may find himself below the target rate of income and stay employed one more period to earn another period wage.[3]

Rephrased for present purposes becomes:

$$\Pr(\text{move}) = P\left(\pi, i, y\right)$$

$$\frac{\partial P}{\partial \pi} \geq 0, \ \frac{\partial P}{\partial i} \leq 0, \ \frac{\partial P}{\partial y}?,$$

(6.3)

It is worth comparing these predictions to those from the standard dualistic view where an above-market clearing formal sector remuneration, y, rations workers into the informal sector where the returns fall to absorb those in the queue. A fall in relative returns of self-employment for salaried work occurs in the context of economic downturns where the informal return must fall to absorb displaced workers. Similarly, to the degree that increased interest rates are associated with recession and the loss of salaried jobs, again, we may expect more movement of the displaced into the informal sector: movement into self-employment would be countercyclical. In both cases, the predicted signs would be the opposite of those implied by the model discussed above.[4]

Data and estimation results

The Mexican National Urban Employment Survey (ENEU) conducts extensive quarterly household interviews in the major metropolitan areas and the data are available from 1987 on. We focus on the pre-1993 period to avoid the lead up to and subsequent crisis at the end of 1994 when classical "queuing" approaches appear more relevant. The ENEU is structured as a rotating panel where in each quarter, a fifth of the sample is dropped and replaced by individuals who will be interviewed for each of the next five quarters. In 24 overlapping panels spanning the period 1987–1993, individual workers can be followed as they move among sectors of work. Individuals are matched by position in an identified household, sex, level of education, and age to ensure against generating spurious transitions. The analysis restricts itself to men aged 16–65 with a high school education or below. It also focuses on formal salaried workers and the "informal" self-employed, including owners of firms with fewer than 16 employees, none of whom have social security or medical benefits and are therefore not protected.[5] Only those who begin in formal salaried employment and move only once over five quarters into self-employment are retained, yielding a sample of 1087 workers. In the estimations, we employ predicted earnings in each sector as a measure of the "own" and "alternate" earnings, given the standard human capital variables, experience, experience squared, education, and education squared. The return to accumulated capital (the opportunity cost of using savings to open a business) is the real 30–60 day deposit rate as calculated from the International Financial Statistics of the IMF deflated by growth of the consumer price index.

A substantial literature exists on limited dependent models in a panel context (see Baltagi, 1996 or Maddala, 1983 for overviews) and continuous dependent variables in an incomplete or rotating panel context (Bjorn and Jansen, 1983; Hsiao, 1986; Nijman et al., 1991). Here we adapt a logit model for use in a rotating panel context.[6]

Table 6.3 presents the results of the estimation of the model set out in the previous section. The results are supportive of the model. The first column

Table 6.3   Determinants of the timing of moving to informal self-employment from salaried employment conditional on moving once, 1987–1993 (Rotating Panel Logit)

	(1)	(2)
Predicted wage (Salaried)	−.642	−.831
	(1.16)	(1.12)
Wage (−1)	1.16	–
	(1.21)	
Predicted earnings (Self)	2.86	2.96
	(.241)	(.228)
Earnings (−1)	−.0208	–
	(.287)	
Interest rate	−8.43 e-3	−8.72 e-3
	(2.40 e-5)	(2.37 e-5)
Interest rate(−1)	−5.83 e-3	7.07 e-3
	(1.88 e-5)	(1.61 e-5)

Note: Standard errors in parentheses.
Nobs=1078, Sample includes 24 complete panels of 5 quarters each spanning 1987–1993.

presents the complete specification and shows that for only the interest rate variable are lagged values significant. The second column presents a more parsimonious specification. Here, self-employed earnings appear very strongly and of the predicted sign, reflecting that as opportunities improve in the informal sector, workers are more likely to open their own businesses. The current wage in the formal sector still enters ambiguously, and is not significant. Again, theory suggests this may be reasonable given that a rise both increases the attractiveness of formal sector employment and raises the savings rate necessary to make a move into self-employment possible. Finally, the interest rate is strongly significant and of the predicted sign, suggesting that a rise in the opportunity cost of the capital used for start up discourages opening up a business. In all cases, the sign is the opposite of that predicted by conventional dualistic views of informal self-employment.

Conclusions

Our results are consistent with workers viewing informal self-employment as a desirable sector, but one that, in the presence of binding credit constraints, requires the accumulation of resources over time to enter. In this sense, we've provided both some theoretical structure and empirical verification of the insights arising from the sociological literature.

The policy implications for labor market analysis are substantial. If a large segment of the informal self-employed sector is, in fact, voluntary as a result of expected higher utility (proxied through expected wages) in the sector, then the design of social protection or other programs that would increase the value of the self-employed expected "package," becomes much more complex. If the sector is the result of segmentation, then any social program directed toward the informal, especially those that are noncontributory, will serve to offset the welfare losses resulting from the wage rigidities and not encourage entry to the informal sector. If not, then workers comparing the discounted present value of likely utility in each sector will view the complete package of attributes in the sector, both wage and nonwage. Hence, if the government implements universal health coverage or provides special services to microenterprises that raise their productivity, the benefits of being informal rise and we would expect to see more workers transiting into that sector. In turn, this shifts the labor supply curve of the formal sector to the left, implicitly levying part of the tax supporting these programs on formal firms.

Although the factors underlying women's decisions to enter the informal sector probably do not follow the same process, nonetheless, the apparent voluntary nature of much entry also suggest that care is required in implementing programs designed to offset the apparent overrepresentation in the informal sector.

Notes

We also thank the Mexican National Institute of Statistics, Geography and Information (INEGI) for the use of the data. INEGI is in no way responsible for any incorrect manipulation of the data or erroneous conclusions drawn from it. Contacts: wmaloney@worldbank.org, paroca@socompa.cecun.uncn.cl

1. Maloney (1999) broadly confirmed these findings with a large sample that allowed linking the rotating panel labor survey with a microenterprise module that tabulated motivations for entering the sector. He finds that at lead two-thirds of those entering informal self-employment report moving voluntarily, citing a desire for greater independence or higher pay as the principal motive even from relatively large formal firms.
2. See Eckstein and Wolpin (1989) for a review of the specification and estimation of dynamic stochastic discrete choice models.
3. By the same token, a worker who suddenly loses his job, that is, y goes to 0, will suddenly see the target level of saving decline and is more likely to move. In this way, the common vision of the informal sector as the reserve army of the unemployed can be seen in somewhat different light.
4. See Maloney (1997) for a discussion of the relative merits of formal vs. informal work and the procyclicality of the latter in Mexico.
5. It is often the case that the informal sector is defined as firms with five or fewer workers. As we are focusing on informality defined as being unprotected by social security or other legislation, we loosen the size limit to the next category tabulated. In practice, the vast majority of small firms in Mexico have fewer than three workers.
6. Fixed effects estimators are not appropriate in this context. The short panel time dimension permits only very imprecise estimates of the individual effect. In the limited dependent variable context, this induces bias into the parameter estimates.

References

Balan, J. (1973) *Men in a Developing Society: Geographic and Social Mobility in Monterrey,* Mexico: Austin University of Texas Press.

Baltagi, B.H. (1996) *Econometric Analysis of Panel Data,* New York: John Wiley and Sons.

Berninghaus, B., and H.G. Seifert-Vogt (1993) "The Role of the Target Saving Motive in Guest Worker Migration," *Journal of Economic Dynamics and Control,* 17, 181–205.

Bjorn, E., and E.S. Jansen (1983) "Individual Effects in a System of Demand Functions," *Scandinavian Journal of Economics,* 85, 461–483.

Blanchflower, D.G., and A.J. Oswald (1998) "What Makes an Entrepreneur?" *Journal of Labor Economics,* 16, 26–60.

Bosch, M., and W. Maloney (2005) "Gross Worker Flows in the Presence of Informal Labor Markets: The Mexican Experience 1987–2002," World Bank Working Paper, Washington, D.C.

Bosch, M., and W. Maloney (2004) "Labor Market Dynamics in Developing Countries: Comparative Analysis using Continuous Time Markov Processes," World Bank Working Paper, Washington, D.C.

Cunningham, W. (1999a) "Mexican Female Small Firm Ownership: Motivations, Returns, and Gender," LCSPG/World Bank, unpublished manuscript, Washington, D.C.

Cunningham, W. (1999b) "Unemployment Insurance in Brazil: Unemployment Duration, Wages, and Sectoral Choice," World Bank Working Paper.

Cunningham, W. (2001a) "Breadwinner versus Caregiver: Labor Force Participation and Sectoral choice over the Mexican Business Cycle," in E. Katz and M. Correia (eds.) *The Economics of Gender in Mexico*, Washington, D.C.: World Bank.

Cunningham, W., and W.F. Maloney (2001) "Heterogeneity in the Mexican Micro-enterprise Sector: An Application of Factor and Cluster Analysis," *Economic Development and Cultural Change*, 5, 131–156.

Eckstein, Z., and K.I. Wolpin (1989) "The Specification and Estimation of Dynamic Stochastic Discrete Choice Models, a Survey," *The Journal of Human Resources*, 24, 562–598.

Evans, D.S., and B. Jovanovic (1989) "An Estimated Model of Entrepreneurial Choice under Liquidity Constraints, *Journal of Political Economy*, 97, 808–826.

Evans, D.S., and L. Leighton (1989) "Some Empirical Aspects of Entrepreneurship," *American Economic Review*, 79, 519–535.

Geldstein, R. (2000) "Non-Labor Market Coping Strategies in Argentina," LCSPG/World Bank, Washington, D.C.

Harris, J.R., and M.P. Todaro (1970) "Migration, Unemployment, and Development: A Two Sector Analysis," *American Economic Review*, 60, 126–142.

Hsiao, C. (1986) *Analysis of Panel Data*, Econometric Society Monograph no. 11, Cambridge: Cambridge University Press.

Johnson, W. (1978) "A Theory of Job Shopping," *Quarterly Journal of Economics*, 92, 261–278.

Jovanovic, B. (1979) "Job Matching and the Theory of Turnover," *Journal of Political Economy*, 87, 972–990.

Maddala, G.S. (1983) *Limited Dependent and Qualitative Variables in Econometrics*, Cambridge: Cambridge University Press.

Maloney, W. (1999) "Does Informality Imply Segmentation in Urban Labor Markets? Evidence form Sectoral Transitions in Mexico," *World Bank Economic Review*, 13, 275–302.

Maloney, W. (2003) "Informal Self-Employment: Poverty Trap or Decent Alternative?" in G.S. Fields and G. Pfeffermann (eds.) *Pathways out of Poverty*, Amsterdam: Kluwer Academic.

Maloney, W.F. (1997) "Labor Market Structure in LDCs: Time Series Evidence on Competing Views," Working Paper Department of Economics, University of Illinois.

Miller, R.A. (1984) "Job Matching and Occupational Choice," *Journal of Political Economy*, 92, 1086–1120.

Nijman, R., M. Verbeek, and A. van Soest (1991) "The Efficiency of Rotating-Panel Designs in an Analysis of Variance Model," *Journal of Econometrics*, 49, 373–399.

Piore, M. (1979) *Birds of Passage*, New York: Cambridge University Press.

7
Institutions and Economic Growth in the Atlantic Periphery: The Efficiency of the Portuguese Machinery of Justice, 1870–1910

Jaime Reis

Introduction

The comparative economic performance of nations over the long run has been a major field of interest for some time now, both in Economic History and in Growth Economics. Thanks to the recent availability of macroeconomic data for many Western countries, its analysis has become possible using endogenous models which take into account the usual variables in the Solow formulation plus control variables, such as human capital, technology, or social capability. While recognizing the relevance of institutional factors, economic historians have appeared reluctant, however, to incorporate them formally into their equations.[1] This is particularly evident in the abundant historical literature on the economics of growth and convergence during the so-called "first era of globalization" (Baumol, 1986; Bordo et al., 2003; O'Rourke and Williamson, 1997; 1999; Pamuk and Williamson, 2000).[2] The classic work by O'Rourke and Williamson (1999), which quantifies in detail the causes of catch-up and convergence within the late nineteenth-century Atlantic economy, dismisses institutional influences on the grounds that open economy forces provide adequate explanation for the differential behavior of these economies. The assumption is that during the nineteenth century "the State took a broadly liberal policy stance" (p. 14) and institutional divergence among nations can therefore be treated as marginal to the problem under consideration.

The available evidence on the European countries that composed the nineteenth-century Atlantic economy does not support, however, this notion of homogeneity. Table 7.1 gathers quantitative data on various aspects of institutional development for 16 of the countries included in the O'Rourke and Williamson (1999) sample.[3] Column 1 presents an indicator of the "openness" of their public decisionmaking arrangements constructed by the University of Maryland's Polity-IV project.[4] Column 2 shows the extent of popular involvement in their political systems, through elections, as measured by the diffusion of the franchise.[5] Column 3 displays an index of "contract-intensive money" (CIM) devised by Clague et al. (1999), which proxies the public's trust in the institutions that protect property rights and enforce contracts.[6] In all of them, we find a considerable dispersion around the mean which suggests that the diversity of institutional endowments may have been considerable. This in turn would mean that institutions might well have a greater role to play in explaining the divergent patterns of long-term economic growth than has been thought likely.

Several difficulties arise, however, when we try to pursue these connections. One is that preliminary tests show that none of the variables in Table 7.1 in fact helps to improve the results of the convergence equations estimated by O'Rourke and Williamson.[7] Other, more appropriate ones must therefore be found. This raises a second problem, which is the

Table 7.1 Institutional characteristics of West European countries

	1	2	4
	Polity. 1870	**Franchise. 1870 (per-cent of population)**	**Contract-intensive money. 1913 (CIM)**
Austria	−4	30.0	0.82
Belgium	6	37.7	0.8
Denmark	−3	29.0	0.91
Finland	8	8.3	0.89
France	8	43.2	0.75
Prussia/Germany	2	38.3	0.91
Greece	10	30.5	na
Ireland	8	28.9	na
Italy	−1	12.3	0.7
Netherlands	−2	21.2	0.66
Norway	10	34.8	0.92
Portugal	2	25.3	0.37
Spain	6	35.7	0.31
Sweden	−4	12.7	0.92
Switzerland	10	28.5	0.92
U.K.	8	28.5	0.97
mean	3.3	17.5	0.78
stan. dev.	1.4	13.4	0.77
max.	10	43.7	0.97
min.	−4	3.5	0.31

Note:Cim=(M2−C)/M2.
Sources: See text.

difficulty of constructing adequate metrics to proxy, retrospectively, the various forms of institutional input which could be important for growth. As has been quite correctly observed, "institutions have to a large extent been left out of the analysis [of economic development for the reason that they are difficult to assess within a strictly defined theoretical framework and equally difficult to measure in quantitative terms" (Gunnarsson, 1991, p. 43). A further twist is that what differentiated nations, in late nineteenth-century Western Europe, was how well these institutions functioned, not so much how well they were structured, a point which has also been made with regard to the present day (Rodrik et al., 2004). Formal distinctions between the institutions of these states certainly existed but were far from substantial. This is not surprising bearing in mind that their respective institutional architectures and philosophies of government were shaped by a common Liberal parliamentary blueprint (Finer, 1997). What we try here therefore is to focus on the more relevant but elusive aspects of institutional quality, rather than on the more measurable but less significant ones of form.

The aim of this paper is to propose an indicator of institutional efficiency which does not suffer from the shortcomings noted above and can be useful to economic historians of institutions in general. It must be objective, quantifiable, and allow comparisons over time and space. We shall try to achieve this by assessing the effectiveness of the judicial system in protecting property rights and enforcing contracts, a key issue in the debate concerning the contribution of institutions to economic growth. This will be carried out in the historical context of Portugal, a small and backward economy of the Atlantic periphery during the "first era of globalization" (1870–1913).[8] The next section of this paper describes the model to be used and justifies the variable – the price of mortgage credit – chosen as a proxy for the "quality" of Portuguese justice in the late nineteenth century. This choice is guided by North's suggestion that "the level of interest rates in capital markets is perhaps the most evident quantitative dimension of the efficiency of the institutional framework" (North, 1990, p. 69). The third section presents the data collected in order to test the relationship under analysis and describes the applicable legal framework. The fourth section presents and discusses the results of the estimation. The last section concludes that the proposed approach provides a credible yardstick for measuring the effectiveness of the Portuguese courts of law and, by extension, of other systems of justice too. Having found that economic agents had a low regard for the ability of the judicial system to ensure the satisfactory enforcement of contracts, it further notes that this perception does not seem to have noticeably improved over time. Finally, it suggests the point at which Portugal may have stood in a rough international ranking of how several countries scored in terms of the quality of their systems of justice.

Background

An adequate protection of property and contractual rights has long been recognized as an essential part of the contribution of institutions to economic performance (Glaeser et al., 2004; Mauro, 1995). As Adam Smith (1776) commented, "commerce and manufactures…can seldom flourish in any state in which there is not a certain degree of confidence in the justice of government." Its absence has a negative effect on investment in fixed and human capital, and in research and technological innovation, which are crucial for growth and development (Nelson and Sampat, 2001). It also deters savers from acquiring stores of wealth and thereby discourages economic agents from pursuing profitable activities and seeking better results from their efforts. Above all, it holds back the spread of the division of labor and specialization which is critical to all modern economic growth (North, 1990).

A satisfactory degree of judicial protection for property and contracts depends on two conditions. It requires, on the one hand, a clear and sufficient body of rules and, on the other, a third-party agency which applies them fairly, expeditiously, and at a low cost. In order that the operation of the courts be facilitated, it is also necessary that arrangements should exist whereby contracts can be easily documented, certified, and registered and, in the case of property rights, that economic agents can identify them and their holders easily and unequivocally. In both these functions, expectations are important. Measures protective of property and contractual rights must therefore not only be "good." They must also be stable over time and predictable, so that economic agents can project past experience in a consistent fashion and thus maximize the beneficial effect of the system of justice.[9]

Assessing the output of a country's machinery of justice is not an easy matter. Judicial proceedings are often complex. The situations under scrutiny and the decisions produced by courts are far from homogeneous, and it is difficult to standardize them for the sake of quantification. Many of the indices used by the practitioners of the New Institutional Economics to quantify judicial efficiency are "subjective." They are based on surveys and polls which ask questions like "how badly do economic agents think the judicial system functions?" and are therefore unsuitable for historical situations. Moreover, typically, they convert qualitative assessments into numbers with the use of arbitrary scales. This poses formidable problems of additivity, interpretation, and comparison over time and space.[10] Another, this time "objective" approach has been used with some success in cases where litigation covers easily defined, repeat events such as eviction orders or check collection, and makes it possible to gauge efficiency simply by means of devices like counting the time it takes to reach or enforce a verdict. This sort of method has been used in several recent studies but not, to my knowledge, in historical contexts in which, in all likelihood, it would be an excessively arduous task to carry out.[11]

An alternative, indirect solution is to estimate judicial output by measuring its impact on the decisions of economic agents who are active in the markets affected by these rulings. A price for a given good or service that was significantly different from what might be expected, should the courts have functioned "normally," would indicate a failure in the protection of contractual rights, for example. Our objective is to apply this reasoning to a field in which abundant and reliable information is available and a certain amount of theoretical reflection has already been undertaken and can help us formulate a suitable model.

We have chosen for this exercise the market for microcredit in a rural setting. This was a common situation throughout nineteenth-century Europe, often bringing together a large number of borrowers and lenders, in operations which were typically small and mostly local. In such atomistic markets, where large participants were absent, it seems fair to assume that "the playing field must have been level" for all involved. Neither creditors nor debtors would have expected to obtain loan prices that deviated from what might be called a "normal" or competitive value.[12] In the first instance, contract enforcement relied to a considerable extent on informal mechanisms associated with reputation and credibility (Guinnane, 1994; 2001). When this failed to resolve situations of noncompliance, however, formal sanctions became necessary since a credit market, where unsanctioned default became easy and habitual, would soon be starved of capital and face rocketing interest rates. Hence the vital importance of courts of law which were able to adjudicate such conflicts rapidly and equitably. In cases where justice was administered slowly, unfairly, and with favoritism, the credit market was bound to function poorly, and the expression of this fact should be discernable in the behavior of the price at which credit was allocated.

In markets plagued by the opportunism of borrowers, lenders have two ways of safeguarding the capital they tie up in loans. One is by requiring safe collateral, which can be executed with the help of third-party enforcement arrangements in the event of failure by the debtor to meet interest and amortization obligations. The other is to do without a real guarantee (which the borrower might be too poor to have, for example) and instead obtain information, at a cost, about the personal attributes of the potential debtor, which might be relevant to the probability of his defaulting. Reputation for honesty, being a hard and productive worker, having a good coguarantor, and so on should enable the lender to form a reasonable expectation concerning the borrower's commitment. This would form the basis on which the decision was taken to enter into a personal, unsecured loan and at what price.

In the present study, we deal only with the first of these alternatives. Mortgage credit between private parties offers an excellent opportunity for an analysis of how well justice protects the rights of lenders. First, it is only through the courts of law, which keep records, that creditors can foreclose on defaulting debtors and recover their principle. Second, to be effective, it requires a legally binding record between the parties, drawn up in accordance with a standard formula, and placed in safekeeping. This means that a considerable amount of reliable, homogeneous information concerning both the contracts and those taking part in them has been generated and remains easily accessible for research.

In the model we outline below, the dependent variable is the market interest rate on this sort of loan, which is normally backed by secure assets, mostly land or buildings. Its main determinants are the cost of risk-free credit, an exogenous variable which is essentially stable over time, and a risk premium, the size and variance of which is governed by several factors. The most important one is the institutional setting, in particular the judicial system and its ability to protect and enforce contracts and property rights adequately. If this functions efficiently, the risk on such loans will be low and the rate charged should be close to the risk-free level. If this protection is perceived as inadequate by market operators, then the risk premium will be substantially greater than zero and the interest rate will rise accordingly. In this event, recognition of a low probability of recovering the loan, given the absence of an efficient independent third-party sanction, forces the lender to consider the personal attributes of the borrower when setting the conditions for the loan.

An adequate protection of the courts is a necessary but maybe not a sufficient condition for mortgage credit to enjoy a low-risk status, however. Historically, there are occasions when the guarantee may be worth less than the principal.[13] This would leave the creditor potentially at a disadvantage, in the event of noncompliance, and, as a result, under the necessity of charging a higher risk premium. One would expect that the smaller the ratio between the guarantee and the amount borrowed, the greater this premium would have to be. Interestingly, although not in a majority of the contracts considered here, many borrowers amongst those studied sought larger loans than their fixed assets could justify. This means that the relationship between the quality of justice and the price of credit is more complex than might be imagined at first sight.

Table 7.2 shows how the loan characteristics discussed above can be assembled into four categories in accordance with the two dichotomous criteria which are fundamental to the working of the mortgage credit market. The first separates operations into those in which the value of the guarantee is large enough to fulfill the contract in the case of default ("adequate guarantee") and those in which it is not ("inadequate guarantee"). The data employed in applying this standard are observable and readily available. The second criterion distinguishes whether loans were made within a framework of effective enforcement of contracts by an independent system of justice

Table 7.2 The model: Four scenarios of institutional/economic interaction in mortgage markets

	Adequate guarantee	Inadequate guarantee
	Panel 1	**Panel 2**
"Good" courts	r: low value, low variance r uncorrelated with g r uncorrelated with A	r: high value. high variance r correlated negatively with g r correlated with A
	Panel 4	**Panel 3**
"Bad" courts	r: high level, high variance r uncorrelated with g r correlated with A	r: high value. high variance r uncorrelated with g r correlated with A

Note: r = rate of interest on loans; g = ratio of mortgage to debt values; A = vector of attributes of borrowers, lenders and contracts.

("good courts") or not ("bad courts"). This is the variable which we cannot observe directly and therefore have to infer. To do so, we submit the loan information at our disposal to three independent statistical tests, which will tell us which of the two institutional alternatives – "good" or "bad" courts of law – best fits the evidence we have gathered. Before we define these tests, however, we must determine the implications, for the profile of this market, of belonging to each one of the panels in Table 7.2.

We begin by looking at what would happen if the courts of law had been capable of giving satisfactory protection to the suppliers of financial services and, at the same time, borrowers had provided adequate collateral on the loans made (panel 1). To begin with, the interest rate level (r) would be typically low and fairly close to its risk-free level, in accordance with the security enjoyed by lenders vis-à-vis their debtors. The personal risk represented by individual borrowers being irrelevant to the determination of the price of the loan, the variance of r would also be low. Consequently, none of the personal attributes of borrowers noted above (vector A) would bear a statistically significant relationship to r either, as they would be unimportant for the recovery of the principal, should a default occur. Finally, the interest rate (r) and the guarantee/debt ratio (g) would be uncorrelated owing to the fact that above a "safe" threshold for g, the risk of the transaction would not be affected by its getting any larger. The lender would always recover his outlay, whatever the magnitude of this ratio.[14]

A second scenario (panel 2) would occur if the ratio g was less than the level that the market judged adequate. Although the judicial system was efficient in enforcing contracts and executing the collateral, in the event of a default, the lender would not recoup fully his loss in this way. This would require an interest rate (r) somewhat above that of a perfectly secure loan to compensate for the greater risk. For this reason also, one would expect that r would show a negative correlation with g. In taking on this risk, however, the lender would also have to take into account the personal attributes (A) of the borrower, since they would affect the latter's capacity to meet the difference between the value of the loan outstanding and that of the security. The interest rate charged ought therefore to correlate with these attributes, and this would imply a higher degree of variance for r than found in panel 1.

A third possibility (panel 3) would be characterized by a high degree of incapacity of the machinery of justice to protect creditors' contractual rights, and by mortgage guarantees being too low to ensure full repayment of the debt. In the event of default, lenders would have a low expectation of receiving any or only some of the collateral in a reasonable delay. This would entail a high-risk premium. The interest rate would be correspondingly high and would not bear any relation to the value of the collateral. Instead, it would be determined by the personal attributes (A) of the borrower, on which the chances of recovery of the principle would be based. In this case, r would also have a high variance.

Panel 4 shows what would happen if the courts failed to play their role properly as protectors of property and contractual rights, but this time with mortgage guarantees in excess of the value of the principal. The result would be both a level and a variance in the interest rate (r) significantly higher than one would expect to meet in a risk-free environment. The ratio g would once again have no influence on the level of r, although not for the same reason as in panel 1. Rather it would be because no matter how great the value of the collateral, its practical importance for the lender's calculation was bound to be very small. In contrast, r would bear a significant relationship to the personal attributes of debtors (A) because these constituted the only information that lenders could rely on when gauging their chances of repayment by borrowers.[15]

This section's central claim then is that three simple quantitative tests arise from the schematic description in Table 7.2 and provide us with the means to infer the "goodness" of the judicial framework within which a given mortgage market might operate. Before applying them to our data, however, it is important to consider the information we shall be using and to summarize the legal context of late-nineteenth-century rural Portugal, which has been chosen as the proving ground for our hypothesis.

Nineteenth-century rural Portugal

Although the nineteenth century expansion of financial services in Europe has been often thought of as an urban phenomenon, there was a rural dimension to it which had considerable significance too. Loans to farmers, landowners, or simply to residents in the countryside, often financed from rural origins too, grew enormously in all countries during this period, and served to satisfy consumption needs, to adjust to life-cycle problems, or to permit investment in additional agricultural capacity and new technology (Guinnane, 2001; Lindgren, 2002; Soto, 2001; Postel-Vinay, 1988). Despite the rapid proliferation of institutional means, such as land banks, rural savings banks, and rural credit cooperatives, much of this flow continued to occur through informal channels, involving only individuals and fairly simple contracts. Even in a "financially sophisticated" country such as Sweden at the end of this century, informal credit was still about as important, in the provinces, as that undertaken by the corporate sector (Lindgren, 2002). Across the continent, mortgage loans, whether in the formal or the informal market, played an important part, but it is impossible to be precise regarding the share of total resources which they absorbed. Around 1900, in Spain, they accounted for 80 percent of all formal rural credit (Carmona and Simpson, 2003, p. 165), while in Italy mortgages outstanding were about equal to the total liabilities of all corporate financial institutions.[16] However, in the absence of data regarding "personal credit," that is, loans with no more backing than the borrower's signature, we cannot gauge what part mortgages were of total rural credit in any of these countries.

Portugal did not diverge from this pattern. Data on both mortgage and personal rural credit are scarce, unreliable, and far from comprehensive. We lack any information on the extent of "personal," unsecured credit, although impressionistic accounts suggest that, in the countryside, it was both substantial and much more expensive than mortgage credit. Indeed, the cry of "usury" was a frequent one in connection with this form of finance (Esteves, 2002; Ulrich, 1908). What little we know regards mortgage credit. Only one national compilation is available, for the period 1852–1862. It shows that a total of about 35,000 *contos*[17] was contracted during this decade in this form,[18] which suggests the existence, by the early 1860s, of a national stock of debt of the same order of magnitude. This can be compared to a total value of landed property at the time of around 400,000 *contos* (Vaz, 1863).

During the following decades, it seems that this portfolio must have grown to a fair extent, both in absolute terms and relative to the value of land. One indication is the creation in 1864 of the Companhia Geral de Crédito Português, to carry out long-term operations (up to 60 years of duration) on the security of large estates (Marques, 1989). Altogether, 40,000 *contos* were loaned by this land bank between 1865 and 1909 and this was only a fraction of all mortgages in rural Portugal, since small and medium property was entirely bypassed by this institution. A second piece of evidence comes from the survey conducted on 54 of the country's c. 300 municipalities, in 1884, showing that between them their notaries had altogether 40,000 *contos* worth of hypothecary loans outstanding on their books (Rodrigues, 1929). A third comes from a handful of local studies which have revealed informal markets for this type of finance in the northern, central, and southern rural parts of the country (Brettell, 1991; da Fonseca, 1977; Fonseca, 1996;

Silva, 1994; Vaquinhas, 1982; Vaquinhas and Fonseca, 1984). The picture they draw is of a high dispersion in loan size, average annual interest rates of about 8 percent, but ranging from 5 to 25 percent, and a length of commitment going from several months to ten years, with a mean of around five years. Borrowers and lenders tended to be local, although some of the capital employed was drawn from farther away.

Loans backed by material guarantees are known to have been practiced in Portugal centuries before the period we are considering. Their legal framework appears, however, to have been quite imperfect and to have made their use difficult and costly prior to its modernization in the 1860s.[19] The compilation of the country's first civil code, in 1867, and the approval, in 1863, of a law establishing a national land registry eliminated many of these imperfections and, in theory at least, created conditions favorable to an expansion of mortgage credit and to its becoming cheaper and easier to use.

The advantages conferred by this new legal package were several.[20] In the first place, the new civil code defined clearly the hierarchy of precedence of all debt obligations and placed mortgages high on this scale, well above most so-called "ordinary credits," thus making them secure. It made the mortgage lien specific to a given asset and did away with the figure of the "general mortgage," which used to fall on all of the debtor's real estate, consequently making it hard to distinguish between the rights of individual creditors. The lender was now able to know exactly which asset was assigned to his particular credit and was thus assured that until the resolution of the contract. This collateral would not serve to meet any other obligation. Creditors' rights were attached to the mortgaged object and no longer to the person of the debtor or to his estate. This meant that in case of a default, all they had to do was seize the guarantee, whoever owned it, an easier task than pursuing judicially the debtor, who might no longer own the asset or be difficult to locate. Finally, in 1867, the civil code abolished the law of 1757 that had fixed the interest rate at 5 percent, and symbolically renamed what used to be called "usury" as an "onerous loan." It also allowed the contracting parties to set the price of money freely.[21] False contractual stipulations that inflated the principle of the loan in order to make it possible to charge higher prices in reality than those allowed by law ceased, and this made the whole process less prone to abuses and irregularities.

To make these dispositions more effective, a national land registry was set up, with offices throughout the country, in which all properties, their attributes and value, their proprietors, and the legal onuses incumbent upon them had to be formally inscribed. The inscription of these legal burdens was to be carried out in chronological sequence, so that precedence of obligations might be easily established and enforced, if necessary. Proper identification of the owners prevented others without authority from attempting to mortgage a property to which they had no legal title. Full publicity was given to the contents of the register. To ensure further transparency, any single property could be entered only in the office of the area where it was located. A specialized body of state functionaries was put in charge of these arrangements, and made liable to penalties in the event of any infringement of the rules.The data to test our model come from the records of mortgage credit transactions carried out between the 1870s and the 1910s and kept by the public notaries of the localities where they took place. They are currently held in the notarial collection of the Portuguese national archive (Arquivo Nacional da Torre do Tombo). Being legal records of contracts which were entered into freely and made before sworn public officials, they must be presumed to be reasonably reliable, particularly as they could serve later as proof in litigation. They cover the vast majority of occurrences of this sort because, with the exception of small amounts, all mortgage deals had to be the object of a notarized contract.

Each entry in the notary's ledger corresponds to a single specific debt. In most cases, it represents a new loan but in a few it was a "confession of a debt" which had been contracted at an earlier date, without formality, and was therefore being restated, with proper legal solemnity, in order to secure the interests of those involved.[22] Each entry usually contains the name, occupation, and residence of the contracting parties. It also provides evidence of their civil status and capacity to sign. Besides this, it includes the interest rate charged, the amount of the debt, often the declared value of the collateral, the number of items of which the latter consisted, and their location. The duration of the loan is mentioned too but rarely with the precision that would render this information useful.[23]

Three benchmarks, for the periods 1874–1876, 1894–1896 and 1910–1913, have been constructed with these data. They cover six counties in the district of Lisbon, namely Torres Vedras, Sintra, Arruda dos Vinhos, Alenquer, Mafra, and Vila Franca de Xira, all of them located between 30 and 55 kilometers from the capital. At the time, the economic base of these administrative units was mainly agricultural, with a marked productive diversification into wine, cereals, olive oil, fruit, and animal husbandry, and a strong orientation towards the market. They were essentially areas of dispersed smallholdings and fairly densely populated. They were quite well connected, by road or railroad, to the small market towns of the region, and ultimately to Lisbon, but in none of these municipalities was there either a branch of a national bank or any local credit institution. Some Lisbon banks had correspondents there, indicating connections with a broader financial world, but they did not carry out credit operations, least of all with the farming community, which was thought too risky and suitable only for mortgage loans, which these institutions did not generally handle (Morais, 1889).

Not all entries are complete. The main lacuna occurs is the value of the collateral. In the cases of collateral consisting of landholdings already entered in the land registry office, notaries did not need to mention this value and recovering the information from the land registry itself has proved impossibly complex. Thus, although the data base contains some 1,750 observations, we can only count on about 1,150 for the tests requiring full information, all the same a satisfactory sample.

The profile which emerges tallies with the characteristics detected in earlier studies of similar regions in Portugal (Vaquinhas and Fonseca, 1984; Fonseca, 1977). On average, loans were not large – between 200,000 and 300,000 reis.[24] The overwhelming majority of participants were local, borrowers and lenders often residing in the same parish, and transactions were entirely between individuals, except for a few involving charitable foundations as lenders. Although borrowers were more numerous than lenders, there would seem to have been no dominant players on either side of the relationship to distort competitive conditions. Having thus established that the conditions called for by the model formulated above appear to be satisfied, we can now turn to the discussion of the results of our three tests.

Results

In comparative terms, Portugal's macroeconomic performance during the years from 1850 to 1913 left much to be desired. Although it had embarked on a process of sustained growth which was common throughout the Atlantic economy, by 1913 it was not only still at the bottom of the ranking in this group, but its per capita GDP had fallen from 60 percent of the average for the most advanced economies to 35 percent of the same (Amaral, 2002). Contemporary public opinion was naturally pessimistic about this economic inadequacy. It was not insensitive either to the institutional roots of these problems, be they in the political system, in the mechanisms of public administration, in the machinery of justice, or in the provision of education (Ramos, 1994).

But were Portuguese institutions responsible to any extent for this comparatively weak economic performance? Were they worse than those of other countries at the time? Could they have delivered a better input in terms of the process of economic growth? In this section we attempt some preliminary answers to these questions, with the help of the results of the three tests outlined above and applied to the data on mortgage contracts assembled for the period between 1873 and 1913. Our aim, first of all, is to determine whether the judicial system functioned poorly in Portugal compared to what might have been reasonably expected. Second, we try to place these findings in a broader international context, by comparing this with what happened elsewhere and therefore should have been practicable anywhere, including Portugal.

The first test focuses on the mean and dispersion of the interest rate charged on mortgage loans. As we saw earlier, one would expect that "bad courts of law" would normally be associated with a high mean and a high variance in this variable. In one instance (Table 7.2, panel 2), however, these characteristics could concur with "good courts," if they coincided with loans in which the ratio (g) of the collateral to the loan value was low. The evidence marshaled in Table 7.3 covers 14 different situations in six counties at different points in time, plus three further benchmarks with incomplete information for Coimbra. It shows interest rate averages lay in a narrow range, from just over 7 to just over 9 percent. In the case of the 1,342 contracts for which we have information on this item, the overall mean is 8.0 percent and the standard deviation is 1.90.

Was this too high a price for low-risk credits such as mortgage loans backed by solid real estate guarantee? Was the implicit risk premium excessive? Three domestic standards may be invoked for comparison. All of them have to do with low-risk financial applications. One comes from the Bank of Portugal, which discounted 90-day commercial paper, in Lisbon, normally at a rate of 5 percent. Although this was first-class paper, with two very good signatures, it was not free from default, and the bank had occasionally to litigate to secure its interests.[25] Nevertheless, it was probably one of the safest financial applications available. A second yardstick is the implicit return on government domestic bonds. This was perhaps a less secure asset and certainly more volatile, despite the state's guarantee, and its rate fluctuated between 4.1 and 6.4 percent over the period (Esteves, 2002). The third was

Table 7.3 Mortgage interest rates: Mean and dispersion

	Mean	Standard deviation	Coefficient of variation	Maximum	Minimum
Alenquer, 1870s	10.7	3.16	0.295	20.0	5.0
Arruda dos Vinhos, 1870s	9.3	2.14	0.230	17.0	5.0
Mafra, 1870s	9.2	2.06	0.223	16.0	4.5
Mafra, 1890s	8.2	1.87	0.227	13.0	5.0
Mafra, 1910s	8.2	1.38	0.168	16.0	4.0
Sintra, 1870s	7.3	1.56	0.214	12.0	4.8
Sintra 1890s	7.8	1.23	0.159	10.0	4.8
Sintra 1910s	7.6	1.28	0.168	10.0	5.0
Torres Vedras, 1870s	8.6	2.69	0.313	16.0	4.5
Torres Vedras, 1890s	7.7	1.48	0.191	12.5	5.0
Torres Vedras, 1910s	7.4	1.15	0.155	10.0	5.0
Vila Franca de Xira, 1870s	9.0	2.83	0.314	17.0	5.0
Vila Franca de Xira, 1890s	9.1	2.42	0.266	15.0	5.0
Vila Franca de Xira, 1910s	8.0	1.86	0.232	10.0	4.0
All	8.0	1.90	0.237	17.0	4.8
Coimbra, 1873	8.4	na	na	na	na
Coimbra, 1878	8.1	na	na	na	na
Coimbra, 1885	7.5	na	na	18.0	5.0

Sources: Arquivo Nacional da Torre do Tombo (Lisbon), Colecção Notários, except for Coimbra/1873 and 1878, which are from Vaquinhas and Fonseca (1983), and Coimbra/1885, which is from Fonseca (1977).

the return on the bonds issued by the Crédito Predial land bank to finance its mortgage loans, which was 6 percent until 1880 and after that between 4 and 5 percent. These claims were backed by a stock of real estate worth at least twice the outstanding loans, as well as by the subscribed shareholder capital, and their market quotation deviated very little from par throughout the period (Marques, 1989). None of these "safe" alternatives could be said to have been much less risky than contractualized mortgages on land and buildings. Significantly, however, their yield was 2 or 3 percentage points lower than the interest rates shown in Table 7.3, a differential which is hard to reconcile with a high standard of judicial efficiency.[26]

As for the dispersion of the price of mortgage, the standard deviation and coefficient of variation data in Table 7.3, at first sight, suggest that these rates were quite "bunched up" around the mean. However, the fact that in all counties the maximum values of the distribution was between double and triple their minimum rates points to the existence of some very distant outliers. Obviously, the institutions that enforced these contracts were unable to countervail the hazard represented by "marginal" borrowers, whose only chance of borrowing was to pay a high-risk premium in a transaction which normally should have been free from this burden.

International comparisons are a second way of looking at the problem. These are not easy to come by in a field of research which has hardly been explored in the perspective adopted here. It is possible, nevertheless, to gather sufficient evidence to support the view that substantial discrepancies in mortgage rates existed between countries that could not be ascribed solely to differences between their respective prevailing interest rates. In the last decades of the nineteenth century, Sweden, Denmark, and the Netherlands, all of them wealthier countries with a reputation for political stability and sound public administration, emerge as quite distinct from Portugal. In the first case, the average interest on mortgages was 5.5 percent, in the second they were 4.86 and in the Netherlands they lay between 4.5 and 5.0 percent. In Sweden, the nearly risk-free discount rate of the Central Bank varied between 4.2 and 5.0 percent, in Denmark it was 3.7 percent on average, while in the Netherlands it was between 3.0 and 3.5 percent. In this group, there was clearly a much smaller risk differential than we find in Portugal.[27]

Spain's experience might be expected to be like that of Portugal. Not only were they similar in cultural, social, and political backgrounds, but in that country too contemporary opinion saw mortgages as a risky business in which the recovery of the principal could be often problematic (Carmona and Simpson, 2003). In fact, a significant risk premium is evident in Spain too. A study of the Mediterranean region of Murcia shows a mean interest rate for mortgages of approximately 9 percent in 1900–1905 (Martinez Soto, 2001). Another, for Navarra, during an earlier period – 1858–1882 – comes up with a mean of 9.4 (Sabio Alcuten, 1996). Throughout the entire period, the discount rate of the Bank of Spain oscillated between 4.5 and 5.0 percent.[28] Similarly, in two counties of the booming coffee-based economy of southern Brazil, a country of young and somewhat unpredictable institutions, we find average interest rates on mortgages of over 11 percent during the years from 1865 to 1887, while rates on "safe" assets were between 5 and 6 percent (Marcondes, 2002).[29]

The conclusion that the Portuguese differential for risk was large and dispersed, both by internal and by international standards within the Atlantic economy, thus validates the situation depicted in panels 2, 3, and 4 of Table 7.2, but does not fit panel 1. Consequently, we turn now, for further clarification of our hypothesis, to our second test, which focuses on two classes of loans: those with a high g and those with a low one. Two issues arise. One is that of the relationship between the rate of interest on mortgage loans (r) and the ratio of guarantee-to-principal values (g). In the case of an "inefficient" judicial system (panels 3 and 4), we would not expect any correlation between these two variables. With "good" courts and a high value of g (panel 1), on the other hand, there would be a complete absence of any significant relationship between r and g – the lender would always recover all of the principle plus outstanding interest thanks to efficient judicial intervention. In contrast, with "good" courts and a low value of g (panel 2), this variable ought to be negatively correlated with interest. Although lenders would anticipate an easy recovery of the guaranteed part of their loan in the event of a default, they still faced some risk, on its uncovered part. This would push the risk premium up somewhat, although less than the premium associated with "bad courts" (panels 3 and 4).

This brings up the second component of this test, which is whether the interest on well-guaranteed loans should be different from that on inadequately guaranteed ones. Mortgages with a low g, if they were in panel 2 should have a lower mean interest than if they were in panel 3, which enjoyed no risk premium reduction. In fact, the latter's interest rate ought to be close to that for loans with a higher g and facing insufficient protection by the courts, namely those in panel 4. Grouping loans by the size of their g ratio and comparing the resultant interest means would therefore constitute another way of sorting our sample in the terms laid out in Table 7.2.

We have considered two thresholds for the guarantee-to-principal ratio. One is a scenario where the ratio is 2.0, corresponding to the requirement imposed by the Portuguese Crédito Predial bank for its operations. In the other, g would be 1.5, reflecting an assumption that local, informal lenders had comparatively better knowledge and consequently needed to protect themselves less from the search costs of the transaction than a Lisbon bank would. We follow the latter approach as being more plausible of the two.

A glance at Table 7.4 shows that for $g < 1.5$ there is no correlation between g and r. This definitely "fails" panel 2 on this count, but satisfies the requirement, in this respect, of panel 3, which is that the two variables be uncorrelated.

Table 7.4   Correlations between the rate
of interest and the g ratio

	Correlation	Sign
g >1.5	**no** (0.004)	–
g < 1.5	**no** (0.006)	+

Note: Value of R2 in brackets.
Sources: The same as for Table 7.3.

When we test this relationship for situations in which the collateral-to-debt ratio is "adequate," both panels 1 and 4 come out well, that is there is no correlation with the interest rate. The second dimension of the test confirms this result. A two-sample z-test on the means of these two groups shows that, at the 5 percent significance level, the null hypothesis is verified. This means that loans with a smaller *g* had the same mean interest rate as those with the larger one and therefore might not be located in panel 2, but rather in panel 3, where rates would be similar to those in panel 4.

At this point, it is difficult to claim that panels 1 and 2, corresponding to "good courts," are completely ruled out, but it is clear that it is the situations involving "bad courts" (panels 3 and 4) that have responded better to the tests conducted so far. We move on therefore to our third and decisive test.

The problem which arises now relates to the informational asymmetry which usually characterizes credit transactions. As a rule, lenders know less than borrowers about the capacity and inclination of the latter to meet their contractual obligations. It is also hard for them to ascertain whether the loan is being used to increase the productive capacity of the borrower and thereby rendering him better able to repay the amount borrowed. Mortgages, if properly enforced, are an efficient device for circumventing this difficulty but in the case we are considering, this remedy may not have been available. Creditors in this case would have had to overcome this knowledge gap by assessing the likelihood of a default directly on the basis of the personal attributes of the borrower. This would involve greater costs, as well as increased risks, both of which would have to be compensated by charging a premium (Guinnane, 2001).[30] Our aim, with this third test, is to find out whether creditors, finding themselves unprotected by the courts of law, did indeed set interest rates which were not only higher but also related to borrowers' characteristics insofar as relevant to the risk they represented.

Three types of characteristics are pertinent to this exercise and jointly constitute vector *A*. One concerns the reputation of debtors for honesty and commitment to contractual obligations. Another refers to their material capacity to meet these obligations. A third has to do with features which were specific to the contract itself and affected transaction costs. It is extremely difficult to gather satisfactory historical evidence regarding the first of these. Nevertheless, we try here two possibilities. One is the participation in the transaction of cosignatories (*cosign*) who pledged their assets and personal reputation to the satisfaction of the borrower's obligation in the event of a default. From this paper's point of view, what is important is that this support may have signaled the borrower's standing in the community, since there would have been little sense in getting a cosignatory to risk his name and assets on behalf of someone whose character was deemed unreliable. On this reasoning, other things being equal, the presence of cosignatories, a dummy variable (=1), should lower the interest rate and make the coefficient negative. The second possibility is the distance (*distance*), in kilometers, separating the abodes of the lender and borrower. This should measure how easy (or difficult) it was for the former to assess accurately the latter's reputation – in some contracts the parties to the contract lived in the same village, in others, 15 or 20 kilometers apart. The expectation is that this coefficient should be positive.

The contracts we have collected also contain items which may be used to proxy the second group of attributes that make up vector *A*. One of them is the amount borrowed (*loan*). A negative sign has been suggested by some of the literature for its coefficient on the grounds that the search cost for loans contained an important fixed element (Guinnane, 2001). Although plausible, this would have represented a very small expense given that the universe of loans was exiguous and therefore search costs were low. Our view instead is that larger loans were taken for investment purposes, by well-heeled borrowers with a good capacity to repay, while smaller ones tended to be contracted for reasons of economic survival and taken by penurious and less creditworthy agents (Hoppe and Langton, 1994; Martinez Soto, 2001; Svensson, 2001). *Loan* is therefore treated here as an indicator of the economic capacity that we are trying to detect in borrowers and its sign should be negative.

Two other personal attributes should contribute to the same end. One is the debtor's civil status (*civ*) – single, married, or widower. The reasoning in this case is that in a peasant society, a married producer was likely to have a larger family labor force at his disposal and therefore be more robust economically (the dummy is =1 for married debtors, and =0 for other situations). The sign for this coefficient ought therefore to be negative. The other is human capital, which we proxy with an indicator of literacy (*litdebt*) (=1 for those able to sign their names and =0 for those signing with a cross). This qualification was still relatively scarce in rural Portugal in contrast with nineteenth-century rural Sweden, where it was strongly associated with financial and productive capacity (Nilsson et al., 1999).[31] We see no reason to think otherwise in the case of Portugal and so, again, an inverse relation with the interest rate and a negative coefficient are expected.[32]

Age, in this context, would be interesting too, although the sign of its coefficient is not unambiguous. It might have proxied physical vigor inversely and therefore productive capacity, but a longer life might also have favored the observation of reputation, as well as the likelihood of a greater accumulation of material wealth and therefore of a greater security in loan transactions. Unfortunately, data for this are available for only a small number of cases and restricted to one county alone – Sintra, in the 1870s – and they yield nonsignificant results anyway.

The interest rate on mortgages might have been affected by factors which were specific to the contracts themselves, rather than to the persons involved. They are worth taking into account nevertheless insofar as they impinged on transaction costs associated with the use of mortgages and would therefore have affected the price of the operation. One of them is the number of separate plots of land or buildings (*nplot*) which composed the collateral that underpinned the transaction. A smaller number would entail lower search costs for the lender and a lower interest rate, conversely, with the result that the coefficient of this variable might be expected to be positive. A second feature of this kind is whether the mortgaged items had been entered into the new land registry (*reg*) created after 1863. Much property in the countryside was not registered until much later, owing to the cost, the bureaucratic difficulty, and the distance from the land office. In the eyes of a lender, such assets would have been perceived as a less reliable guarantee, given the many forms of malfeasance to which the lack of registration could give rise. In these cases, credit would have been relatively more expensive. With registered collateral, a mortgage would have attracted a lower rate of interest and hence we should expect a negative coefficient for this variable.

To make this analysis complete, it is necessary to consider whether geography had any influence on interest rates, a point suggested by the rate differences between localities shown in Table 7.3. The question is whether there were locational specificities which determined these variations in the price of credit, despite the physical proximity and socioeconomic similarity between them. Could this be an aspect of institutional conditions or was it simply the result of market segmentation and contrasting local supply and demand conditions? To try and answer this question we used dummies for the four main towns in the sample, namely Torres Vedras (TV), Sintra (SNT), Vila Franca de Xira (VFX) and Mafra (MAF).

From the point of view of the present analysis, the results of the OLS estimation presented in Table 7.5 are important. All coefficients are individually significant at least at the 10 percent level and two-thirds of them are at the 1 percent level. All but one (*civ*) have the expected sign and the F statistic allows us to reject the null hypothesis of the coefficients being jointly equal to zero. The R2 is not particularly high, as one might expect given this is a panel data exercise, but suggests a reasonable explanatory power for the equation. It should be borne in mind that it is derived from historical data

Table 7.5 Determinants of the interest rate of mortgage contracts, 1870s to 1910s Dependent variable: Interest rate (OLS regression)

Explanatory variables (expected signs in brackets)	
C	10.067***
	(54.13)
Loan (–)	–0.807***
	(–4.821)
Civ (–)	0.212*
	(1.799)
Litdebt (–)	–0.487***
	(–3.903)
Nplot (+)	0.062*
	(1.651)
Reg (–)	–0.211*
	(–1.716)
TV	–2.095***
	(–10.004)
SNT	–2.154***
	(–10.682)
MAF	–1.748***
	(.8.806)
VFX	–1.147***
	(–5.412)
R2	0.161
F-statistics	24,298
Prob (F-statistic)	0.000
N	1153

Notes: *t*-statistics in brackets; loans in millions of *reis*; civ dummy – married =1, single or widower=0; lit dummy – can sign =1, cannot sign =0; reg dummy – registered collateral =1, not registered collateral = 0; cosign dummy – has cosignatory =1, no cosignatory =0; TV – Torres Vedras; SNT – Sintra; MAF – Mafra; VFX – Vila Franca de Xira.

Sources: See text.

which were gathered by small-town notaries, who were often insufficiently qualified and may have worked according to not very consistent standards of exactitude (Silva, 1911). The implication is that mortgage interest rates were indeed influenced by the personal attributes of borrowers, who were made to pay a risk premium which reflected the risk they represented for their creditors. This is associated with the fact that lenders attached little value to the role of collateral in the mortgages they subscribed, a consequence, in turn, of their lack of trust in the judicial system. In terms of the model in Table 7.2, this means placing our data in panels 2, 3 and 4, but not in panel 1.

Besides personal attributes, interest rates emerge as being surprisingly influenced by locational specificities too, even though there was such a narrow geographic compass. Other things being equal, mortgages were dearer in Vila Franca de Xira and Mafra than in Sintra and Torres Vedras. It is tempting to invoke social and economic circumstances to explain these disparities but even the most obvious ones do not seem to provide a suitably coherent analysis. Distance from, and accessibility to, the large pool of savings in nearby Lisbon is a case in point and would proxy the supply side of this story, yet it fits poorly with the data. Greater proximity to the capital was not matched by cheaper credit. Per capita revenue from direct taxation is a variable that might have proxied demand side conditions convincingly, but also fails in practice to support a plausible interpretation.[33] Alternatively, we might contemplate an institutional formulation according to which courts of law did significantly and consistently better in some places than others. This would be coherent with the main hypothesis of this study, namely that the machinery of justice in late-nineteenth-century Portugal was of poor quality. In this view, judicial inefficiency would not only mean underperforming in the enforcement of rights and contracts. It would also include a component of doing so in an erratic and unpredictable fashion. The conclusion would be that strongly significant locational dummies were just another manifestation of overall judicial inefficiency.

Three of the variables initially considered – *civ*, *dist*, and *cosign* – failed to yield the expected outcome. In the case of the civil status of borrowers (*civ*), the problem may be the misspecification of the variable. A married farmer and a widowed farmer may not have differed much after all in terms of the number of useful working relatives in the family. On the other hand, a young married farmer with small children could have been in a worse situation than a widower living with adult sons and daughters. Likewise, borrowers who were single and living in a "fraternity," could have been better off too. The age/physical vigor of the head of family would have been a better characteristic to use, but unfortunately this was unobservable, as already noted.

The irrelevance to the model of the distance between lender and debtor is probably the result of two distortions in the way in which we have measured *Dist*. One is that it was taken from a GPS reading between the head sites of the parishes to which the two parties belonged, rather than by measuring the distance between the true locations of their respective abodes. The extreme case is the value of zero attributed to pairs of contracting parties who lived in the same parish but who may have lived several kilometers apart. The second difficulty is that present day GPS paths probably differ from the historical trajectory between any two points to an extent that we cannot know today.

The failure of the cosignatory variable (*cosign*) to help explain the determination of the mortgage rate can best be seen as a problem of endogeneity.

As formulated above, the existence of a third-party guarantee could only affect lenders' perceptions of risk if they believed that the machinery of justice would deal efficiently with any defaulter, including the cosignatory. If they did not, the value to the creditor of the extra guarantee would have been minimal since anyone acting as a guarantor in a debt transaction, no matter how respectable, might behave just as opportunistically as the defaulting borrower given the lack of credible sanctions. Perhaps for this reason, this was not a commonly used mechanism. Only 12 percent of all contracts in our sample included cosignatories.

In contrast, registration of mortgaged property at the land office (*reg*) evoked the expected response. Why does this not contradict the "judicial inefficiency" thesis or raise another problem of endogeneity? The fact that an asset was officially described, with all its liens, and could be consulted did not in itself improve the likelihood of a successful foreclosure on a defaulting party. But it did provide the lender, at little cost, with reliable information on the status of the collateral. As a result, it lowered, not the risk premium, but the search cost of the transaction, which also had an impact on the mortgage rate. For this to occur land offices must have been "institutionally efficient," a condition which the market apparently considered to have been met, even if the courts of law themselves functioned poorly. The positive and significant coefficient of the *reg* variable, in Table 7.5, attests to this.

To sum up, Table 7.6 gathers all the test results for our sample of mortgage contracts and organizes them into the panels in Table 7.2. It is clear that the data fit properly the requirements only of panels 3 and 4, in other words, the situations in which courts were deemed to be "bad." This corroborates the view, shared by commentators and participants in the mortgage market of the late nineteenth century, that the existing machinery of justice performed poorly in protecting property rights and enforcing contracts. Indeed, in setting loan conditions, economic agents did not conduct their business as if they expected the full and prompt recovery of the principle in the event of a default. Institutions did matter and in this case their impact was negative.

Table 7.6   Statistical test results and the panels of Table 7.2

	Test1	Test 2	Test 3
Panel 1	no	yes	no
Panel 2	yes	no	yes
Panel 3	yes	yes	yes
Panel 4	yes	yes	yes

Sources: See text.

Conclusions

It is widely believed that the institutional systems of the developed nations of the late-nineteenth-century Atlantic economy were basically similar. It is thought that these countries were molded by the same blueprint and that whatever discrepancies existed, they were hardly sufficient to explain differences in economic performance. The present study contends that these countries were institutionally more diverse than has been supposed and that this may have contributed to some of the divergence in growth observed between them. To clarify this issue, we have focused on the efficiency of the machinery of justice. This is of interest not only because its design displayed a notable appearance of uniformity among polities, but also because neoinstitutionalists have held the judicial system to be a key institutional factor for growth.

Given the parsimony of information in this field of historical research, the topic has had to be explored by indirect means. Its limits were drawn around the behavior of economic agents in small-scale mortgage credit markets, with our data coming from six counties in provincial Portugal, between the 1870s and the 1910s. Based on nearly 1800 mortgage contracts, three tests were devised to allow us to determine whether lenders found that judicial institutions were good at enforcing contracts and enforcing property rights. The conclusions from such a narrow area of analysis can arguably be extended to the machinery of justice in Portugal as a whole, and the method seems robust enough that it can serve for comparative, international purposes too.

All three tests show that the loan policy followed by these moneylenders was contradictory with a high level of trust in the efficiency of the courts. In the first place, interest rates were excessively high, and there was too much dispersion around the mean. This implies that they were set in the expectation that the collateral would not give adequate security in the event of default. In this respect, Portugal differed sharply from Sweden, Denmark and the Netherlands and was very similar to Spain and Brazil, suggesting that a North-South divide was already then present in terms of institutional quality.

The second and the third tests confirm this perception. Creditors negotiated their loans in the same way, whether the security pledged was adequate or not to cover the risk of the operation. This leads us to infer that they expected relatively little from the third-party contract enforcement power of the courts. This is corroborated by the fact that creditors showed themselves sensitive to the personal attributes of borrowers as indicators of the likelihood of a successful settlement of the loan. The interest rate was lower for borrowers whose attributes indicated a greater capacity and willingness to repay, and higher for those who seemed less promising from this point of view. This research has still a long way to go, namely by extending it to other countries along the lines developed here. In the meantime, two final questions should be posed. The first is whether any evolution occurred in terms of institutional quality during the four decades which we have scrutinized? It is tempting to read an improvement in judicial efficiency into the gradual reduction in mean interest rates from the 1870s to the 1910s registered in Table 7.3. But there are other circumstances to consider. Land registration was spreading rapidly during this timespan – in Vila Franca de Xira, for example, it rose from 35 to 86 percent of all real estate pledged – and this would account for at least some of the reduction in mean interest rates. In the second place, it is not unlikely that access to financial resources in nearby Lisbon was on the rise, as communications improved and financial institutions developed. The specific contribution of improvements at the level of the courts may therefore have been rather slight.

The second question seeks to reconcile the existence of an active mortgage market with the poor showing of the courts of law which were supposed to underpin its operation. In this matter, two issues commend themselves to our attention. One is that the courts may have functioned imperfectly, but they were not inexistent. Some remedy was obtainable from them against prevaricators, but we suppose it cost a considerable amount of time and money. The high interest rates we have detected reflect the high costs associated with default because of an adverse institutional environment. It does not imply that these economic agents were struggling in a Hobbesian environment. At the same time, lenders apparently welcomed borrowers who owned adequate collateral, and were prepared to charge them less than they would have for "personal" unsecured credit, protected by nothing other than the reputation of the debtor. Undoubtedly, these courts made some difference after all. Even though mortgage contracts were probably more costly to both parties, and certainly more complicated bureaucratically, they may have seemed a useful selection mechanism for lenders. For borrowers who owned assets, they offered a chance of a lower interest rate. In a world of small peasants, many of whom needed finance but had nothing to pledge, there was nothing left but to pay a "usurious" interest rate, the only one that in their case the market would bear.

Notes

The author is grateful to Helena Monteiro and Rui Lopes for research into archival sources. For useful advice and comments, he is indebted to Patrick Svensson, Dan Andersen, Timothy Guinnane, Hans Christian Johansen, Anders Perlinge, Ingrid Henriksen, Juan Carmona, and Hadi Esfahani, as well as to the participants in the Economic History seminar at the Universidad Carlos III, Madrid.

1. For an excellent survey of the potential and missed opportunities of this literature, see Crafts (2000).

2. For interesting exceptions, see the papers by Foreman-Peck (1995), Foreman-Peck and Lains (2000), and Allen (2003).
3. To avoid problems of endogeneity, we relate these data to 1870, the start of the observed process of growth and convergence.
4. On a scale from -10 to +10, Polity-IV measures to what degree the political system suppresses or fosters the competitive political participation of the citizenry in the choice of leaders and policies and ensures the protection of civil liberties. See Marshall and Jaggers (2002) and, for the data, http://www.cidcm.umd.edu/polity/.
5. Data for the franchise as a percentage of the adult population are obtained from Rose (2000), except in the case of Greece, which were kindly provided by Professor Anne Couderc.
6. "Contract-intensive money" is defined as the ratio of noncurrency money to total money supply, that is, CIM= (M2–C)/ M2). The closer its value is to 1, the greater the trust that the public will have in the protection that institutions give to contractual rights. It is estimated using data from Mitchell (1996).
7. See Reis (2005a). In the case of CIM, the results of the estimation are suggestive but a problem of endogeneity is posed in this context by "contract-intensive money." For a different view of this issue, see Prados and Sanz (2006).
8. Two studies have been seminal in their treatment of the links between institutions and long-term economic development, namely Acemoglu et al. (2001; 2002). The present analysis differs from their approach in several ways. It considers a much shorter time span – 40 as opposed to 500 years. Its object of study is not a sample of ex-colonies of the West which adopted imported institutions, but rather European countries which set up and developed their own. Most important, it employs measures of institutional efficiency which are appropriate to the historical situation, rather than yardsticks drawn from the late twentieth century or from the Polity project, none of which seem suitable to the context examined. For a recent critique of this approach, particularly regarding the institutionalist assumption of country-specific and time-invariant institutions and legal codes, see Sgard (2006).
9. The present study, while recognizing the importance of distinguishing between the quality of rules and the quality of their application, does not attempt to unbundle them. This would be an arduous task that would not fit into the compass of this paper which engages solely in the outcome of the courts' efforts from the point of view of the consumers of this service.
10. For studies which illustrate the difficulties of assessing the quality of government in a sample of countries in this fashion, see La Porta et al. (1999), Kauffman et al. (2002) and Cabral and Pinheiro (1999). For the same problem regarding the phenomenon of "corruption," see Mauro (1995).
11. For an illustration of the enormous effort required to produce an "objective" indicator, see Djankov et al. (2003), which employs 38 variables to assess comparatively how well, during the 1990s, the courts of 115 countries functioned.
12. We are not interested therefore in situations in which rural credit markets had become strongly influenced by financial institutions. Since the latter would enjoy economies of scale, they could lower the interest rate without this signifying an institutional improvement and this would invalidate the comparison we are trying to establish.
13. Although not a majority, cases like this are not infrequent in the database we are employing here.

14. The situation depicted in panel 1 is not an "ideal" one. As we shall see below, in several countries in late-nineteenth-century Europe, although not in Portugal, mortgage credit actually seems to have conformed quite closely to these characteristics.
15. It has to be accepted that lenders might not be uniformly regarded by the courts of law. Given the imperfections of the judicial system, some might be better at obtaining judicial protection than others. For this reason, in the third section we include in vector A a variable that reflects possible differences of treatment of litigants by the courts.
16. Data on mortgages for Italy are from the *Annuario Statistico del Regno d'Italia* for 1900. The total of corporate financial liabilities is from Reis (2005b).
17. The conto was a Portuguese unit of account worth 1,000,000 reis. The real (plural reis) was the basic unit of the monetary system. At this time, one conto was the equivalent to £222 sterling.
18. The real (plural reis) was the official monetary unit. To simplify, the conto (= 1,000,000 reis) was also used as a unit of account. At this time, one conto was equivalent to £222 sterling approximately.
19. Ibid.
20. This section is based on Vaz (1863), Sousa (1866), and the civil code itself. For a recent perspective, see Hespanha (2004).
21. See Hespanha (2004). Portugal followed most of Europe, where usury laws were abolished during the 1850s and 1860s. An exception was France, which kept the 5 percent ceiling until 1918! See Postel-Vinay (1998).
22. This was a common practice in eighteenth-century France too. See Hoffman et al. (2000, ch.3).
23. Not infrequently this stipulation was "at the will of the lender," at other times "for the rest of the life of the borrower," and more often still "for a year and beyond."
24. The equivalent to between £44 and £66 sterling. In every county studied, there were a few large loans above one conto, that is £222.
25. This discount rate was raised now and then but this was out of consideration for money market conditions rather than due to the riskiness of the paper taken.
26. The case of a large Alentejo landowner who, in 1890, was lending on mortgage at between 6 and 9 percent, but placed money on deposit at the bank at 5 percent, corroborates the existence and scale of a risk premium on mortgage loans relative to more secure placements (Fonseca, 1992).
27. Central Bank discount rates are from Homer and Sylla (1996) except for Denmark which are from Johansen (1985). Mortgage rates for Sweden are from Hellgren (2003), Hoppe and Langton (1994), and Perlinge (2005); for the Netherlands, from the Dutch Statistical Yearbook; and for Denmark from data collected at the Landsarkivet for Sjaelland, Copenhagen. The available data on available mortgage interest rates do not allow us to comment on measures of dispersion, except for Denmark, where the coefficient of variation on 100 contracts between 1879 and 1895, in southern Zeeland was 0.108, less than half of the Portuguese figure.
28. Even though based on a small sample of countries, a geographic pattern of "judicial efficiency" comes to light from this exercise in comparison, and is suggestive because it matches other possibly relevant spatial distributions. Sweden and the Netherlands had not only better justice but were also substantially richer than their Iberian counterparts. Moreover, their institutions, in general, were highly considered. On the other hand, Portugal and Spain were beset with reputations

for political instability, clientelism, corruption, and low human capital endowment, and their level of GDP per capita was of course much lower.
29. For the Brazilian "safe" rate, we used the yield on public gold bonds given by http://eh.net/databases/finance. There was no protocentral bank at this time in Brazil.
30. Creditors were also less familiar with the nature and true worth of the collateral than the persons who pledged it. However, since these features were physical and directly observable, we assume that evaluating them would have had a far smaller cost than that of assessing the personal attributes of borrowers and would not have raised the price of mortgage credit much.
31. In the late nineteenth century, the Portuguese literacy rate was 25 percent. The borrowers in our data base did about 15 percentage points better than this but lenders were about 70 percent literate.
32. We have included a dummy for the literacy of lenders, because it might be presumed that better educated lenders would be better at navigating through the intricacies of the machinery of justice and would therefore charge less on their loans. On the other hand, if this were the case, they could always charge the same as their less educated rivals and simply pocket the difference as a rent. In any case, this variable was tried and proved nonsignificant.
33. Data for either are drawn from the Portuguese Statistical and Fiscal Yearbooks.

References

Acemoglu, D., S. Johnson, and J.A. Robinson (2001) "The Colonial Origins of Comparative Development: An Empirical Investigation," *American Economic Review*, 91, 1369–1401.
Acemoglu, D., S. Johnson, and J.A. Robinson (2002) "Reversal of Fortune: Geography and Institutions in the Making of the Modern World Income Distribution," *Quarterly Journal of Economics*, 117, 1231–1294.
Allen, R.C. (2003) "Progress and Poverty in Early Modern Europe," *Economic History Review*, 56, 403–443.
Amaral, L. (2002) "How a Country Catches Up: Explaining Economic Growth in Portugal in the Post-War Period (1950s to 1973)," Ph.D. dissertation, European University Institute.
Baumol, W. (1986) "Productivity Growth, Convergence and Welfare: What the Long-Run Data Show," *American Economic Review*, 76, 1072–1085.
Bordo, M.D., A.M. Taylor, and J.G. Williamson (eds.) (2003) *Globalization in Historical Perspective*, Chicago, IL: University of Chicago Press.
Brettell, C.B. (1991) "Moral Economy or Political Economy? Property and Credit Markets in 19th Century Rural Portugal," *Journal of Historical Sociology*, 12, 1–28.
Cabral, C., and A. Pinheiro (1999) "Credit Markets in Brazil: The Role of Judicial Enforcement and other Institutions," Inter-American Development Bank Working Paper R-368, Washington, D.C.
Carmona Pidal, J., and J. Simpson (2003) *El Laberinto de la Agricultura Española: Instituciones, Contratos y Organizacion entre 1850 y 1936*, Zaragoza: Prensas Universitárias de Zaragoza.
Clague, C., P. Keefer, S. Knack, and M. Olson (1999) "Contract-Intensive Money: Contract Enforcement, Property Rights and Economic Performance," *Journal of Economic Growth*, 4, 181–211.

Crafts, N.R.F. (2000) "Institutional Quality and European Development before and after the Industrial Revolution," Paper presented at the World Bank Summer School, Washington, D.C., July 17–19.

Djankov, S., R. La Porta, F. Lopez-de-Silanes, and A. Shleifer (2003) "Courts," *Quarterly Journal of Economics*, 118, 453–517.

Esteves, R.P. (2002) *Finanças Públicas e Crescimento Económico. O Crowding Out em Portugal da Regeneração ao Final da Monarquia*, Lisbon: Banco de Portugal.

Finer, Samuel (1997) *The History of Government, vols I–III*, Cambridge: Cambridge University Press.

Fonseca, F.T. da (1977) "O Crédito Privado em Coimbra no Ano de 1885 Visto a Partir dos Actos Notariais: Alguns Aspectos," *Boletim do Arquivo da Universidade de Coimbra*, 3, 161–225.

Fonseca, H.A. (1992) *Economia e Atitudes Económicas no Alentejo Oitocentista*, Ph.D. dissertation, University of Évora.

Fonseca, H.A. (1996) *O Alentejo no Século XIX. Economia e Atitudes Económicas*, Lisboa: Imprensa Nacional.

Foreman-Peck, J. (1995) "A Model of Later Nineteenth Century European Economic Development," *Revista de Historia Economica*, 13, 441–471.

Foreman-Peck, J., and P. Lains (2000) "European Economic Development: The Core and the Southern Periphery, 1870–1910," in J.G. Williamson and S. Pamuk (eds.) *The Mediterranean Response to Globalization before 1950*, London and New York: Routledge.

Glaeser, E., R. La Porta, F. Lopez-de-Silanes and A. Shleifer (2004) "Do Institutions Cause Growth?" *Journal of Economic Growth*, 9, 271–303.

Guinnane, T. (1994) "A Failed Institutional Transplant: Raiffeisen''s Credit Cooperative in Ireland, 1894–1914," *Explorations in Economic History*, 31, 38–61.

Guinnane, T. (2001) "Cooperatives as Information Machines: German Rural Credit Cooperatives, 1883–1914," *Journal of Economic History*, 61, 366–389.

Gunnarsson, C. (1991) "What is New and What is Institutional in the New Institutional Economics? An Essay on Old and New Institutionalism and the Role of the State in Developing Countries," *Scandinavian Economic History Review*, 39, 43–67.

Hellgren, H. (2003) *Fasta Förbindelser. En Studie av Låntagare hos Sparbanken och Informella Kreditgivare I Sala 1860–1910*, Uppsala: Uppsala Studies in Economic History.

Hespanha, A.M. (2004) *Guiando a Mão Invisível: Direitos, Estado e Lei no Liberalismo Monárquico Português*, Coimbra: Almedina.

Hoffman, P.T., G. Postel-Vinay, and J-L. Rosenthal (2000) *Priceless Markets. The Political Economy of Credit in Paris, 1660–1870*, Chicago, IL and London: University of Chicago Press.

Homer, S., and R. Sylla (1996) *A History of Interest Rates*, 3rd ed., New Brunswick, NJ: Rutgers University Press.

Hoppe, G., and J. Langton (1994) *Peasantry to Capitalism. Western Östergötland in the Nineteenth Century*, Cambridge: Cambridge University Press.

Johansen, H.C. (1985) *Dansk Økonomisk Statistik 1814–1980*, Copenhagen: Gyldendal.

Kauffman, D., A. Kraay, and P. Zoido-Lobaton (2002) "Governance Matters II. Updated Indicators for 2000/01," World Bank Policy Research Working Paper 2772, Washington, D.C.

La Porta, R., F. Lopez-de-Silanes, A. Shleifer, and R. Vishny (1999) "The Quality of Government," *Journal of Law, Economics and Organization*, 15, 222–279.

Lindgren, H. (2002) "The Modernization of Swedish Credit Markets, 1840–1905: Evidence from Probate Inventories," *Journal of Economic History*, 62, 810–832.

Marcondes, R.L. (2002) "O Financiamento Hipotecário da Cafeicultura no Vale do Paraíba Paulista (1865–1887)," *Revista Brasileira de Economia*, 56, 147–170.

Marques, A.H. de O. (1989) *Companhia Geral de Crédito Predial Português*, 125 Anos de História, Lisbon, n.e.

Marshall, M.G., and K. Jaggers (2002) "Polity IV Project. Political Regime Characteristics and Transitions 1800–2002," Center for International Development and Conflict Management, University of Maryland.

Martinez Soto, A.P. (2001) "La 'Tela de Araña'. Mercados Informales de Financion Agrária, Usura y Crédito Hipotecário en la Region de Múrcia (1850–1939)," *Áreas. Revista de Ciências Sociales*, 21, 185–220.

Mauro, P. (1995) "Corruption and Growth," *Quarterly Journal of Economics*, 110, 681–712.

Mitchell, B.R. (1996) *British Historical Statistics*, Cambridge: Cambridge University Press.

Morais, P. (1889) *Inquérito Agrícola. Estudo Geral da Economia Rural da 7ª Região Agrícola*, Lisbon: Imprensa Nacional.

Nelson, R.R., and B.N. Sampat (2001) "Making Sense of Institutions as a Factor Shaping Economic Performance," *Journal of Economic Behaviour and Organization*, 44, 31–54.

Nilsson, A., L. Pettersen, and P. Svensson (1999) "Agrarian Transition and Literacy: The Case of Nineteenth Century Sweden," *European Review of Economic History*, 3, 79–96.

North, D.C. (1990) *Institutions, Institutional Change and Economic Performance*, Cambridge: Cambridge University Press.

O'Rourke, K.H., and J.G. Williamson (1997) "Around the European Periphery 1870–1913: Globalization, Schooling and Growth," *European Review of Economic History*, 1, 153–190.

O'Rourke, K.H., and J.G. Williamson (1999) *Globalization and History: The Evolution of a Nineteenth Century Atlantic Economy*, Cambridge, MA: MIT Press.

Pamuk, S., and J.G. Williamson (eds.) (2000) *The Mediterranean Response to Globalization before 1950*, London and New York: Routledge.

Perlinge, A. (2005) *Sockenbankirerna. Kreditrelationer och Tidig Bankversamhet: Vånga Socken I Skåne 1840–1900*, Stockholm: Nordiska Museets Förlag.

Postel-Vinay, G. (1998) *La Terre et l'Argent. L'Agriculture et le Crédit en France du XVIIIe au Début du XXe Siècle*, Paris: Albin Michel.

Prados de la Escosura, L., and I. Sanz Villaroya (2006) "Contract Enforcement and Argentina's Long-Run Decline," Working Paper WP 06–06, Department of Economics, Universidad Carlos III, Madrid.

Ramos, R. (1994) *A Segunda Fundação. História de Portugal, vol.VI*, Lisbon: Estampa.

Reis, J. (2005a) "Institutional Factors and Economic Growth during the First Era of Globalization: What Can We Do with Them?" Inaugural Lecture, VIII Congress of the Spanish Association of Economic History, Santiago de Compostela, September 1316.

Reis, J. (2005b) "Los Sistemas Financieros de la Periferia: Una Comparacion entre Escandinavia y el Sur de la Europa durante el Siglo XIX," Papeles de Economia 105/6, 109–129.

Rodrik, D., A. Subramanian, and F. Trebbi (2004) "Institutions Rule: The Primacy of Institutions over Geography and Integration in Economic Development," *Journal of Economic Growth*, 9, 131–165.

Rodrigues, J.A. de S. (1929) *A Companhia Geral do Crédito Predial Portuguez. Estudo Descritivo e Crítico da sua Vida*, Lisbon: Sociedade Nacional de Tipografia.

Rose, R. (2000) *International Encyclopedia of Elections*, Basingstoke: MacMillan.

Sabio Alcuten, A. (1996) *Los Mercados Informales de Credito y Tierraen una Comunidad Aragonesa*, Madrid: Banco de España.

Sgard, Jerome (2006) "Do Legal Origins Matter? The Case of Bankruptcy Laws in Europe 1808–1914," *European Review of Economic History*, 10, 389–419.

Silva, E. (1911) *Os Escrívães-Notários perante as Reformas Judiciais e do Notariado*, Lisbon: Libanio da Silva.

Silva, M.J. de O. (1994) *Crédito Hipotecário em Santarém durante a Regeneração (1851–56)*, Santarém: Câmara Municipal de Santarém.

Smith, A. (1776, 1990) *An Inquiry into the Nature and Causes of the Wealth of Nations*, London: Encyclopedia Britannica.

Sousa, J.C.B de (1866) *Crédito*, Lisbon: Typographia Franco-Portuguesa.

Svensson, P. (2001) *Agrara Entreprenörer. Böndernas Roll i Omvandlingen av Jordbruket i Skåne 1800–1870*, Lund: Lund Studies in Economic History.

Ulrich, J.H. (1908) *O Crédito Agrícola em Portugal*, Lisbon: Ferin.

Vaquinhas, I.M. (1982) "O Credito Hipotecário em Coimbra no Ano de 1866. Tentative de Integração no Desenvolvimento Capitalista do Século XIX," *Boletim do Arquivo da Universidade de Coimbra*, IV, 39–84.

Vaquinhas, I.M., and F.T. da Fonseca (1984) "Formas de Investimento de Capital. Crédito Privado e Crédito Publico em Coimbra no Terceiro Quartel do Século XIX," *Revista Portuguesa de Historia*, 20, 99–139.

Vaz, J.J.F. (1863) *Do Crédito Predial. Resposta aos Pontos propostos pela Faculdade de Direito da Universidade de Coimbra*, Combra: Typographia da Universidade.

8

An Evaluation of the Contractionary Devaluation Hypothesis

Ricardo Bebczuk, Arturo Galindo, and Ugo Panizza

Introduction

Throughout his sharp writings and lucid presentations on Latin American economies, Professor Werner Baer has shown a vivid interest in exchange rate policy and its growth and welfare consequences. In particular, he has consistently been concerned with how macroeconomic strategies shape the income distribution and the level of unemployment in developing countries.[1]

Part of the research on macroeconomic adjustment has focused on the role of exchange rates. As a key relative price in the economy, the real exchange rate may not only alter the country's external balance but also other more socially sensitive variables such as income distribution, poverty, and employment. This explains the relentless effort on the part of scholars and policymakers to provide a reliable answer as to whether real devaluations boost or hinder economic growth. A better understanding of this link would certainly have useful implications for exchange rate, fiscal, and monetary policies. This paper contributes to this debate by offering new empirical macrolevel evidence on the impact of real exchange rate devaluations on growth for a large sample of countries during the period 1976–2003, using newly constructed measures of dollarization and various interaction effects.

Table 8.1 summarizes the complex effects that real devaluations have on economic activity. Let us consider the following flows across domestic sectors that include exportable and nontradeable producers, as well as households – we rule out the government for simplicity (the effect, if any, would be similar to that on a nontradeable producer) and the domestic financial sector by taking it as a mere intermediary between households and firms. It is expected that any decline in current and prospective cash flows for firms and households will translate into a decline of aggregate investment and consumption, respectively.

The traditional view posing that a real devaluation improves the trade balance emerges from the first two rows, which show that exportable producers

Table 8.1   Real devaluation effects on sectoral cash flows

Foreign currency denominated variables	Exportable producing firms	Nontradeable producing firms	Households
Trade channel			
Exportable goods	+	−	−
Imported goods	−	−	−
Financial channel			
Gross debt	−	−	−
Gross assets	+	+	+

are better off after devaluation. Not only does the supply of exports increase but also a depressed aggregate demand for imports for consumption and investment purposes ensues and, as long as the Marshall (1923)-Lerner (1944) conditions are satisfied, a real devaluation will have a positive effect on the trade balance. Subsequent developments such as the popular Mundell (1963)-Fleming (1962) model adopted this approach, implying that devaluations are expansionary. Of course, as shown in the first two columns of the upper panel in Table 8.1, this model assumes that the beneficial revenue effect for tradeable-producing industries outweighs the detrimental one for nontradeable producers and the negative impact on the tradeable sector that arises from more expensive imported inputs.

An income effect adds to the previous substitution effect: as long as nominal wages do not fully adjust to the new price level, household disposable income is negatively affected, with a deleterious impact on aggregate consumption coming from inflation in the tradeable consumption basket.[2] Diaz-Alejandro (1965) and Krugman and Taylor (1978) give theoretical support to this early contractionary devaluation mechanism brought about by income distribution considerations. Lizondo and Montiel (1988) and Larrain and Sachs (1986) are in-depth explorations within this framework.

Modern contributions have placed more emphasis on a financial channel rather than on the standard trade channel. In light of the dollarization process taking place in a number of emerging economies over the last decades, this research stresses the mismatch between foreign currency denominated debt and domestic currency denominated revenues (see, among others, Céspedes et al., 2004; Frankel, 2005; and Krugman, 1999). Going back to Table 8.1, this is reflected in the first line of the lower panel. Nevertheless, it must be borne in mind that the sign and magnitude of the effect is linked to the net, as opposed to the gross, foreign denominated debt. Looking at the second row of the lower panel, gross assets might be owned by firms and households in countries having suffered massive capital flights in the past. Moreover, when it comes to domestic dollarization, it is clear that dollar denominated debts are partly financed with dollar denominated instruments.

The rest of the paper reviews the related empirical evidence in the next section and then discusses the findings; some conclusions complete the paper.

Empirical literature review

The critical role of the exchange rate in the economy, especially during currency and financial crises, has stimulated a substantial empirical research effort. We start with some macrolevel evidence. Edwards (1986) finds a moderate short-run effect but no long-run effect of exchange rate depreciations on GDP level and growth for a panel of 12 developing countries. Kamin and Klau (1998) find similar results for a sample of 27 developing and industrialized countries. More recent contributions focus on financial factors arising from currency mismatches that turn real devaluations contractionary. These papers argue that balance sheet effects are the cause of the contractionary effect of devaluations in emerging countries since the 1990s.[3] In short, a depreciation in the real exchange rate increases the value of financial obligations in foreign currency vis-à- vis the value of revenues in the domestic currency, causing liquidity and solvency problems that hinder growth possibilities for firms.

Regarding country case studies, Amman and Baer (2003) contend that Brazil's devaluation in 1999 had a positive growth effect, as some analysts claim with regard to the post-2001 crisis Argentine experience. In contrast, Bonomo et al. (2003) find that in firms with high liability dollarization those results are reversed. Domac (1997) reaches the same conclusion looking at the Turkish economy over the period 1960–1990.

Recently, many empirical studies have resorted to microlevel data to assess the impact of real exchange rate depreciations in the presence of currency mismatches. These studies have analyzed the impact of real exchange rate fluctuations on the dynamics of investment and employment. Bleakley and Cowan (2002) use a sample of 480 firms from five Latin American countries (Argentina, Brazil, Chile, Colombia, and Mexico) during the years 1991–1999, to test if real exchange rate devaluations have influenced investment decisions. They do not find conclusive evidence regarding a contractionary effect of exchange rate depreciations on investment.

Further country-specific work summarized by Galindo et al. (2003) finds different results. In a study of Mexican firms, Pratap et al. (2003) find that exchange rate depreciations have a negative effect on firm performance, measured using the investment rate. This result confirms previous research on Mexico by Aguiar (2005) and Martinez and Werner (2002). Benavente et al. (2003), Carranza et al. (2003), Echeverry et al. (2003), and Galiani et al. (2003) find similar results for Peru, Argentina, Colombia, and Chile, respectively.[4]

In a study analyzing the effect of real exchange rate depreciations on employment in the presence of liability dollarization, Galindo et al. (2005) use a panel dataset on industrial employment and trade for nine Latin

American countries, and find that real exchange rate depreciations impact employment growth positively in countries with high trade openness, but this effect is reversed as liability dollarization increases. In industries with high liability dollarization, the overall impact of real exchange rate depreciations is negative.

Empirical methods and results

Building on a standard growth regression, and in light of recent firm-level evidence and of the cumbersome relationship between devaluations and growth, we incorporate interaction terms to evaluate the contractionary devaluation hypothesis in a cross-country econometric framework. We test whether the presence of dollar denominated debt is important for the effect of real depreciations on GDP growth estimating the following model:[5]

$$GROWTH_{i,t} = \alpha + \beta_1 X_i + \beta_2 Z_{i,t} + \gamma DRER_{i,t-1} + \delta DOLL_{i,t-1} +$$
$$\phi(DRER_{i,t-1} * DOLL_{i,t-1}) + \varepsilon_{i,t} \qquad (8.1)$$

where the dependent variable is the growth rate of GDP per capita measured in PPP dollars (we use PPP dollars in order to avoid an automatic relationship between GDP growth and changes in the real exchange rate), X is a matrix of country-specific time-invariant characteristics (which we will later substitute with country-fixed effects), Z is a matrix of country-specific time-variant characteristics,[6] DRER is the percentage change in the real exchange rate (we use the bilateral real exchange rate with respect to the U.S. dollar, with a positive sign indicating a depreciation), and DOLL is a measure of dollarization to be precisely defined momentarily. Our coefficients of interest are γ and ϕ. As the standard Mundell-Fleming model assumes that devaluations are expansionary, we expect γ to be positive, but the balance sheet effect literature suggest that the expansionary effect of devaluations should be smaller in countries with high levels of dollarization and so we expect ϕ to be negative. We also interact DRER with trade openness (exports plus imports to GDP) in order to account for the magnitude of the trade channel presented in the Introduction.

We use three measures of dollarization: external dollarization and two alternative measures of domestic dollarization. We define external dollarization as follows:

External dollarization = OSIN*external debt/GDP   (8.2)

where OSIN is the Original Sin measure built by Eichengreen et al. (2005), which measures the currency composition of external debt (we use their OSIN3 index, which equals 1 minus the volume of external debt in local currency to the volume of external debt in foreign currency, with 1 corresponding to a fully dollarized external debt) and external debt/GDP is the country's total external debt measured as a share of GDP. As OSIN has limited overtime variability, all the overtime variability of external dollarization comes from external debt/GDP. External dollarization takes high values for countries which have high levels of external debt and for which there is no international market for local currency debt (for instance, Argentina), but has low values for countries that have low levels of external debt (such as, Guatemala, for instance) and hence have a low value of external debt or countries (such as South Africa) for which there is a substantial market of domestic currency international debt and hence low values of OSIN.

Note that we obtain our external debt data from the World Bank's Global Development Finance (GDF) database. As GDF does not report data for industrial countries, we assume that these countries have zero external debt and, hence, implicitly that they do not have external dollarization. In the robustness analysis, we will explore the consequences of this assumption.

We define domestic dollarization 1 as the share of dollar bank deposits of GDP. Formally:

$$\text{Domestic dollarization 1} = \text{deposit dollarization}^*(\text{bank deposits/GDP}). \tag{8.3}$$

We obtain data on deposit dollarization from the database assembled by Levy Yeyati (2006). Although deposit dollarization is available for a large number of countries – a clear advantage for empirical research, its interpretation may be doubtful. As mentioned in the Introduction, deposits are on the assets side for a large segment of residents, so a devaluation against the dollar may indeed have a beneficial impact on wealth, depending on the net position of local agents. Moreover, if banks are able to pursue better diversification strategies than individuals, dollar deposits should not necessarily have any contractive effect. In order to expand our number of observations, we assume that domestic dollarization is constant within countries.[7]

Our second measure of domestic dollarization (domestic dollarization 2) is what Calvo et al. (2006) call domestic liability dollarization (DLD), a measure similar to the previous one but rather than focusing on the structure of bank liabilities (i.e. deposits), it focuses on the structure of bank assets (i.e. loans). In particular, Calvo et al. (2006) build the domestic dollarization measure as follows. For industrial economies they use BIS reporting banks' local asset positions in foreign currency as a share of GDP. For emerging economies, they add dollar deposits and bank foreign borrowing (IFS line 26c) and then assume that banks match their liabilities with their assets.

$$\text{Domestic dollarization 2} = \text{loan dollarization}^*(\text{bank loans/GDP}). \tag{8.4}$$

Table 8.2 Baseline regressions: Dependent variable – GDP per capita growth rate

	(1)	(2)	(3)	(4)	(5)	(6)
Gross fixed capital formation/GDP	0.163	0.189	0.205	0.195	0.191	0.333
	[0.021]***	[0.028]***	[0.040]***	[0.028]***	[0.034]***	[0.077]***
Population growth	−0.002	0.002	−0.005	0.000	0.004	−0.009
	[0.002]	[0.003]	[0.004]	[0.003]	[0.002]*	[0.008]
Log(GDP per capita 1974)	−0.008	−0.008	−0.005	–	–	–
	[0.002]***	[0.003]***	[0.004]			
Secondary schooling/Total population	0.010	0.022	0.019	−0.011	−0.005	0.049
	[0.010]	[0.017]	[0.016]	[0.017]	[0.019]	[0.065]
Log(Population)	0.001	0.002	−0.002	0.007	−0.004	0.035
	[0.001]	[0.001]	[0.002]	[0.010]	[0.010]	[0.066]
Government consumption growth	0.025	0.031	0.033	0.020	0.025	0.009
	[0.013]*	[0.013]**	[0.021]	[0.014]	[0.014]*	[0.023]
Freedom index	−0.003	−0.004	−0.002	−0.002	−0.001	0.002
	[0.001]**	[0.002]**	[0.003]	[0.002]	[0.002]	[0.005]
D terms of trade	0.007	−0.011	0.058	0.010	−0.010	0.058
	[0.014]	[0.013]	[0.045]	[0.014]	[0.012]	[0.045]
D real exchange rate	0.028	0.007	−0.021	0.029	0.002	−0.016
	[0.016]*	[0.015]	[0.018]	[0.016]*	[0.015]	[0.020]
Openness	0.028	0.026	−0.022	0.036	0.026	0.010
	[0.009]***	[0.010]**	[0.017]	[0.013]***	[0.013]**	[0.030]
D real exchange rate * Openness	−0.033	−0.039	0.514	−0.031	−0.016	0.440
	[0.060]	[0.082]	[0.140]***	[0.060]	[0.087]	[0.134]***
External dollarization [t–1]	−0.009	–	–	−0.007	–	–

Continued

Table 8.2 Continued

	(1)	(2)	(3)	(4)	(5)	(6)
D real exchange rate * External dollarization [t–1]	[0.004]** −0.028	–	–	[0.005] −0.031	–	–
Domestic dollarization [t–1]	[0.013]** –	0.0000 [0.000]	–	[0.014]** –	–	–
D real exchange rate * Domestic dollarization [t–1]	–	0.0000 [0.001]	–	–	0.000 [0.001]	–
Domestic dollarization 2 [t–1]	–	–	−0.030 [0.030]	–	–	−0.061 [0.047]
D real exchange rate * Domestic dollarization 2 [t–1]	–	–	−0.504 [0.060]***	–	–	−0.477 [0.056]***
SAFRICA dummy	−0.014 [0.007]*	−0.018 [0.007]***	–	–	–	–
LATAM dummy	−0.003 [0.004]	−0.006 [0.004]	0.003 [0.007]	–	–	–
ECA dummy	−0.005 [0.009]	0.000 [0.009]	0.003 [0.016]	–	–	–
Observations	1416	1324	289	1416	1324	289
Number of countries	57	56	29	57	56	29
Estimation method	Random effects	Random effects	Random effects	Fixed effects	Fixed effects	Fixed effects

Note: Robust standard errors in brackets.
  * significant at 10%; ** significant at 5%; *** significant at 1%.

We estimate the model using an unbalanced panel of 57 countries (22 industrial and 35 developing) over the 1976–2003 period.[8] Column 1 of Table 8.2 reports our baseline regression for external dollarization (we estimate the equation using a random effects model). As expected, we find that real depreciations are associated with higher growth. The effect is economically significant as the point estimates suggest that, in countries with no external dollarization, a 20 percent real devaluation is associated with an increase in per capita GDP growth of approximately half a percentage point. We also find that external dollarization does reduce the expansionary effect of devaluations. In particular, the point estimates suggest that in countries where external dollarization is greater than 0.84 (countries that have dollar denominated external debt greater than 84 percent of GDP), currency devaluations become contractionary. This corresponds to the top decile of the distribution of observations in the whole sample and to the top 20 if we restrict the sample to developing countries.

Column 2 repeats the experiment by focusing on domestic dollarization (again we use random effects). In this case, we still find that the coefficients have the right sign but they are not statistically significant. This is consistent with the fact, underlined in the first section, that domestic dollar debts are partially held by residents, particularly by depositors, so the aggregate effect of a real exchange rate devaluation is unclear.

Column 3 uses the measure of domestic liability dollarization assembled by Calvo et al. (2006). This reduces the sample to 29 countries (18 industrial and 11 developing), but we still find a large negative effect caused by depreciations in countries with high levels of domestic liability dollarization. In particular, the point estimates indicate that the effect of depreciations becomes negative for countries with values of domestic liability dollarization of above 0.5, which is just above the median value for DLD in our sample.

In column 4, we repeat the experiment of column 1, but substituting the time-invariant country-specific variable with a set of country-fixed effects, and the results remain mostly unchanged. This is done in order to control for a variety of country-specific effects that might have been ignored in the empirical specification. We still find that devaluations are expansionary in countries with low levels of external dollarization and contractionary in countries with high levels of external dollarization. Column 5 repeats the experiment of column 2 using fixed effects, but even though the coefficients have the correct sign, they are not statistically significant. Column 6 repeats the experiment of column 3 using fixed effects without finding major changes. In all cases, we include an interaction term of real depreciation with the trade openness coefficient under the hypothesis that the former will have more powerful effects in more open economies, and this is confirmed in columns 3 and 6.

In Table 8.3a we explore the consequences of our assumption that industrial countries have no external dollarization (without reporting, from now on, the whole control set and focusing on external dollarization and the only significant domestic dollarization measure – domestic dollarization 2). We do this in two ways. In columns 1 and 2 we interact real depreciation with a dummy variable that takes value 1 for industrial countries (column 1 uses random effects and column 2 uses fixed effects).[9] This should allow us to separate the effect of dollarization from that of being an industrial country. We find that this interaction has a negative and not significant coefficient,[10] but what is more interesting for our purposes is that the coefficients of γ and are unchanged (if anything increases in absolute value). Our second strategy consists of dropping all industrial countries from the sample (columns 3 and 4 of Table 8.3a use random and fixed effects, respectively): once more the results are unchanged. Table 8.3b repeats the experiment using domestic dollarization, and again we find that the results are robust to dropping industrial countries. Notice that the domestic dollarization measure correctly captures the possibility of liability dollarization in

Table 8.3a Separating the effect of industrial countries (using external liability dollarization) dependent variable: GDP per capita growth rate

	(1)	(2)	(3)	(4)
D real exchange rate [t–1]	0.031	0.03	0.037	0.032
	[0.017]*	[0.018]*	[0.021]*	[0.021]
Openness	0.031	0.035	0.041	0.047
	[0.009]***	[0.013]***	[0.016]***	[0.025]*
D real exchange rate * Openness	–0.032	–0.028	–0.07	–0.046
	[0.060]	[0.060]	[0.087]	[0.086]
External dollarization [t–1]	–0.008	–0.006	–0.009	–0.006
	[0.004]**	[0.005]	[0.004]**	[0.005]
D real exchange rate * External dollarization [t–1]	–0.03 [0.015]**	–0.032 [0.016]**	–0.03 [0.015]**	–0.032 [0.016]**
Industrial countries	0.013			
	[0.009]			
D real exchange rate * Industrial countries	–0.008 [0.016]	–0.005 [0.016]		
Observations	1416	1416	828	828
Number of countries	57	57	35	35
Estimation method	Random Effects	Fixed Effects	Random Effects	Fixed Effects

Note: The regressions include the same controls as in Table 8.1, but are not reported in order to save space.

Robust standard errors in brackets. * significant at 10%; ** significant at 5%; *** significant at 1%.

Table 8.3b   Separating the effect of industrial countries (using domestic liability dollarization) dependent variable: GDP per capita growth rate

	(1)	(2)	(3)	(4)
D real exchange rate [t–1]	–0.021	–0.015	–0.037	–0.018
	[0.018]	[0.018]	[0.036]	[0.044]
Openness	–0.02	0.047	–0.057	0.073
	[0.018]	[0.038]	[0.155]	[0.197]
D real exchange rate * Openness	0.479	0.207	0.777	0.259
	[0.160]***	[0.174]	[0.623]	[0.817]
Domestic Dollarization [t–1]	–0.024	–0.056	0.021	0.035
	[0.031]	[0.047]	[0.047]	[0.065]
D real exchange rate * Domestic dollarization [t–1]	–0.506 [0.061]***	–0.485 [0.056]***	–0.522 [0.067]***	–0.543 [0.072]***
Industrial countries	0.004	–	–	–
	[0.017]			
D real exchange rate * Industrial countries	0.012 [0.026]	0.06 [0.032]*	–	–
Observations	289	289	112	112
Number of countries	29	29	11	11
Estimation method	Random effects	Fixed effects	Random effects	Fixed effects

Note: The regressions include the same controls as in Table 8.1, but are not reported in order to save space.

Robust standard errors in brackets. * significant at 10%; ** significant at 5%; *** significant at 1%.

industrial countries and in this case we observe that the DRER*IND interaction has the expected positive sign.

Next, we explore the role of outliers. In columns 1 and 2 of Table 8.4a, we estimate the model for our external dollarization measure (again using random and fixed effects) after dropping all observations where $|\varepsilon_{i,t}| \geq 3\sigma_\varepsilon$.[11] Again, we find that the coefficients are unchanged. Finally, we use the robust regression routine of STATA (this is the RREG command which uses two types of iterations to put less weight on outliers). In column 3 we run regular robust regression and in column 4 we also include a set of country-fixed effects. The results are basically identical to those of our baseline regression. Table 8.4b repeats the experiment for domestic liability dollarization and again confirms the result.

After having established that our baseline result is extremely robust, we now move to test whether the effect documented above goes through

Table 8.4a   The role of outliers (using external liability dollarization) dependent variable: GDP per capita growth rate

	(1)	(2)	(3)	(4)
D real exchange rate [t–1]	0.031	0.028	0.029	0.033
	[0.013]**	[0.013]**	[0.011]***	[0.011]***
Openness	0.027	0.043	0.019	0.046
	[0.009]***	[0.010]***	[0.007]***	[0.012]***
D real exchange rate *	–0.051	–0.043	–0.054	–0.063
Openness	[0.055]	[0.055]	[0.048]	[0.047]
External dollarization [t–1]	–0.011	–0.01	–0.012	–0.011
	[0.002]***	[0.002]***	[0.002]***	[0.002]***
D real exchange rate * External	–0.026	–0.029	–0.024	–0.029
dollarization [t–1]	[0.007]***	[0.007]***	[0.008]***	[0.008]***
Observations	1390	1388	1416	1416
Number of countries	57	57	57	57
Estimation method	Random effects	Fixed effects	Robust regression	Robust regression with fixed effects

Note: The regressions include the same controls as in table 8. 1, but are not reported in order to save space.

   Robust standard errors in brackets. * significant at 10%; ** significant at 5%; *** significant at 1%.

Table 8.4b   The role of outliers (using domestic liability dollarization) dependent variable: GDP per capita growth rate

	(1)	(2)	(3)	(4)
D real exchange rate [t–1]	–0.025	–0.013	–0.026	–0.022
	[0.018]	[0.020]	[0.018]	[0.016]
Openness	–0.024	0.009	–0.025	0.011
	[0.017]	[0.030]	[0.021]	[0.029]
D real exchange rate * Openness	0.52	0.386	0.505	0.369
	[0.138]***	[0.126]***	[0.148]***	[0.129]***
Domestic dollarization [t–1]	–0.032	–0.056	–0.037	–0.017
	[0.029]	[0.042]	[0.022]	[0.030]
D real exchange rate * Domestic	–0.499	–0.493	–0.477	–0.433
dollarization [t–1]	[0.059]***	[0.054]***	[0.065]***	[0.056]***
Observations	288	284	289	288
Number of countries	29	29	29	29
Estimation method	Random effects	Fixed effects	Robust regression	Robust regression with fixed effects

Note: The regressions include the same controls as in Table 8.1, but are not reported in order to save space.

   Robust standard errors in brackets. * significant at 10%; ** significant at 5%; *** significant at 1%.

Table 8.5 Investment growth dependent variable: Growth of investment in PPP dollars

	(1)	(2)	(3)	(4)
Population growth	0.000	0.001	0.002	−0.005
	[0.001]	[0.002]	[0.003]	[0.006]
Log(GDP per capita 1974)	−0.002		0.000	
	[0.001]**		[0.002]	
Secondary schooling/Total population	0.001	−0.016	0.001	0.029
	[0.007]	[0.013]	[0.011]	[0.036]
Log(Population)	0.001	0.003	0.000	0.013
	[0.000]*	[0.006]	[0.001]	[0.047]
Government consumption growth	0.023	0.021	0.000	−0.001
	[0.007]***	[0.008]***	[0.014]	[0.016]
Freedom index	−0.002	−0.002	0.001	0.003
	[0.001]**	[0.001]*	[0.002]	[0.003]
D terms of trade	−0.033	−0.032	−0.012	−0.008
	[0.008]***	[0.008]***	[0.027]	[0.028]
D real exchange rate	−0.001	−0.002	−0.023	−0.026
	[0.009]	[0.009]	[0.019]	[0.020]
Openness	0.011	0.018	−0.004	−0.013
	[0.005]**	[0.007]**	[0.011]	[0.018]
D real exchange rate * Openness	0.037	0.039	0.159	0.159
	[0.039]	[0.042]	[0.098]	[0.099]
External dollarization [t−1]	0.001	−0.001	–	–
	[0.001]	[0.002]		
D real exchange rate * External dollarization [t−1]	−0.026	−0.025	–	–
	[0.004]***	[0.004]***		
Domestic dollarization [t−1]	–	–	−0.058	−0.101
			[0.020]***	[0.038]***
D real exchange rate * Domestic dollarization [t−1]		–	−0.149	−0.134
			[0.084]*	[0.080]*
SAFRICA dummy	0.001	–	–	–
	[0.004]			
LATAM dummy	0.001	–	−0.002	–
	[0.002]		[0.004]	
ECA dummy	−0.002	–	−0.002	–
	[0.003]		[0.007]	
Observations	1415	1415	289	289
Number of countries	57	57	29	29
Estimation method	Random effects	Fixed effects	Random effects	Fixed effects

Note: Robust standard errors in brackets.
  * significant at 10%; ** significant at 5%; *** significant at 1%.

investment or consumption growth. In Table 8.5, we run a set of regressions similar to those of Table 8.1 but with the growth rate of investment as the dependent variable. In columns 1 and 2, we carry out the regressions for external dollarization (with random and fixed effects, respectively), concluding that the balance sheet effect is very strong. The effect of domestic dollarization is tested in columns 3 and 4, and the estimate turns out to be highly positive and significant at a 10 percent level. To save space, we do not present the consumption growth regressions, but they decisively reject the presence of an effect as the one detected for GDP and investment growth.

Conclusions

In this chapter we explore the role of liability dollarization in the way that real exchange rate devaluations impact economic growth. Our research follows recent research pieces that have shown that at a microeconomic level balance sheet effects arise in the presence of liability dollarization and lead to negative impacts of real exchange rate devaluations on firms' performance. Our research complements the microeconomic research by showing how at a macrolevel the results hold and are economically significant.

We find that in countries with no external dollarization, a 20 percent real devaluation increases per capita GDP growth by approximately half a percentage point (although this estimate is not significant at conventional levels in some of our exercises). The chief finding, nevertheless, is that the devaluation-dollarization interaction variable is highly significant across most of the regressions. As dollarization increases, the expansionary effect of devaluations diminishes. In countries where the external dollarization measure used in the text is greater than 0.84 (countries that have dollar denominated external debt greater than 84 percent of GDP), currency devaluations become contractionary. This corresponds to the top decile of the distribution of observations in the whole sample and to the top 20 if we restrict the sample to developing countries.

Similar results are obtained when using a measure of domestic liability dollarization. In short, for most of the developing country sample, the contractionary effect of devaluations seems to dominate the expansionary effect that is brought in though the standard trade channels of the Mundell-Fleming model. These results are robust to several specification changes, including separating the effect of industrial and developing countries, and dealing explicitly with possible outliers.

Our study also confirms that investment is the main channel through which macroeconomic adjustment is achieved following a real exchange rate devaluation. Microeconomic research had shown that firms with dollarized liabilities adjust capital expenditure negatively when faced with devaluations while other firms respond positively. This paper shows that at the macrolevel the adjustment also comes through investment rather than consumption.

Notes

The authors thank Hadi Esfahani, Giovanni Facchini, and Geoffrey Hewings for the invitation to participate in the conference "Economic Development in Latin America" in honor of Professor Werner Baer. Bebczuk and Galindo are very grateful for Professor Baer's inspiration, especially during their graduate school years. Professor Baer was a member of both of their dissertation committees. We also appreciate the comments received during the conference, and especially the insightful suggestions from Hadi Esfahani. Of course, all remaining errors are ours. The views in this document are those of the authors and do not reflect those of the Inter-American Development Bank nor its board of directors.

1. See for example Amman and Baer (2003) or Baer and Maloney (1997).
2. It must be noted that while the price of tradeables normally keeps track of the exchange rate in an open economy, nontradeables might also do so in dollar-indexed economies.
3. See Galindo et al. (2003) for an empirical survey.
4. Harvey and Roper (1999) find that balance sheet effects played a significant role in propagating the crisis.
5. We use dollar debt and dollarization as a short-cut for foreign currency debt.
6. We use the same set of country characteristics used by Levy Yeyati and Sturzenegger (2002), who also address the exchange rate-growth nexus: Investment over GDP, Population and Population Growth, Secondary Enrollment, lagged Government Consumption, Civil Liberties, change in Terms of Trade, the Frankel and Romer index of openness, and three regional dummies. Although these variables are often included in growth exercises, it is also known that few variables have turned out to be consistently robust. In any case, some unreported regressions with combinations of these controls yield otherwise similar results on our variables of interest.
7. Our results do not change if we relax this assumption.
8. Endogeneity might appear in this model as a result of potential simultaneous causation between the dependent variable and some right-hand side ones. We partially address this drawback by using lagged values of most regressors. One way of dealing with this is to use internal instruments through GMM methods. However, this is not bullet-proof either, because, on the one hand, results are frequently quite sensitive to the chosen lag structure and, on the other hand, the endogeneity bias may worsen as long as the instruments are weak.
9. The regressions include the same set of controls as in Table 8.1, but, in order to save space we only report the variables of interest.
10. While the negative coefficient may seem puzzling, this can be easily rationalized with the observation that we are forcing all industrial countries to have zero dollarization but some balance sheet effects are likely to be at work there and we would capture them if we could measure external dollarization in these countries. Since we cannot measure these effect the DRER*IND interaction just captures their average effect.
11. We proceed in two steps: estimate the model, recover the residual, and compute their variance, and then reestimate the model dropping all observations for which the above condition holds.

References

Amman, E., and W. Baer (2003) "Anchors Away: The Costs and Benefits of Brazil's Devaluation," *World Development*, 31, 1033–1046.

Aguiar, M. (2005) "Investment, Devaluation, and Foreign Currency Exposure: The Case of Mexico," *Journal of Development Economics*, 78, 95–113.

Baer, W., and W. Maloney (1997) "Neoliberalism and Income Distribution in Latin America," *World Development*, 25, 311–327.

Benavente, J., C. Johnson, and F. Morandé (2003) "Debt Composition and Balance Sheet Effects of Exchange Rate Depreciations: A Firm-Level Analysis for Chile," *Emerging Markets Review*, 4, 397–416.

Bleakley, H., and K. Cowan (2002) "Dollar Debt and Devaluations: Much Ado About Nothing?" Working Paper # 02–5, Federal Reserve Bank of Boston.

Bonomo, M., B. Martins, and R. Pinto (2003) "Debt Composition and Exchange Rate Balance Sheet effect in Brazil: A Firm Level Analysis," *Emerging Markets Review*, 4, 368–396.

Calvo G., A. Izquierdo, and R. Loo-Kung (2006) "Relative Price Volatility under Sudden Stops: The Relevance of Balance Sheet Effects," *Journal of International Economics*, 69, 231–254.

Carranza, L., J. Cayo, and J. Galdón-Sanchez (2003) "Exchange Rate Volatility and Economic Performance in Peru: A Firm Level Analysis," *Emerging Markets Review*, 4, 472–496.

Céspedes, L., R. Chang, and A. Velasco (2004) "Balance Sheets and Exchange Rate Policy," *American Economic Review*, 94, 1183–1193.

Diaz-Alejandro, C. (1965) *Exchange Rate Devaluation in a Semi-Industrialized Country*, Cambridge, MA: MIT Press.

Domac, I. (1997) "Are Devaluations Contractionary? Evidence from Turkey," *Journal of Economic Development*, 22, 145–163.

Echeverry, J., L. Fergusson, R. Steiner, and C. Aguilar (2003) "'Dollar' Debt in Colombian Firms: Are Sinners Punished During Devaluations?" *Emerging Markets Review*, 4, 417–449.

Edwards, S. (1986) "Devaluation and Aggregate Economic Activity: An Empirical Analysis of the Contractionary Devaluation Issue," Working Paper No. 412, Los Angles, CA: Department of Economics, UCLA.

Eichengreen, B. and R. Portes (2005) "Globalization and Economic and Financial Instability," in H.P. Gray and J. Dilyard (eds) *The Globalization of the World Economy* vol. Elgar Reference Collection. Cheltenham, U.K. and Northampton, MA: Elgar, 3–51.

Fleming, M. (1962) "Domestic Financial Policies under Fixed and under Floating Exchange Rates," *IMF Staff Papers*, 9, 369–379.

Frankel, J. (2005) "Contractionary Currency Crises in Developing Countries," *IMF Staff Papers*, 52 (2).

Galiani, S., E. Levy Yeyati, and E. Schargrodsky (2003) "Financial Dollarization and Debt Deflation under a Currency Board," *Emerging Markets Review*, 4, 340–367.

Galindo, A., A. Izquierdo, and J. Montero (2005) "Real Exchange Rates, Dollarization and Industrial Employment in Latin America," Working Paper No. 0601, Madrid: Banco de España.

Galindo A., U. Panizza, and F. Schiantarelli (2003) "Debt Composition and Balance Sheet Effects of Currency Depreciation: A Summary of the Micro Evidence," *Emerging Markets Review*, 4, 330–339.

Harvey, C., and A. Roper (1999) "The Asian Bet," in A. Harwood, R. Litan, and M. Pomerleano, (eds.) *The Crisis in Emerging Financial Markets*, Washington, D.C.: Brookings Institution Press, 29–115.

Kamin, S., and M. Klau (1998) "Some Multi-Country Evidence on the Effects of Real Exchange Rates on Output," *International Finance Discussion Paper*, No. 611, Washington, D.C.: Board of Governors of the Federal Reserve System.

Krugman, P. (1999) "Balance Sheets, the Transfer Problem, and Financial Crises," *International Tax and Public Finance*, 6, 459–472.

Krugman, P., and L. Taylor (1978) "Contractionary Effects of Devaluations," *Journal of International Economics*, 8, 445–456.

Larrain, F., and J. Sachs (1986) "Contractionary Devaluation, and Dynamic Adjustment of Exports and Wages," NBER Working Paper No. 2078.

Lerner, A. (1944) *The Economics of Control*, New York: Macmillan.

Levy Yeyati, E. (2006) "Financial Dollarization: Evaluating the Consequences", *Economic Policy*, 45, 61–110.

Levy Yeyati, E., and F. Sturzenegger (2002) "To Float or to Trail: Evidence on the Impact of Exchange Rate Regimes," mimeo, Department of Economics, Universidad Di Tella, Argentina.

Lizondo, S., and P. Montiel (1988) "Contractionary Devaluation in Developing Countries: An Analytical Overview," IMF Working Paper No. 51, Washington, D.C.

Marshall, A. (1923) *Money, Credit, and Commerce*, London: Macmillan.

Martínez, L., and A. Werner (2002) "The Exchange Rate Regime and the Currency Composition of Corporate Debt: The Mexican Experience," *Journal of Development Economics*, 69, 315–334.

Mundell, R. (1963) "Capital Mobility and Stabilization Policy under Fixed and Flexible Exchange Rates," *Canadian Journal of Economics and Political Science*, 29, 475–485.

Pratap, S., I. Lobato, and A. Somuano (2003) "Debt Composition and Balance Sheet Effects of Exchange Rate Volatility in Mexico: A Firm Level Analysis," *Emerging Markets Review*, 4, 450–471.

Part II

Income Distribution and Economic Development

9
Interpreting Brazilian Income Distribution Trends

Don Coes

Introduction

In his long career teaching so many of us to ask the important questions about the Brazilian economy, Werner Baer has often focused on its unequal distribution of income. The persistence of inequality for so much of its history has troubled him, as it has so much of the Brazilian economics profession. It would be optimistic to think that we will soon have much better answers or better policies than we currently do, but surely an important step on that journey begins by asking the right questions. Werner's intellectual style has always been to look at the actual numbers, rather than try to extract some delicate hypotheses from a theoretical model.

This chapter attempts to follow that tradition in asking how we should interpret some of the income distribution numbers that we do have. That large task, as he has often shown us, begins by asking a lot of questions. A few of the many ones he might ask are the focus of our discussion here. The chapter begins with a brief summary of recent trends in the Brazilian distribution of personal income. The next section turns to the question of how we might weight the welfare of the different groups that receive Brazil's income, suggesting the use of "stochastic dominance" criteria for making welfare judgments for data like those from Brazil. In the next section we look at some of the demographic, age structure, and geographic issues that arise in the interpretation of Brazil's income distribution data. We conclude, as Werner often has, with as many questions as when we started, but hopefully, more informed ones.

Structure and trends in the distribution of Brazilian income

Brazilian income data before the 1980s have many limitations. These became apparent in the 1970s, as tabulations of census information from the Instituto Brasileiro de Estatística e Geografia (IBGE)'s decennial censuses taken in 1960 and 1970 seemed to indicate that the gap between the highest income earners and those at lower levels had actually widened. Table 9.1 shows real income for each decile in the census years of 1960, 1970, and 1980, as well as the annual growth rates of income in each decile over the two subperiods and over the whole period.

The table reveals a number of features of the Brazilian experience between 1960 and 1970 that provided support for both the defenders of the military regime that seized power in 1964 and its critics.[1] Average real income for most deciles of income distribution rose modestly over the period, with only the seventh deciles average income showing a small loss. One of the interesting features of this decade's experience was that it does not appear to be the poorest in Brazil who failed to accompany the highest income groups' gains, but those Brazilians in the middle (fourth through seventh) deciles of income distribution.

That was small consolation for the poorest, however, whose mean real incomes even in 1970 remained at only about 2.5 percent of those of the highest decile, despite annual growth about in line with the overall growth of income. The biggest beneficiaries by far were those in the highest decile, whose incomes appear to have increased at almost double the overall rate. It is not surprising, therefore, that critics of the post-1964 regime viewed the 1970 numbers as an indictment of the economic policies enacted by the military government. Inequality clearly increased, with the Gini coefficient rising from 0.54 to 0.59. Given the political climate of the times, however, open discussion of the increasing inequality in Brazil was limited.

In retrospect, it may be the case that the IBGE decennial data was too limited to bear the weight of the political discussion that it engendered in the

Table 9.1   Brazilian income by decile, 1960–1980

Decile	Annual real income (in September 1960 Cr$)			Annual growth rate 1960–1970	Annual growth rate 1970–1980	Annual growth rate 1960–1980
	1960	1970	1980			
1	689	852	1702	2.1	7.2	4.6
2	1366	1506	2929	1.0	6.9	3.9
3	2013	2203	4256	0.9	6.8	3.8
4	2737	2798	5151	0.2	6.3	3.2
5	3621	3687	6363	0.2	5.6	2.9
6	4509	4531	8051	0.0	5.9	2.9
7	5540	5295	10345	−0.5	6.9	3.2
8	6387	7307	14254	1.4	6.9	4.1
9	8648	11126	22161	2.6	7.1	4.8
10	23348	34128	69094	3.9	7.3	5.6
Mean	5886	7343	14431	2.2	7.0	4.6

Source: Ramos and Mendonça (2005); primary source, IBGE.

1970s. Among other limitations, in addition to its relatively limited coverage, was the vulnerability of real income comparisons to the price data used over a decade of high inflation. Inflation accelerated in the early 1960s, with the general price level rising more than eightfold between 1960 and the end of 1964. Despite the stabilization program of the post-1964 period and the resulting fall in the inflation rate, price levels still more than tripled over the remainder of the decade, resulting in a price level in 1970 of over 25 times that of 1960.

For this reason, comparisons of real income changes for different groups over the 1960–1970 period are highly vulnerable to the price data used to deflate the nominal income data of each census year. If we assume that the same price deflator can be used for each decile of income distribution, then conclusions about the observed worsening of relative inequality are robust to high inflation rates. Conclusions about absolute changes in the mean real incomes of different deciles, however, are highly suspect. Given that the reported mean real income of all Brazilians rose about 2 percent, with that of the middle deciles hardly changing at all, it seems difficult to make the strong arguments about real income changes in the 1960–1970 period that critics and defenders of the post-1964 regime sometimes made.[2]

Table 9.2   Brazilian income by decile, 1981–2002

	Mean real income (in October 2002 reais)			Annual growth rate		
Decile	1981	1992	2002	1981–1992	1992–2002	1981–2002
1	27	19	29	–3.5	4.3	0.4
2	54	49	65	–1.0	2.9	0.9
3	78	74	96	–0.5	2.6	1.0
4	105	103	131	–0.2	2.4	1.1
5	137	137	171	0.0	2.2	1.1
6	177	178	224	0.1	2.3	1.2
7	233	233	291	0.0	2.2	1.1
8	322	314	399	–0.3	2.4	1.1
9	499	477	617	–0.4	2.6	1.1
10	1418	1342	1803	–0.5	3.0	1.2
Mean	305	292.6	382.6	–0.4	2.7	1.1

Source: Ramos and Mendonça (2005); primary source: IBGE – *Pesquisa Nacional de Amostra por Domicílios.*

Higher rates of economic growth between 1970 and 1980, despite the slowdown in growth as Brazil's external constraints tightened in the later part of the decade, make real income change conclusions somewhat more reliable in this second period. As may be seen in Table 9.1, mean real income rose by about 7 percent in this period, with all deciles of the income distribution sharing in these gains. The worsening of relative inequality that had occurred in the preceding decade, however, was not reversed, and the Gini coefficient in 1980 was virtually unchanged from that of 1970, rising slightly to 0.60.

One of the few benefits of the heated debate over the IBGE census data and what it seemed to show was a marked improvement in Brazil's income distribution data after 1980. In 1981 IBGE began annual publication of a large-scale household sample survey (the PNAD, or *Pesquisa Nacional por Amostra de Domicílios*). By 2000, this national survey was based on more than 350,000 households, permitting much more reliable conclusions to be drawn about Brazilian income trends. Table 9.2 summarizes data from the PNAD for 1981, 1992, and 2002.

In contrast to the earlier census data, the PNAD data available beginning in 1981 permit us to draw conclusions about Brazilian income level and distribution trends with considerably more confidence. The famous "lost decade" of the 1980s – for most Brazilians painfully more than a decade – is apparent in the data. Real income fell or stagnated for almost all deciles of income distribution, with the cruelest blow falling on Brazil's poorest. With the recovery of the economy after the successful stabilization of the Plano Real, real incomes for all deciles rose enough in the second half of the 1990s to offset fully the macroeconomic disasters of the preceding decade. In contrast to the earlier period of high growth in the late 1960s and early 1970s, the lowest deciles of the income distribution saw their incomes grow more rapidly than did overall mean income.[3]

Welfare interpretations of the Brazilian income distribution data

Simple descriptive interpretation of the Brazilian income data is an obvious first step, but few of us would want to stop there. Implicit – and sometimes explicit – in the controversies over income trends in Brazil is the assumption that we might be concerned more with the lowest deciles of the distribution than with the highest.

Critics of the apparently worsening inequality of the 1960s, for example, placed little or no weight on the fact that some already economically favored Brazilians' real incomes had increased significantly. This occurred without any significant fall in the incomes of the lower half of income distribution. In the jargon of economics, or "bom economês," as it is known in Brazil, this would be called a "Pareto improvement," since some gained without anyone losing. Indeed, some of the defenders of the post-1964 regime's policies suggested that a rising tide would eventually lift all boats, and that as long as mean trends in income growth were positive, it was pointless to worry about worsening relative inequality.

This is clearly an extreme position. Not only economic theory, but Brazilian political discourse and policy have generally embodied the view that the value of one more or less cruzeiro or real of the income of those who have less of it is greater than that of those who have more of it. A formalization of this view in an economic context is that the marginal utility of income is not only positive, but decreasingly positive.

This restriction provides some justification for the focus of many commentators on Brazilian income trends over the past four decades on relative inequality, rather than on absolute levels of income. Since overall welfare would be increased by transferring income from the rich to the poor when the marginal utility of income is decreasing, an other-things-equal increase in relative inequality is clearly bad.

The problem with this reasoning, however, is that other things – most importantly the levels of income – are not equal. As Tables 9.1 and 9.2 both show, there appear to have been significant changes in income levels in at least three of the four subperiods considered. In the 1970s and again in the 1990s, Brazilian mean real incomes clearly increased, even if we allow for considerable imprecision in both the underlying nominal income data and in the price data used to deflate them in the earlier pre-PNAD data. In the 1980s real incomes for most groups decreased, even though those changes were small for most deciles of the distribution. Given our uncertainties about the earlier data, an exclusive focus on relative inequality might be justifiable for the period 1960–1970, as discussions in the 1970s sometimes seemed to assume, but it does not work for the dataset as a whole.

What is needed is a way to evaluate income changes when both the location and shape of the income distribution change simultaneously. If everyone's incomes rise by the same amount, without any change in relative inequality, we would consider that an unambiguous improvement in welfare. In a parallel fashion, if average incomes were unchanged, but the dispersion of incomes about this mean were to increase, we would regard that as a negative outcome.

One way of dealing with such simultaneous changes in income distributions that has received some attention from economists in recent years is the use of stochastic dominance rankings of distributions.[4] If the incomes of some members of the economy increase, without any others falling, the new income distribution is said to be superior to the previous one by a "First Degree Stochastic Dominance" (FSD) rule. In the distributions of Tables 9.1 and 9.2, all ten deciles' mean incomes increased in the 1970–1980 period and again in the 1992–2002 period, permitting us to judge the income distribution at the end of each subperiod as superior in welfare to the beginning, regardless of any changes in relative inequality. The only restriction on preferences that this conclusion requires is that the marginal utility of income be positive.

Evaluations of the welfare changes in income distributions are sometimes not this straightforward. If we make the widely accepted assumption noted above, that the marginal utility of income is not only positive, but decreasing in income, however, then additional rankings are possible using a "Second Degree Stochastic Dominance" (SSD) rule. Such a rule leads to a larger ordering of different distributions. In the case of the data in Table 9.2, for example, it shows that welfare fell for Brazilians between 1981 and 1992.

The difficulty with these and even higher-order SD rules is that they do not always permit us to judge whether welfare has risen or fallen. But this may be a strength, rather than a weakness, in comparison with simple numerical rankings based on mean income or on measures of relative inequality, such as the Gini coefficient, since the impossibility of ranking is really telling us that for reasonable variations in preferences, some individuals would rank pairs of distributions in opposite ways. If one is willing to accept the data of Table 9.1 for the 1960–1970 period as correct, for example, then a ranking is not possible for lower-order SD rules. The intuition of this result is that although there were minor positive gains for most income deciles, the small probability that real incomes would fall (as they did for those in the seventh decile) would require a higher-order SD rule, based on additional restrictions on preferences.

At an operational level, there are some additional difficulties with SD rankings of the kind of income distribution data considered. One of them arises from aggregation of the hundreds of thousands of actual households now in the PNAD into ten groups, which we have implicitly treated as if they were ten individuals. Finer disaggregation might maintain the ranking, but it is also possible that small downward changes in a smaller group (for example, a percentile) in a group of otherwise upward changes could make the overall distribution change we are considering fail the FSD test. Higher-order rules might resolve this indeterminacy, but this is not guaranteed.

Age, geography, and consumption in Brazilian economic inequality

In any empirical measure of income inequality, even in highly egalitarian societies, there will be some spurious inequality arising from the varying ages of the individuals or households studied. This point becomes more obvious if we consider a hypothetical society formed of individuals of equal "life-cycle" incomes in the Modigliani sense. Inclusion of households of varying ages in the sample from such a society would show a degree of inequality, despite our assumption of perfect equality over the life cycle, if income varied with the age and experience of the primary earners in the household. This would be a trivial problem in a welfare sense if capital markets permitted costless transfers of income between different periods to "smooth" the consumption of households over their equal-income life cycles. Even in the U.S., however, these kinds of capital markets do not exist. This assumption is clearly not valid in Brazil, where borrowing rates offered in financial markets are sometimes a multiple of the rates available to net savers. As a result, younger households' consumption is likely to be constrained to the income currently received.

If the age structure of the Brazilian population were not changing, then the spurious inequality that is generated by age-dependent income could be ignored. In a society whose age structure is changing, however, this may in turn have an effect on inequality. In 1950, 41.7 percent of the population was under 15, with only 2.5 percent over 65. By 1980, those under 15 made up only 38.2 percent of the population, while those over 65 were 4.0 percent. IBGE estimates for 2000 were 28.3 and 5.6 percent respectively.

The effect of this aging of the Brazilian population on income distribution is complex. If the rise in average age of the household is positively correlated with income, then some rise in real income may be down to the fall in the share of dependent children, as well as the increased age-dependent income itself. Further aging of the population, however, may have an increasing effect on the aged share of the population, possibly having the reverse effect.[5]

In a country the size of Brazil, the spatial dimension of income inequality is another obvious complication. Table 9.3 shows the relative per capita income of each of the five IBGE-classified regions of Brazil over the past half-century. The underlying data are from population censuses and estimates of national product by region in current prices.

Two features of these data are apparent. First, there is still a significant degree of inequality in per capita income across the five regions, with per capita income in the poor Northeast less than half that of the higher-income Southeastern states, even in 2000. Second, there has been some reduction in these disparities over the past half-century. This trend toward slightly less regional inequality might be explained in several ways. In the 1950s and 1960s large-scale internal migration moved many of Brazil's poor from the Northeast to major Southeast labor markets, notably São Paulo. More recently, many poor have moved from the South and Southeast to high-growth areas in the Center-west. In addition to the effect of this "reallocation" of the poor to higher-income regions, that is, slightly reducing Brazil's regional economic inequality, the net effect of Brazilian federal government tax and expenditure policies may have favored poorer regions, although not necessarily the poorest in those regions.

The data of Table 9.3 may overestimate both regional income inequality and poverty for several reasons. The regions are not equal in size; the

Table 9.3   Relative per capita income by region, 1949–2000

	1949	1959	1970	1980	2000
North	0.48	0.56	0.56	0.63	0.60
Northeast	0.40	0.45	0.39	0.41	0.47
Southeast	1.55	1.49	1.53	1.44	1.36
South	1.01	0.98	0.94	1.06	1.19
Center-west	0.52	0.57	0.71	0.87	1.01
Brazil	1.00	1.00	1.00	1.00	1.00
Stan. dev. across regions (unweighted)	0.48	0.43	0.44	0.40	0.38

North: Rondônia, Acre, Amazonas, Roraima, Pará, Amapá, Tocantins; *Northeast*: Maranhão, Piauí, Ceará, Rio Grande do Norte, Paraíba, Pernambuco, Alagoas, Sergipe, Bahia; *Southeast*: Minas Gerais, Espírito Santo, Rio de Janeiro, São Paulo; *South*: Paraná, Santa Catarina, Rio Grande do Sul; *Center-west*: Mato Grosso do Sul, Mato Grosso, Goiás; *Federal District*.

Sources: 1949–1980: Coes (1995), calculated from IBGE, *Anuário Estatístico do Brasil* (various); 2000: calculated from data at www.ibge. gov.br

relatively wealthier Southeast accounted for about 43 percent of Brazil's in population in 2000, with the North and Center-west each about 7 percent. Recent studies of the PNAD surveys, moreover, suggest that respondents in poorer households may understate income in kind, which would tend to make poorer regions appear to have even lower incomes than the data of Table 9.3 suggest. An additional complication is that there are significant net transfers of income from the higher-income states like São Paulo to poorer ones. Unadjusted data like that of Table 9.3 do not reflect the welfare effects of such net transfers.

Even with these caveats, however, it is clear why discussion of income inequality in Brazil along regional lines has long been a feature of Brazilian political debate. The obvious pitfall here in substituting regional inequality for inequality among people or among households in the political debate is that not all of the poor are in the Northeast, nor all of the wealthy in São Paulo or other Southeast states. Although geographical inequality is an imperfect proxy for inequality among people, this has not been an obstacle to the political system. Federal government net transfers, coming from both tax and expenditure policies, reflect this substitution of concern about regional inequality for inequality among persons.

A third complication in evaluating Brazilian income distribution data is suggested by these transfers. The data of Tables 9.1 and 9.2 tell us what income was received, not who finally benefited from it. Many might argue that it is not income itself, but the current and future consumption that income permits that should be the focus of any welfare analysis of income distribution. Even though these two variables are highly correlated in any economy, they are not identical. The presence of significant income transfers, both between persons and across regions, in Brazil suggests that consumption might be somewhat less inequitably distributed than in income.

When we focus on consumption inequality, rather than income inequality, there may be some reasons to believe that inequality in Brazil diminishes slightly. Brazilian capital markets severely limit the degree to which households can move spending power from one time period to another in order to smooth consumption. Even though such transfers in Brazil are limited to fairly short time periods, they do occur in both organized and in informal markets. This possibility implies that consumption may be a better variable to measure the standard of living (and hence welfare) than are the income measures, like the PNAD, that have been the focus of most investigation.[6]

An additional reason to prefer consumption to income as the true index of welfare is that among lower income groups, especially those who are the beneficiaries of transfers from other family members or of public transfers, consumption is clearly a better measure of that person's standard of living than is reported income. In rural areas, where home-produced food and housing services are important, consumption may be both easier to measure and less likely to be underreported.

It is difficult to estimate the effect of public expenditure policy in possibly diminishing consumption inequality relative to income inequality in Brazil. Some transfers, such as public support for university education – some of it for graduates of private secondary schools – has a negative effect. Other such "perverse" transfers may arise from Brazil's pension system. But there is little question that other kinds of public expenditures improve consumption inequality relative to income inequality. Among them are a number of expenditures that received more emphasis in the past decade, such as preschool and primary school expenditure, or the provision of basic health and sanitation infrastructure in favela areas.[7]

Conclusion: What should we be asking about inequality?

Any serious look at the large amount of data available for a number of years in Brazil suggests a high and persistent degree of inequality. Why it is so high, and why so persistent, are probably the most important questions that we can ask. The existing data provide some clues, but they also raise many unanswered questions.

Conventional measures of income inequality, such as the Gini coefficient, are easy to calculate from the available data. They probably give us a spuriously precise result, however, since they order income distributions that from an economic theory point of view cannot really be ordered without additional restrictions on preferences (if they can be ordered at all), as our discussion of the application of stochastic dominance rules in the second section of this paper suggests. Another difficulty from a welfare theoretic point of view is that these relative inequality measures divorce the effects of greater dispersion about measures of central location, such as mean real income, from the location measures themselves. This too provides an argument for approaches like stochastic dominance that combine the effects of both the mean of the distribution and its shape. It would be useful to know more about the empirical implementation of this approach, and how large a set of income distributions it effectively orders in economies like that of Brazil.

At an empirical level, we must ask how price information affects our evaluation of income distribution trends. Although this may be a less serious problem in post-Plano Real Brazil than it was in the days of high inflation, real income comparisons over time remain vulnerable to the price deflators that are used. This problem is further complicated in long-term welfare comparisons by the introduction and availability of new goods – be they soybean oil or cellphones – that have become more important for Brazilian consumers over the past few decades. A related empirical problem arises when we attempt to assess the effects of the provision of public goods on individual welfare. It is clear that in Brazil these have both positive and negative effects on inequality, depending on the goods provided.

One of the most important questions, both theoretically and empirically, is whether we should be measuring income inequality or consumption inequality. The latter variable is probably more defensible in terms of economic theory, but most of the data available to date in Brazil, such as those in PNAD, focuses on measures of income. For a number of reasons, consumption may actually be easier to measure in some household survey contexts.

Even if we succeed in answering a number of the preceding questions, we are still left with what may be the largest one of all: what do we – or what should we ask of policy in dealing with it? But as Werner Baer would rightly tell us, that would be an interesting new paper.

Notes

1. See Bacha and Taylor (1978) or Fishlow (1972) for a discussion of some of this controversy. Among those who attempted to explain the trend toward worsening inequality as a natural consequence of the acceleration of growth was Langoni (1973). For a more recent summary of Brazilian income distribution trends in both this period and subsequently, see Ramos and Mendonça (2005).
2. Welfare judgments based on "poverty lines" in Brazil are quite sensitive to the price index used. See, for example, Beckerman and Coes (1980).
3. See Dollar and Kray (2002) as an example of the argument that the welfare consequences for the poor of higher rates of real income growth are at least as important as reductions in relative inequality.

4. Key contributions in the earlier literature on stochastic dominance and related concepts include Hadar and Russell (1969), Rothschild and Stiglitz (1970), and Whitmore (1970). Discussions of this approach in analyzing income inequality include Atkinson (1970), Foster and Shorrocks (1988), and Sen (1997). For its use with Brazilian data, see Barros and Mendonça (1995) and Ramos and Mendonça (2005).
5. Some relations between age, household structure, and consumption and income inequality are discussed in De Ferranti et al. (2004).
6. Methods for combining relatively small-sample consumption expenditure data from Brazil with the large-sample PNAD income-focused data have been developed by Elbers et al. (2004).
7. The relation of a number of these public expenditures to inequality is discussed in the World Bank country study (2004).

References

Atkinson, Anthony B. (1970) "On the Measurement of Inequality," *Journal of Economic Theory*, 2, 244–263.

Bacha, Edmar, and Lance Taylor (1978) "Brazilian Income Distribution in the 1960s: Facts, Model, Results, and the Controversy," *Journal of Development Studies*, 14, 271–297.

Barros, Lauro, and Rosane Mendonça (1995) "A evolução do bem-estar, pobreza e desigualdade ao longo das últimas três décadas – 1960–1990," *Pesquisa e Planejamento Econômico*, 25.

Beckerman, Paul, and Donald V. Coes (1980) "Who Benefits from Economic Growth?" *American Economic Review*, 70, 246–249.

Coes, Donald V. (1995) *Macroeconomic Crises, Policies, and Growth in Brazil, 1964–90,* Washington, D.C.: The World Bank.

De Ferranti, David, Guillermo E. Perry, Francisco H.G. Ferreira, and Michael Walton (2004) *Inequality in Latin America: Breaking with History?* Washington, D.C.: The World Bank.

Dollar, David, and Aart Kraay (2002) "Growth is Good for the Poor," *Journal of Economic Growth,* 7, 195–225.

Elbers, Chris, Jean Olson Lanjouw, Peter Lanjouw, and Phillippe G. Leite (2004) "Poverty and Inequality in Brazil: New Estimates from Combined PPV-PNAD Data," in *Inequality and Economic Development in Brazil,* World Bank.

Fishlow, Albert (1972) "Brazilian Size Distribution of Income," *American Economic Review*, 62, 391–402.

Foster, James E., and Anthony Shorrocks (1988) "Poverty Orderings," *Econometrica*, 56, 173–177.

Hadar, Josef, and William Russell (1969) "Rules for Ordering Uncertain Prospects," *American Economic Review*, 69, 25–34.

Langoni, Carlos G. (1973) *Distribuiçao de Randa e Desenvolvimento Econômico no Brasil,* Rio de Janeiro: Espressão e Cultura.

Ramos, Lauro, and Rosane Mendonça (2005) "Pobreza e Desigualdade de Renda no Brasil," in Giambagi et al. (ed.) *Economia Brasileira Contemporânea (1945–2004),* Riode Janeiro: Elsevier, 355–377.

Rothschild, Michael, and Joseph Stiglitz (1970) "Increasing Risk: A Definition," *Journal of Economic Theory*, 2, 225–243.

Sen, Amaryta (1997) *On Economic Inequality* (revised edition), Oxford and New York: Clarendon/Oxford University Press.

Whitmore, G.A. (1970) "Third Degree Stochastic Dominance," *American Economic Review*, 60, 457–459.

World Bank (2004) *Inequality and Economic Development in Brazil* (World Bank Country Study), Washington, D.C.: The IBRD/World Bank.

10
The Evolution of Agriculture and Land Reform in Brazil, 1960–2006

Charles Mueller and Bernardo Mueller

Introduction

The impressive work of Werner Baer on Brazil is a major landmark in the study of the development of the country he chose to analyze. This is particularly the case regarding his interpretation of development based on industrialization in the post-World War II period. A major text on this is his *Industrialization and Economic Development in Brazil* (1965), which was translated into Portuguese and published in Brazil under the title *A Industrialização e o Desenvolvimento Econômico do Brasil* (several editions). This book was an important source of study for a generation of Brazilian economists. In it, he focuses on the role of agriculture in the development of Brazil and, particularly, of the limitations this sector experienced as import substitution industrialization was reaching its climax in the late 1950s and early 1960s; he also examines Brazil's agrarian problem in the period. Similarly, in his major opus, *The Brazilian Economy – Growth and Development* (2001) which is now on its fifth edition (a sixth edition is in the making), Werner Baer offers us a keen analysis of the more recent developments in the agricultural and agrarian scenes.

The purpose of our chapter is to discuss, against the backdrop of Werner Baer's analyses, the factors that enabled Brazilian agriculture to progress from the awkward position in which it was found in the late 1950s and early 1960s to the modern and dynamic segment of the Brazilian economy of our days, in spite of the fact that, until recently, there was no land reform to speak of. In fact, we will examine how land reform was postponed for so long and why when it began to take place, it was based mostly on distributional considerations and land reform ceased to be recommended as a major tool for the expansion of agricultural production and of productivity.

The development of Brazilian commercial agriculture after World War II

Discussing the performance of Brazilian commercial agriculture after World War II the above-mentioned texts by Werner Baer identify roughly two phases: (1) from the end of the war to the early 1970s, a phase of horizontal agricultural expansion; and (2) from the early 1970s to the late 1980s, a period of officially induced conservative modernization. He would probably agree, however, that there is a third phase: from the early 1990s to the present: a 'free market' period of a remarkable performance in commercial agriculture.

The phase of horizontal expansion

In *Industrialization and Economic Development* the analysis of agricultural development is discussed by Werner Baer in the context of the urban-biased import substitution industrialization strategy adopted after the war. Agriculture was then identified with backwardness, deserving attention only because of some of the key roles it played in the ISI strategy. Urban bias took place mainly through considerable manipulation of agricultural prices in favor of the urban-industrial sector. As a result, there was a substantial transfer of income from agriculture to the latter sector (Oliveira, 1981). Werner Baer showed that, notwithstanding this, the performance of agriculture was adequate. Production increased enough to assure that, by and large, the sectoral terms of trade did not negatively affect the urban-industrial sector (Baer, 1983, table 7.2; 2001, 358–361), in spite of the very rapid pace of import substitution activities and of the growth in urban demand for food. Moreover, in spite of a consistently overvalued foreign exchange, agriculture originated most of the country's export earnings.

As stressed by Werner Baer (1965, ch. 7; 2001, ch. 15) Brazilian agriculture remained extremely primitive during this phase; yields remained very low by world standards and almost unchanged. The agricultural sector remained largely the same and policies for modernizing it were almost nonexistent, oneexception to this being the efforts by organizations of the state government of São Paulo to improve the production of coffee, cotton, and sugar cane, the effects of which were limited to portions of that state (Pastore et al., 1976). As acknowledged by Baer – and also by his then colleague at Vanderbilt University, the expert in Brazilian agriculture William Nicholls (1972) – the expansion in production of this period was the result mainly of road building programs; new roads enabled farmers to bring more land into cultivation, under practically the same very low yield methods.

Indeed, employing shift share analysis to the growth of the vegetable crop sector, Patrick (1975) determined that between 1949 and 1968 that 82.5 percent of the 4.3 percent annual growth in output of this sector resulted from the expansion in the area cultivated – the area effect – and only 17.5 percent came increases in yields – the yield effect. He estimated also that in the state of São Paulo the proportions were almost the reverse; the area effect on this state's agricultural growth was 15.5 percent, but the yield effect was 85.5 percent, a reflection of the above-mentioned technological advances.

In sharp contrast, in the Northeast the area effect was 115.9 percent and the yield effect was –15.9 percent; the area cultivated had to expand more than the increase in production so as to make up for consistent reductions in yields in this depressed region.

However, towards the end of the period, the stock of fertile lands at the agricultural frontier had diminished considerably. There were ample unused lands in the Cerrado (the Brazilian huge savannas), but there was no technology available for their utilization. Fearing problems resulting from an inadequate performance of the agricultural sector, the 1964–1985 military government acted to create conditions for more intensive exploitation of areas already settled; occupation of land in the frontier was to continue but now with geopolitical motivations.

It is interesting to note, regarding Baer's mid-1960s analysis of agriculture (the first edition of his *Industrialization and Economic Development* is from this period), that he avoided placing the blame for the sluggish growth of agricultural productivity on the fashionable structuralist view prevalent in Brazil at this time. According to the structuralists, the problems agriculture was then facing resulted from of an inbuilt failure on the part of Brazilian farmers to respond to the demands from the budding urban-industrial sector. Accordingly, the main structuralist policy prescription was that of a drastic agrarian reform, involving confiscating land from the *latifundistas* and placing it in the hands of small farmers who were seen as more responsive to the requirements of urban-industrial development. The structuralist view had been demolished by one of its own ranks (see Castro, 1979) but it took considerably longer for the truth to be accepted. Avoiding the fashion of the day, Werner Baer acknowledged the highly concentrated land ownership distribution of the period (which remains to the present), and saw an important role for modernizing agrarian reform. But the main impact of such a reform would be redistributive, although in some regions it might be a factor in putting into use idle land of very large, poorly exploited landholdings (Baer, 1983). Having traveled extensively in Brazil and knowing the country better than many Brazilian experts, Werner Baer refused to embark on simplistic explanations and suggestions, based on imported doctrinaire positions. His main policy prescriptions stressed the need to develop the country's agricultural marketing capabilities, to induce technical change in agriculture, and to develop adequate incentive policies for the expansion of agriculture.

The period of officially induced conservative modernization

This period began with the inception of the military regime. Emphasizing the strategic role of an adequate performance in agriculture in terms of production for the domestic market and as a source of much needed foreign exchange, the first military government, almost immediately after it got into power, introduced a far-reaching reformulation of the country's agricultural strategy. The main elements in this were:

- the establishment of a rural credit system, providing abundant financing, at very generous terms, to commercial agriculture;
- the implementation of a broad-based research system in tropical agriculture – the EMBRAPA system;
- improvement of the instruments and of the administration of the minimum price policy;
- inducements for the formation and expansion of *agribusiness complexes*; and
- marked changes in the legislation governing land reform (see below).

The nature and the results of the changes in the agricultural strategy are appropriately discussed in the fifth edition of Werner Baer's *The Brazilian Economy*. There we see that, by far, the main instrument of the system of inducements was agricultural credit. The rationale for the reformists in the mid-1960s was that abundant credit at low interest rates would induce farmers to improve their production methods by purchasing modern inputs and implements. Accordingly, the availability of subsidized credit expanded markedly, and until the mid-1980s, it was accompanied by considerable expansion of agricultural production (see Figure 10.1). However, in the 1980s, the efficacy of agricultural credit in expanding output began to weaken, and the rural credit system became increasingly regarded as wasteful and distorting (Sayad, 1984). Moreover, it had turned into an obstacle for the implementation of macroeconomic policy (da Mata, 1982). So, agricultural credit was considerably curtailed and the real interest rates on farm loans became positive.

In the second half of the 1980s the incentives and subsidies of the credit policy were replaced with those provided by the minimum price policy;

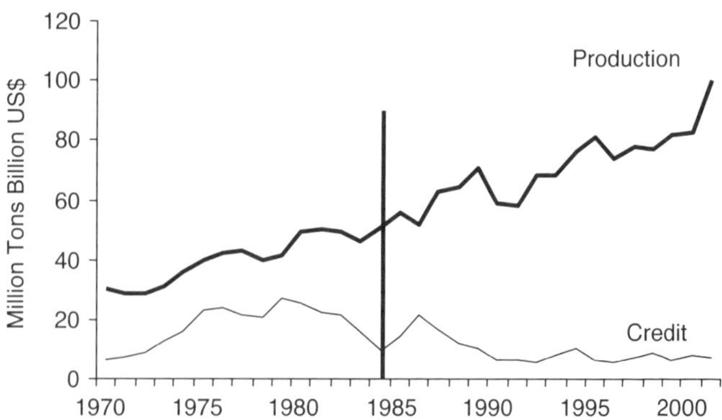

Figure 10.1   Production of grains and agricultural credit, 1970–2001

Sources: Production: CONAB, Ministério da Agricultura; Agricultural credit: Banco Central.

this policy became aggressively employed to induce production. In fact, the minimum price policy, together with the devaluations of the 1980s, brought about a considerable expansion and diversification of agricultural exports. However, this policy soon became unsustainable, as it involved the accumulation of huge government stocks of agricultural products. These problems, together with the effects of the 1988 Constitution on the capacity of the federal government to intervene, led to a significant decline in direct official involvement in agricultural promotion in the 1990s.

A negative feature of the conservative modernization period was its hectic policy setting: as argued by Dias and Amaral (2000) and as extensively documented by Rezende (2003),[1] there were frequent policy changes, caused not only by macroeconomic constraints and changes in priorities. At certain times, the main aim was to have the domestic market well supplied to avoid inflationary pressures caused by food shortages; at other periods the emphasis was on the generation of export revenues associated with balance of payments problems. Moreover, the agricultural sector became increasingly subject to complex and distorting interventions, such as price controls and barriers to agricultural exports. Also, policy changes were not only frequent during the period, but the policies and interventions themselves became increasingly unsustainable. As a result, as shown below, the 1990s saw a substantial change in direction regarding agricultural strategy.

Performance of agriculture in the conservative modernization period

Considering the economic instability and the policy shifts of the 1980s, the performance of agriculture was quite adequate. The output of grains and oilseeds,[2] for instance, increased from 22.4 million tons in 1965, to 58.1 million tons in 1985 and to 71.5 million tons in 1989. As for the value of agricultural exports,[3] it increased from US$1.3 billion in 1965, to 5.0 billion in 1975 and to 10.1 billion in 1985. After this there was a minor reduction in the value of agricultural exports, to US$9.6 billion in 1990, because of falling international commodity prices.

However, in the conservative modernization period agricultural exports increased at a much slower pace than the country's total exports; while in 1965 they represented 82.6 percent of the total exports, their share declined to 39.3 percent in 1985 and to 30.5 in 1990. Moreover, the diversification of agricultural exports increased substantially. In 1965 coffee alone accounted for 50.6 percent of the total value of agricultural exports; in 1990 its share fell to only 12.3 percent. The exports of other agricultural products – notably soybeans and soy meal, orange juice, poultry and beef – greatly expanded in the period. No doubt, this was the result of the policies then adopted; they were costly and unsustainable, but they produced considerable changes in the Brazilian agriculture.

Moreover, as acknowledged by Baer (2001, p. 376), modernization of agriculture together with the advance of agribusiness complexes led to considerable, although selective, increases in productivity in the period for both the crop and the livestock sectors. Commodities which were integrated into agribusiness complexes showed important productivity changes while crops which were not integrated in this way remained stagnant (Mueller, 1992). As a matter of fact, it was this integration that enabled the agricultural sector to strive and finally prosper after, in the 1990s, the encumbered government support and intervention system had to be abandoned.

Period of rapid expansion and modernization with sharply declining official backing

We begin by highlighting the main positive legacies of the previous period. They include:

- the consolidation and expansion of an effective system of agricultural research;
- increasing professionalization of commercial farmers; and
- development of agribusiness complexes; as already stressed, most of the success stories of the Brazilian agriculture are related to such complexes.

It is worth discussing further the main impacts of the policy changes of the early 1990s: it was then that the country's productive sectors – including its agriculture – became increasingly exposed to international competition. Tariffs were reduced, import prohibitions and export quotas ceased to be employed and the foreign trade bureaucracy was streamlined. Thus, many of the distorting interventions of the past were phased out.

Regarding agricultural financing, for instance, the main changes were:

- the *direct* government funding of commercial agriculture was substantially reduced, and the interest rate for public agricultural credit was consistently maintained at positive, although often below market rates;
- most of the remaining official financing was channeled to small farmers and to land reform settlement projects; and
- for most of the commercial agriculture, other sources of finance, usually private, were developed. By and large the government retreated to the coordination of the provision of adequate financing for agriculture.

As mentioned, however, the policy changes of this period did not evolve smoothly; there were ups and downs, which engendered some turbulence for the sector. Deserving emphasis, in this respect, is the 1994–1999 period, which saw the strong appreciation of the real – a key policy instrument of the Real Plan (Baer, 2001, ch. 10). The strong real negatively affected agricultural exports and increased agricultural imports; and this happened in a period of slack in international commodity prices. Agriculture received an important boost in 1999 when the foreign exchange rate was allowed to float freely, producing a sharp devaluation of the real. Together with increasing trends in world commodity prices, the new exchange rate policy induced a considerable expansion of Brazil's agricultural and agribusiness exports.

In examining the events of this period it is convenient, therefore, to focus separately on the 1991–1998 period, which began with acute macroeconomic problems and saw the implementation of the Real stabilization plan with the overvalued real; and the 1999–2004 period, starting with the introduction of the floating foreign exchange rate regime, which brought about a sizeable devaluation of the real. Between 1991 and 1998 the annual rate of growth of real agricultural GDP averaged a modest 2.4 percent, in line with the rate of growth of GDP for the whole economy (2.8 percent annually). After initial very low or negative rates, agricultural growth rates increased in the euphoric period after the implementation of the Real Plan, but declined considerably in 1997 and 1998. In contrast, between 1999 and 2004, the annual agricultural growth rate averaged an impressive 5.4 percent; moreover, growth remained high in almost every year of the period. Very seldom in the past had agriculture experienced a six-year streak of substantial expansion. In contrast, the country's GDP real growth averaged only 1.8 percent between 1999 and 2004.

The data on grain and oilseed production confirm these developments (see Figure 10.2). Between 1991 and 1998 output increased moderately, from 57.9 million tons to 76.6 million. Starting in 1999, there was a sharp upturn, and production continued increasing year after year, reaching 123.2 million tons in 2003. Overall, the grain and oilseed output increased by 32.3 percent in the seven years between 1991 and 1998, but by 55.4 percent in the six-year period from 1999 to 2004. It is worth stressing, moreover, that this expansion in output was obtained with only a relatively small addition to the land under cultivation; between 1991 and 2005, the area in grains and oilseeds increased by only 25.1 percent, from 37.9 million to 47.4 million hectares. Most of the substantial increase in output resulted from gains in yield. As indicated, technological change was a major factor in this performance; and it reached not only the grains and oilseeds sector, but also products such as sugarcane and coffee, and – with impressive results – the beef, poultry, pork, eggs, and milk sectors. It is important to bear in mind that this performance was substantially assisted by external markets that have recently been very favorable.

Further, this performance had important repercussions on Brazil's international trade. The value of agribusiness exports – including only commodities and semimanufactured goods[4] – increased from US$21.2 billion in 1997 to 43.6 billion in 2005 (see Figure 10.3). The impact of this achievement on the country's external accounts was considerable. To give an idea, in 2005

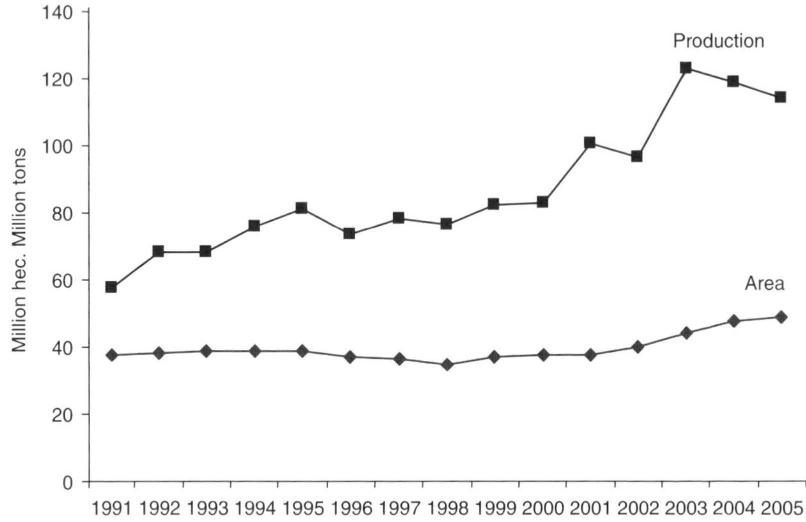

Figure 10.2   Area cultivated and production of grains, 1991–2005
Source: CONAB, Ministério da Agricultura, Pecuária e Abastecimento.

Brazil's balance of trade totaled US$44.8 billion, of which 38.4 billion came from the agribusiness sector. According to ERS/USDA and FAO data,[5] in 2003 Brazil had become the leading world exporter of soybeans, sugar, meat from beef cattle, coffee, orange juice, and tobacco; the second large exporter of soy meal, oil from soybeans, and poultry; and the fourth largest exporter of pork, corn, and cotton.

The recent progress of the meats sector (beef, poultry, and pork) and of the sugar and alcohol sector of Brazil's agribusiness is also reflected on the foreign trade data. In the ten years between 1996 and 2005, the value of exports of beef, poultry, and pork increased more than five times, from US$1.4 billion to 7.7 billion. In addition, sugar and alcohol exports increased from an yearly average of US$1.7 billion in the period 1991–1993 to 4.9 billion in 2005, with a substantial contribution, of late, from ethanol exports.

It is important to remember that all this was attained with a considerably reduced official support. According to a recent OECD survey of governmental support to agriculture (OECD, 2005a), between 2002 and 2004 Brazil provided support to the agricultural producers amounting to 3 percent of the gross value of agricultural output. In this period, of the major agricultural countries, only New Zeeland had a lower level of support (2 percent). This contrasted sharply with the levels of support granted by the US (17 percent), the OECD countries (30), the EU (34), and Japan (58).

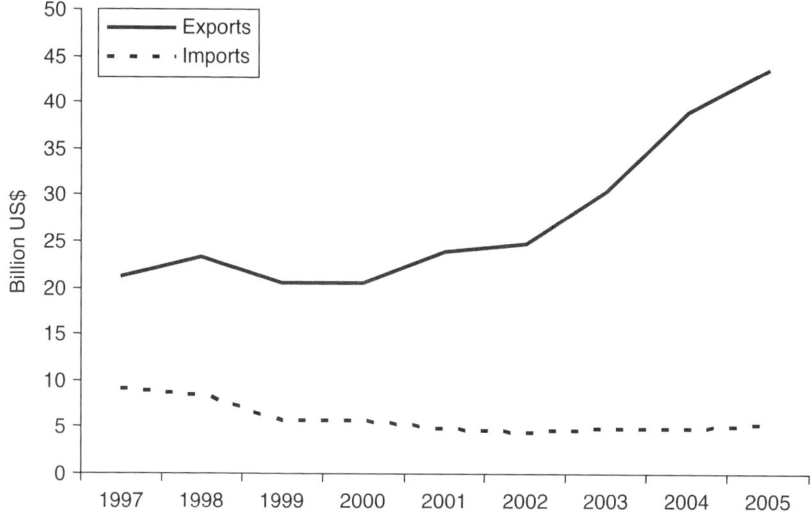

Figure 10.3   Agribusiness foreign trade, 1997–2005

Source: SECEX, Ministério do Desenvolvimento, Indústria e Comércio.

Recent problems

An observer of the Brazilian scene a couple of years back would be impressed by both the recent performance of Brazil's agribusiness complex – a modern, dynamic sector of the economy – and the state of mind of almost everyone involved with the agricultural component of the complex and with agricultural policymaking. The atmosphere was euphoric and the impression was that the sector could stand entirely on its own, with minimal governmental support. The perception would be less strong, however, if one considered that this performance was substantially assisted by recent very favorable external markets for products of the soy, sugar and alcohol, orange juice, and meats complexes, keeping in mind that – if the future is to replicate the past – this is liable to change.

As a matter of fact, in 2005 and 2006 such reverses severely hit the soybean, corn, and cotton sectors. World prices for these commodities experienced considerable declines, the Brazilian currency became increasingly strong, and the agriculture of the South in 2005, and of the South and the Center-West in 2006, suffered considerable losses as a result of a severe drought. Additionally, a series of internal obstacles cast some doubt on the ability of Brazilian agriculture to continue expanding when the situation returns to near normality. We examine, below some of the most important among these problems.

Problems highlighted by recent climatic events

In 2004 a severe but localized drought in Brazil's extreme south led to a reduction in the production of grains (Figure 10.2). Moreover, in 2005 a more extended drought – reaching the country's southern states and parts of the Center-West – reduced production further. In December 2004, when the 2004/05 crops had just been planted, CONAB's forecast was that of a grain harvest of 131.9 million tons for 2005 (*Agroanalysis*, March, 2005), but the drought brought about a reduction in the forecast to 113.9 million tons. This occurred during a phase when world prices for grains were declining[6] and the Brazilian currency was appreciating rapidly.[7] These events brought about a substantial decline in agricultural incomes – the 2005 preliminary data on national accounts show a decline of 0.8 percent in real agricultural GNP, in sharp contrast to the 5.3 percent average agricultural growth of the 2001–2004 period. That the 2005 result was not worse was because of the good performance of the sugarcane-alcohol, coffee, citrus, and, with some problems, the meats sectors.

These events generated some disturbing long-term effects. The very favorable 2001–2004 period induced farmers to borrow heavily, both for investment and for the purchase of inputs.[8] It is estimated that early in 2006 some one-third of the agricultural debt of R$ 36.85 billion (some US$16.6 billion) was overdue.[9] As a result, the government portion of the sums due (mostly relating to loans by the Banco do Brasil and BNDES) had the repayment date extended. New lines of credit at favored interest rates were established, but the farmers considered these measures to be too little and to late. They demanded more; they pressed for further extensions on dates of repayment and even amnesties of portions of the sums due. The economic team in government, however, was not willing to embark on policies involving additional expenditure.

The previous debt crisis faced by the Brazilian agricultural sector occurred in 1995–1996, and was solved by a federal government-sponsored program of securitization of the debt (it transformed farmers' short- and medium-term debts into long-term debt, backed by the issue of certificates). Now the farmers want more of the same; but it is not easy to apply this solution in the present; in 1995 most of the agricultural debt was held by official banks (Banco do Brasil, Banco do Nordeste, Banco da Amazônia, BNDES) facilitating securitization. Now, however, most of the overdue debt of commercial agriculture is with input suppliers or with private financial institutions and the federal government has no hold over these organizations (Gazeta Mercantil, March 28, 2006, p. b-12). A solution on these lines would require the passage of a special law by Congress, involving a complicated set of arrangements.

Infrastructure deficiencies

Paradoxically, however, the 2004–2005 events provided respite to a looming problem faced by Brazilian agriculture: that of the inadequate state of the infrastructure servicing the Brazilian agribusiness sector (roads and ports). By 2005 this infrastructure was considered to be completely inadequate. In fact, a "logistical blackout" was foreseen for this year; it failed to materialize thanks to the decline in production brought about by the drought. The impacts of this critical deficiency have been felt more strongly on the agricultural frontier of the Center-West and Northern regions, but it is also affecting settled agricultural areas.[10] Infrastructure deficiencies mean high transportation costs for agriculture[11] and threats of disruption in transportation and commercialization at the harvest's peak.

A central difficulty in this area is the lack of a clearer definition regarding who should be responsible for investment in infrastructure in Brazil. In the past such investment was undertaken mainly by the public sector, but at present the latter has not only lost the capacity to invest, but it has also failed to create conditions for the private sector to do so. The Lula government has been toying with the concept of Public-Private Partnerships (PPPs) to overcome the government's lack of capacity for investment, but the necessary institutional changes to enable PPPs to make an impact are yet to be created.

Problems of the meat sector

In late 2005 and early 2006 the dynamic meat sector began to experience difficulties which have the potential to dampen its recent strength. The beef cattle segment was affected by foot-and-mouth disease (FMD) outbreaks. A surge of FMD in 2004 in the Northern state of Pará had already blocked exports to a few countries, but in the second semester of 2005, just as Brazil began removing these export restrictions, the first of four further FMD outbreaks occurred. To make things worse, these took place in the states of Mato Grosso do Sul and Paraná, two major cattle producing areas.[12] In spite of the fact that the spread of the disease was still quite limited and regardless of the immediate containment measures undertaken by the Brazilian animal health authorities, 56 importing countries imposed partial or total bans on the importation of meat from beef cattle from Brazil. Early in 2006, this ban was being partially lifted thanks to the efforts of containment of FMD, but some countries were still unwilling to comply.[13]

The history of the fight against FMD in Brazil deserves some notice. Until the mid-1970s the country virtually ignored the disease. Vaccines for the disease were sold, but they were basically used by cattle ranchers in a few more advanced cattle regions. In most of the country FMD was considered a fact of life. The annual number of FMD surges remained very large; in 1976, for instance, the number of registered surges peaked at more than 10,000.[14] Because of the loss of export revenues caused by the disease, the federal government began intensifying FMD vaccination; at the same time, domestic capacity for the production of vaccines was expanded. As a result of these measures, the number of reported surges declined sharply. However, the annual rate stabilized at something below 2000 between 1983 and the early

1990s, as the control of the disease in the more remote cattle areas remained largely ineffective.

Prompted by the export barrier imposed by this situation, in 1992 the federal Plan for the Eradication of Foot and Mouth Disease (PEFMD) was instituted, as a joint effort by the government and the cattle producers; the incidence of vaccination increased, encompassing the main producing regions; the quality of the vaccines was improved; and cattle ranchers were induced to vaccinate regularly. As a result, in 2004 some 97 percent of the Brazilian herd was vaccinated, against only 64 percent ten years earlier (Lima et al., 2005, p. 25). The number of annual outbreaks of FMD went sharply down; in 2000 there were only 47 outbreaks; in 2001, 37; and in 2002 and 2003, there were no outbreaks. The situation seemed under control at the time of the first of the mentioned incidents in 2004, but the 2005 surges were especially worrying because of the geographical area of incidence.

International control over FMD in producing countries is wielded by the World Animal Health Organization (WAHO). In 2004 this organization considered that a few states of Brazil's Southern region composed an area free of FMD without the need to vaccinate; a larger area – most of the states of the Southeast and the Center-West regions – was considered free of FMD with vaccination, but in most of the Northern and Northeastern states the disease had not yet been controlled. At any rate, the situation seemed under control in 16 states. The 2004 surges of FMD were in the Northern region, so it was not regarded with much concern; some importing countries imposed bans on Brazilian beef, but most of these were gradually lifted. This was not the case with the 2005 surges; a worrying aspect of that year's outbreaks was that they took place in the area which WAHO regarded by as free of FMD with vaccination.

How did FMD reappear in areas considered free from the disease? The federal government and the cattle farmers lay the blame on each other. The farmers were accused of negligence in vaccination and of illicitly importing cattle from infected areas of neighboring countries. The government was blamed for reducing expenditure on animal health programs as a result of expenditure cuts stemming from the strict fiscal policy. This led to insufficient action in disease control.[15] There was an element of truth in both arguments. The problem in early 2006, however, was whether or not the spread of FMD was effectively contained by the animal health authorities. The recent FMD areas were quarantined, cattle herds in the infected areas were slaughtered, and vaccination was intensified.

Brazil aims, in the long run, to completely eradicate FMD; the problem, however, is the sheer size of the country and the fact that beef cattle are found everywhere. Moreover, the country has extensive borders with countries that do not carry out adequate control of FMD. In early 2006 demand was strong and there was a 180-day ban on beef cattle meats exports by Argentina, so the restrictions of many importing countries were relaxed; as a result, the value of beef cattle meat exports actually increased (Rosa et al., 2006). However, a decline in world demand or another surge of FMD outbreaks would severely hurt the prospects of this promising sector of Brazil's agribusiness.

Another sector hurt by the FMD was that of the production and export of pork. Pig production in Brazil progressed very rapidly from a precarious situation of low productivity and low quality products, to a modern and highly productive stage. A result from this was a rapidly increase in pork exports. Exports increased markedly after 2002, and in 2005 their value exceeded US$1 billion. But in 2005, this part of the meat sector also felt the impact of the FMD outbreaks. One of the consequences was that Russia, which imported some 65 percent of the volume of Brazil's pork, imposed a ban on all meat imports from the country. This led to reductions in prices and on revenues.[16] Early in 2006, there were hopes that Russia would soon lift its ban on pork from Brazil, but this was far from certain.

The poultry segment has also experienced problems recently. In 2005, Brazil was the main world exporter of poultry meat, exporting 9.3 million tons to 148 countries, at a total value of US$3.5 billion.[17] Brazil's share of world poultry exports was almost 40 percent. This is, by far, the more advanced and competitive area of the country's meat sector; nevertheless, in 2006, it also began feeling adverse impacts from health problems, albeit not of its own making. The main concern was with the impact of bird flu (BF), and efforts were being made to shield the Brazilian poultry flock from this disease.

Brazil has been free from this disease, but there is no guarantee that it will not reach the country. However, the main problem early in 2006 was the scare created worldwide by BF and by the possibility that a mutation of the virus might result in human infection. As a result of this scare, there has been an appreciable reduction of the demand for poultry meat. In early 2006, this outcome was already evident in the European Union. The spread of the BF scare is worrying the Brazilian producers who have began to face cancellations of orders. A sharp decline in demand would have distressing consequences. The effect of the BF scare on demand were already having negative impacts, not only production at the farm level, but also on the employment in the packing industries, on the demand for corn and soy meal for poultry feed, and on the sales of other inputs (*Gazeta Mercantil*, March 23, 2006, p. A1 and B12).

International negotiations and the demands facing Brazil's agribusiness

The future of agribusiness in Brazil depends not only on an effective solution of the short-term and structural problems mentioned above, but also on a steady expansion of the world demand for commodities and products such as grains, meats, sugar, ethanol, and orange juice. Therefore, the results of ongoing international negotiations can be expected to have important effects. Among those, the results of the Doha round of negotiations of the World Trade Organization (WTO), which began in 2001 and are due to end in 2006, are considered of special importance by agribusiness and by the Brazilian government. In fact, during the boom years, before the recent problems it now faces, the most important claim of agribusiness on public policy was a strong involvement on the part of the government in the negotiations, and both the Fernado Henrique Cardoso and the Lula administrations have conformed. The international competitiveness and export growth of the agribusiness complex are seen as depending crucially on the outcome of such negotiations.

The WTO rounds of talks aim at establishing rules and conditions for a fairer and less distorting, and thus more efficient, international trade. Talks to this end intensified in the Uruguay round of negotiations (1989–1992). These were heralded as a turnaround for the heavily protected and distorted markets for agricultural commodity and products, but in fact the result of the negotiations was a stalemate. There was some progress regarding trade in industrial products but almost none on the subject of agricultural trade. The Doha negotiations were expected to bring considerable progress in this area.

The main problem, responsible for the Uruguay round stalemate, was that the major OECD importing countries – especially the United States and the European Union (EU) – were unwilling to abandon practices involving considerable trade distortions, such as heavy subsidization of domestic agricultural production and exports, and the imposition of strong tariff and nontariff barriers to trade. Subsidies were particularly distorting; the OECD estimated that at the beginning of the millennium the equivalent of some US$300 billion of subsidies were being granted to the OECD's farmers.[18] Such massive subsidies discriminated against agricultural exporting countries such as Brazil since they were mostly granted based on land use, resulting in excess production, and ultimately to subsidized dumping on international markets, generating low world prices and reducing developing countries' exports. The WTO Doha round – officially labeled the Doha Development Program – gave some priority to the reduction of barriers and distortions regarding agricultural trade. However, the political will for change continues to be countered by the action of powerful vested interests which stand to lose if significant progress is to be achieved.

An important recent change was the latest reform of the Common Agricultural Policy (CAP) of the EU. It altered the concession of subsidies based on production or on exports, to subsidies based on factors such as the conservation of landscape, the protection of the environment, or on cultural contributions of rural areas, considered acceptable by the WTO. The distorting subsidies are to be gradually scaled down. After previously resisting changes to their subsidy schemes the EU agreed to back the abolition of distorting subsidies by 2013 (with substantial advances by 2010).

The United States also conceded large amounts of subsidies on agriculture. In 2002, for instance, the country's Farm Bill was the most protectionist ever,[19] in spite of its involvement in the WTO rounds. As a matter of fact, both the U.S. and the EU are pressing for reductions of trade barriers on industrial products and services but they are willing to concede little in exchange by significantly reducing their agricultural trade barriers. Moreover, there were disputes between the United States and the EU, so that much needed to be accomplished by 2006 – the year in which the Doha round is scheduled to end – in order to attain the rounds' minimum objectives.

As a major interested party, Brazil has played an active role in the Doha round. Together with India, it leads the G20, a group of major agricultural exporting developing countries pressuring for substantial reductions of barriers for agricultural trade. The G20 and, of course Brazil, would obviously gain from reductions in distorting subsidies in the United States and the EU and on the improvement of access to these countries' markets for agricultural commodities. However, the United States and the EU assert that for this to happen, the G20 countries would have to agree to lower substantially their tariffs and other barriers on industrial and services trade.

As things stood in mid-2006, the G20 was pressuring for a sharp reduction in distorting agricultural subsidies and in tariff and nontariff barriers affecting agricultural trade, both from the United States and from the EU, but was willing to agree only to a modest reduction in their barriers on industrial and services trade. The EU, in turn, requires substantial concessions regarding the latter and wants the United States to reduce its agricultural subsidies drastically. The United States wants fewer tariff and nontariff barriers, on the part of both the G20 nations and the EU (Chaddad and Jank, 2005. See also note 15, which has a reference to Chaddad et al. (2005); note 18, which has a reference to Chaddad et al. (2006), note 19, which has Chaddad and Jank (2005)). However, major concessions on the part of the main negotiating blocs were far from being offered. In fact, early in August 2006 the Doha round reached another and apparently definitive stalemate.

In addition to its involvement in the WTO negotiations, Brazil's vitality in the area of agricultural trade is revealed by two major victories in disputes filed at the Dispute Settlement Board (DSB) of the WTO: against U.S. cotton subsidies and EU sugar export subsidies. In the case of U.S. cotton subsidies the DSB agreed that these were causing serious losses to the Brazilian cotton sector since they depressed world prices of the commodity and led Brazil to lose its share of the market. And in the case of the EU sugar subsidies, the DSB agreed that the EU was providing subsidies far above those allowed by the GATT agreement, with negative impacts on Brazil's sugar exports. Although both the EU and the United States dragged their feet in complying with the decisions stemming from these two test cases, they had important impacts in terms of increasing the Brazilian resolve (Chaddad and Jank, 2005, p. 6).

Evolution of land reform policy in Brazil, 1960–2006

The preceding section has presented a picture of remarkable change and evolution of commercial agriculture in Brazil in the past 50 years. Throughout this entire period, land reform was generally seen as a major issue that needed to be urgently addressed, although the justification for this changed over time from issues of productive efficiency to that of social justice. It is thus remarkable that despite this perception of the importance of land reform, and despite several attempts over the years to attack the problem, land ownership concentration has barely budged. The Gini coefficient for land ownership concentration was 0.836 in 1967 and remained practically stable over the next 20 years, moving to 0.837 in 1972, 0.854 in 1975, 0.831 in 1992, and 0.843 in 1998 (INCRA, 2001). In 2000 it did slightly shift downward to 0.802 although that change is partially a result of the change in methodology in calculating the index introduced by INCRA (2001). This lack of impact on land ownership concentration is not because of inaction. Throughout this period, there has always been a land reform program in place and much redistribution has been done. Table 10.1 shows that in the past decade more than 43 million hectares of land (more than the area of Germany) were redistributed by the government's official land reform program to over 800,000 families (over 3 million people) at a cost of over R\$ 17 billion (approximately US.\$7.7 billion at the August 2006 exchange rate).

How can it be that so much effort has been directed toward land reform with such paltry results? This section of the paper will answer this question by focusing on the political institutions that determine the incentives of the actors involved in land reform policy in Brazil. It is argued that these institutions do provide the incentives and the means for land reform policy to be pursued, but that the type of land reform program that has emerged as an equilibrium from these interactions has been one that is effective at redistributing land but ineffective at transforming landless peasants into productive smallholders.

In Brazil there is a commonly held perception that land reform does not get accomplished because there is a lack of "political will." This notion comes intuitively in a country that simultaneously contains a large number of landless peasants and vast amounts of idle land in private and public ownership. This perception is, however, incorrect. Since the 1960s several governments have actively pursued genuine land reform policies. However, despite the fact that political institutions in Brazil provide for strong presidential powers (Alston and Mueller, 2006), both during the military dictatorship, (1964–1985) and in the civilian governments since, all land reform

Table 10.1   Number of families settled, 1995–2005

Year	President	No. families settled	INCRA expenditure (1000 R\$)	Land distributed (hectares)
1995	F.H. Cardoso	42,912	1,278,891	
1996	F.H. Cardoso	62,044	1,424,635	
1997	F.H. Cardoso	81,944	2,020,126	
1998	F.H. Cardoso	101,094	1,956,124	
1999	F.H. Cardoso	85,226	1,303,987	
2000	F.H. Cardoso	92,986	1,160,012	
2001	F.H. Cardoso	82,449	1,154,510	
2002	F.H. Cardoso	60,000[φ]	1,244,567	
Total		608,685	11,542,852	19,662,093
2003	Lula	36,301	1,245,836	
2004	Lula	81,254	2,167,729	
2005	Lula	127,506	2,250,400	
Total		245,061	5,663,965	22,487,475

[φ] Estimate.
Source: Ondetti (2006).

efforts have failed. The latest manifestation of this phenomenon is particularly telling. The election of President Lula of the Worker's Party brought to power in 2003 the first left-wing government in Brazil. Given the new President's personal history as well as his party's long held positions, it was widely expected that an effective land reform would finally be realized. Land reform had long been a banner of the opposition and there can be no doubt about the President's desire to pursue these policies. Furthermore, in Brazil the shape and scope of land reform essentially depends on the President, who controls the appointment procedure and determines the budget of the Ministry of Land Reform as well as the federal land reform agency INCRA. Nevertheless, despite the will and the means to pursue the land reform that he had always clamored for as opposition leader, what has materialized in the first two-andone-half years in office has been a disappointment and a puzzle to those who expected drastic change and striking results. The new government cut expenditure to a greater extent than the previous one, producing one of the lowest budgets for land reform in the recent past and resulting in only 36,000 new families settled from a target of 60,000 for 2003.[20]

It is thus apparent that land reform, as other policies, does not depend exclusively on the political will of the President and his/her government. Obviously, the choice of which policies to pursue and how much effort and resources to dedicate to each is constrained by opportunity costs, formal and informal institutions, and fiscal constraints, as well as by the actions of other political actors, such as Congress, the Judiciary, interest groups, and voter preferences. In this section, we will provide an integrated picture of the political institutions that determine land reform policy in Brazil.

Our analysis focuses on the period since 1993, which is when the landless peasant movement (MST) started to change the policymaking game in land reform in Brazil. Prior to this period there had been several attempts at land reform, but these had generally been blocked or drastically scaled down by landowners as an interest group. An example is the PNRA (*Plano Nacional de Reforma Agrária*) of 1985, the program created by the first civilian government after the military dictatorship. Because land reform was a symbolic policy that encapsulated the new democratic spirit, the plan started out with ambitious targets, for the first time making the use of expropriation of unproductive private land the central instrument for obtaining land for redistribution. However, very early on the government realized that the program brought more opposition from aggrieved landowners than it did support from those who stood to gain, and in less than a year it was drastically scaled down.[21] As noted in Dean (1971), this outcome has far-reaching historical roots and is general to several other Latin American countries.

Concentration of land ownership has been one of Latin America's most striking social and economic handicaps. The predominance of large estates, arising in the colonial period, was not eliminated by the governments of the newly independent nations, despite clear evidence of the superior economic viability of smallholdings that was observable in Western Europe and the United States. Even though the liberals of Latin America sought to apply other lessons expounded by their European mentors, sometimes ruthlessly, and often at considerable cost, they allowed their countries to experience for the most part an increasing concentration of land ownership during the nineteenth century. Why was there so little effective reform? "(I)n the case of Brazil…government sought consciously to deal with land concentration and to counter the power of the great land owners. The final failure of these efforts is an interesting example of the difficulty of reform from within a political system dominated by the landed elite." (Dean, 1971, p. 606)

The first point to be explored here is how to account for the change from the landowner dominated policymaking game described by Dean to the landless-peasant dominated game which has prevailed since 1993? What is it that led to such a sharp shift in the interest group which policy catered to? In order to understand these issues, three fundamental characteristics of this policymaking area in Brazil have to be taken into account. The first is that society as a whole (and more importantly, voters) in Brazil are sympathetic towards land reform. Although Brazilian society is predominantly urban and has more pressing concerns, such as unemployment and safety, it is aware of the blatant inequality of landownership and perceives land reform as a costless solution (to themselves) as it supposedly merely involves taking land from owners of large idle farms and distributing it to landless peasants.[22] Second, the President is seen as being responsible for land reform and is held accountable by voters for results or lack of them in this policy arena. Furthermore, this perception is correct as political institutions give the President the instruments to set the policy agenda in this area and pursue it or not. Finally, the third crucial characteristic is the large information asymmetry between society, as the principal that demands land reform, and the government, as the agent that implements it. This information asymmetry implies that society cannot correctly judge the truthfulness of the government's claims to be doing all that is possible regarding land reform given the existing constraints. Every government institutes a land reform program, establishes targets, and appoints committed land reform ministers and INCRA presidents. The public receives the announcements of achievements made by the government with skepticism, but has little means to sort out how much is true. As in any principal-agent relationship, the information asymmetry provides the agent with informational rents. In this case, the rents accrue to the government that can implement less of the costly land reform than it would if there were complete information.

The change in the policymaking game in Brazil took place because of the effect that the MST had on the amount of information received by the public on the real efforts of the President toward land reform.[23] Although the MST was founded in 1985, it took several years for the movement to get organized on a national scale and to devise the strategy of occupation as a means of pressuring for land reform. Furthermore, the institutional basis for that strategy was only put in place in 1993 when the ordinary laws were passed that complemented the land reform-related dispositions in the 1988 Constitution. By establishing that land must fulfill its "social function," included in which is reaching preordained and regional-specific levels of productivity, the laws provided a legal basis for invading private and public land as a means of pressuring the government to step up its land settlement programs. This strategy proved to be tremendously successful as can be seen in the sharp increase in the number of occupations and settlements occuring after 1993, in Figure 10.4.

The essence of the MST's strategy is not that of force, although the invasions and occupations do often result in conflict and violence. The essence is to explore the leverage provided in favor of land reform in the Constitution and legislation, so as to pressure the government to dedicate more political and financial resources toward that end. The actual pressure for more land reform is not exerted directly by the MST, but rather indirectly through the voters, who, as noted above, are sympathetic towards the cause. What the MST is actually doing when it invades or performs other actions, such

Figure 10.4   Occupations and settlements, 1988–2004[24]

Note: Data for number of families settled from 1988 to 1994 is the average for each government; Sarney (1988–1989), Collor (1990–1991), Franco (1992–1994).

Source: Ministério do Desenvovlvimento Agrário (2004, p. 20), Comissão Pastoral da Terra (2004, p. 13).

as blocking roads, occupying government offices, undertaking a march, or making declarations in the press, is to reduce the information asymmetry that the voters have of the amount of effort the government actually puts in to land reform (Alston et al., 2006). These actions impart information to the public that the government's claims regarding its efforts are not accurate. This aspect of the role of the MST is effective because the public finds the group's actions credible, stemming partly from the fact that the landless peasants are among the poorest and most destitute groups in society. This is not to say that the public approves of everything the MST does. In fact Brazilian society tends to be conservative and does not approve of the seizure of private property. Nevertheless, this does not contradict the fact that when the MST's antics create a commotion in the nation's life the voters tend to question the government's land reform efforts, thus exerting pressure for more to be done.

Tables 10.2 and 10.3 provide some evidence of this interpretation of the channels through which the MST exerts its influence. Table 10.2 shows the results of a regression that seeks to explain the determinants of presidential popularity in Brazil. Following the literature on presidential popularity, general macroeconomic variables were included, such as interest rates, exchange rate, and inflation, as well as lagged popularity (monthly observations).[25] In addition to these conventional variables, the number of occupations in the previous month was found to have a positive and significant effect on the President's popularity. This result shows that MST action (as well as that

Table 10.2   Presidential popularity and land reform (Dependent Variable: Popularity)

Popularity$_{t-1}$	0.879***
	(13.84)
Occupations$_{t-1}$	–0.02**
	(–2.05)
Exchange rate$_{t-1}$	–0.042*
	(–1.76)
Inflation	0.028***
	(0.44)
Interest$_{t-1}$	–0.047***
	(–2.63)
Constant	0.616**
	(2.27)
N	71
$F(5, 65)$	104.32
Prob>F	0.0000
H_0: No Cointegration (ADF 2 lags, const.)	–6.043***

Notes: Ordinary least squares with Newey-West standard errors in parentheses. 1% ***, 5% **, 10%*. All variables in logarithms. All variables $I(1)$. Residual based cointegration test uses ADF with critical values from Charemza and Deadman (1997) lower bound = –6.01, upper bound = –5.83.

Source: Alston et al. (2006)

other smaller groups) does have an impact through voters in an area that is particularly dear to the President; his/her popularity. Whereas Table 10.2 provides information on the long-term relationship between these variables, Table 10.3 shows, through an error correction framework, that the same result holds for short-term relationships, that is, increases in occupations lead to reduced popularity.

Given that in the argument above the final effect of the MST's actions is that society gets more of what it wants, there is the temptation to conclude that the MST is providing a valuable service to society. Furthermore, the argument thus far has not shed any light on the paradox of why all the land reform that gets done does not translate into lower land ownership concentration. Note however, that what has been shown above is simply that the MST is successful in pushing the government to expend more effort toward land reform, while nothing has been said about the form that this effort takes. The problem with land reform in Brazil in the past two decades is that its evaluation has been cast in terms of the number of families that are settled, which turns out to be a deceptive measure for gauging how much the true objective of transforming landless peasants into emancipated and self-sustaining smallholders has been accomplished. This has been noted

Table 10.3 Error correction model of presidential popularity (Dependent Variable: ΔPopularity)

ΔPopularity$_{t-1}$	0.547***
	(2.81)
ΔOccupations$_{t-1}$	−0.025***
	(−2.62)
Exchange rate$_{t-1}$	−0.200
	(1.45)
ΔInflation$_{t-1}$	0.018**
	(−2.37)
ΔInterest$_{t-1}$	−0.013
	(−0.27)
Error correction term	−0.597**
	(−2.60)
Constant	0.0006
	(0.09)
N	70
F(6, 63)	4.05
Prob>F	0.0017

Note: Newey-West *t*-stats in parentheses.1% ***, 5% **, 10%*. Δ refers to first difference.
Souce: Alston et al. (2006).

for example in a government-sponsored analysis of the quality of the settlement projects in 2003:

> The methods which the government adopts to evaluate land reform (quantitative, counting the families that have been settled and the destination of resources), has the power to evaluate land reform through only a very simplified point of view. Through this view … the numbers are favorable. Thus, why invest in other important aspects if they will not enter the evaluation of the government's achievements? Why spend resources, dedicate managerial energy, implement actions that are out of the restricted lens under which its actions will be analyzed? The natural tendency is to invest in land acquisition (where it is more easily available or where the social movements are more active); to provide the minimal conditions to install the families in the projects and meet the quantitative targets suggested by the central administration. Aspects such as quality of life, economic development of the projects, environmental impacts, regional benefits and benefits to the local community outside the projects; take a secondary role under this form of evaluating performance. (Sparovek, 2003, p. 169)

This critique is deeper than the usual cliché that "it is not enough to give land, the government must also give credit, extension services, infrastructure, etc." Recent land reform programs in Brazil have been providing much in the way of these ancillary services and still the success rates in the settlement projects have been disappointing.[26] The critique here is that by choosing the wrong measure to set targets and evaluate the government's efforts, the type of land reform that gets implemented is one that has very little impact on what society really wants to achieve. The debate over how much land reform the government is doing centers on the number of settled families, and thus gives an incentive for the government to look for land and landless to match with little regard as to whether that match will be conducive to emancipated smallholders in the future. In order to meet the ambitious targets the government sets itself to appease society's demand for land reform, and which the MST will certainly contest and the media avidly disseminate, the government has an incentive to use both land and people that have no natural inclination or comparative advantage for the purpose. Thus even distant land with poor soils is turned into settlement projects to be populated with poor and needy people who have no experience of, or aptitude for, rural life, and this has proven time and again to be a recipe for disaster for the goal of creating a class of emancipated smallholders. For many of the people involved the prospect of joining a settlement project is attractive not because they intend to become smallholders and live by farming, but because they stand to receive land and credit which are valuable in their own right from the government. The credit sustains the families for long periods of time and the land can be sold despite the formal prohibition on doing so. Given that a large fraction of the Brazilian population is mired in poverty and has low opportunity costs of time, there is a considerable reserve of candidates willing to undergo the hardships involved in the long process of participating in an invasion and the subsequent settlement project.[27]

It has been argued (Graziano, 2004) that there are no longer any true landless peasants in Brazil, that is, people with real aptitude for agriculture and available to be settled. What exists is a large mass of poor and deprived who need assistance but have little probability or inclination of becoming productive rural landholders. Similarly it is argued (Graziano, 2004) that there is few unproductive latifundia left, given the massive expropriations of the past decade and the growth of agricultural productivity, so that further land reform can only proceed if it uses land that is already in productive use. This assessment might be too harsh; nevertheless, it is correct in stressing the fact that the current land reform program based on expropriation and settlement projects has become obsolete. Although this fact is obvious to the government, it is not easy to change the program as the MST and other movements are effective at maintaining public pressure for the program to continue, as described above. Interestingly the MST is not that interested in acquiring more settlement projects as it already commands a large stock of families in those it has. Its major concern now is to assure that the government duly pays out the credit and other benefits to which the settlers have a right, and which often fail or are delayed. Thus the MST has shifted somewhat the focus from invading land to invading government offices, blocking roads, and other actions to assure its share in the fight for scarce public resources.

It is undeniable that land reform in Brazil has effectively produced a redistribution of resources toward some of the poorest strata of the population, which is a commendable achievement in a country with such high inequality as Brazil and that has proved so impervious to attempts at redistribution throughout its history. Furthermore this distribution benefits not only the members of the settlement projects but to some extent also the neighboring community.[28] Nevertheless the fact remains that this redistribution is done in a most inefficient way. The process of distributing wealth in the form of land that will likely be sold and credit for activities that will probably not really be undertaken is a roundabout and wasteful means of transferring resources. For each Real that is redistributed to a landless peasant through the government's land reform program an amount certainly much larger (there are no estimates) is dissipated in the process. The deadweight loss of a direct transfer would be considerably smaller and would result in fewer of the pernicious side effects that result from land reform programs, such as the environmental damage caused by the settlement projects[29] and the weakening of property rights and land rental markets that could otherwise contribute towards a more efficient use of land in the country.[30]

Given that land reform programs in Brazil have been so highly fraught with inefficiencies, there must be opportunities for Pareto improving changes. The question thus rises of why the country persists in the pursuit of a model of land reform (based on expropriation and settlement projects) that has yielded an insignificant number of emancipated settlement projects out of a huge number of projects that remain dependent on governmental credit to remain viable? Why does the issue of land reform continue to be debated in terms of the number of families that are settled each year, when it is clear that these numbers do not translate into an effective measure of land reform? The reason is probably that it is convenient for both the MST and for the government to keep the game under these rules. For the government the measure provides a simple unit that it can put into government programs and then claim to have met. In addition, it is easier to simply settle large number of families than to follow through with all the additional work necessary for transforming landless peasants into small farmers. The number of families that the government can realistically herd through such a transformation, given any reasonable budget constraint, is a small fraction of the total number of landless ones, so the shortcomings in the extent to which the government would be addressing the landless problem effectively would be all too apparent. Settling hundreds of thousands of families, on the other hand, allows the government to claim actually to be solving much of the entire problem.

For the MST, on the other hand, the current setup has proven to be very successful. The large numbers of settled families in thousands of settlement projects that receive credit from the government provide resources and the means to command further occupations and thus extend its reach.[31] For the MST the measure is also useful as it provides an easy means of criticizing the government's efforts in the eyes of the voters. For these reasons it is not in the interests of the MST for the concept of land reform to be changed to consideration of the program's actual effect in reducing concentration of landownership or the effectiveness of transforming landless into producers. Evidence of this is the fierce resistance by the MST to any attempt by the government to pursue land reform by alternative means such as the land tax or the Land Bank, where groups of landless are financed to purchase land rather than being settled on land expropriated by the government. Thus, by using their extraordinary capacity as an interest group to restrict the land reform debate to the current terms, the MST obfuscates the true issues and detracts from the true goal of reducing landownership concentration.

Conclusions

In the past two decades the process of public policymaking in Brazil has undergone drastic transformations, with important impacts on both agriculture and land reform. One of the most striking transformations has been the adoption of fiscal discipline as the guiding principal in macroeconomic policy. In 1999 the Real suffered a sharp devaluation and all bets were that the hard-earned stability of the previous five years would be lost. Only fiscal rectitude and governmental restraint would prevent the onslaught of inflation and economic decline, and Brazil was notorious for its shortcomings in both of those qualities. Surprisingly, what has prevailed since then has been orthodox fiscal and monetary policy and the achievement of impressive primary surpluses that have stabilized the debt/GDP ratio and contributed to reducing drastically the country's risk ratings, even though actual economic growth has remained mediocre. This behavior has proved to be long lasting as it has weathered several internal and external shocks and even the shift to a left-wing President. As it is reasonable to expect this policy scenario to persist in the coming years, it is useful to close this chapter by examining what this means to the policy areas of agriculture and land reform.

The main instrument used by the government to achieve the primary surpluses to which it has proved so committed are the *contingenciamentos*, through which it withholds the execution of expenditure authorized in the budget, with the resources channeled to paying of interest on the national debt. Approximately 95 percent of the budget is protected through constitutional hardwiring of expenditure (mostly social security, civil service wages, health, and education) so that the *contingenciamentos* take place in the remaining discretionary expenditures that include programs such as land reform, poverty alleviation, environment, and infrastructure, such as roads. The *contingenciamentos* affect programs and activities in all ministries and public organizations and have become a daily aggravation to those who work in or depend on the public sector. Agriculture and land reform have been no exception. In 2003 budgetary law conceded to the Ministry of Agriculture R\$ 740 million, but by the end of the year 310 million had been impounded for primary surplus purposes so that only 59 percent of the original expenditure could be realized.[32] For the Ministry of Agrarian Development the initial budget contained R\$ 1116 million but in the end only 709 million were actually spent. The same levels of cuts were observed in other areas (although agriculture and land reform are above the mean) and have been consistent over the years.

If this budgetary environment does in fact persist in the future the impact on agriculture and land reform should be markedly different, given the characteristics of these policy areas as described in this paper. In the second section, it was noted that the current state of agriculture is one of reasonably free markets and little dependence on government policy. The sector has been able to achieve remarkable growth and progress despite the lack of several basic government services. It is interesting that the sector is assigned fewer budgetary resources than land reform, despite the importance of agriculture to the economy as a whole. The fiscal policy game described above may present several stumbling blocks to this sector in the future, in particular the poor state of infrastructure, which will continue to bear the brunt of the *contingenciamentos*. However, in spite of its current predicament, the agricultural sector will likely continue to overcome the difficulties it now faces and to thrive as it has in the past.

Land reform, on the other hand, is not similarly impervious to the fiscal crunch. The President will remain locked in the game of announcing ambitious targets for how many families will be settled each year. The information asymmetries, described in the third section, that make it difficult for voters to evaluate what the government's policy has truly achieved, allow some scope for creative accounting and temporary settlements (that eventually reconsolidate). In the end however, the government will remain torn between its fiscal imperatives and the indirect pressure from the MST through voters for more resources, with an increasing emphasis on credit rather than land. If interest rates decline and GDP grows, the debt/GDP ratio will fall and primary surplus targets will loosen, allowing more resources for this kind of policy. If interest rate reductions and economic growth do not materialize, land reform expenditure will likely remain constrained and MST confrontation will increase. Either way, as long as policy insists on the same style of land reform program, it will continue to be the case that whatever resources are spent will represent a costly and wasteful means of distribution compared to one not focused mostly on the number of settled families.

Notes

1. See also, Baer (2001) pp. 373–376.
2. This is an indicator commonly used in Brazil of the performance of agriculture. It is routinely estimated and made public by CONAB, of the Ministry of Agriculture.
3. Data on agricultural exports, from SECEX, Ministério do Desenvolvimento, Indústria e Comércio.
4. Foreign trade data for the agribusiness complex, from SECEX, Ministério do Desenvolvimento, Indústria e Comércio (www.mdic.gov.br). The data for the complex's exports include semimanufactured products, but not products manufactured from those (for instance, they include the exports of hides but not of shoes).
5. Compiled by Marcos S. Jank, "O Sucesso recente," Notes from a lecture given at the XLIII Congresso Brasileiro de Economia e Sociologia Rural. Ribeirão Preto, July 27, 2005.
6. According to USDA (2005) the year ended with large world stocks of soybeans, corn, and cotton, and the 2004/05 estimates of world production were substantial. The international prices of these commodities began to decline almost at the time the Brazilian 2004/05 summer crops were being planted. In fact, the declines in prices were, in part, contained by the reductions in the Brazilian harvest brought about by the drought.
7. By mid-2005 the phase of appreciation of the real accelerated. This meant lower prices in the domestic currency even for exports with non declining world prices.
8. See Lopes and Lopes (2006).
9. See *Agroanalysis*, FGV 25, December 2005, p. 43.
10. See Borges (2005).
11. For instance, the cost of transportation of soybeans in Brazil averages $50 per ton, in comparison to $20 per ton in the U.S. *Conjuntura Economica* 59, May 2005).
12. An interesting analysis of the FMD in Brazil – of its incidence, spread, containment, and almost total eradication – is in Lima et al., 2005.
13. See Rosa et al. (2006).
14. Lima et al. (2005) p. 12.
15. An interesting analysis of government expenditure on farm programs in Chaddad and Jank (2005). There we see that there has been a continuous decline in strategic agricultural programs, such as research and development and sanitary surveillance. But there has been a consistent increase in expenditure on land reforms and related programs, and on credit for small family farming.
16. See Pereira (2006).
17. See Lauandos (2006).
18. References regarding the WTO rounds of negotiations and to the policies they aim to change are from: OECD (2005), Tangermann (2006), Chaddad and Jank (2005) and "2013: o fim dos subsídios à exportação," *Agroanalysis* 25, December 2005, pp. 12–14.

19. Agricultural subsidies in the U.S. jumped from US$7 billion in 1997 to US$20 billion in 2004 (Chaddad and Jank, 2005, p. 6).
20. Of these only 9217 families were accommodated in new settlement projects. The remaining 75 percent of the families were settled in preexisting projects created by the previous government. To save expenditure the Lula government settled many in the Amazon region where the cost of settling is lower but so too are success rates.
21. For details on the PNRA and other early land reform programs see Mueller (1994) and Alston et al. (1999).
22. Evidence to back these claims on the preferences of society will be provided below.
23. This argument is formalized in Alston et al. (2006).
24. Data on the number of families settled are highly controversial as this is the main indicator in the public debate on how much land reform the government has achieved. The numbers in Figure 10.4 are from the Lula government and revise downward the claims by the Cardoso government for 1995–2002.
25. Unemployment was not significant and GDP was found to be I(0) (stationary) in the sample period and was thus not included in the cointegration analysis. When the stationarity was ignored and GDP included, it was positive and significant.
26. See Ondetti (2006) for data on the provision of credit, technical assistance, and infrastructure to settlement project beneficiaries.
27. For details of life in an MST camp and settlement project see Wright and Wolford (2003).
28. Measuring this effect is currently an active theme in the literature.
29. Brandão Jr. and Souza Jr (2006) analyzed a sample of 343 settlement projects in the Amazon, out of a total of 1354, covering 36,383 square kilometers, and found the deforestation rates to be four times greater than the Amazon average. One of the reasons for the high rate of deforestation is the availability to the settlement project beneficiaries of subsidized credit.
30. See Rezende (2006) for an analysis of the effect of rural conflicts on land rental markets.
31. The MST charges from its members a portion (usually 3–5 percent) of the credit they receive from government (Harnecker, 2003, ch. 5).
32. Data and analysis of the budgetary cuts is available at the Consultoria de Orçamento e Fiscalização Financeira of both the House and the Senate: www.camara.gov.br/internet/orcament/principal/ and www.senado.gov.br/sf/orcamento/.

References

Alston, L., and B. Mueller (2006) "Pork for Policy: Executive and Legislative Exchange in Brazil," *The Journal of Law Economics and Organization*, 22, 87–114.

Alston, L., G. Libecap and B. Mueller (1999) "Titles, Conflict and Land Use: The Development of Property Rights and Land Reform on the Brazilian Amazon Frontier," Ann Arbor: The University of Michigan Press.

Alston, L., G. Libecap, and B. Mueller (2006) "How Interest Groups can Influence Political Outcomes Indirectly through Information Manipulation: The Landless Peasants Movement in Brazil," Working Paper, Dept. of Economics, Universidade de Brasília.

Baer, W. (1965) *Industrialization and Economic Development in Brazil*, Homewood, IL: Richard D. Irwing.

Baer, W. (1983) *A Industrialização e o Desenvolvimento Econômico do Brasil*, 5th ed. Rio de Janeiro: Editora da Fundação Getúlio Vargas.

Baer, W. (2001) *The Brazilian Economy: Growth and Development*, Westport, CO: Praeger.

Borges, E. (2005) "Um setor a beira do colapso," *Conjuntura Econômica*, 59, 24–25.

Brandão Jr., A., and C. Souza Jr. (2006) "Desmatamento nos Assentamentos de Reforma Agrária na Amazônia," *O Estado da Amazônia*, Belém, IMAZON, June No. 7.

Castro, A. (1979) *7 Ensaios Sobre a Economia Brasileira – Volume I*, Rio de Janeiro: Forense, section 2.

Chaddad, F., and M. Jank (2005) "Policy Coherence for Development: Issues for Brazil," Paper presented at the Global Forum on Agriculture: Policy Coherence for Development. Paris, November 30 and Dececember 1, 2005.

Dean, W. (1971) "Latifundia and Land Policy in Nineteenth-Century Brazil," *Hispanic-American History Review*, 51, 606–625.

Dias, G., and C. Amaral (2000) "Mudanças estruturais na agricultura brasileira, 1980–1998" in R. Baumann (ed.) *Brasil: Uma Década em Transição*, Rio de Janeiro: CEPAL/CAMPUS.

da Mata, M. (1982) "Credito rural: caracterização do sistema e estimativas dos subsídios implícitos," *Revista Brasileira de Economia*, 36, 215–245.

Graziano, X. (2004) *O Carma da Terra no Brasil*, São Paulo: Girafa.

Harnecker, M. (2003) *Landless People: Building a Social Movement*, São Paulo: Editora Expressão Popular.

INCRA (2001) *Índice de Gini*, Brasília: Incra, May, annex 18.

Lauandos, I. (2006) "Cinco grandes desafios," *Agroanalysis*, 26, 25–26.

Lima, R., S. Miranda, and F. Galli (2005) "Febre Aftosa – impacto sobre as exportações brasileiras de carnes e o contexto mundial das barreiras sanitária," São Paulo: ICONE and CEPEA-ESALQ/USP, October.

Lopes, M., and I. Lopes (2006) "Os desafios da próxima safra agrícola," *Conjuntura Econômica*, 60, 36–37.

Mueller, B. (1994) "The Economic History, Political Economy and Frontier Settlement of Land in Brazil," unpublished Ph.D. dissertation, Urbana-Champaign: Dept. of Economics University of Illinois.

Mueller, C. (1992) "Dinâmica, Condicionantes e Impacto Socioambientais da Evolução da Fronteira Agrícola no Brasil," *Revista de Administração Pública*, 26, 15–34.

Nicholls, W. (1972) "The Brazilian agricultural economy: recent performance and policy," in R. Roett (ed.) *Brazil in the Sixties*, Nashville, TN: Vanderbilt University Press.

OECD (2005) *Agriculture and Development: The Case for Policy Coherence.* OECD, November 8.

OECD (2005a) "Análise das políticas agrícolas no Brasil," *Revista de Política Agrícola*, 14 (Special ed.), 5–16.

Oliveira, J. (1981) "An analysis of transfers from agricultural sector and Brazilian development, 1950–1974," unpublished Ph.D. thesis, England: University of Cambridge.

Ondetti, G. (2006) "Lula and Land Reform: How Much Progress?" Paper presented at the 2006 Meeting of the Latin American Studies Association, March 15–18, San Juan.

Pastore, J., G. Castro, and C. Manoel (1976) "Condicionantes da produtividade da pesquisa agrícola no Brasil," *Estudos Econômicos*, 6, 147–181.

Patrick, G. (1975) "Fontes de crescimento na agricultura brasileira: o setor de culturas," in C. Contador (ed.) *Tecnologia e Desenvolvimento Agrícola*, Rio de Janeiro: IPEA/INPES, 89–110.

Pereira, F. (2006) "Suínos: cenário menos favorável," *Agroanalysis*, 26, 21–23.

Rezende, G. (2003) *Macroeconomia e Agricultura no Brasil*, Porto Alegre: Editora UFRGS/ IPEA.

Rezende, G. (2006) "Pobreza e Desigualdade no Brasil: O Papel Adverso das Políticas Trabalhista, Fundiária e de Crédito Agrícola," Working Paper, IPEA, Rio de Janeiro.

Rosa, F., L. Alencar, and T. Alcides Jr. (2006) "Mudanças na exportação de carnes," *Agroanalysis*, Rio de Janeiro, FGV 26, 15–20.

Sayad, J. (1984) *Crédito Agrícola no Brasil: Avaliação das críticas e das propostas de Reforma*, São Paulo: Pioneira, part I.

Sparovek, G. (2003) *A Qualidade dos Assentamentos de Reforma Agrária Brasileira*, São Paulo: Páginas e Letras Editora e Gráfica.

Tangermann, S. (2006) "The WTO negotiations: what interests are the OECD countries pursuing?" *Agriculture and Rural Development*, 1, 7–9.

Wright, A., and W. Wolford (2003) *To Inherit the Earth: The Landless Movement and the Struggle for a New Brazil*, Oakland, CA: Food First Books.

11
Human Capital and Income Concentration in Brazil

Mirta N. S. Bugarin

Introduction

High income concentration and poverty in Brazil have been intensively studied by Paes de Barros et al. (2000a; 2000b). In their words, "... Brazil is not a poor country, but a country with too many poor people ...." Their careful research clearly shows that high poverty rates are the result mainly of the high concentration of income and "unequal opportunities for social and economic inclusion." Although international comparisons show that between 1978 and 1998 almost 70 percent of countries have a per capita income below Brazil's, 10 percent of the richest families in the country have access to 50 percent of the aggregate family income, whereas 50 percent of the poorest households have only 10 percent of the same aggregate income.

An obvious factor influencing unequal earnings is the heterogeneous level of education among the labor force, for education can be understood as a means to attain improvements in labor productivity and consequently in family income. This line of argument, based on the theory of human capital first developed by Becker (1964), Lucas (1988), Schultz (1989), and Uzawa (1964), among others, regards formal education as a means of investment for better future earnings through the improvement in labor productivity it could bring about, with a positive impact in the economy's growth rate. On the other side, many empirical studies have been conducted that link the unequal distribution of schooling as the factor most contributing to the high income concentration. Fishlow (1972) conducted a study analyzing the main factors contributing to this in Brazil during the 1960s. Based on the Brazilian Demographic Census, the author's results showed that the control variable that most explained the high income concentration of the sample was the educational difference, which accounted as much as 20 percent of the phenomenon. Other control variables such as economic activity, regional distribution, and age groups did not contribute as much to an explaination of the empirically observed income concentration. Langoni (1973) also showed that education was the factor most contributing to the high and increasing Brazilian income concentration during the 1970s. Reis and Barros (1990) based on PNAD[1] data studied the Brazilian regional distribution of earnings for the 1976–1986 period. Among different Brazilian regions quite different patterns of distribution of education prevailed and the educational factor alone explained almost 50 percent of the earnings differences observed in the country's different regions. Lam and Levinson (1991) used different PNAD data to study the evolution of schooling and earning distribution in Brazil during the 1970s and 1980s, finding that the younger the analyzed group the better the improvement in the distribution of both education and earnings. Barros and Ramos (1992), also analyzing PNAD data, found that for Brazil the return for a year of schooling is higher than for other countries, increasing with the level of schooling and decreasing with the level of regional development. Although there are many other factors affecting the income distribution of a given country,[2] those factors are subsidiary in explaining high income concentration in Brazil resulting from the unequal distribution of schooling in the population of the country as suggested by Cacciamali and Freitas (1992) and Bonelli and Ramos (1993) in their static decomposition analysis, and Franco (2001).

Based on the evidence above, the present study aims to construct a recursive general equilibrium model where a high income concentration can be generated through differences in the human capital stock available to different types of agents. The agents of the model economy are heterogeneous for they differ in the level of education, and according to this differential they face different employment opportunities, and this evolves according to a stochastic process described by a two-state Markov chain. The associated transition probability matrices reflect the fact that more educated agents face a higher probability of remaining employed in the next period if they are currently employed and, if they are actually unemployed they also have a higher probability of being employed in the next period than do less educated agents. The steady state analysis shows that this model economy can generate a high concentration of income as suggested by the Brazilian empirical evidence.

The paper is organized as follows. The next section presents the model economy as well as the definition of the recursive equilibrium which is numerically computed. The following section describes the parameters and the data sources used for calibrating the model. The next section analyses the steady state distribution of income generated by the model. The conclusion presents the main findings and the extensions that could be incorporated in the study.

The model economy

The model economy extends Aiyagari's (1994) formulation to include a large number of ex ante heterogeneous agents trading in incomplete markets.

Agents are identical in their preferences but differ in their level of education: type 1 agents represent the labor force with 12 or more years of education and type 2 includes all agents with less than 12 years of education.[3] These differentiated levels of education determine, in turn, the differentiated Markov process governing the agent's employment opportunities, hence, the type 1 (type 2) agent's labor income at time t, s_t^1 (s_t^2), evolves according to a two-state Markov chain with transition probability matrix P^1 (P^2), such that the respective elements $[P_{ij}]$, $i, j = e(employed),u(unemployed)$ denote the probability of a type 1 (type 2) agent being at state j in the next period given that she/he is currently facing state i.[4]

If the realization of the process at t is $s_t^1 = e$ ($s_t^2 = e$), the agent of type 1 (type 2) is employed and receives a labor income $w^1 s_t^1 = w^1$ ($w^2 s_t^2 = w^2$), where $w^1 > w^2$, the productivity of type 1 labor exceeds the productivity of type 2 labor. Otherwise, if $s_t^1 = u$ ($s_t^2 = u$), the agent of type 1 (type 2) is unemployed. Notice that, for each agent of the same type, the histories of employment opportunities they have had can differ, consequently changing the capital, k_t^i, $i = 1,2$, she/he had accumulated.

The agents are constrained to hold a single asset, capital, among a grid of positive values $\kappa = [0 < k_1 < ... < k_n]$, hence they are not able to borrow/lend in any period. Moreover, if any type of agent is unemployed in any period t, she/he can finance her/his current expenditure in consumption, c_t^i, and/or investment, x_t^i, with a resource given by θw_t^i, which could be understood as resources obtained from home production, equivalent to a fraction θ of the income if she/he were employed, w_t^i, as well as the return from capital services, $r_t k_t^i$, of accumulated capital in the past. Then, for each type of agent $i = 1,2$, the maximum problem can be summarized as follows:

$$\max_{k_{t+1}^i} E_0 \left\{ \sum_{t=0}^{\infty} \beta^t \left[(1/(1-\sigma))(c_t^i)^{1-\sigma} \right] \right\} \tag{11.1}$$

such that,

$$c_t^i + x_t^i \leq w_t^i s_t^i + r_t k_t^i, \text{ for } t \in [0,\infty), \text{ if } s_t^i = e$$

$$c_t^i + x_t^i \leq \theta w_t^i + r_t k_t^i, \text{ for } t \in [0,\infty), \text{ if } s_t^i = u$$

$$c_t^i \geq 0$$

$$k_{t+1}^i \in \kappa$$

given (k_0^i, s_0^i) and the law of motion for capital formation $k_{t+1}^i = (1-\delta)k_t^i + x_t$, where β is a discount factor, δ a depreciation rate of capital, and σ a risk aversion parameter.

The Bellman equation for each type of agent, $i = 1,2$, each employment state $s \in m/m = \{e,u\}$, and each possible capital value $k_j \in \kappa$ is given by the expression below.

$$v^i(k^i_j,s^i_m) = \max_{k^i_{t+1} \in \kappa}\left\{\left(\frac{1}{1-\sigma}\right)[(1-\delta-r_t)k^i_t + w^i_t s^i_{mt} - k^i_{t+1}] + \beta\sum_{m=1}^{2}P_{i,m}v(k^{i'},s^i_m)\right\} \quad (11.2)$$

The above equation is solved for a value function $v^i(k,s)$ and an associated policy function $k^{i'} = g^i(k^i,s^i)$ mapping this period (k^i,s^i) pair into an optimal choice of capital to carry into next period, $k^{i'}$. The solution of the above problem, for each type of agent, induces a stationary distribution $\lambda^i(k,s)$: starting with a particular distribution $\lambda^i_0(k,s)$ at $t=0$, the distribution of agents of the same type over individual state variables, (k^i,s), remains constant over time even while the employment status of the individual agent of the corresponding type is itself a stochastic process. Thus, the average level of capital across agents of the same type i, $i = 1,2$, is given by:

$$K^i = \sum_{k^i,s^i}\lambda^i(k^i,s^i)g(k^i,s^i) \quad (11.3)$$

and, the average level of capital across agents of the economy by the following aggregation,

$$K = qK^1 + (1-q)K^2 \quad (11.4)$$

where the parameter q represents the proportion of agents of type 1 within the unitary mass of workers.

The average level of employment for each type of agents is:

$$L^i = \sum_{k^i}\lambda^i(k^i,s^i = e) \quad (11.5)$$

so that the average level of employment for the economy is given by the expression below.

$$L = qL^1 + (1-q)L^2 \quad (11.6)$$

The Markov process governing the employment opportunities differs according to the type of agent, hence the associated transition probability matrices are given by:

$$P^1 = \begin{bmatrix} a_{ee} & a_{eu} \\ a_{ue} & a_{uu} \end{bmatrix} \quad P^2 = \begin{bmatrix} b_{ee} & b_{eu} \\ b_{ue} & b_{uu} \end{bmatrix}$$

where:

$$\begin{cases} a_{ee} > a_{eu} \\ a_{ue} < a_{uu} \end{cases} \quad \begin{cases} b_{ee} > b_{eu} \\ b_{ue} < b_{uu} \end{cases} \quad \text{and} \quad \begin{cases} a_{ee} > b_{ee} \\ a_{eu} < b_{eu} \\ a_{ue} > b_{ue} \\ a_{uu} < b_{uu} \end{cases}$$

The elements of the above matrices reflect the fact that the more educated the agent, the higher is his/her probability of remaining employed in the next period if he/she is already employed and the higher his/her probability of being employed in the next period if currently unemployed.

The competitive firms of the model economy produce according to a technology described by a Cobb-Douglas production function of the following form:

$$Y_t = AK_t^{\alpha_1} L_t^{1,\alpha_2} L_t^{2,(1-\alpha_1-\alpha_2)} \tag{11.7}$$

The factor's markets are competitive, hence, their real returns are given by their respective marginal physical products, according to the first order conditions of the firm's profit maximization problem. They are given by:

$$w_t^1 = A\alpha_2 K_t^{\alpha_1} L_t^{1,\alpha_2-1} L_t^{2,(1-\alpha_1-\alpha_2)} \tag{11.8}$$

$$w_t^2 = A(1-\alpha_1-\alpha_2)K_t^{\alpha_1} L_t^{1,\alpha_2} L_t^{2,(-\alpha_1-\alpha_2)} \tag{11.9}$$

$$r_t = A\alpha_1 K_t^{\alpha_1-1} L_t^{1,\alpha_2} L_t^{2,(1-\alpha_1-\alpha_2)} \tag{11.10}$$

where factor share parameters are assumed to be $\alpha_1 \in (0,1)$, $\alpha_2 \in (0,1)$ such that $(\alpha_1+\alpha_2)<1$. Therefore, if in the economy type 2 (less educated) labor is more abundant than type 1, that is, $L_t^2 > L_t^1, \forall t \geq 0$, the real return of the latter will be necessarily higher than of the former, that is, $w_t^1 > w_t^2, \forall t \geq 0$.

Recursive equilibrium

The recursive equilibrium for the above model economy consists of:

- a set of policy functions for each type of agent, $g^i(k^i,s^i)$;
- a set of stationary probability measures $\lambda^i(k^i,s^i)$, $i = 1,2$, describing the distribution of agents across the state variables (k,s), for each type of agent; and
- a set of positive numbers $(K,r,w^1,w^2) \in R_+$,

such that,

(a) prices satisfy $w_t^1 = \partial Y_t / \partial L_t^1$, given by (11.8); $w_t^2 = \partial Y_t / \partial L_t^2$, given by (11.9) and, $r_t = \partial Y_t / \partial K_t$, given by (11.10);
(b) each policy function $g^i(k^i, s^i)$, $i = 1,2$, is the solution to the respective agent's maximization problem (11.1);
(c) each probability distribution $\lambda^i(k, s)$, $i = 1,2$, is a stationary distribution associated with he policy functions $g^i(k^i, s^i)$, $i = 1,2$ and the probability transition matrices P^i, that is,

$$\lambda^i(k,s) = \sum_{s^i} \sum_{k^i} \lambda^i(k^i, s^i) P^i(s^i, s^{i'})$$

(d) the aggregate capital stock of the economy is determined by the average behavior of the agents, that is,

$$K = q\lambda^1(k^1, s^1) g(k^1, s^1) + (1-q)\lambda^2(k^2, s^2) g(k^2, s^2)$$

(e) the average employment of the economy is given by the aggregate employment status for both types of agents.

$$L = q\lambda^1(k^1, s^1 = e) + (1-q)\lambda^2(k^2, s^2 = e)$$

Calibration

In order to obtain a numerical solution to the model and generate a steady state income distribution, we need to choose particular values for the parameters of the model. The calibration of the model was made under the assumption that the model period is one week. The parameter α_1 corresponds to the capital's share in production. Following Araújo and Cavalcante Ferreira (1999) the value of this parameter is taken to be 0.49, being this value consistent with the National Account Tables data.[5] The depreciation factor for capital stock, $1-\delta$, is set to 0.88, which implies an annual rate of depreciation, δ, of 12 percent. To describe fully the production function we still have to set the value of the parameter α_2, the educated labor's share in production.

From equations (11.8) and (11.9) one may conclude that:

$$\frac{w_1}{w_2} = \frac{\alpha_1}{1-\alpha_1-\alpha_2} \frac{L^2}{L^1} \tag{11.11}$$

Data from the Pesquisa Mensal de Empregos (PME)[6] covering the period from 1991 to 1997 shows that the wage of workers with 12 or more years of education is about 3.50 times the wage of workers with less than 12 years of education. The same data source shows that the participation of the less educated workers in the total labor force in total is 5.25 times the participation of the more educated workers. These informations and equation (11.11) above imply a value of α_2 of approximately 0.31. The reason to choose 12 years of education as the threshold between educated and less educated worker comes from Tables 11.1 and 11.2.

Table 11.1 displays two jumps, the first between 0–4 and 5–8 years of education, the second and clearest between 9–11 and 12 or more years of education. Table 11.2 displays only one clear cut and it is located between 9–11 and 12 or more years of education. Since the model allows for two types of agents the most appropriated classification is the one which separates individuals with more than 12 years of education from the others.

The elements of the transition probability matrices are based on the statistics computed by Curi and Menezes Filho (2006). This study shows that

Table 11.1   Average unemployment rate by years of education (%)

	0–4	5–8	9–11	≥12
1991	3.86	6.96	5.35	2.56
1992	4.67	8.72	6.65	2.63
1993	4.34	7.29	6.17	2.50
1994	3.93	6.94	5.87	2.39
1995	3.61	6.55	5.69	2.32
1996	4.18	7.23	6.63	2.79
1997*	4.42	7.85	7.37	2.69

Note: * January to April.

Source: Mercado de Trabalho: Conjuntura e Análise; Ministério do Trabalho e IPEA (Table A.4.6).

Table 11.2   Average income by years of education (R$ of December 1995)

	0–4	5–8	9–11	≥12
1991	291.18	341.86	546.45	1,269.67
1992	241.19	281.97	457.39	1,036.24
1993	262.11	308.73	500.92	1,173.25
1994	263.14	315.05	525.61	1,286.70
1995	298.73	354.33	552.34	1,359.21
1996	315.51	362.69	569.12	1,396.33
1997*	317.81	362.44	542.07	1,336.71

Note: * January to April.

Source: Mercado de Trabalho: Conjuntura e Análise; Ministério do Trabalho e IPEA (Table A.7.6).

during the 1990s the transition probability of an economically active, formally employed agent of the Brazilian economy to be employed in the next period is 77.24 percent and of an economically active unemployed worker to continue unemployed in the next period is 14.9 percent. They also compute the marginal impact of various factors on the transition path. Taking the mean value of the workers with less than 11 years of education and comparing it with the marginal value corresponding to workers with more than 11 years of education, we observed that the transition from state e to state u is 62 percent higher for less educated workers. On the other side, the marginal effect on the transition from state u to state e is 11.66 percent higher for more educated workers than for the less educated ones. Taking these numbers into consideration, the transition probability matrices can be calibrated as follows.[7]

The transition probability matrices are then given by:

$$P^1(s,s') = \begin{bmatrix} .77 & .23 \\ .94 & .06 \end{bmatrix} \quad and \quad P^2(s,s') = \begin{bmatrix} .63 & .37 \\ .83 & .17 \end{bmatrix}$$

where s is the current state and s' is the next period state.

There exists a wide range of empirical estimations for the intertemporal elasticity of substitution,[8] $1/\sigma$, and there is also a large set of studies dealing with the estimation of the intertemporal elasticity of substitution for Brazil, most of them applying econometric approaches to estimate this parameter or to identify some facts related with its value.[9] Although most of the empirical literature deals with credit restriction and may produce values consistent with our model, we have chosen to use the value proposed in Barreto and Schymura (1995), since, like us, they work with a calibrated dynamic general equilibrium model. So we set the value of σ at 1.43, which corresponds to an intertemporal elasticity of substitution of 0.7.

The discount rate β was taken from Araújo and Cavalcante Ferreira (1999) and is set to an annual value of 0.96. Finally, the parameter θ, was set to 0.05 following Aiyagari (1994).

Steady state analysis

Table 11.3 reports the average level of the real variables for the model economy at the steady state for each type of agent and the prices of the three factors of production as well. The exercise shows that capital stock corresponding to the type 1 agent is approximately 21 percent higher than the capital stock corresponding to the second type. This result seems to reflect the fact that the former have a labor income more than 20 times higher than the latter, as well as a higher probability of being employed. Moreover,

Table 11.3   Steady state variables values

Variables	type 1	type 2
Capital stock	18.070	14.922
Employed mass	0.8132	0.7071
Wage type 1	2.9946	0.1406
Capital rent	0.0740	0.0740

Table 11.4   Sensitivity analysis (steady state values)

Variables	$\sigma = 1.2$	$\sigma = 1.43$	$\sigma = 1.6$	$\sigma = 2$	$\alpha_1 = 0.33$
Capital stock type 1	18.169	18.070	17.923	17.613	7.2756
Capital stock type 2	15.243	14.922	15.024	15.865	1.8665
Capital rent	0.0734	0.0740	0.0740	0.0737	0.0600
Wage type 1	3.0209	2.9946	2.9970	3.0094	0.8435
Wage type 2	0.1418	0.1406	0.1407	0.1413	0.7118

the model economy produces an employment mass of type 1 workers 15 percent higher than the corresponding mass for the type 2.

Table 11.4 shows in turn the sensitivity analysis results adopting (i) different values for the risk aversion parameter, σ (inverse of the intertemporal elasticity of substitution), and alternatively (ii) a different value for the capital income share, α_1, noticing that the values in the third column correspond to the original calibration above.[10]

The sensitivity results shows that the obtained long-run equilibrium values are fairly robust to the adopted elasticity of substitution calibration. Whereas, the steady state equilibrium variable values change drastically using the capital income share of 0.33 based on international evidence and keeping the elasticity of substitution parameter to 0.7 as the initial calibration, in this case, we can observe that the capital stock decreases in absolute terms but the differential between the two types of agents increases drastically. Type 1 agents have 1.21 times more capital stock than type 2 using the initial calibration. On the other side, adopting the alternative capital share of 0.33, the capital stock pertaining to the type 1 appears to be approximately 3.89 times higher than the capital stock allocated to the type 2 in equilibrium.

Income distribution analysis

Using the model economy described in the second section, calibrated with the parameters presented in the third section, the stationary distribution of agents type 1 and 2 over the aggregate income level generated by the model economy is shown in Figure 11.1.

As Figure 11.1 reveals, this model generates a high concentration of income, as expected. First the figure shows the high concentration of type 2 agents at lower levels of income and a relatively small mass of type 1 agents at high income levels, indicating a high concentration of income the model with heterogeneous human capital (schooling) can generate. Moreover, the maximum income level for type 1 agents is approximately 1.5 times higher than the maximum income for type 2 agents and, the difference between the minimum income for both types increases drastically such that type 1 minimum income can be as high as 15 times the minimum income for type 2.

Secondly, only a small mass of the agents of the model economy corresponding to the more educated type are located at the top level of income whereas a considerable mass of less educated workers attains the average income level of this type.

Finally, we can also observe the distribution of income within groups generated by the model economy. Income is more equally distributed within the agents of type 1, with more than 12 years of schooling, whereas the income within the second type, with less than 12 years of schooling, is much more unequally distributed.

The above results are generated by the model, first, because the marginal product of the more educated agents, reflected in their wage rate, is more

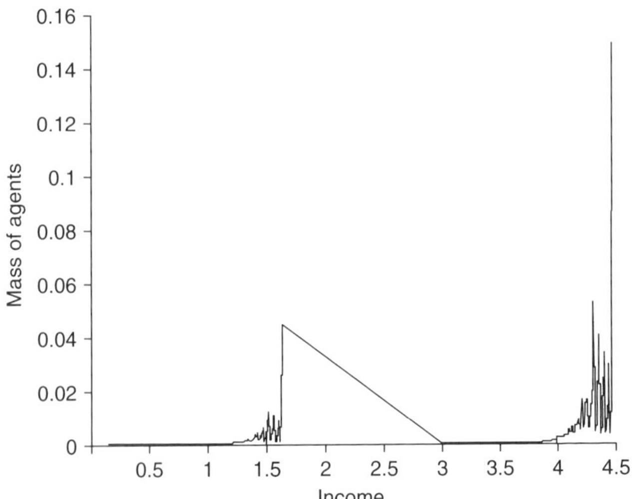

Figure 11.1   Distribution of agents over income

than 21 times higher than the one corresponding to less educated agents and, second, by the fact that the former faces a higher probability of being employed than the latter, independent of the state they are currently facing.

Empirically, the above results could be sustained by various studies conducted by the IDB (1998). Their main findings – on the magnitude of inequalities among Latin American countries – shows that the high unequal distribution of schooling is the factor contributing most to the high Gini coefficient of those countries. According to their data, this coefficient, which for Brazil reaches almost 0.6 (the highest among Latin American countries), improves considerably, to 0.45 approximately, if the richest 10 percent of the economy are discounted. Moreover, this group has ten or more years of education, whereas the poorest 30 percent of the population have at most (only) two years of schooling, strongly suggesting a very important role for unequal human capital distribution in explaining the country's high income concentration.

Conclusion

The model economy constructed in this study aimed to capture an important factor to explain the high concentration of income in Brazil. Agents with 12 or more years of education represent only 15 percent of the labor force in the country, thus qualified labor turns out to be the scarcest resource of the economy and, consequently, the corresponding productivity which dictates their income is as much as 3.5 times that of the less educated workers. Along this line of argument, the model economy introduces two types of agent, differing in their years of schooling (human capital). In addition, the model incorporates another relevant empirical fact: the more educated the worker, the higher his/her probability of being employed. Therefore, the individual shocks of employment opportunities differ between the two types of agent.

The introduction of the above elements in the model generates a highly concentrated income distribution at the recursive equilibrium, which is supported by the Brazilian empirical evidence. The artificial economy generates a very high concentration of less educated agents at low levels of income and a relatively small mass of agents around the highest level of income. Moreover, the simulations have shown a much more unequal income distribution among agents with less than 12 years of education than among the more educated ones. At the steady state distribution, the model also generates a maximum income 1.5 times higher for the more educated workers than for the less educated ones and, a minimum income 15 times higher for the former than for the latter.

Given the above results, an extension of this study to include a transfer mechanism between different types of agent seems to be in order as a topic for future research. This scheme could allow the less qualified, hence less productive, agents to be able to accumulate more human capital, improving in turn the income distribution among the agents of the economy.

Notes

Professor Werner Baer has long been a great contributer to the academic training of generations of Latin American economists, in particular from Brazil. Even though this study is quite insufficient to show my true appreciation, I would like to dedicate it to him, wishing that his dynamic work could continue to spill over so many of us for many years to come.

1. Pesquisa Nacional de Amostra Domiciliar, IBGE.
2. See for instance the theory of efficiency wages and the theory of labor market segmentation.
3. For justification of this cut line, please refer to the third section below.
4. Please see below for detailed description of the transition probability matrix $P^1(P^2)$.
5. This value for the capital's share based on the Brazilian National Accounts data is high compared to international evidence. Nonetheless, this parameterization is adopted because we are not dealing with a balanced growth model. For a detailed analysis of the long-run implication of this data please refer to Gomes et al. (2005).
6. Monthly Emplyment Inquiry.
7. The above study uses data from the monthly employment survey of the Brazilain main metropolitan regions (Pesquisa Mensal de Emprego) publisehd by the Instituto Brasiliero de Geografia e Estatstica, IBGE.
8. This seems also to be the case even for the U.S. economy, see Imrohoroglu et al. (1998), among others.
9. See Cavalcanti (1993), Issler and Rocha (1999), and Reis et al. (1998).
10. Since there is no change in the calibration of the transition probability matrices, employed labor in the long-run equilibrium for both types of agents is not reported in Table 11.4.

References

Araújo, C., and P. Cavalcante Ferreira (1999) "Reforma Tributária, Efeitos Alocativos e Impactos de Bem Estar," *Revista Brasileira de Economia*, 53, 133–166.

Aiyagari, S.R. (1994) "Uninsured Idiosyncratic Risk and Aggregate Savings," *Quarterly Journal of Economics*, 109, 659–684.

Barreto, F., and L.G. Schymura (1995) "Aplicação de um modelo de gerações superpostas para a reforma da previdência no Brasil: uma análise de sensibilidade no estado estacionário," *Annals of XVII meeting of the Brazilian Econometric Society*.

Barros, R. Paes de and L. Ramos (1992) "A Note on the Temporal Evolution of the Relationship between Wages and Education Among Brazilian Prime-Age Males: 1976–1989," Discussion text, IPEA, Rio de Janeiro, Brazil.

Barros, R. Paes de, R. Henriques, and R. Mendonça (2000a) "Education and Equitable Economic Development," *Economica*, 1, 111–144.

Barros, R. Paes de, R. Henriques, and R. Mendonça (2000b) "Desigualdade e Pobreza no Brasil: retrato de uma estabilidade inaceitável", *Revista Brasileira de Ciências Sociais*, 15, 123–142.

Becker, G. (1964) *Human Capital*, New York: Columbia University Press.

Bonelli, R., and L. Ramos (1993) "Distribuição de renda no Brasil: avaliação das tendências de longo prazo e mudanças nas desigualdades desde meados dos anos 70," *Revista de Economia Poltica*, 13, 76–97.

Cacciamali, M., and P.S. Freitas (1992) "Do capital humano ao salário eficiência: uma aplicação para analisar os diferenciais de salários em cinco ramos manufactureiros da Grande São Paulo," *Pesquisa e Planejamento Econômico*, 22, 343–368.

Cavalcanti, C. (1993) "Intertemporal Substitution in Consumption: An Empirical Investigation for Brazil," *Brazilian Review of Econometrics*, 13, 203–229.

Curi, A.Z., and Menezes Filho, N.A. (2006) "O Mercado de Trabalho Brasileiro é Segmentado? Alterações no Perfil da Informalidade e nos Diferenciais de Salários nas Décadas de 80 e 90," *Estudos Econômicos*, 36, 867–899.

Fishlow, A. (1972) "On the Emerging Problems of Development Policy: Brazilian Size Income Distribution," *American Economic Review*, 62, 391–402.

Franco, R.C. (2001) "A Relação entre a desigualdade eduacional e desigualdade salarial nos Estados brasileiros," Universidade de Braslia, Departamento de Economia: mimeo.

Gomes, V., M.N.S. Bugarin, and R. Ellery Jr. (2005) "Long-run Implications of the Brazilian Capital Stock and Income Estimates," *Brazilian Review of Econometrics*, 25, 67–88.

Imrohoroglu, A., S. Imrohoroglu, and D. Jones (1998) "A Dynamic Stochastic General Equilibrium Analysis of Social Security," in T. Kehoe. and E. Prescott (eds.) *The Discipline of Applied General Equilibrium*, Heidelberg: Springer-Verlag.

Issler, J.V., and F. Rocha (1999) "Consumo, restrição a liquidez e bem estar no Brasil," *Annals of the XXI meeting of the Brazilian Econometric Society*.

Lam, D., and D. Levinson (1991) "Declining Inequality in Schooling in Brazil and Its Effects on Inequality on Earnings," *Journal of Development Economics*, 37, 199–225.

Langoni, C.G. (1973) *Distribuição de renda e desenvolvimento econômico do Brasil*, Rio de Janeiro, RJ: Editora Expressão e Cultura.

Lucas, R.E. Jr. (1988) "On the Mechanics of Economic Development," *Journal of Monetary Economics*, 22, 3–42.

Marimon, R., and A. Scott (eds.) (1999) *Computational Methods for the Study of Dynamic Economies*, Oxford: Oxford University Press.

Reis, E., J.V. Issler, F. Blanco, and L. Carvalho (1998) "Renda permanente e poupança precaucional: evidências empricas para o Brasil no passado recente," *Pesquisa e Planejamento Econômico*, 28, 233–272.

Reis, J.G., and R. Paes de Barros (1990) "Desigualdade salarial e distribuição da educação: a evolução das diferenças regionais no Brasil," *Pesquisa e Planejamento Econômico*, 20, 415–478.

Schultz, T.P. (1989) "Returns to Womens Education," PHRWD Background Paper 89/001, Washington, D.C.: World Bank, Population, Health, and Nutrition Department.

Uzawa, H. (1964) "Optimal Growth in a Two-Sector Model of Capital Accumulation," *Review of Economic Studies*, 31, 1–24.

Part III

Regional Aspects of Economic Development

12

Structural Analysis of Employment in the Brazilian Economy: 1996 and 2002 Compared

Joaquim J.M. Guilhoto, Silvio Massaru Ichihara, and Márcio Guerra Amorim

Introduction

This chapter takes as its analytical base, and is inspired by, the seminal book of Prof. Werner Baer, *The Brazilian Economy*. This work has shaped and influenced the thought of Brazilian and Brazilianist economists for generations and as a consequence has helped to promote better understanding of the Brazilian economy and its evolution to a more developed and better country. The present work assumes that one has a basic knowledge of *The Brazilian Economy* (Baer, 2001) and from there makes an analysis of how the changes in the structure of the Brazilian economy has had an impact on employment. Following Baer (2001), the evolution of the Brazilian job market has been affected by different periods in the nation's political and economic historical course. In this respect, state intervention has to a greater or lesser extent been a constant presence.

Since the 1930s, the state has adapted executive and legislative policies intended to establish the conditions necessary for industrial development. In this process, the successive public policies that have been adopted have consolidated the national urban job market. However, a rural exodus and social inequality emerged as unintended consequences of the goal of economic growth.

In the recent past, the state was able to assume the responsibility for implementing a basic industrial structure (steel industries, metallurgy, energy, etc.) and, simultaneously, raising enough resources to sustain the period called the "Brazilian miracle" ("*milagre brasileiro*"). Nevertheless, in recent decades, the shortage of resources and the emergence of political and economic crises have weakened the government, reducing its capacity for solving the problems surrounding unemployment and the informal job market.

It is up to the state and other organizations to look carefully for more precise and, at the same time, effective measures for reducing unemployment and social inequality. In this case, precision is a requirement dictated by the shortage of available resources, while greater efficiency implies consideration not only of the direct, but also the indirect, impacts. Analyses that consider the linkages between all the productive sectors make the measurement of the direct and indirect effects resulting from employment-based policies possible. In this sense, the input-output table and associated model are very useful tools, because they portray the entire economic relations framework that determines national production.

However, it is also necessary to interpret the technological and trade changes occurring over time. Although input-output analyses consider countless details of the economic structure, they are often static since they refer to a specific time period. An alternative way to apprehend these changes in the productive structure consists in comparing two or more matrices estimated for different years. Furthermore, this analysis, associated with indicators based on national accounts such as gross value of production, imports of intermediary inputs, and imports to households' consumption, among others, makes possible a better comprehension of changes in the productive structure.

The most recently national input-output data published by the Brazilian National Institute of Statistics (IBGE), the official institution responsible for the release of the National Input-Output tables, refers to 1996. Hence our analysis was constrained by data availability; a set of input-output accounts was constructed for a more recent year to enable analysis of structural changes and the concomitant changes in employment. Accordingly, a table was constructed for 2002 using the estimation methodology of the national input-output table, presented by Guilhoto and Sesso Filho (2005), and the System of National Accounts, released by IBGE.

After the estimation of the national input-output table for 2002, the structure of the job market in the Brazilian economy was analyzed, with an emphasis on the differences in employment generation and the demand for labor. The analysis focuses on the determination of employment coefficients and their changes from 1996 to 2002.

The next section will deal with the theoretical background used in the paper. Thereafter, the results for the estimated employment multipliers are discussed, in association with an analysis of the key sectors in the economy. In the final section, some concluding comments are presented.

Theoretical background

The intersectoral flows in a given economy can be represented by the following system

$$X = AX + Y \tag{12.1}$$

where X is an (nx1) vector with the value of the total production in each sector, Y is an (nx1) vector with values for the final demand, and A is an (nxn) matrix with the technical coefficients of production (Leontief, 1951). In this model, the final demand vector can be treated as exogenous to the system, such that the level of total production can be determined by final demand, that is,:

$$X = BY \tag{12.2}$$

$$B = (I - A)^{-1} \tag{12.3}$$

where B is a the (nxn) Leontief inverse matrix.

From equation (12.2) it is possible to evaluate the impact of final demand on total production, and from there, on employment, imports, wages, etc.

To estimate the induced effect, that is, how much an increase in employment would generate, for example, on production in the economy given the consumption of newly employed people, one can make family consumption endogenous to the model, such that one has:

$$\bar{A} = \begin{bmatrix} A & H_c \\ H_r & 0 \end{bmatrix} \tag{12.4}$$

where $\bar{A}$ is the new matrix of technical coefficients with size $(n+1)$x$(n+1)$, H_r is a (1xn) vector with the income coefficient in each sector, and H_c is an (nx1) vector with the family consumption coefficients.

The new vectors of production and final demand would be given, respectively, by ($\bar{X}(n+1)$x1), and by ($\bar{Y}(n+1)$x1). They would be represented as:

$$\bar{X} = \begin{bmatrix} X \\ X_{n+1} \end{bmatrix} \tag{12.5}$$

and

$$\bar{Y} = \begin{bmatrix} Y* \\ Y*_{n+1} \end{bmatrix} \tag{12.6}$$

The Leontief system would then be represented by:

$$\bar{X} = \bar{B}\bar{Y} \tag{12.7}$$

$$\bar{B} = \left(I - \bar{A}\right)^{-1} \tag{12.8}$$

where $\bar{B}$ is an $((n+1)\times(n+1))$ matrix of the Leontief inverse, taking into consideration the induced effect.

Multipliers

From the multipliers' results it is possible to measure the direct and indirect effects of a change in final demand on production, income, employment, etc. (see Miller and Blair, 1985). From the Leontief inverse matrix (B) defined above one has that the production multiplier of type I for each economic sector is given by:

$$P_j = \sum_{i=1}^{n} b_{ij}$$
$$j = 1,...,n$$

(12.9)

where P_j is the production multiplier for sector j and $b_{ij} \in B$.

The production multiplier of type II, which takes into consideration the induced effect of the income-consumption linkage, is given by:

$$\bar{P}_j = \sum_{i=1}^{n} \bar{b}_{ij}$$
$$j = 1,...,n$$

(12.10)

where $\bar{P}_j$ is the production multiplier for sector j and $\bar{b}_{ij} \in \bar{B}$.

To estimate the employment multipliers, one first defines the employment/output coefficients, w_j:

$$w_j = \frac{e_j}{X_j}$$

(12.11)

where e_j is the total employment in sector j, and X_j is the level of production in sector j.

The total employment rates of types I (E_j) and II ($\bar{E}_j$), generated in sector j are given by:

$$E_j = \sum_{i=1}^{n} w_i b_{ij}$$

(12.12)

$$\bar{E}_j = \sum_{i=1}^{n} w_i \bar{b}_{ij}$$

(12.13)

The employment multipliers, that is, how much employment is generated in the economy for each person employed in a given sector, for the cases of type I (W_j) and type II ($\bar{W}_j$) are:

$$W_j = \frac{E_j}{w_j} \qquad (12.14)$$

$$\bar{W}_j = \frac{\bar{E}_j}{w_j} \qquad (12.15)$$

The Rasmussen/Hirschman approach

The work of Rasmussen (1956) and Hirschman (1958) led to the development of indices of linkage that have now become part of the generally accepted procedures for identifying key sectors in the economy. Defining b_{ij} as a typical element of the Leontief inverse matrix, B, B^* as the average value of all elements of B, and if $B_{\bullet j}$ and $B_{i\bullet}$ are the associated typical column and row sums, then the indices may be developed as follows:

Backward linkage index (*power of dispersion*): $U_j = \left[B_{\bullet j}/n \right] / B^*$ (12.16)

Forward linkage index (*sensitivity of dispersion*): $U_i = \left[B_{i\bullet}/n \right] / B^*$ (12.17)

One of the criticisms of the above indices is that they do not take into consideration the different *levels* of production in each sector of the economy; this is accomplished by the pure linkage approach presented in the next section.

The pure linkage approach

Following Guilhoto et al. (2005) the pure linkage approach can be used to measure the relative importance of the sectors in terms of production generation in the economy. Consider a two-region input-output system represented by the following block matrix, A, of direct inputs:

$$A = \left(\begin{array}{c|c} A_{jj} & A_{jr} \\ \hline A_{rj} & A_{rr} \end{array} \right) \qquad (12.18)$$

where A_{jj} and A_{rr} are the quadrat matrices of direct inputs within the first and second regions and A_{jr} and A_{rj} are the rectangular matrices showing the direct inputs purchased by the second region and vice versa.

From (12.18), one can generate the following expression:

$$B = (I - A)^{-1} = \begin{pmatrix} B_{jj} & B_{jr} \\ B_{rj} & B_{rr} \end{pmatrix} = \begin{pmatrix} \Delta_{jj} & 0 \\ 0 & \Delta_{rr} \end{pmatrix} \begin{pmatrix} \Delta_j & 0 \\ 0 & \Delta_r \end{pmatrix} \begin{pmatrix} I & A_{jr}\Delta_r \\ A_{rj}\Delta_j & I \end{pmatrix} \qquad (12.19)$$

where:

$$\Delta_j = \left(I - A_{jj}\right)^{-1} \tag{12.20}$$

$$\Delta_r = \left(I - A_{rr}\right)^{-1} \tag{12.21}$$

$$\Delta_{jj} = \left(I - \Delta_j A_{jr} \Delta_r A_{rj}\right)^{-1} \tag{12.22}$$

$$\Delta_{rr} = \left(I - \Delta_r A_{rj} \Delta_j A_{jr}\right)^{-1} \tag{12.23}$$

By utilizing this decomposition (12.19), it is possible to reveal the processes of production in an economy as well as to derive a set of multipliers/linkages.

From the Leontief formulation:

$$X = (I - A)^{-1} Y \tag{12.24}$$

and using the information contained in equations (12.19) through (12.23), one can derive a set of indexes that can be used to (a) rank the regions in terms of their importance in the economy and (b) to see how the production process works in the economy.

From equations (12.19) and (12.24) one obtains:

$$\begin{pmatrix} X_j \\ X_r \end{pmatrix} = \begin{pmatrix} \Delta_{jj} & 0 \\ 0 & \Delta_{rr} \end{pmatrix} \begin{pmatrix} \Delta_j & 0 \\ 0 & \Delta_r \end{pmatrix} \begin{pmatrix} I & A_{jr}\Delta_r \\ A_{rj}\Delta_j & I \end{pmatrix} \begin{pmatrix} Y_j \\ Y_r \end{pmatrix} \tag{12.25}$$

leading to the definitions for the Pure Backward Linkage (PBL) and for the Pure Forward Linkage (PFL) as:

$$PBL = \Delta_r A_{rj} \Delta_j Y_j$$
$$PFL = \Delta_j A_{jr} \Delta_r Y_r \tag{12.26}$$

where the PBL will reveal the pure impact on the rest of the economy of the value of the total production in region j, $(\Delta_j Y_j)$, that is, the impact that is free from the demand inputs that region j makes from region j and the feedbacks from the rest of the economy to region j and vice versa. The PFL will yield the pure impact on region j of the total production in the rest of the economy (ΔY_r).

As the PBL and PFL are shown in current values, the pure total linkage (PTL) can be obtained by adding the two previous indices:

$$PTL = PBL + PFL \qquad\qquad (12.27)$$

The pure linkage indices can also be normalized by the average value of the sectors in the economy such that the normalized indices show how many times larger or smaller than the average sector in the economy a sector is. In such a way, it is possible to use these indices for a direct comparison of the productive structure of economies with different sizes and currencies or a comparison for the same economy at two or more points in time.

Results

In this section, the results of the employment effects will be presented first. In this way, the coefficients are interpreted together with the descriptive analysis based on the data extracted from the input-output tables.

Employment generation

Recalling the remarks in the previous section, the values of the direct, indirect, and induced employment generation coefficients relate the number of jobs to the monetary value of production, expressed in the Brazilian currency (reals in constant prices of 2002). The values of the input-output table for the year 1996 are also expressed in value terms of 2002, ensuring that the employment generation coefficients are expressed in comparable units for 1996 and 2002 (jobs generated per R$ 1 million at 2002 values). By definition, the employment effects are classified into three types: (1) direct employment effect, that determines how many jobs are generated by a given sector when its production increases; (2) indirect employment effect, that determines how many jobs are generated in all the other sectors when the production of a given sector is increased; and (3) induced employment effect, that determines how many jobs are generated as a result of households' consumption, following an increase in their income, given the increase of direct, indirect, and induced jobs. Figure 12.1 displays, for 2002, the value of the direct employment effect for each sector, represented by the bars (with the scale on the left axis). The diamonds and their lines are associated with the right axis that indicates the difference of the direct employment effect between the years (2002 effect minus that of 1996).

For example, the first of the 42 sectors considered in this chapter is agriculture. This sector, in 2002, presented a direct employment generation coefficient of around 64 jobs for every R$1 million at 2002 rates. However, between 1996 and 2002, there was a decrease of 35 jobs (represented by the line from zero on the right axis down to the diamond). This means that in 1996 the direct employment effect for agriculture was recorded as 99 jobs generated for each R$ 1 million of production in 2002.

In Figure 12.1, the bar for private households with employed persons is especially significant. This sector demands a great deal of labor, but its participation in the national gross output is very low (0.62 percent in 2002). Obviously, an incentive to increase production in the sector results numerically in the generation of a large number of jobs. In practice, however, this does not represent a reasonable policy in the context of a strategic plan for employment generation, since this sector neither is a prominent producer nor has a great capacity for the indirect stimulation of national production.

Looking at the changes indicated in Figure 12.1, agriculture showed the largest fall by 2002, with its value reduced to two-thirds of that of 1996. In contrast, the footwear industries showed an increase of 12 jobs for every R$1 million of increased production, relative to 1996. In the general, in 2002, 30 sectors showed decreased values for the direct employment effect in relation to the year 1996. Moreover, in only five sectors had this value increased by more than two jobs per R$ 1 million, between 1996 and 2002. Clearly, labor productivity increases were the dominant characteristic of structural changes over this period.

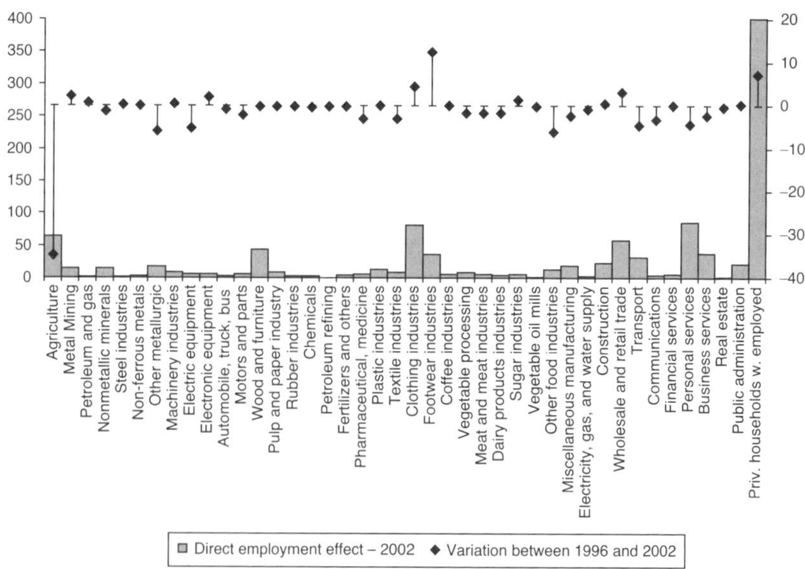

Figure 12.1   Direct employment effect in 2002 and its variation in relation to 1996

Decreases and increases in the direct employment effect can be associated with the following main factors. In the case of decreases, it is the adoption of new technology in the sector that stirs production to become more capital intensive and concomitantly reduce the labor requirement (for example, the introduction of agricultural machinery that requires fewer workers but maintains or increases production). In the case of increases, the restructuring of the sector, leading it to become momentarily more labor-intensive (for example, the installation of an industrial park for electronic equipment demands labor recruitment but does not meet the expected levels of production in this investment stage).

In Figure 12.2, the indirect employment effect is cumulatively added to the direct effect. The extensions above the previous bars correspond to the indirect employment effect and the variations represented by the diamonds and lines reveal the difference of both effects between the two years in analysis (the sum of the 2002 direct and indirect effects minus those of 1996). It can be observed that the secondary sectors have the largest values of indirect employment generation, given an increase of R\$ 1 million in their areas of production. These sectors, located between textile industries and miscellaneous manufacturing, are supplied by other sectors.[1] Therefore, such production increase depends upon an expansion in primary production, and thus generates larger indirect employment effects.

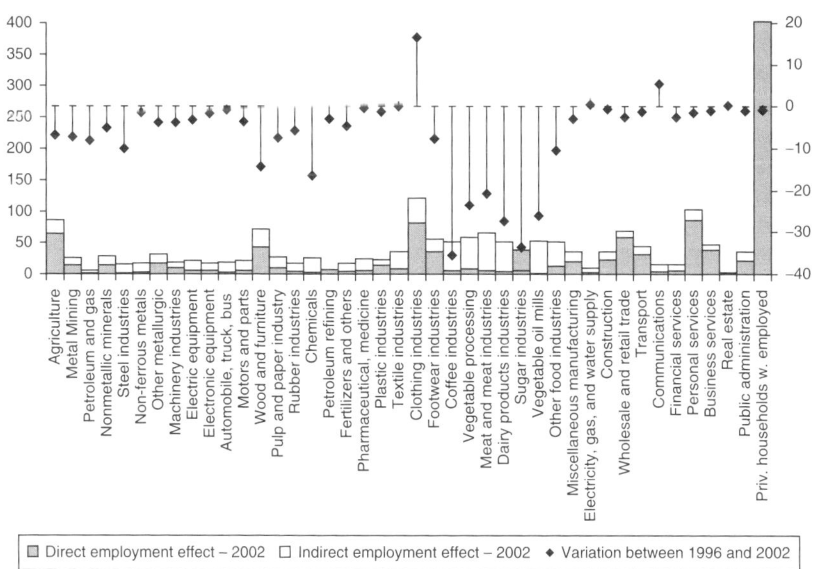

Figure 12.2   Indirect employment effect in 2002 and its variation in relation to 1996

When both effects (direct and indirect employment generation) are summed and compared with those of 1996, the variations are negative in most of the cases. For the cases when the totals decreased, the reasons can be ascribed to:

- The adoption of capital intensive technology or
- increased imports of inputs to the productive sectors (for example, the substitution of national plastic packaging by imported sources, causing a decrease in the indirect employment effect of food industries).

In case of increases, the causes might be:

- temporary increases in labor associated with restructuring
- increased relations with other sectors (for example, the expansion of the communications market, increasing the demand for other products of more labor intensive sectors in the national economy). Such expansion in these types of relationships can result from the reduction of imported inputs (for example, the substitution of imported textiles by a similar domestic ones for the production of clothing).

In similar fashion to Figure 12.2, Figure 12.3 adds the induced employment effect to the two other effects. The second extension above the bars aggregating the direct and indirect values corresponds to the induced employment effect. The diamonds, in turn, characterize the variation of the sum

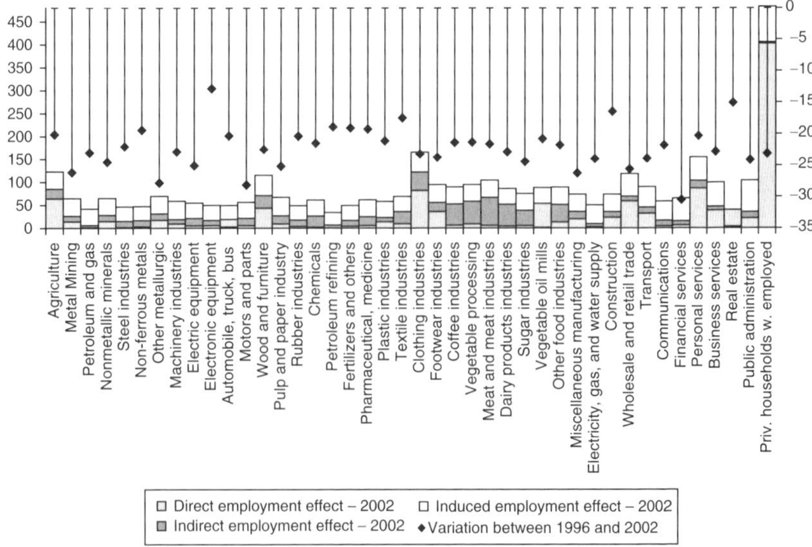

Figure 12.3 Induced employment effect in 2002 and its variation in relation to 1996

of the three effects between the years (the sum of the 2002 direct, indirect, and induced effects minus those for 1996).

An increase of R\$ 1 million in 2002 in the private household sector, will give a direct expansion of 402 jobs. This sector, however, demands few inputs for its production and shows an insignificant indirect employment effect (three jobs). On the other hand, the increased income of the 402 additional employed persons will lead to enhanced consumption that stimulates the production of other sectors, generating 78 new jobs in the economy. The total employment effect will be 483 jobs; in other sectors, the indirect effects turn out to be much larger than the induced effect (see Figure 12.3).

In 2002, in relation to the total employment effect (the sum of the direct, indirect, and induced employment generation), no sector increased its impact compared to 1996. The reduction of the total employment effect is mainly associated with:

- all the considerations mentioned above in the cases of decreases in the direct and indirect employment effects;
- adoption of more capital-intensive technology;
- increased consumption of imported intermediate inputs; and
- decreases in workers' purchasing power (for example, a sector maintains the same number of workers but pays lower wages, reducing their income and purchasing power).

The following discussion addresses these items in more detail.

Expansion of the capital intensive production technology and reduction of the compensation of employees

The expansion of capital intensive production technology results in a negative impact on the generation of direct, indirect, and induced employment. Obviously, the expansion of labor intensive technology has the opposite effect but this was not a dominant characteristic in the economy's restructuring between 1996 and 2002. The analysis conducted here utilizes the variation of the direct employment generation coefficients between the years 1996 and 2002, associating it with other two variations:

- the variation of the ratio of compensation to gross domestic output (GDO) of each sector and
- the variation of the ratio of compensation to the value added (VA) in each sector.

These combinations work as branches of a decision tree, each of them determining what sectors expanded the utilization of capital intensive technology, between the years 1996 and 2002. The tree referred to is outlined in Figure 12.4.

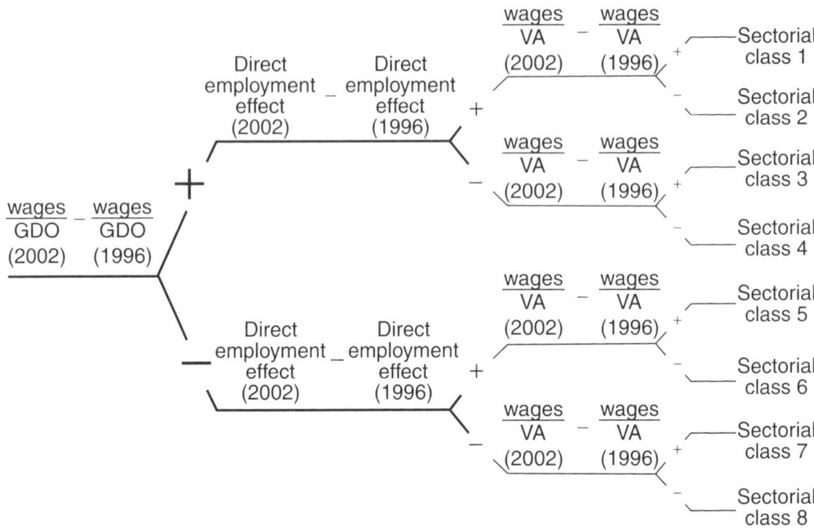

Figure 12.4   Sector classifications based on the relations between direct employment effect, compensation, gross domestic output (GDO), and value added (VA)

In Figure 12.4, the first stage is defined by the ratio of compensation to gross domestic output (GDO). If the variation between the years 1996 and 2002 is positive, it means that wages were a larger share of GDO in the latter year. A negative value indicates a decline in this share. The second stage divides the sectors into two groups depending on whether their direct employment generation coefficients grew or not. Finally, the third stage separates the sectors that expanded compensation value relative to the value added (VA) from those sectors where this proportion was reduced.

The compensation of employees is included in the VA, which, added to the intermediary consumption (IC), results in the GDO. In the cases in which the compensation value increased at rates larger than those of the VA, the gross operational surplus (GOS) retained in the sector was smaller, in other words, the profitability of the activity was reduced. By means of these combinations, eight groups could be defined. Table 12.1 classifies the sectors according to these groups and makes inferences about what happened in each of them between 1996 and 2002.

Imports destined for intermediary and household consumption

The technological variable provides insights into changes in direct employment in each sector. However, this is not sufficient for anunderstanding of the effects of indirect and induced employment generation. In these cases, in addition to the employed persons in a given sector, one is concerned

Table 12.1 Sector classifications and interpretations

Group	Sectors	Explanation
1	Electronic equipment; Construction; Private households with employed persons.	Expansion in labor utilization with an increase in compensation as a share of GDO and VA, indicating the reduction of GOS and profit margins.
2	No sector.	
3	Plastic industries; Personal services; Wood and furniture; Real estate.	Reduction in labor utilization with an increase in the share of compensation in GDO and VA, indicating the employment of fewer persons, but for higher wages.
4	No sector.	
5	Wholesale and retail trade; Public administration.	Expansion in labor utilization with a decrease in the share of compensation in GDO, but with an increased participation in VA, indicating either the employment of lower paid workers and/or reduction of profit margins.
6	Clothing industries; Machine industries; Petroleum and gas; Steel industries; Metal Mining; Footwear industries; Sugar industries.	Expansion in labor utilization, but with a decrease in the share of compensation in GDO and VA, indicating the employment of more people and an increase in profit margins.
7	Textile industries; Automobile, truck and bus industries; Dairy products industries; Transport; Other food industries; Communications; Electric equipment industries; Motors and parts for vehicle industries.	Reduction in labor utilization with a decrease of compensation share of GDO, but not of VA, indicating the employment of fewer persons and a possible increase in intermediary consumption, reducing VA (sectors that reduced employment and profit margins, possibly under strong competitive pressure).
8	Pharmaceutical and medicinal industries; Other vegetables-processing; Business services; Agriculture; Meat and meat industries; Nonmetallic mineral industries; Nonferrous metals; Chemicals; Coffee industries; Vegetable oil mills; Fertilizer and others chemical industries; Other metallurgic industries; Petroleum refining; Rubber industries; Miscellaneous manufacturing; Pulp and paper industries; Electricity, gas, and water supply; Financial services.	Reduction in labor utilization with a decrease in compensation's share of GDO and VA, indicating the employment of fewer persons. Possible substitution of labor with capital intensive technology.

about the jobs generated by the consumption of this sector in relation to the production of others. From this point of view, when the sector stops buying in the domestic market, increasing dependence on imported inputs, there is no stimulus to national production or, as a consequence, indirect employment generation. The growth of imports also reduces the demand for national products by households, furthering limiting the induced effects.

The ratio of total imports of inputs by a given sector to its GDO measures the participation of imported goods in the production process. In Figure 12.5, the sectors that show the largest share of imported inputs in their production are classified in the highest deciles. For example, the following sectors are in this group: electronic equipment industries; the automobile, truck and bus industries; petroleum refining; fertilizer and others chemical industries; and miscellaneous manufacturing. In contrast, the sectors located in the first (lowest) decile (those which have the smallest share of imported inputs in relation to the GDO) are coffee industries; meat and meat industries; financial intermediation; real estate; and private households with employed persons.

According to Figure 12.5, the vast majority of the sectors imported more inputs in 2002, compared to 1996. Only nine sectors, represented by the downward arrows, reduced their consumption of imported inputs. Of this group, five sectors are contained in the highest decile (mentioned above) in both 1996 and 2002, notwithstanding this reduction. The figures are not very different in relation to the other sectors among this group, in other words, there changes were modest.

An expressive structural difference was noticed only in the sector of other food industries (that includes beverage manufacturing), which fell from the sixth to the third decile. The reduction of its consumption of imported inputs was apparently small, around 0.9 percent, but it is a significant value in a sector that imports 4 percent of its GDO. Unfortunately, the substitution by national inputs, in this sector and most of the others, did not contribute to an increase in employment generation. However, one can infer that at least two sectors had their respective employment generation coefficient enhanced by the reduction in imports: textile industries and electricity, gas, and water supply. In both sectors, the variation is negative for the direct employment effect,[2] but positive for the indirect one,[3] possibly because of the substitution of imported inputs by domestic ones.

The opposite case is observed in 11 of the 12 sectors[4] for which positive direct employment generation coefficients became negative when added to the indirect employment effect. In these 11 sectors, an increase in the import volume occurred and, possibly, this is the cause of the reduction in the indirect employment effect. Note that only the clothing industries showed a positive variation in direct and indirect employment effects despite the growth in imports.

Sectors	1996	T	2002
Agriculture and related services	■■□□□□□□□□	⇧	■■■■■□□□□□
Metal Mining	■■■■■□□□□□	⇧	■■■■■■□□□□
Petroleum and gas mining	■■■□□□□□□□	⇧	■□□□□□□□□□
Nonmetallic mineral industries	■■■■■□□□□□	⇧	■■■■■□□□□□
Steel industries	■■■■■■■■□□	⇧	■■■■■■■■□□
Non-ferrous metals metallurgy	■■■■■■■■■□	⇩	■■■■■■■■■□
Other metallurgic industries	■■■■□□□□□□	⇧	■■■■■■□□□□
Machinery and tractors industries	■■■■■■□□□□	⇧	■■■■■■□□□□
Electric equipment industries	■■■■■■■■■□	⬆	■■■■■■■■■□
Electronic equipment industries	■■■■■■■■■■	⬇	■■■■■■■■■■
Automobiles, trucks and buses industries	■■■■■■■■■■	⇩	■■■■■■■■■■
Motors and parts for vehicles industries	■■■■■■■□□□	⬆	■■■■■■■■■■
Wood and furniture industries	■■■■□□□□□□	⇧	■■■□□□□□□□
Pulp and paper industries	■■■■■■■■□□	⇧	■■■■■■□□□□
Rubber industries	■■■■■■■■■□	⇧	■■■■■■■■□□
Chemicals	■■■■■■□□□□	⇧	■■■■■□□□□□
Petroleum refining	■■■■■■■■■■	⇩	■■■■■■■■■■
Fertilizers and others chemical industries	■■■■■■■■■■	⇩	■■■■■■■■■□
Pharmaceutical and medicine industries	■■■■■■■■■■	⇩	■■■■■■■■□□
Plastic industries	■■■■■■■■□□	⬆	■■■■■■■■■■
Textile industries	■■■■■■■■■□	⇩	■■■■■■■■□□
Clothing industries	■■■■■□□□□□	⇧	■■■■□□□□□□
Footwear industries	■■■■■■■□□□	⇧	■■■■■■□□□□
Coffee industries	■□□□□□□□□□	⇧	■□□□□□□□□□
Other vegetable processing	■■■■■■■□□□	⇧	■■■■■■■□□□
Meat and meat industries	■□□□□□□□□□	⇧	■□□□□□□□□□
Dairy products industries	■■■□□□□□□□	⇧	■■□□□□□□□□
Sugar industries	■■■□□□□□□□	⇧	■■□□□□□□□□
Vegetable oil mills	■■■■■■□□□□	⇧	■■■■□□□□□□
Other food industries	■■■■■■■□□□	⇩	■■■□□□□□□□
Miscellaneous manufacturing	■■■■■□□□□□	⬆	■■■■■■■■■□
Electricity, gas, and water supply	■■■■■■□□□□	⇩	■■■□□□□□□□
Construction	■■■□□□□□□□	⇧	■■■■□□□□□□
Wholesale and retail trade	■■□□□□□□□□	⇧	■■□□□□□□□□
Transport	■■■■■■■□□□	⇧	■■■■■■□□□□
Communications	■■■■□□□□□□	⇧	■■■■■■□□□□
Financial services	■□□□□□□□□□	⇧	■■□□□□□□□□
Personal services	■■□□□□□□□□	⇧	■■■■■■□□□□
Business services	■■□□□□□□□□	⇧	■■■□□□□□□□
Real estate	■□□□□□□□□□	⇧	■□□□□□□□□□
Public administration	■■■■□□□□□□	⇧	■■■■□□□□□□
Private households with employed persons	■□□□□□□□□□	⇧	■□□□□□□□□□

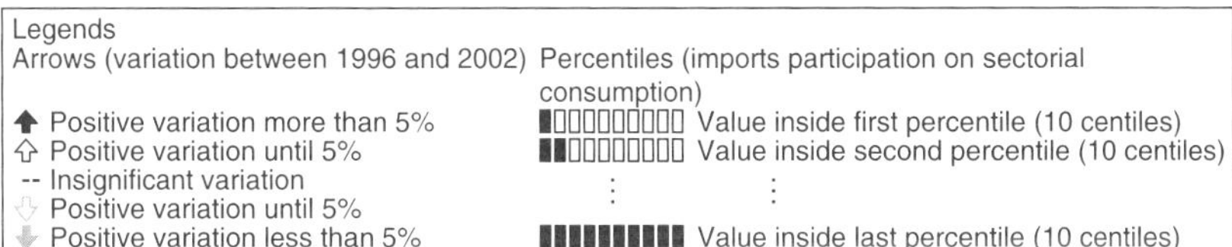

Figure 12.5 Classification of sectors based on the ratio of imported inputs to GDO, 1996 and 2002

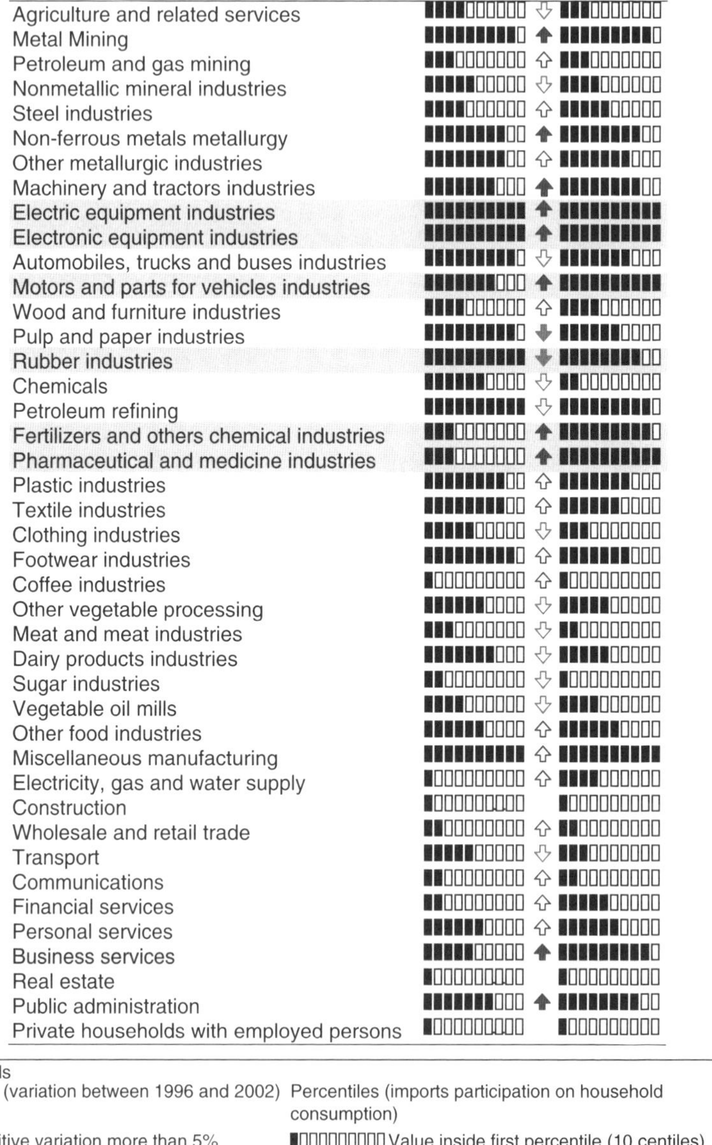

Figure 12.6 Classification of sectors for imported goods in total households' consumption, 1996 and 2002

Households demand for imported goods also increased in most sectors. In Figure 12.6, the most important changes in imports share of households consumption are highlighted. Such increases in the relative importance of import consumption range from 16.6 percent, in the fertilizer and others chemical industries, to 48 percent, in electronic equipment industries.

While 14 sectors reduced their imports of goods destined for household consumption (the downward arrows in Figure 12.6), together these make up less than 30 percent of the national households' budget, indicating the important share of imports to households between 1996 and 2002. In turn, this change contributed negatively to the induced employment effect between those years.

Increase in linkage between a given sector and the other sectors of the economy

To measure the degree of linkage between one sector and the other sectors of economy, the Rasmussen-Hirschman (RH) indicators and the pure linkage indicators were used.

The Rasmussen-Hirschman (RH) backward and forward linkages

Figure 12.7 shows four series of results, namely the values of the RH backward and forward linkages of 1996 compared to those of 2002. The points above the axis with a value of zero represent forward linkages, while those below correspond to backward linkages. Closed figures correspond to 1996 and opened figures to 2002. In all of these cases, the farther the distance from the point to the zero horizontal axis, the greater is the linkage's value, forward as well as backward. Note that values below this axis should not be interpreted as negative.

The backward linkages denote how much one sector demands from the other sectors. Sectors like the steel industries and those related to food (sugar, coffee, dairy products, meat, and other food products) have high backward linkages while, at the same time, activities related to services, public administration, and institutions (sectors on the right side of the figure) have little dependence on inputs from other sectors.

There were no major changes in the structure of backward linkages between 1996 and 2002. Some sectors such as the textile industry, meat and meat industries, wholesale and retail trade, and transport modified their technological coefficients and started to demand more inputs, in contrast to what occurred with the steel, metal mining, and footwear industries. However, in general terms, backward linkages were not significantly modified over this time period.

In relation to forward linkages, they determine how much the output of one sector is demanded by other sectors. The dispersion of forward linkages is greater than that observed for backward linkages and it can also be observed that agriculture is extremely important in comparison to others, because of its high potential to supply inputs to others sectors of the national economy. Comparing the data of 1996 and 2002, note that the importance of petroleum refining, industrial services of public utilities and wholesale and retail trade has became even greater in 2002. Others sectors like communications and petroleum and gas extraction also showed high indicators in contrast to sectors such as agriculture, the textile industry, and services.

Industrial production technology became even more dependent on energy sources over this period. With the greater use of refined petroleum products, the use of gross products from petroleum and gas mining also grew. Growth in sectors like wholesale and retail trade, industrial services of public utilities, and communications is also perceived – their outputs were more in demand by other sectors of economy in 2002 in comparison to 1996.

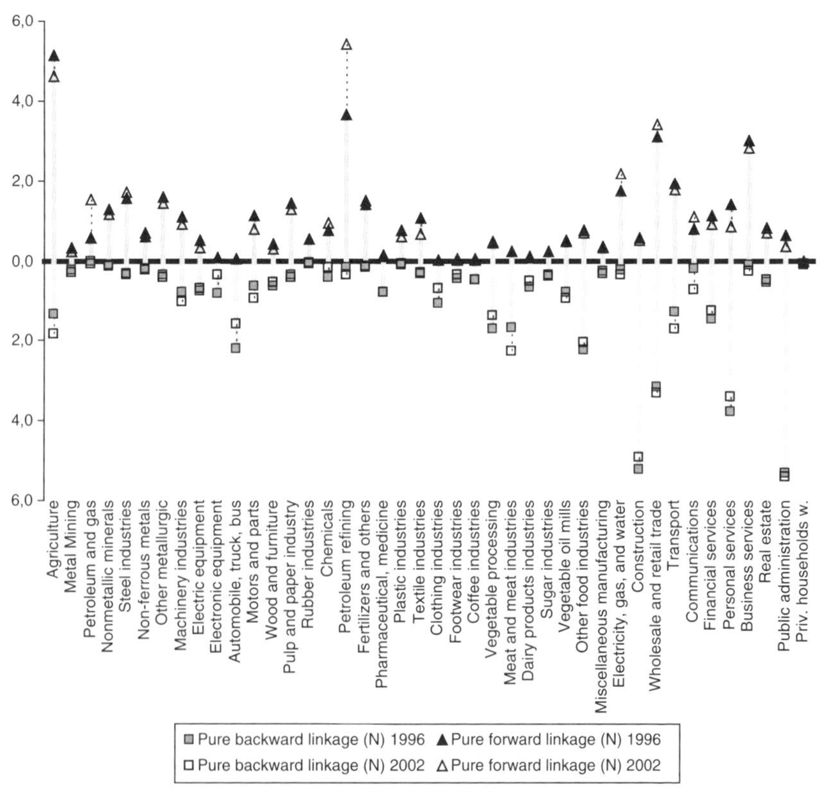

Figure 12.7　Rasmussen-Hirschman backward and forward linkage, Brazil, 1996 and 2002

Pure backward and forward linkages

RH indicators do not consider the full economic importance of a sector since they only measure production coefficients. The pure backward linkage indicator also takes into consideration the importance exerted by the sector on others in terms of volume; therefore, the order of importance given to each sector may be different. For example, the sector that shows the greatest RH forward linkage indicator – vegetable oil mills – is the only the fourteenth most important sector to the pure normalized backward linkage. The analysis using pure linkages complements the results obtained by means of RH linkage indicators. Figure 12.8 shows the values of pure forward and backward linkages in the same way they were presented in Figure 12.7.

Comparing the results shown in Figures 12.7 and 12.8 (regarding the backward linkages), it is observed that public administration, construction, and the wholesale and retail trades are strong buyers from other sectors,

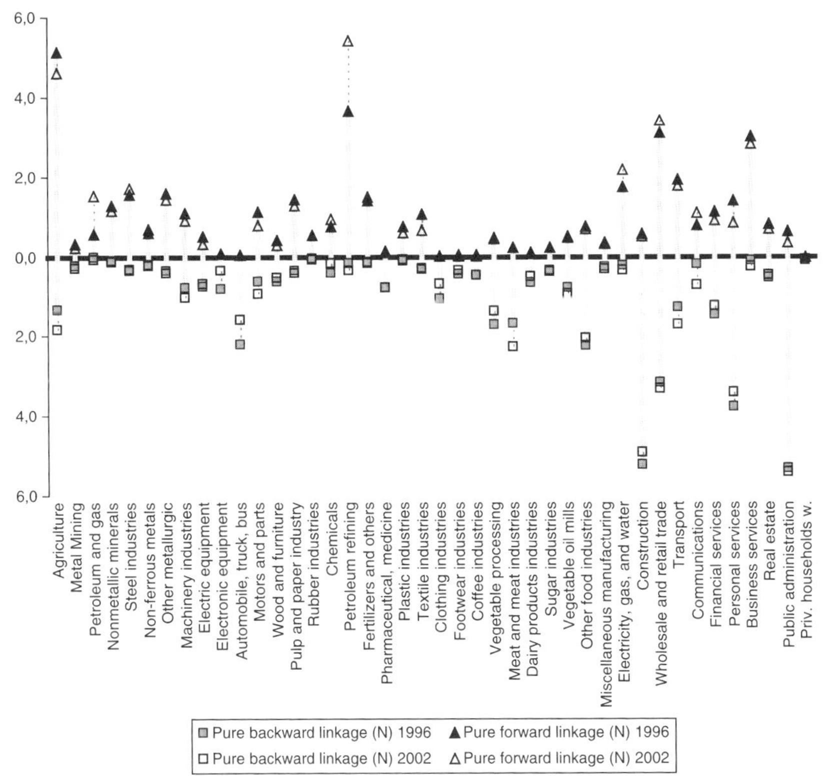

Figure 12.8   Pure backward and forward linkages, Brazil, 1996 and 2002

according to the pure linkage indicator (Figure 12.8). Their representation in relation to the other sectors is significantly different to those observed in Figure 12.7, because of the size of the monetary flows with which they are involved. For forward linkages, there is greater correspondence between the sectors with the higher pure linkage indicators and those with the highest HR forward linkages.

Regarding the totality of the pure linkages, note that the prominent sectors that have increased their relations are: refined petroleum; petroleum and gas; communications; meat and meat industries; industrial services of public utilities; and wholesale and retail trade. The main sectors that reduced their relations with the rest of the economy are: personal services; automobiles, trucks and buses; electronic equipment; and vegetable processing.

It is important to point out that, in 2002, the communications sector showed a reduction in the direct employment effect (Figure 12.1), but an increase in the indirect effect (Figure 12.2). This can be explained by the more intense relationship between the sector and the economy, evidenced the changes in the backward and forward linkages. In other words, the communications sector not only started to be more in demand from other sectors, as a consequence, it also demanded more from them (Figures 12.7 and 12.8), raising its capacity for indirect job generation.

In the case of the clothing industry, the RH backward linkage was not modified and the pure indicator was reduced. The increase of imports can explain this fact (Figure 12.5), but the unusual increase in the indirect employment effect (Figure 12.2) may then be the result of a reorganization of the sector in 2002.

Final comments

In general terms, all sectors have seen a reduction in the total employment effect (summing the direct, indirect, and induced effects). It would appear that technological changes and increased dependence on imports have reduced the demand for labor. The consequences of those facts provoked the reduction of the value of labor income to production in 35 of the 42 productive activities discussed here. The distribution of employed persons was modified in this period. While agriculture is still the biggest user of labor (19 percent of employed persons), its participation has been reduced, while the wholesale and retail trade and services sectors have gained.

The sectors related to petroleum and gas extraction have become more important in national production. Apparently, extractive production (the petroleum and gas sector) grew with the generation of more jobs, but these jobs demanded less qualified peoples with lower wages, since the multiplying effect of this sector was reduced together with the share of relative remuneration to VBP and VA. In the case of petroleum refining, the sector also grew in importance, but its development was characterized by greater capital utilization, reducing the employment effect (jobs generated by R$ 1 million at the 2002 rate) and the number of persons employed in the sector.

Households consumption of imported electronics increased and the sector itself became less important in the domestic economy, although there was an increase in the direct job generation coefficient in this sector. The clothing industries were the only ones to show positive direct and indirect employment effects, even with the increase of imported inputs and the reduction of its relations with the other sectors of economy. This sector's transformation requires further research. The wholesale and retail trade sector gained strength and perhaps added more labor than most other sectors over the time period studied.

The textile industries and the industrial services of public utilities increased in importance in the indirect employment effect, because of the substitution of foreign inputs by national ones. The communications sector grew its production significantly, but its evolution was based on the addition of intensive capital technology, reducing its capacity to offer direct jobs.

The construction sector kept its prominent position in the economy and even increased its capacity to absorb more labor. The processing sector of food production (food industries) gained prominence because of its capacity for indirect employment generation, but its potential in employment generation was reduced. This fact must be attributed mainly to the increase of technology in agriculture, which supplies the inputs. Further, these industries have increased the import of necessary inputs for their products but there was a reduction of processed foods imports destined for household consumption in 2002.

It is clear that the total employment effect (negative variation in all of the sectors) has been influenced strongly by technological developments in agriculture. The substantial reduction of the direct employment effect in agriculture (98 to 64 jobs generated by R$ 1 million at the 2002 rate) goes far beyond the indirect relations of job generation in food processing industries generated by household demand.

Notes

The authors would like to thank the students Denise Imori and Marina Assumpção for the English translation of the original paper in Portuguese. Of course, the remaining mistakes are still our responsibility.

This paper is the result of a research conducted under the support of the *Trends and Forecasting Unit/National Department of SENAI (National Service of Industrial Education)*.

1. Such sectors tend to show large backward linkage indices. However, considering them by the GHS method, the index tends not to be very expressive for most of these sectors, given their importance in terms of production generation.
2. See Figure 12.1.
3. See Figure 12.2.

4. Footwear industries; Private households with employed persons; Wholesale and retail trade; Metal mining; Electronic equipment industries; Sugar industries; Petroleum and gas extraction; Construction; Machinery and tractor industries; Public administration; Steel industries; and Clothing industries.

References

Baer, W. (2001) *The Brazilian Economy: Growth and Development*, 5th ed., Westport: Praeger.

Guilhoto, J.J.M., M. Sonis, and G.J.D. Hewings (2005) "Linkages and Multipliers in a Multiregional Framework: Integration of Alternative Approaches," *Australian Journal of Regional Studies*, 11, 75–89

Guilhoto, J.J.M., and U.A. Sesso Filho (2005) "Estimação da Matriz Insumo-Produto à partir de Dados Preliminares das Contas Nacionais," *Economia Aplicada*, 9, 277–299

Hirschman, A.O. (1958) *The Strategy of Economic Development,* New Haven, CT: Yale University Press.

Leontief, W. (1951) *The Structure of the American Economy*, 2nd ed., New York: Oxford University Press.

Miller, R.E., and Blair, P.D. (1985) *Input-Output Analysis: Foundations and Extensions,* New Jersey: Prentice Hall.

Rasmussen, P. (1956) *Studies in Intersectoral Relations*, Amsterdam: North Holland.

13
Trade Liberalization, Space, and Regional Development

Eduardo Haddad

Introduction

Despite some remarkable improvements in the last few years, trade liberalization in Brazil is still modest compared to other countries. The Brazilian international trade coefficient, measured by the sum of imports and exports, is still much lower than that observed for countries with a similar national income. This factor (although not alone) has restricted the growth of the Brazilian economy. One of the major elements of the trade liberalization process the Brazilian economy has undergone is concerned with its trading relationships in a growing context of regionalism. This was energized after the creation of MERCOSUR in the early 1990s, and is still in the process of negotiation, aimed at the geographic expansion of trade agreements with partner countries. For either economic or political reasons, Brazil has sought different regional integration strategies in an attempt to foster economic development.

Given the negotiation approaches to the future of the region, Brazil contemplates three alternatives for the creation of trading blocs. First, Brazil is directly involved in the creation of the Free Trade Area of the Americas (FTAA), resuming the process started in 1994 that proposed the integration of Western Hemisphere economies in a one-of-a-kind free trade agreement. Second, interested parties have already shown political commitment toward a trade agreement between MERCOSUR and the European Union, despite the fact that its implementation has stumbled upon specific problems that are difficult to address in the short run. Third, the Doha round of the World Trade Organization (WTO) has launched a more general round of multilateral negotiations, highlighting the role of Brazil as a global trader. In general, these scenarios may define resource allocation anew in the Brazilian economic space, with potential winners and losers throughout the process. Effects associated with trade creation and diversion constitute the core mechanisms for the transmission of changes in trade patterns of the Brazilian economy and their consequences on the Brazilian economic space. In this chapter, some important factors are outlined that may help elucidate the relationship between trade liberalization and space in the context of economic development in Brazil.

In the next section, an overview of the recent structure of Brazilian international trade flows is presented, focusing on its regional dimension. A discussion of spatial aspects of Brazil's trade policy follows, and, then, a digression on the role of spatial interdependence in the productive system is presented in the context of the process of trade liberalization in the country. Concluding remarks address some of the policy implications from a spatial perspective.

Overview on the international participation of Brazilian states

Comparative advantage has been regularly used to explain the trade pattern of a given region. The Ricardian theory explains comparative advantage in terms of differences in supply resulting from technologies and resource availabilities that are specific to the regions involved in the trade process (Bowen et al., 1998). The Brazilian economy is not internally homogeneous, with striking variations across regions and sectors. When analyzing the international trade framework of Brazilian states, one should bear in mind the specific characteristics of each state, that is, its productive structure, the availability of natural resources, government incentives, the tax system, transportation costs, and easy access to external markets, among other factors. These are determining factors for the trade pattern of each state. Coupled with these factors, there are also tariff and nontariff barriers, agreements, and trade preference systems between countries that discourage the use of comparative advantages of states for the trade in specific products.

Table 13.1 shows a balance among the major Brazilian trading partners in the 1996–2002 period. The destination of approximately 27 percent of Brazilian exports was the EU, 26 the rest of the world, 25 NAFTA, 13 MERCOSUR, and 8 the rest of the FTAA. The import pattern was well balanced across the five regions. Approximately 32 percent of Brazilian imports were from the European Union, 29 from NAFTA, 17 from MERCOSUR, 15 from the rest of the world, and 5 from the rest of the FTAA. A more in-depth data analysis allows us to assert that the trade framework of Brazilian states is not so well balanced as the Brazilian trade framework as a whole. Such difference can be explained, for instance, by the discrepancies in transportation costs, economies of scale, and factor endowments across Brazilian states.

The main markets for Northern region's products were the EU and the rest of the world, which accounted for 67.96 percent of the total amount exported by the region. For the state of Pará, the major trade partners were the EU and the rest of the world (40.69 and 39.07 percent, respectively). As for the source of goods, the rest of the world was remarkably important.

Table 13.1 Trade direction: Exports and imports of Brazilian states according to source and destination (1996/2002) (%)

	MERCOSUR		NAFTA		Rest of the FTAA		European union		ROW	
	Exp	Imp	Exp	Imp	Exp	Imp	Exp	Imp	Exp	Imp
North	6.19	1.69	20.17	16.45	5.67	5.75	33.58	13.29	34.38	62.82
AC	15.32	7.42	25.85	17.00	13.57	0.94	33.97	68.35	11.29	6.30
AP	2.74	0.26	7.17	15.26	4.12	15.38	31.41	30.39	54.55	38.70
AM	24.55	1.01	33.02	5.98	24.71	5.67	5.17	13.47	12.55	73.87
PA	1.79	4.48	17.27	73.16	1.18	5.29	40.69	10.06	39.07	7.02
RO	13.31	8.07	27.30	46.07	3.47	6.02	17.33	27.34	38.59	12.50
RR	0.01	0.07	4.09	3.20	50.44	74.88	10.98	10.97	34.48	10.87
TO	0.57	19.68	26.90	12.82	0.20	0.60	49.22	24.20	23.12	42.71
Northeast	11.76	16.98	31.71	26.83	4.50	12.78	26.16	14.83	25.88	28.58
AL	1.65	14.82	22.93	49.69	0.80	0.28	7.12	7.81	67.50	27.40
BA	15.24	16.06	32.19	30.50	5.11	14.31	24.79	11.82	22.67	27.30
CE	11.92	21.97	53.73	30.59	8.90	11.71	16.90	12.93	8.54	22.80
MA	7.68	2.32	21.79	25.07	0.33	19.99	42.02	14.91	28.19	37.72
PB	8.46	12.76	46.56	24.82	5.32	1.41	23.29	26.35	16.38	34.65
PE	11.81	25.24	22.11	9.46	6.24	12.29	21.20	20.91	38.65	32.10
PI	1.84	5.87	32.03	48.47	1.81	1.39	49.25	16.03	15.06	28.24
RN	5.67	12.22	39.61	45.19	5.48	2.01	35.07	16.90	14.16	23.68
SE	23.97	44.17	13.09	5.31	7.80	1.52	49.43	34.95	5.71	14.06
Southeast	15.05	16.33	27.36	31.73	9.91	4.66	23.29	42.62	24.39	4.66
ES	3.89	29.20	33.20	36.13	2.47	6.20	28.31	22.28	32.13	6.20
MG	8.48	16.29	20.65	40.50	4.44	3.48	35.57	36.25	30.86	3.48
RJ	12.87	22.68	25.64	21.42	16.53	3.72	15.71	48.46	29.25	3.72
SP	19.11	13.72	29.13	30.97	12.09	4.82	19.15	45.66	20.52	4.82
South	13.04	24.70	23.24	30.12	6.11	3.04	29.03	23.17	28.58	18.97
PR	10.18	23.73	14.17	17.36	4.57	3.67	38.63	34.85	32.45	20.39
SC	13.48	19.74	26.37	45.19	6.88	2.26	27.99	20.74	25.29	12.07
RS	15.11	27.13	28.97	35.10	6.96	2.81	21.89	14.81	27.06	20.17
Center-West	4.55	14.33	4.52	9.53	3.40	12.22	60.88	29.35	26.64	34.57
DF	0.89	3.43	9.44	0.43	0.75	1.46	39.20	58.24	49.72	36.44
GO	4.46	24.46	12.34	18.33	2.42	4.60	55.95	16.16	24.83	36.46
MT	1.22	12.96	1.68	16.52	3.15	8.46	66.64	17.12	27.31	44.94
MS	15.77	14.56	1.69	3.46	5.86	51.26	50.44	10.76	26.24	19.95
Brazil	13.42	17.11	25.43	29.23	8.06	5.37	26.88	32.76	26.21	15.53

Source: MDIC (elaborated by the author).

Its share of the total amount imported by the Northern region reached 62.82 percent.

For the Northeast region, NAFTA was the major trade partner, with a 31 percent share of the total amount exported by the region. Exports from the states of Ceará, Paraíba, and Piauí concentrated on specific goods. Ceará

Table 13.2 Share of total exports and imports according to destination and source (1996–2002) (%)

	MERCOSUR		NAFTA		Rest of the FTAA		European union		ROW		Total	
	Exp	Imp	Exp	Imp	Exp	Imp	Exp	Imp	Exp	Imp	Exp	Imp
North	2.67	0.83	4.32	8.62	3.77	8.34	6.95	3.18	7.47	15.24	5.55	7.21
AC	0.01	0.00	0.00	0.00	0.01	0.00	0.01	0.02	0.00	0.00	0.00	0.01
AP	0.02	0.00	0.03	0.03	0.05	0.14	0.12	0.05	0.21	0.06	0.10	0.04
AM	1.93	0.43	1.12	7.96	2.98	6.84	0.20	2.66	0.52	14.83	0.99	6.61
PA	0.62	0.31	3.04	0.37	0.63	1.12	6.53	0.36	6.58	0.25	4.34	0.44
RO	0.09	0.04	0.10	0.25	0.04	0.08	0.06	0.06	0.14	0.03	0.09	0.06
RR	0.00	0.00	0.00	0.00	0.04	0.15	0.00	0.00	0.01	0.00	0.01	0.01
TO	0.00	0.05	0.02	0.01	0.00	0.00	0.03	0.03	0.01	0.05	0.02	0.03
Northeast	7.11	10.68	9.54	3.91	4.26	24.57	7.40	4.74	7.61	9.14	7.63	8.06
AL	0.06	0.24	0.55	0.05	0.05	0.02	0.14	0.07	1.39	0.24	0.54	0.19
BA	4.55	4.55	4.68	1.73	2.39	12.01	3.44	1.67	3.26	3.86	3.73	3.32
CE	0.75	2.20	1.78	0.70	0.91	3.58	0.52	0.67	0.27	1.19	0.83	1.24
MA	0.83	0.17	1.12	0.13	0.05	4.85	2.01	0.58	1.41	1.42	1.30	0.99
PB	0.10	0.26	0.29	0.07	0.11	0.09	0.15	0.29	0.10	0.40	0.17	0.26
PE	0.58	2.55	0.56	0.66	0.49	3.85	0.49	1.09	0.94	1.67	0.63	1.64
PI	0.01	0.03	0.14	0.08	0.02	0.02	0.19	0.04	0.06	0.07	0.11	0.05
RN	0.11	0.20	0.39	0.29	0.17	0.10	0.34	0.14	0.14	0.20	0.26	0.18
SE	0.11	0.48	0.04	0.20	0.06	0.05	0.12	0.20	0.01	0.08	0.07	0.20

Southeast	63.83	54.01	62.13	76.99	71.12	49.98	49.94	74.21	53.57	60.26	57.73	66.72
ES	1.42	8.34	6.50	5.34	1.51	5.99	5.12	3.48	6.03	5.76	4.88	5.40
MG	7.90	6.90	10.78	3.21	7.04	4.92	16.76	8.15	15.02	3.42	12.75	5.61
RJ	3.98	7.76	4.12	10.95	8.11	3.93	2.38	8.42	4.38	10.36	4.05	9.27
SP	50.53	31.02	40.73	57.48	54.46	35.14	25.68	54.17	28.13	40.72	36.04	46.44
South	25.09	32.86	23.37	8.94	19.42	12.70	27.75	16.12	27.90	13.32	25.62	15.98
PR	7.00	11.63	4.69	4.10	5.03	5.64	12.93	9.01	11.16	5.28	8.95	7.02
SC	5.36	4.16	5.53	1.15	4.63	1.54	5.61	2.27	5.17	1.37	5.37	2.00
RS	12.73	17.07	13.16	3.70	9.77	5.52	9.21	4.83	11.58	6.67	11.30	6.97
Center-West	1.30	1.62	0.63	1.54	1.42	4.41	7.96	1.76	3.45	2.03	3.47	2.03
DF	0.00	0.13	0.01	0.99	0.00	0.18	0.04	1.17	0.05	0.70	0.03	0.89
GO	0.34	0.99	0.45	0.26	0.27	0.63	1.91	0.36	0.86	0.80	0.91	0.59
MT	0.21	0.18	0.13	0.07	0.73	0.39	4.87	0.12	1.96	0.31	1.94	0.22
MS	0.75	0.31	0.04	0.21	0.42	3.22	1.13	0.11	0.58	0.22	0.60	0.33
Total	100.00	100.00	100.00	100.00	100.00	100.00	100.00	100.00	100.00	100.00	100.00	100.00

Source: MDIC (elaborated by the author).

exported 53 percent to NAFTA; Paraíba exported 46 percent to the NAFTA, and Piauí exported 49 percent to the EU. Imports had a more even distribution, though.

NAFTA was also the main destination for exports from the Southeast region, although the EU and of the rest of the world received 23 and 24 of these, respectively. Exports were better distributed in the states of São Paulo and Rio de Janeiro while exports from Minas Gerais concentrated on specific destinations. The EU and the rest of the world were the major partners of this state (66 percent).

MERCOSUR was not the major trade partner of Southern states, despite their proximity. Only 13 percent of the total exported from the Southern region went there. Imports from MERCOSUR, however, amounted to 24 percent.

The Center-West region showed a highly concentrated distribution of exports. The EU's share of in the region's value of total exports reached 60 percent. The European Union was also the main destination of exports from the states of Goiás (56 percent), Mato Grosso (66), and Mato Grosso do Sul (50).

Table 13.2 shows a large regional concentration in the framework of Brazilian international trade during the study period. The Southeast and Southern regions accounted for 83 percent of exports and for 82 of imports. The share of the Southeast region in the total export and import values corresponded to over 50 percent for all five regions considered. The state of São Paulo accounted for 50 percent of exports to MERCOSUR and for 54 percent of exports to the rest of the FTAA. The Southeast and Southern regions accounted for 89 percent of total exports to MERCOSUR. The states of São Paulo and Rio Grande do Sul were the main exporters.

Spatial aspects of Brazilian trade policy

Regional (subnational) and sectoral impacts of the trade liberalization process have been constantly discussed in the regional context. Haddad and Hewings (2000) analyzed the short-term and long-term regional effects of trade liberalization policies, represented by simulations of tariff reductions, on the Brazilian economy. The B-MARIA model (Haddad, 1999) was used, yielding estimates for three Brazilian macroregions. A larger disaggregation of macroregional results was proposed at the state government level and implemented in Haddad and Azzoni (2001); estimates for 26 sectors are provided in 27 Brazilian states. By using the results to assess the changes to the center of gravity of sectoral production, one can note that the more open policies of the 1990s caused a geographic movement towards the Central and Southern regions, increasing regional disparities.

A study developed by Haddad et al. (2002) assessed the macroeconomic, sectoral, and regional impacts of three alternative strategies for trade integration of the Brazilian economy, namely: (a) implementation of the FTAA; (b) implementation of a free trade area with the EU; and (c) implementation of a general free trade area with all of Brazil's trade partners. The results, generated from a computable general equilibrium model combined with an interstate trade model, revealed a continuation of the concentration of economic activity in the Brazilian Southern and Southeastern regions.

Domingues (2002) assessed the short-term and long-term sectoral effects of trade liberalization in the context of an FTAA agreement. The results of simulation exercises show that positive effects of FTAA liberalization on the growth of Brazil's GDP and on the trade balance should be expected. However, the results suggest that the interaction of market forces in the Brazilian economy is beneficial for the state of São Paulo.[1]

Quite recently, two studies, developed by Haddad (2004) and Haddad and Perobelli (2005), have drawn some attention to the spatial effects of transportation costs in a context of larger trade liberalization in the Brazilian economy. In Haddad (2004), the main results indicate a "spatial trap distribution" polarized by the center of gravity of the Brazilian economy,

Figure 13.1   Major Brazilian ports
Source: Brazilian Ministry of Transport.

Table 13.3 Ports of entry for Brazilian state imports (percentage distribution)

												Destination															
		AC	AP	AM	PA	RO	RR	TO	AL	BA	CE	MA	PB	PE	PI	RN	SE	ES	MG	RJ	SP	PR	SC	RS	DF	GO	MT	MS
Port of entry	AC	0.4	0.0	0.0	0.0	0.0	0.0	0.0	0.0	0.0	0.0	0.0	0.0	0.0	0.0	0.0	0.0	0.0	0.0	0.0	0.0	0.0	0.0	0.0	0.0	0.0	0.0	0.0
	AP	0.0	33.9	0.0	0.0	0.0	0.0	0.0	0.0	0.0	0.0	0.0	0.0	0.0	0.0	0.0	0.0	0.0	0.0	0.0	0.0	0.1	0.0	0.0	0.0	0.0	0.0	0.0
	AM	4.3	0.9	99.5	0.0	38.9	4.0	0.0	0.0	0.0	0.0	0.0	0.0	0.0	0.0	0.0	0.0	0.0	0.0	1.1	0.0	0.0	0.0	0.0	0.0	0.0	4.3	0.0
	PA	0.0	28.2	0.0	68.0	0.0	0.0	0.0	0.0	0.0	0.0	0.2	0.0	0.0	0.0	0.0	0.0	0.0	0.0	0.0	0.0	0.0	0.0	0.0	0.0	0.0	0.0	0.0
	RO	0.0	0.0	0.0	0.0	0.5	0.0	0.0	0.0	0.0	0.0	0.0	0.0	0.0	0.0	0.0	0.0	0.0	0.0	0.0	0.0	0.0	0.0	0.0	0.0	0.0	0.0	0.0
	RR	0.0	0.0	0.0	0.1	0.0	93.7	0.0	0.0	0.0	0.0	0.0	0.0	0.0	0.0	0.0	0.0	0.0	0.0	0.0	0.0	0.0	0.0	0.0	0.0	0.0	0.0	0.1
	TO	0.0	0.0	0.0	0.0	0.0	0.0	0.0	0.0	0.0	0.0	0.0	0.0	0.0	0.0	0.0	0.0	0.0	0.0	0.0	0.0	0.0	0.0	0.0	0.0	0.0	0.0	0.0
	AL	0.0	0.0	0.0	0.0	0.0	0.0	0.0	84.5	0.0	0.0	0.0	0.0	0.2	0.0	0.0	0.4	0.0	0.0	0.0	0.0	0.1	0.0	0.0	0.0	0.0	0.0	0.0
	BA	0.0	0.0	0.0	0.0	0.0	0.0	0.0	8.6	91.6	0.1	0.0	0.4	5.8	10.0	1.4	31.0	0.2	0.0	0.0	0.2	0.0	0.0	0.0	0.4	0.0	0.0	0.0
	CE	0.0	0.0	0.0	0.1	0.0	0.0	4.2	0.5	0.2	98.1	0.5	22.4	0.1	56.7	4.5	0.0	0.0	0.0	0.0	0.0	0.0	0.0	0.0	0.5	0.0	0.0	0.0
	MA	0.0	0.0	0.0	25.6	0.0	0.0	0.0	0.0	0.0	0.0	98.9	0.0	0.4	7.2	0.0	0.0	0.0	0.2	0.0	0.0	0.0	0.0	0.0	0.0	0.0	0.0	0.0
	PB	0.0	0.0	0.0	0.0	0.0	0.0	0.0	0.0	0.6	0.0	0.0	25.9	0.6	2.6	0.3	0.0	0.0	0.0	0.0	0.0	0.0	0.0	0.0	0.0	0.0	0.0	0.0
	PE	0.0	0.0	0.0	0.1	0.0	0.0	0.0	2.3	0.0	0.1	0.1	33.2	88.0	0.9	16.0	19.9	0.0	0.2	0.0	0.0	0.0	0.0	0.0	0.0	0.0	0.0	0.0
	PI	0.0	0.0	0.0	0.0	0.0	0.0	0.0	0.0	5.2	0.0	0.0	0.0	0.0	0.0	0.0	0.0	0.0	0.0	0.0	0.0	0.0	0.0	0.0	0.0	0.0	0.0	0.0
	RN	0.0	0.0	0.0	0.0	0.0	0.0	0.0	0.0	0.0	0.0	0.0	0.0	0.0	0.0	62.9	0.0	0.0	0.0	0.0	0.0	0.0	0.0	0.0	0.0	0.0	0.0	0.0
	SE	0.0	0.0	0.0	0.0	0.0	0.0	0.0	0.0	0.0	0.0	0.0	0.0	0.0	0.0	0.0	21.4	0.0	0.0	0.0	0.0	0.0	0.0	0.0	0.0	0.0	0.0	0.0
	ES	0.0	0.0	0.0	1.0	0.0	0.0	0.0	0.0	0.2	0.0	0.1	0.1	0.2	0.1	0.0	0.7	83.2	28.4	0.2	0.0	0.0	0.0	0.0	0.1	16.3	1.0	0.0
	MG	5.9	0.0	0.0	0.0	0.0	1.3	0.4	0.1	0.3	0.0	0.0	0.0	0.0	0.0	0.0	0.0	0.1	6.9	0.1	0.1	0.1	0.1	0.0	0.2	0.2	1.1	0.0
	RJ	0.0	0.8	0.2	1.5	23.0	0.0	2.6	0.4	0.0	0.0	0.0	1.4	0.1	0.7	2.4	4.2	5.5	32.0	91.0	0.8	0.4	0.6	0.1	16.5	2.8	0.0	0.3
	SP	29.4	35.4	0.2	2.5	2.7	1.1	84.0	2.2	0.0	0.7	0.0	12.5	3.5	13.9	10.8	15.5	8.9	25.4	5.1	91.8	6.7	6.9	3.5	35.7	58.2	20.6	9.1
	PR	60.0	0.0	0.0	0.0	19.6	0.0	6.4	0.6	0.0	0.1	0.0	1.6	0.1	0.1	0.7	6.0	1.0	1.5	0.6	1.5	75.9	17.5	0.5	2.1	17.4	42.1	5.3
	SC	0.0	0.0	0.0	0.0	0.0	0.0	0.0	0.0	0.0	0.0	0.0	0.0	0.1	0.0	0.0	0.0	0.5	0.8	0.1	0.4	12.3	63.2	1.2	0.3	1.1	4.7	0.4
	RS	0.0	0.8	0.0	1.1	14.4	0.0	2.4	0.9	0.0	0.9	0.0	2.4	0.8	4.7	1.0	0.7	0.6	4.6	1.6	5.0	3.7	11.5	94.6	0.3	3.7	5.5	9.6
	DF	0.0	0.0	0.0	0.0	0.0	0.0	0.0	0.0	0.0	0.0	0.0	0.0	0.0	0.0	0.0	0.0	0.2	0.0	0.0	0.0	0.0	0.0	0.0	43.8	0.1	0.0	0.0
	GO	0.0	0.0	0.0	0.0	0.0	0.0	0.0	0.0	0.9	0.0	0.0	0.0	0.0	0.0	0.0	0.0	0.0	0.0	0.0	0.0	0.0	0.0	0.0	0.0	0.0	0.0	0.0
	MT	0.0	0.0	0.0	0.0	0.2	0.0	0.0	0.0	0.9	0.0	0.0	0.0	0.0	0.0	0.0	0.0	0.0	0.0	0.0	0.0	0.0	0.0	0.0	0.0	0.0	20.5	0.0
	MS	0.0	0.0	0.0	0.0	0.7	0.0	0.0	0.0	0.1	0.0	0.0	0.0	0.0	3.1	0.0	0.0	0.0	0.0	0.0	0.1	0.7	0.3	0.0	0.0	0.1	0.0	75.2
	Total	100.0	100.0	100.0	100.0	100.0	100.0	100.0	100.0	100.0	100.0	100.0	100.0	100.0	100.0	100.0	100.0	100.0	100.0	100.0	100.0	100.0	100.0	100.0	100.0	100.0	100.0	100.0

Table 13.4 Ports of exit for Brazilian state exports (percentage distribution)

		Place of production																									
		AC	AP	AM	PA	RO	RR	TO	AL	BA	CE	MA	PB	PE	PI	RN	SE	ES	MG	RJ	SP	PR	SC	RS	DF	GO	MT	MS
Port of exit	AC	0.0	0.0	0.1	0.0	0.0	8.0	0.0	0.0	0.0	0.0	0.0	0.0	0.0	0.0	0.0	0.0	0.0	0.0	0.0	0.0	0.0	0.0	0.0	0.0	0.0	0.0	0.0
	AP	0.0	91.5	0.0	0.0	0.0	0.0	0.0	0.0	0.0	0.0	0.0	0.0	0.0	0.0	0.0	0.0	0.0	0.0	0.0	0.0	0.0	0.0	0.0	0.0	0.0	0.0	0.0
	AM	5.7	0.0	72.5	0.0	1.2	0.0	0.0	0.0	0.0	0.0	0.0	0.0	0.0	0.0	0.0	0.0	0.0	0.0	0.0	1.9	0.0	0.0	0.0	0.0	0.0	10.1	0.0
	PA	7.6	6.3	0.2	65.9	1.9	0.0	0.0	0.0	0.0	0.1	1.9	0.0	0.0	0.0	0.0	0.0	0.0	0.0	0.1	4.5	0.0	0.0	0.0	0.0	0.0	1.2	0.0
	RO	0.0	0.0	0.1	0.0	0.7	0.0	0.0	0.0	0.0	0.1	0.0	0.0	0.0	0.0	0.0	0.0	0.0	0.0	0.0	0.0	0.0	0.0	0.0	0.0	0.0	0.1	0.5
	RR	0.0	0.0	2.0	0.0	0.4	81.3	0.0	0.0	0.0	0.0	0.0	0.0	0.0	0.0	0.0	0.0	0.0	0.0	0.0	0.0	0.0	0.0	0.0	0.0	0.0	0.0	0.0
	TO	0.0	0.0	0.0	0.0	0.0	0.0	0.0	0.0	0.0	0.0	0.0	0.0	0.0	0.0	0.0	0.0	0.0	0.0	0.0	0.0	0.0	0.0	0.0	0.0	0.0	0.0	0.0
	AL	0.0	0.0	0.0	0.0	0.0	0.0	0.0	97.9	0.0	0.0	0.0	0.0	0.0	0.0	0.0	0.0	0.0	0.0	0.0	0.0	0.0	0.0	0.0	0.0	0.0	0.0	0.0
	BA	0.0	0.0	2.4	0.1	0.0	0.0	0.5	1.3	83.1	0.2	0.0	1.6	12.0	0.8	0.4	31.0	0.2	0.1	0.5	0.1	0.0	0.0	0.0	0.0	0.0	0.0	0.0
	CE	0.0	0.4	0.1	0.2	0.0	0.3	0.0	0.2	0.5	86.9	0.7	31.7	10.0	66.9	44.5	0.0	0.0	0.0	0.1	0.0	0.0	0.0	0.0	0.0	0.0	0.0	0.0
	MA	0.0	0.0	0.0	32.8	0.0	0.0	87.9	0.0	0.0	0.0	96.7	0.0	0.0	23.4	0.0	0.0	0.0	0.0	0.1	0.0	0.0	0.0	0.0	0.0	0.0	0.0	0.0
	PB	0.0	0.0	0.0	0.0	0.0	0.0	0.0	0.0	0.4	0.0	0.0	13.4	1.2	0.9	1.3	0.0	0.0	0.0	0.0	0.0	0.0	0.0	0.0	0.0	0.0	0.0	0.0
	PE	0.0	0.0	0.0	0.0	0.0	0.0	0.0	0.4	0.4	1.0	0.0	36.0	56.8	0.0	7.0	0.1	0.0	0.0	0.2	0.5	0.0	0.0	0.0	0.0	0.0	0.0	0.0
	PI	0.0	0.0	0.0	0.0	0.0	0.0	0.0	0.0	0.0	0.0	0.0	0.0	0.0	0.0	0.0	0.0	0.0	0.0	0.0	0.0	0.0	0.0	0.0	0.0	0.0	0.0	0.0
	RN	0.0	0.0	0.0	0.0	0.0	0.0	0.0	0.0	0.1	0.6	0.0	1.0	1.2	0.0	41.7	0.0	0.0	0.0	0.1	0.1	0.0	0.0	0.0	0.0	0.0	0.0	0.0
	SE	0.0	0.0	0.0	0.0	0.0	0.0	0.0	0.0	0.0	0.0	0.0	0.0	0.0	0.0	0.0	48.4	0.0	0.0	0.0	0.0	0.0	0.0	0.0	0.0	0.0	0.0	0.0
	ES	0.0	0.0	0.0	0.1	1.8	0.0	0.0	0.0	7.2	0.2	0.0	0.2	0.0	0.0	0.0	0.0	96.9	38.2	0.6	0.0	0.1	0.0	0.0	53.7	25.3	8.8	0.6
	MG	0.0	0.0	0.0	0.0	0.0	0.0	0.0	0.0	0.0	0.0	0.0	0.0	0.0	0.0	0.0	0.0	0.0	0.7	0.0	0.0	0.0	0.0	0.0	0.1	0.0	0.0	0.0
	RJ	0.8	1.6	1.0	0.0	0.5	0.2	0.1	0.0	1.4	0.7	0.3	0.4	1.4	6.2	0.6	1.7	1.4	31.1	74.4	1.2	0.5	0.1	1.1	9.3	0.3	0.0	0.0
	SP	2.3	0.1	20.1	0.5	16.3	2.6	8.0	0.1	3.8	6.5	0.3	14.3	13.2	1.8	3.5	9.0	0.7	25.4	20.6	79.2	7.1	4.2	7.1	29.4	58.9	40.9	26.3
	PR	35.3	0.1	0.3	0.3	64.1	7.7	3.5	0.0	0.4	1.3	0.0	0.2	1.4	0.0	0.1	3.2	0.2	1.4	0.5	3.0	73.5	9.3	2.4	1.3	6.4	23.2	29.9
	SC	29.0	0.0	0.0	0.0	9.9	0.0	0.0	0.0	0.0	0.0	0.0	0.0	0.0	0.0	0.5	0.0	0.0	0.6	0.3	1.3	14.6	80.2	6.7	4.3	8.0	13.9	27.8
	RS	19.2	0.0	1.0	0.1	3.3	0.0	0.0	0.0	2.6	1.8	0.1	0.9	2.6	0.0	0.1	5.5	0.5	2.1	2.0	7.1	4.0	5.7	82.0	1.0	0.9	0.5	0.2
	DF	0.0	0.0	0.0	0.0	0.0	0.0	0.0	0.0	0.0	0.0	0.0	0.0	0.0	0.0	0.0	0.0	0.0	0.0	0.0	0.1	0.0	0.0	0.0	0.9	0.0	0.0	0.0
	GO	0.0	0.0	0.0	0.0	0.0	0.0	0.0	0.0	0.0	0.0	0.0	0.0	0.0	0.0	0.0	0.0	0.0	0.0	0.0	0.0	0.0	0.0	0.0	0.0	0.0	0.0	0.0
	MT	0.0	0.0	0.1	0.0	0.0	0.0	0.0	0.0	0.1	0.2	0.0	0.0	0.0	0.0	0.0	0.4	0.0	0.0	0.0	0.2	0.0	0.0	0.1	0.0	0.0	0.4	0.0
	MS	0.0	0.0	0.2	0.0	0.0	0.0	0.0	0.0	0.1	0.5	0.0	0.4	0.1	0.0	0.1	0.7	0.0	0.3	0.2	0.6	0.3	0.4	0.5	0.0	0.2	0.9	14.5
	Total	100.0	100.0	100.0	100.0	100.0	100.0	100.0	100.0	100.0	100.0	100.0	100.0	100.0	100.0	100.0	100.0	100.0	100.0	100.0	100.0	100.0	100.0	100.0	100.0	100.0	100.0	100.0

strengthening the results of previously mentioned studies. In other words, the central position of the state of São Paulo and its surroundings still has a strong influence on spatial processes in the Brazilian economy. In the short run, this influence can be noticed by the role of São Paulo's state economy as the key convergence point of accessibility that optimizes the welfare and efficiency of peripheral economies. Regional welfare gains, as well as regional efficiency gains, are strongly associated with easier access to Southeastern markets, especially São Paulo; furthermore, in terms of system efficiency, the reduction of transaction costs between the Southeastern and Southern states, which offers the possibility of exploring increasing returns of scale, turns out to be the major trigger of Brazil's growth. In the long run, relocation effects, combined with the expansion of dynamic regional markets, seem to strengthen the concentration of economic activities.

Haddad and Perobelli (2005) explicitly introduced transportation costs between the ports of entry and exit of international flows and the consumption and production sites in the Brazilian territory. This paper assessed the regional impact of the elimination of barriers to international trade in the context of an integrated interstate system. More specifically, the authors analyzed the spatial hindrances that have a negative effect on the domestic transmission of trade liberalization benefits, for instance, high transportation costs from remote regions. In 2003, over 80 percent of the total international trade flows occurred via the sea. Based on the location of ports (Figure 13.1), the authors showed that coastal regions have a geographic advantage that allows larger gains associated with a wider integration between Brazil and other countries. The spatial distribution of the ports of entry to state imports (see Table 13.3) and of the ports of exit to state exports (Table 13.4) shows that some state economies largely depend on ports outside their borders. Thus, for remote regions, that is, those with difficult access to international markets, the transportation system is of paramount importance to the assessment of relative regional performance associated with the trade liberalization process.

These results – obtained in these and other studies – suggest the existence of a "spatial trap distribution" in the Brazilian economy that is reinforced by the existing transportation system and regional production specialization combined with the spatial production interdependence arising from it. Thus, in a wider context of trade liberalization, the traditionally highly developed regions have a privileged starting point.

Note on the productive integration of the Brazilian industry and the spatial interdependence of its exports

In the case of exports, there seems to be some agreement that their importance is not restricted only to the positive effects they can bring to the generation of trade surplus, or to the creation of jobs and income. By encouraging national production, exports create direct jobs (and income) in the export sectors, and indirect jobs as a result of the existing links in the production chain. In addition, the net foreign currency inflow results in the so-called income effect, that is, the effect on production and jobs arising from consumption by economic agents whose income is generated by the export activity.

The increase in job openings and in income resulting from exports is remarkable, but this relationship is not exhaustively dealt with in this quantitative dimension. To take part in the international market and to export goods and services, companies should be prepared to face fiercer competition, and should therefore increase their productivity, reduce their production costs, and increase their efficiency. Zockun (2002), analyzing data on São Paulo's state economy, found that after the main variables are controlled for, exporting companies tend to generate more added value, to pay better salaries, and to have a productivity differential 72 percent higher than nonexporting companies.

In this case, one may infer that exports affect the labor market not only in terms of job openings, but also because they are associated with workforce qualification, there is a clearly defined relationship with productivity levels. In other words, the export-job opening dyad has a clear qualitative dimension. On the one hand, this is because exporting companies need qualified personnel in order to increase their productivity and compete in the global economy; on the other hand, it is because they end up having a remarkable effect on the labor market as their demand tends to concentrate on better educated workers, that is, supposedly those who are better qualified.

Therefore, incentives to export translate not only into the creation of direct and indirect jobs through an increase in production along the whole production chain, but also into its effects on the relative demand for the workforce, based on qualification levels.[2] In this regard, since exporting companies use very modern technologies, they tend to have better educated workers. Also, the *geographic concentration* of these exporting companies has some impact on the profile of the workforce.

In a recent study assessing the regional impacts of state exports on the creation of jobs, Chahad et al. (2004) demonstrated that the qualified workforce was concentrated in Southern and Southeastern Brazilian states. With this qualified workforce concentrated in these regions, it is possible to find elements for empirical evidence for the Heckscher-Ohlin theorem in the Brazilian subnational space, especially with regard to the theoretical aspects associated with the characteristics expected from state exports.[3]

One of the key elements of studies that assess industrial competitiveness associated with the Brazilian international trade flows concerns the spatial interaction across regional production frameworks: economic changes in a given region have possible effects on other regions. This finding is extremely important to the assessment of the effects of export-encouraging policies on the regions of a country. Leakages of regional income/output, from spatially well-defined initial shocks, have been a major concern to governors: how is it possible to guarantee that tax/financial efforts required to stimulate productive units within the borders of a given Brazilian state will result in income and jobs for its own inhabitants?

Figure 13.2 shows the regional distribution of industrial multipliers for each Brazilian state. The multipliers were calculated using the interstate input/output matrix for the year 1996, developed by FIPE (Institute of Economic Research Foundation). The graph shows the distribution of net effects of the industrial multiplier of Brazilian states into two economic spaces, the state itself (intraregional) and the rest of Brazil (interregional).

These results indicate the importance of interregional leakages in the Brazilian economy, especially to the Northern and Northeastern states. In these cases, on average, over 50 percent of the net multiplier effect impacts on other Brazilian states. In the better developed Southeastern states, these leakages are lower than 25 percent. The states of Ceará and São Paulo are good examples of this phenomenon. In the state of São Paulo, 88 percent of the (net) multiplier effect is absorbed by the state itself; whereas in Ceará, only 44 percent is. State interdependence, in case of Brazilian industry, is quite remarkable. Characterized by a polarization between the Central and Southern regions, this spatial configuration shows a large production dependence of the states located in peripheral regions.

In the specific case of state exports, this situation persists. The study by Chahad et al. (2004) revealed employment multipliers (according to six qualification levels) of standard export units of each Brazilian state and, by using decomposition techniques, showed the level of intraregional and interregional job creation. The analysis of regional impacts on the job

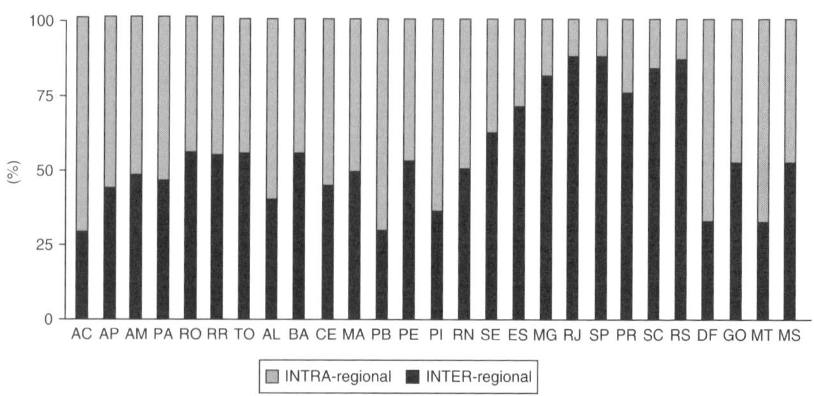

Figure 13.2   Distribution of industrial multipliers, Brazil 1996

Source: Domingues et al. (2001).

creation resulting from state exports revealed some concentration of qualified workforce in Southern and Southeastern states. The most developed states benefit from Brazilian exports, meeting, either directly or indirectly, the demand for better qualified workers. In short, one may say that the state of Ceará exports a qualified workforce from São Paulo, and the state of São Paulo exports an unskilled workforce from Ceará.

Final remarks

All the discussion above focused on the role of trade as a growth factor at the regional level. Several theories advocate the positive view that links trade with economic development, highlighting the direct gains from international specialization, in addition to further impacts on the development of a country through a series of multiplier effects absorbed by the domestic economy (Meier, 1989). From the subnational space point of view, the principles of the export base theory and *pôles de croissance* (Perroux, 1955) underpin several regional development models.

Recently, however, given the great importance of issues related to the globalization process and to the implicit assumption that the future of a region is strictly connected to its capacity to compete in external markets, international trade has commanded attention from all regional analysts. In the Brazilian case, as shown, this importance is readily perceived in only some Brazilian states. Would the other states be challenged with an obsolete trade framework, based on the export of poor-quality products targeted at specific markets? Would the regional concentration of international trade flows be irreversible, since liberalization indicates that this phenomenon has been intensified?

In our opinion, the answer to these questions is no. First, we should consider the current tendency toward expansion of trade agreements involving Brazil (aimed at the gradual reduction of trade restrictions, with increasingly wider geographic areas) as a general equilibrium phenomenon that is complex and dynamic, and whose effects extrapolate into the long-term future. The regional integration process involves issues that link growth with technology, learning, externalities, political economy, and political agreements (Devlin and French-Davis, 1997), the consequences of whichon the subnational space can be redefined by public policies. According to the current stage of development of the Brazilian economy, market forces tend to have economic activity focused on the Central and Southern regions, but the government can still intervene in order to ease the situation. It is necessary however to set regional planning guidelines for the efficient use of the potential of peripheral regions and for the promotion of development and consolidation of dynamic comparative/competitive advantages in all regions.

Second, interstate trade plays a key role in state economies. Interregional interactions should be taken into account in order better to understand how regional economies are affected, both in international and domestic markets, since the performance of better developed regions has a pivotal role in smaller economies.

The usual characterization of spatial interaction, which considers the region *versus* the rest of the world, does not take into account two of its major properties for the elucidation of an interregional system: feedbacks and hierarchy. Interstate trade can potentially trigger the dissemination of feedback effects, which, quantitatively, can be larger than the effects produced by international trade.However, the impact of feedback effects will be partly determined by the hierarchical structure of the regional economic system. In the Brazilian case, for instance, the impacts of the interstate trade

Table 13.5   Interstate and international export coefficients: Brazilian states, 1997

	Interstate exports/ GDP (A) (%)	International exports/ GDP (B) (%)
Acre	25.7	0.1
Alagoas	30.8	4.6
Amapá	5.3	3.4
Amazonas	87.7	1.9
Bahia	30.5	4.4
Ceará	28.9	2.1
Distrito Federal	10.4	0.0
Espírito Santo	90.2	5.6
Goiás	52.6	2.3
Maranhão	13.1	8.7
Mato Grosso	76.5	7.9
Mato Gr. Sul	41.6	2.6
Minas Gerais	57.5	7.6
Pará	14.5	14.0
Paraíba	27.5	0.9
Paraná	59.1	7.7
Pernambuco	31.2	1.1
Piauí	13.5	1.2
Rio Gr. Norte	23.8	1.4
Rio Gr. Sul	36.1	7.6
Rio de Janeiro	32.3	1.6
Rondônia	17.6	1.0
Roraima	13.8	0.3
Santa Catarina	61.7	7.9
São Paulo	49.0	5.4
Sergipe	39.1	0.6
Tocantins	20.5	0.6

Sources: (A) Gross data from Confaz and IBGE; (B) MDIC and IBGE (elaborated by the author).

of São Paulo on the Brazilian economy are expected to be different from the impacts produced by other states.

Table 13.5 shows some important characteristics of the Brazilian regional system. Interstate and international export coefficients are provided for all Brazilian states. Notably, interstate exports for all states outnumber, to a greater or lesser extent, international exports. In general, interstate flows have a larger relative importance to less developed states.[4] These estimates reveal the importance of interstate trade flows to state economies. Nevertheless, it is necessary to investigate further thetrade flows across Brazilian states in order to make generalizations about the types of trade involved, the change in their composition over time as Brazilian economy develops, and the implications of these structural differences for the design and implementation of development policies.[5]

Thus, the conclusion is that the future of many Brazilian regions might not be closely related to their performance in international markets, but rather to their relationship with other domestic markets. Once again, there is room for public intervention through actions targeting the modernization of Brazil's transportation network, establishing a more efficient interaction between producers and consumer markets, thus maximizing the effects of Brazilian trade policy strategies. Thus, mechanisms for the dissemination of feedback effects would be created, and the competitive edge of Brazilian products in the international market would be increased.

Notes

The original ideas behind this paper are outlined in E.A. Haddad, and F.S. Perobelli, (2005) "Integração Regional e Padrão de Comércio dos Estados Brasileiros," in Anita Kon (org.), *Unidade e Fragmentação: A questão regional no Brasil*, Editora Perspectiva; E.A. Haddad, E.P. Domingues, and F.S. Perobelli (2002) "Regional Effects of Economic Integration: The case of Brazil," *Journal of Policy Modeling*, 24; and E. Haddad, (2004) "Retornos Crescentes, Custos de Transporte e Crescimento Regional," FEA/USP, Postdoctoral (Habilitation) dissertation. I am also grateful to Geoffrey J.D. Hewings for stimulating our discussions on this topic in recent years.

1. The simulations were performed according to the context of two regions: São Paulo and rest of Brazil.
2. See Domingues et al. (2001) for a spatially aggregate impact analysis.
3. When measuring the effect related to workforce qualification on state exports, one finds an important element in characterizing international trade flows from Brazilian states, which sheds some light upon the interpretation of such trade model in the subnational space context.
4. Exceptions include the states of Amapá, Maranhão, and Pará, whose transportation and communications systems are predominantly destined to the outflow of mineral exports.
5. It should be noticed that that some of the interstate flows may be generated by international exports, as revealed in Hewings and Paar (2008).

References

Bowen, H.P., A. Hollander, and J.M. Viaene (1998) *Applied International Trade Analysis*, Ann Arbor: The University of Michigan Press.

Chahad, J.P.Z., A.E. Comune, and E.A. Haddad (2004) "Interdependência Espacial das Exportações Brasileiras: Repercussões sobre o Mercado de Trabalho," *Pesquisa e Planejamento Econômico*, 31, 93–122.

Devlin, R., and R. French-Davis (1997) "Towards an Evaluation of Regional Integration in Latin America in the 1990's," Occasional Paper #1, Inter-American Development Bank, Integration, Trade and Hemispheric Issues Division, Washington, D.C.

Domingues, E.P. (2002) "Dimensão Regional e Setorial da Integração Brasileira na Área de Livre Comércio das Américas," Tese de Doutorado, São Paulo: FEA/USP.

Domingues, E.P., F.L.L. Leon, and E.A. Haddad (2001) "Impactos das Exportações sobre a Estrutura Setorial e de Qualificação do Emprego no Brasil," *Economia*, 2 (1), 259–290.

Haddad, E.A. (1999) *Regional Inequality and Structural Changes: Lessons from the Brazilian Experience*, Aldershot: Ashgate.

Haddad, E.A. (2004) "Retornos Crescentes, Custos de Transporte e Crescimento Regional," Tese de Livre Docência, São Paulo: FEA/USP.

Haddad, E.A., and C.R. Azzoni (2001) "Trade Liberalization and Location: Geographical Shifts in the Brazilian Economic Structure," in J.J.M. Guilhoto and G.J.D. Hewings (eds.) *Structure and Structural Change in the Brazilian Economy*, Aldershot: Ashgate.

Haddad, E.A., E.P. Domingues, and F.S. Perobelli (2002) "Regional Effects of Economic Integration: The Case of Brazil," *Journal of Policy Modeling*, 24, 453–482.

Haddad, E.A., and G.J.D. Hewings (2000) "Trade and Regional Development: International and Interregional Competitiveness in Brazil," in B. Johansen and R. Stough (eds.) *Theories of Regional Development: Lessons for Policies of Regional Economic Renewal*, Heidelberg: Springer-Verlag.

Haddad, E.A., and F.S. Perobelli (2005) "Trade Liberalization and Regional Inequality: Do Transportation Costs Impose a Spatial Poverty Trap?" São Paulo, FEA/USP: mimeo.

Hewings, G.J.D., and J.B. Parr (2008) "The Changing Structure of Trade and Interdependence in a Mature Economy: The US Midwest," in P. McCann (ed.) *Technological Change and Mature Industrial Regions: Firms, Knowledge, and Policy*, Cheltenham: Edward Elgar.

Meier, G.M. (1989) *Leading Issues in Economic Development*, 5th ed., Oxford: Oxford University Press.

Perobelli, F.S. (2004) "Análise das Interações Econômicas entre os Estados Brasileiros," Tese de Doutorado, São Paulo: FEA/USP.

Perroux, F. (1955) "Note sur la Notion de Pôle de Croissance," *Economie Appliquée*, 8, 307–320.

Zockun, M.H. (2002) "Diferenciais de Produtividade na Indústria," in J.P. Chahad and R. Fernandes (eds.), *O Mercado de Trabalho no Brasil: políticas, resultados e desafios*, São Paulo: MTE/FIPE/Dept. de Economia FEA/USP.

14
Regional and Demographic Determinants of Poverty in Brazil

Andre P. Souza, Carlos R. Azzoni, and Veridiana A. Nogueira

Introduction

Why are some areas poor? One possible reason could be that they exhibit high concentrations of households with the "wrong" characteristics, such as a low level of education, larger families, etc. If households were free to migrate, any social policy aimed at improving educational levels in these areas, for example, would end up stimulating migration. As a result, the inequality observed after the adjustment process would indicate a scenario of no geographical differences in living standards (income, living conditions, etc.). It would be completely explained by the different sets of personal characteristics across regions. In this case, there would be no place for targeting a specific region in the implementation of policy measures: there would be no need for "regional" policies. On the other hand, moving can be costly and risky for poor people, because of transportation costs and other personal (emotional, noneconomic) factors. As Ravallion (1993) points out, it could be difficult for policymakers to target household characteristics, indicating that geographic targeting could be needed, even after factoring in migration. Park et al. (2002) evaluated the effectiveness of the regional targeting of a large-scale, Chinese poverty alleviation program, and found out that political factors affected targeting and that leakage grew as a result of increased coverage. Bird and Shepherd (2003) tested social and political exclusion variables and typical geographical variables in explaining rural poverty in Zimbabwe, and showed that proximity to urban areas is an important factor.

This discussion points out the importance of determining whether or not observed regional inequality results completely from differences in mobile, nongeographic characteristics, such as education, family size, etc. or if, even after controlling for these variables, a "regional" residual would still be present. Brazil is a country with huge and persistent regional inequalities, as described in Azzoni (2001), Baer (2001), and Haddad (1999) and is thus an interesting case to study the subject. Azzoni and Servo (2002) have shown

"

that metropolitan differentials in wage income are important, even after controlling for personal and sectoral characteristics of households, plus cost-of-living differences, with similar results for the variables of interest over time (measured in years). That study was limited in the sense that only households from the 11 official metropolitan areas were compared. In this chapter, we cover all 27 of Brazil's states, including households in urban (metropolitan and nonmetropolitan) and rural areas. In this study we use information from the Population Census of 2000, while Azzoni and Servo (2002) had to rely on household surveys, since the census was not available at the time.

We applied different decomposition techniques in assessing the role of demographic and geographical variables in explaining income inequality in Brazil, following Ravallion and Wodon (1999). Since we have a larger number of observations, we were able to estimate regressions for each state, improving on the results of both studies. The next section presents the database and provides some information on the regional distribution of poverty in Brazil. In the third section, we regress the log of real income values in the states against personal characteristics and regional dummies, allowing for a first statement of the importance of regional factors. A step forward in the decomposition of the factors influencing regional inequality is presented in the following section, in which both the influence of characteristics and of returns to characteristics is determined. Thereafter, we develop geographic and concentration profiles, using national parameter estimates to predict the income of households in different states. Finally, some conclusions from the study are offered.

Database

The incidence of poverty in different regions can be measured in many different ways, as the height-to-age ratio, weight, infant mortality, health conditions, access to public utilities, per capita income, etc. Following Ravallion (1993), we use the log of the "welfare ratio" (W) to measure the standard of living in different states in Brazil. This is defined as nominal per capita income deflated by a state-specific poverty line, incorporating cost-of-living differences. It is assumed that a vector of household characteristics X, with parameters that vary geographically, defines this welfare ratio. We use microdata from the 2000 population census, considering 3,918,674 urban, and 1,141,359 rural, households across Brazil's 27 states. For each household, we calculate average per capita income from all sources. As for household characteristics, we use: number of children (age < 5), number of adolescents (age 5–18), number of adults (age 18–65), number of elderly people (age > 65), years of schooling, maximum number of years of education in the household, gender, age, race, marital status, type of occupation (managers, directors; arts and sciences; middle-level occupations; administrative services;

agricultural works; manufacturing; maintenance; military; others), and age and years of schooling of the head of household's partner.

Poverty line values were taken from Rocha (1997), and translated into July 2000 monetary figures using an adequate price index. Since Rocha does not provide estimates for some rural areas, especially in the North region, we have made some adaptations based on her work. The figures for poverty lines consider different urban and rural cost-of-living in the states, therefore they are net of regional differences at those levels. The average values for income are R\$ 402.71 and R\$ 140.89,[1] for urban and rural areas, respectively, giving a ratio of 2.86. After discounting for the cost-of-living, the ratio drops to 1.26, since the cost-of-living in rural areas is much lower than in urban areas. Table 14.1 presents the percentage of households below the poverty

Table 14.1 Proportion of households under poverty and indigence lines (%)

	Proportion of indigent			Proportion of poor		
State	Urban	Rural	Total	Urban	Rural	Total
Brazil	8.63	15.72	10.23	28.47	36.38	30.25
Rondônia	7.47	10.92	8.93	21.43	20.50	21.04
Acre	12.26	19.15	14.74	30.15	34.22	31.62
Amazonas	16.68	32.80	20.68	35.89	53.54	40.27
Roraima	9.19	28.69	14.88	23.67	40.10	28.47
Pará	14.31	17.42	15.38	37.00	35.96	36.65
Amapá	14.72	18.34	15.22	33.13	32.26	33.02
Tocantis	15.73	21.79	17.62	37.42	34.98	36.65
Maranhão	17.77	30.63	23.26	45.13	60.62	51.74
Piauí	17.33	28.78	22.10	48.62	56.48	51.89
Ceará	16.15	29.15	20.23	45.70	56.24	49.01
Rio Grande do Norte	11.75	23.83	15.45	31.70	48.17	36.75
Paraíba	15.28	23.34	18.00	44.88	50.53	46.78
Pernambuco	16.87	23.88	18.72	47.20	51.51	48.34
Alagoas	12.39	28.57	17.91	29.98	58.84	39.82
Sergipe	14.09	20.06	16.12	41.75	50.15	44.60
Bahia	16.37	21.64	18.26	46.53	48.91	47.39
Minas Gerais	5.56	9.41	6.48	25.73	27.18	26.08
Espírito Santo	5.80	4.62	5.51	26.78	20.59	25.26
Rio de Janeiro	8.65	5.23	8.47	27.68	26.69	27.63
São Paulo	5.85	5.66	5.83	21.20	17.95	20.89
Paraná	5.29	9.08	6.20	20.18	26.78	21.77
Santa Catarina	2.89	4.98	3.50	10.02	15.38	11.59
Rio Grande do Sul	4.62	5.80	4.91	14.40	17.91	15.26
Mato Grosso do Sul	5.49	6.60	5.72	32.99	26.95	31.71
Mato Grosso	5.40	10.87	6.75	30.88	30.30	30.74
Goiás	5.77	7.07	6.00	36.53	26.77	34.77
Distrito Federal	5.15	3.96	5.07	27.03	17.31	26.37

line in each state; it also shows the number of households under the indigence line (also taken from Rocha, 1997). For the country as a whole, 30.2 percent of households can be considered poor, with 10.2 percent indigent, but the proportion of poor households varies significantly across states: it is almost 52 percent in the poor Northeastern states of Maranhão and Piauí, and only 12 in the Southern state of Santa Catarina.

Regression results

Following Ravallion and Wodon (1999), our estimated regressions correlate the log of the welfare ratio (W) to characteristics of the households in general. We linearly regress *log*W on a vector of nongeographic variables (X) and a vector of state fixed effects (D). We estimate equations of the form:

$$\log W_i = \alpha + \beta X_i + \delta D_i + \varepsilon_i \qquad \forall i = 1,...,27 \tag{14.1}$$

The error terms ε are assumed to be independently distributed, with a zero mean. Separate equations are estimated for rural and urban households.[2]

The results are shown in Table 14.2. As the basis for comparison for the dummy variables, we use unemployed, black, married women in the state of São Paulo. Thus, the regression coefficients must be interpreted as income gains/losses relative to this reference. The intercept indicates that such urban households had an average income of only 37 percent[3] of the poverty line, and similar rural households had only 71 percent of the poverty line. The coefficients for the nongeographic variables are statistically significant and presented the expected signs: per capita household income declines with number of children, adolescents, and elderly people in the household (squared terms are also included); men make more money than women; age and age squared indicate the typical life cycle profile; white people earn more than people of other races; education is positively associated with income, etc.[4]

Comparing urban and rural households, the coefficients are quite different in general. For example, the number of adults is not as important a negative factor for rural households (the coefficient is almost half that of the urban equation); the number of elderly is positive for rural households, probably indicating the importance of pension payments for people of that age in the rural setting.[5] As for the state dummies, they are all significant, indicating that, controlling for all nongeographic characteristics included in the X vector, there are significant differences in the welfare ratio across states. This is a first indicator that geography does matter.

Comparing areas

We turn now to the analysis of the determinants of differences between urban and rural households. Writing separate equations for urban and rural

Table 14.2 Regression of real income on characteristics and geographical variables (Dependent variable = Log W)

	Urban		Rural	
	Coefficient	Standard deviation	Coefficient	Standard deviation
Intercept	−1.0006	0.0051	−0.3363	0.0093
State Dummies				
Rondônia	0.3450	0.0046	0.4930	0.0060
Acre	0.2252	0.0071	0.2977	0.0100
Amazonas	0.1655	0.0034	0.1620	0.0065
Roraima	0.3858	0.0087	0.2534	0.0141
Pará	0.0614	0.0025	0.2188	0.0041
Amapá	0.2894	0.0072	0.2670	0.0188
Tocantis	0.0324	0.0042	0.1122	0.0068
Maranhão	−0.2760	0.0029	−0.4475	0.0039
Piauí	−0.2268	0.0032	−0.4891	0.0046
Ceará	−0.1881	0.0021	−0.4649	0.0039
Rio Grande do Norte	−0.2183	0.0036	−0.2979	0.0050
Paraíba	−0.1929	0.0027	−0.4101	0.0045
Pernambuco	−0.2972	0.0019	−0.3186	0.0039
Alagoas	−0.1596	0.0044	−0.3214	0.0052
Sergipe	−0.0829	0.0028	−0.3156	0.0046
Bahia	−0.2339	0.0017	−0.2631	0.0032
Minas Gerais	0.0542	0.0013	0.0350	0.0030
Espírito Santo	−0.0111	0.0027	0.1253	0.0053
Rio de Janeiro	−0.1997	0.0013	−0.2000	0.0054
Paraná	0.0777	0.0016	−0.0660	0.0035
Santa Catarina	0.2917	0.0022	0.1696	0.0039
Rio Grande do Sul	0.2108	0.0015	0.0102	0.0034
Mato Grosso do Sul	−0.1422	0.0032	−0.0749	0.0065
Mato Grosso	−0.0377	0.0040	−0.0192	0.0075
Goiás	−0.2213	0.0020	−0.1059	0.0047
Distrito Federal	−0.0893	0.0033	0.1637	0.0124
Household Characteristics				
Number of children under 5	−0.3862	0.0013	−0.3184	0.0021
Number of childern under 5 squared	0.0482	0.0005	0.0377	0.0007
Number of adolescents	−0.3499	0.0007	−0.3017	0.0011
Number of adolescents squared	0.0285	0.0002	0.0229	0.0002
Number of adults	−0.1799	0.0010	−0.0990	0.0018
Number of adults squared	0.0189	0.0001	0.0113	0.0002
Number of elderly	−0.0287	0.0023	0.1915	0.0041

Continued

Table 14.2 Continued

	Urban		Rural	
	Coefficient	Standard deviation	Coefficient	Standard deviation
Number of elderly squared	−0.0030	0.0011	−0.0504	0.0019
Maximum number of schooling years in the household	0.0529	0.0002	0.0232	0.0003
Head of Household Characteristics				
Dummy masculine	0.0856	0.0012	0.0647	0.0029
Age	0.0189	0.0002	0.0137	0.0003
Age squared	−0.0001	0.0000	−0.0001	0.0000
Dummy white	0.1495	0.0008	0.1029	0.0016
Years of schooling	0.0219	0.0003	0.0226	0.0007
Years of schooling squared	0.0018	0.0000	0.0027	0.0001
Dummy not-married	0.5568	0.0051	0.5467	0.0092
Spouse characteristics				
Age	0.0152	0.0002	0.0078	0.0004
Age squared	−0.0001	0.0000	0.0000	0.0000
Years of schooling	0.0109	0.0004	0.0148	0.0007
Years of schooling squared	0.0018	0.0000	0.0028	0.0001
Head of Household Occupation				
Director, manager	0.9409	0.0020	0.7381	0.0052
Arts and sciences	0.6652	0.0022	0.5540	0.0099
Middle-level technicians	0.5006	0.0018	0.4785	0.0068
Administrative services	0.3488	0.0020	0.5015	0.0093
Service sector	0.2595	0.0011	0.3581	0.0031
Agriculture	0.2167	0.0017	0.1697	0.0020
Manufacturing goods and services	0.3692	0.0012	0.4876	0.0029
Maintenance	0.3892	0.0025	0.5092	0.0087
Military	0.6205	0.0039	0.7898	0.0201
Unespecified	0.5377	0.0038	0.2256	0.0056
R^2	0.5737		0.4792	
Number of observations	3,918,674		1,141,349	

households, and taking their expectations, the urban-rural differential in mean welfare ratio is

$$E\left[\log W_i \ / \ i \in U, X_i = X_U\right] - E\left[\log W_i \ / \ i \in R, X_i = X_R\right]$$
$$= \left(\alpha_U - \alpha_R\right) + \left(\beta_U X_{i,U} - \beta_R X_{i,R}\right) + \sum_k \left(s_{U,k}\delta_{U,k} - s_{R,k}\delta_{R,k}\right) \tag{14.2}$$

where X_U and X_R are the sample means for urban and rural areas, and $S_{U,K}$ and $S_{R,K}$ are the proportions of state k's population in each sector for urban and rural areas. The first term on the right-hand side of equation (14.2) is the difference in intercepts. In this case, it shows the difference between the predicted *log*W for an unemployed, nonwhite, married women in São Paulo state between urban and rural areas. The second term indicates the differential impacts of nongeographic variables in urban and rural areas. The third term provides the difference resulting from the geographical distribution of population between urban and rural areas.

The results of this decomposition are presented in Table 14.3. The difference in the intercept indicates that unemployed nonwhite married women living in the rural area of São Paulo state are better off, comparatively, than those living in the urban area. As for the nongeographic variables, the largest influence comes from the urban-rural differences in education variables, but differences in demographics also play a role. The difference in geographic dummy variables indicates that, on average, and controlling for

Table 14.3 Contributing factors to average levels of living and urban-rural disparities

	Urban	Rural	Difference
Mean log welfare ratio	0.66	0.42	0.23
Decomposition			
Constant term	−1.00	−0.34	−0.66
Geographic dummy variables	−0.04	−0.12	0.08
Household characteristics	−0.66	−0.56	−0.10
Returns			−0.22
Characteristics			0.12
Demographics	0.61	0.37	0.24
Returns			0.09
Characteristics			0.14
Education variables	0.82	0.32	0.51
Returns			0.14
Characteristics			0.37
Occupation variables	0.27	0.20	0.07
Returns			−0.02
Characteristics			0.10

other characteristics, the gap between the rural areas of São Paulo state and other similar areas in the country is higher than is the case for urban areas. This effect is of the same magnitude as those of differences in occupational variables.

The above comparison between urban and rural areas does not tell the interesting part of the story, for the differences could result from either differences in characteristics or from the varying returns to those characteristics across states. For example, the difference in education could result from different years of schooling across states and/or to the varying returns to each school year in different states. In order to advance further in the analysis, since the model parameters differ between the rural and urban models, we compute the expected gain in welfare from living in urban areas of a given state over rural areas, given that the household has the national means of all characteristics, X^*. For the *j*th state, this is given by:[6]

$$E\left[\log W_i/i \in \mathrm{U}, D_i = D^j, X_i = X^*\right] - E\left[\log W_i/i \in \mathrm{R}, D_i = D^j, X_i = X^*\right]$$

$$= \left(\alpha_U - \alpha_R\right) + \left(\beta_U - \beta_R\right) X^* + \left(\delta_{U,j} - \delta_{R,j}\right) \tag{14.3}$$

Only the third term on the right-hand side of equation (14.3) varies across states. The first term shows the effect of unexplained sectoral differences between rural and urban areas, as well as differences in the excluded dummies. The second term presents the effect of urban-rural differences in the returns to household characteristics, that is, the difference in welfare for a household with the national set of average characteristics, if the location were urban or rural. The results of this decomposition are also presented in Table 14.3. Of the −0.10 difference in household characteristics, returns to characteristics account for −0.22, while the profile of characteristics in the rural area presents a positive effect of 0.12. Thus, the comparative disadvantage of rural areas in terms of household characteristics results mainly from the lower return to characteristics in the rural setting. As for demographics, the most important share belongs to the characteristics (58 percent), with returns at a lower level, although positive. That is, on average, rural households present a more adequate set of characteristics than urban households, although returns are also higher in the rural areas. A similar situation is observed for education, in this case the share of characteristics is higher, 72 percent, indicating that, on average, households living in rural areas present a more adequate set of characteristics. As for differences in the last term of equation 14.3, the gap between urban areas of São Paulo state and other urban areas in the country favors this state, and is around one-third of the same gap involving rural areas, indicating that both sectors do better in São Paulo, but that the rural sector is in better shape, relatively, than its urban sector.

We have estimated regressions for households within each state, and the regional dummies were, of course, eliminated. From these equations, the same decomposition of equation (14.3) was estimated for households within each state, and the results are presented in Table 14.4. Column (B) indicates the urban-rural income differential for a household with the national average of characteristics, subject to the returns of those characteristics in each state. As Figure 14.1 indicates, the urban-rural return to household characteristics (column B) is inversely related to aggregate income levels; the higher the share of a state in national production, the lower the premium for living in the urban areas. Or, put another way, the rural sector in large state economies is more developed, comparatively, than in small states. For example, in the case of São Paulo state (35 percent of national GDP), the difference in returns between urban and rural households is only 0.9, from a total of 0.54. The highest share in the explanation comes from differences in characteristics of rural households (column E).

Table 14.4 Oaxaca decomposition: Comparing urban and rural areas within states

State	$(\alpha_U - \alpha_R)$ (A)	$(\beta_U - \beta_R) X^*$ (B)	$(X_U - X^*) \beta_U$ (D)	$(X^* - X_R) \beta_R$ (E)	Difference (F)
Rondônia	−1.02	0.53	0.12	0.36	−0.01
Acre	−0.97	0.47	0.14	0.45	0.10
Amazonas	−0.87	0.48	0.14	0.47	0.23
Roraima	−1.22	0.84	0.14	0.50	0.27
Pará	−0.60	0.04	0.12	0.42	−0.02
Amapá	−1.37	0.95	0.14	0.46	0.18
Tocantis	−1.15	0.64	0.14	0.45	0.07
Maranhão	−0.74	0.41	0.15	0.52	0.34
Piauí	−0.69	0.43	0.16	0.55	0.45
Ceará	−0.43	0.24	0.17	0.49	0.47
Rio Grande do Norte	−0.66	0.27	0.13	0.47	0.21
Paraíba	−0.46	0.19	0.16	0.49	0.38
Pernambuco	−0.48	0.05	0.13	0.48	0.18
Alagoas	−0.49	0.10	0.13	0.52	0.27
Sergipe	−0.58	0.37	0.16	0.46	0.41
Bahia	−0.69	0.30	0.13	0.47	0.21
Minas Gerais	−0.66	0.22	0.13	0.49	0.18
Espírito Santo	−0.75	0.22	0.12	0.43	0.03
Rio de Janeiro	−0.28	−0.17	0.12	0.48	0.16
São Paulo	−0.54	0.09	0.13	0.49	0.17
Paraná	−0.43	0.14	0.14	0.49	0.33
Santa Catarina	−0.42	0.17	0.15	0.48	0.37
Rio Grande do Sul	−0.20	−0.04	0.15	0.56	0.46
Mato Grosso do Sul	−0.97	0.60	0.12	0.36	0.12
Mato Grosso	−1.12	0.72	0.11	0.42	0.14
Goiás	−0.76	0.26	0.12	0.43	0.06
Distrito Federal	−0.64	−0.11	0.14	0.57	−0.03

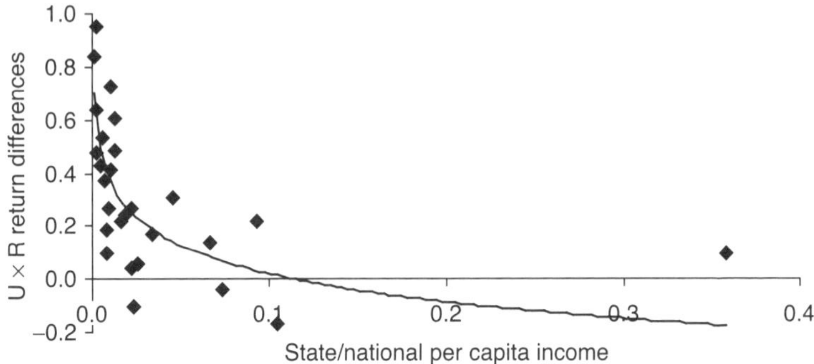

Figure 14.1   Urban x rural return differences across states

Geographic profiles

Another way of assessing the importance of geographic effects is by comparing actual income with values contingent on other characteristics. The first measure uses the estimated state parameters in each sector to predict the income of a household with the national characteristics, that is:

$$\log \hat{W}_U = \alpha_U^j + \beta_U^j X^* \text{ and } \log \hat{W}_R = \alpha_R^j + \beta_R^j X^* \tag{14.4}$$

Thus, if the estimated income value for state *j* resulting from equation (14.4) is lower than the observed (unconditional) value, households in that state experience higher returns to characteristics, compared to the national average return. This measure was named "geographic profile" by Ravallion and Wodon (1999), and isolates the purely geographical effects.

Figures 14.2 and 14.3 show the ratio of unconditional to the estimated incomes ("geographic") in relation to per capita income levels in states (national per capita income level = 1). The figures indicate that the richer the state, the higher the ratio, meaning that rich states tend to experience higher returns to characteristics than poor states, in both sectors.

Another measure is given by:

$$\log \tilde{W}_U^j = \alpha^* + \beta^* X_U^j \text{ and } \log \tilde{W}_R^j = \alpha^* + \beta^* X_R^j \tag{14.5}$$

with:

$$\alpha^* \equiv s_U(\alpha_U + \sum_k s_{U,k}\delta_{U,k}) + s_R(\alpha_R + \sum_k s_{R,k}\delta_{R,k}) \text{ and } \beta^* = s_U\beta_U + s_R\beta_U$$

being weighted national averages. It uses overall national parameters to estimate income values for each state, highlighting the concentration of

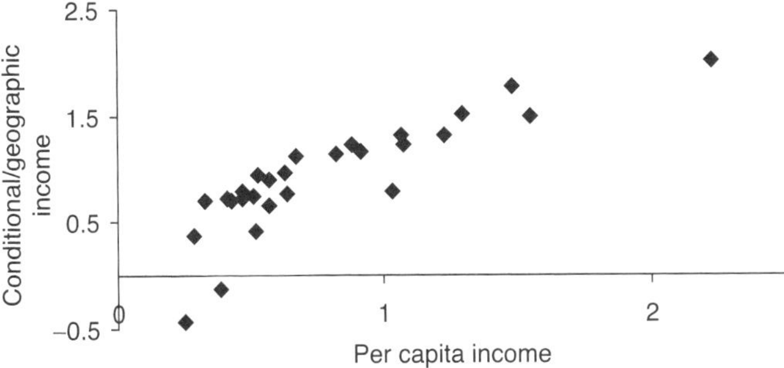

Figure 14.2   Urban unconditional over geographic

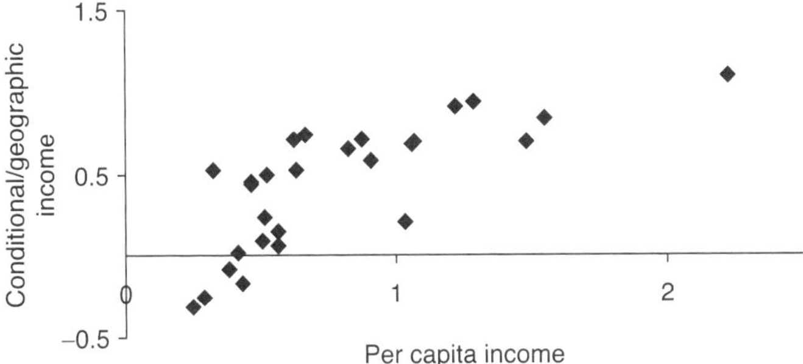

Figure 14.3   Rural unconditional over geographic

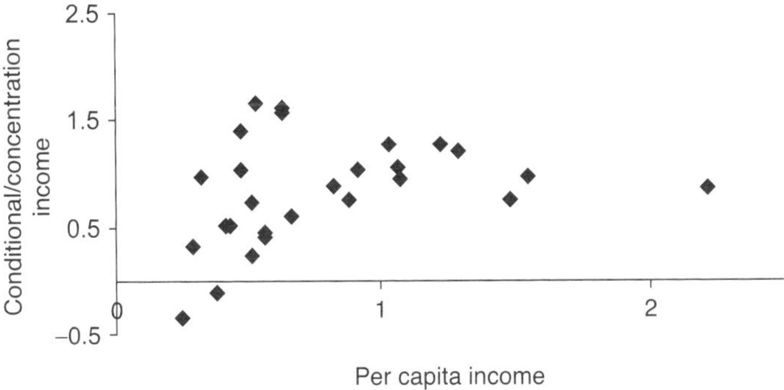

Figure 14.4   Urban conditional over concentration

geographic characteristics, and is called by Ravallion and Wodon the "concentration profile." When the predicted value is larger than the observed (unconditional) value, there is a more favorable set of characteristics in that state, or good characteristics are concentrated in that region.

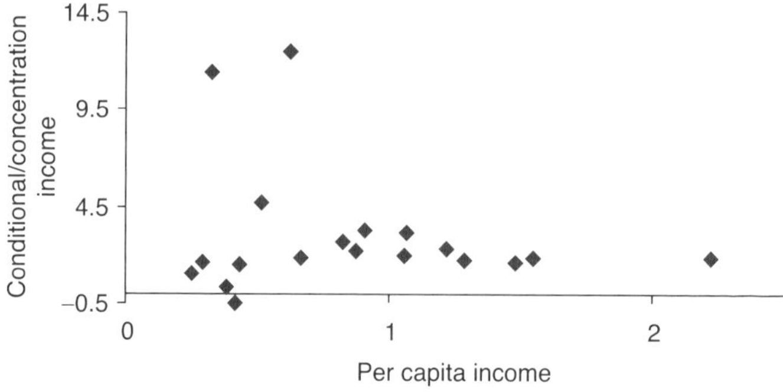

Figure 14.5   Rural conditional over concentration

As Figures 14.4 and 14.5 indicate, the variation of the concentration profile across states does not provide such an evident relationship as does the
geographic profile. Nonetheless, the urban sector presents an increasing
trend as per capita income grows for the poorer group of states, although the
overall dispersion seems to be independent of the income level of a state. For
the rural sector, this conclusion is even stronger.

Conclusions

We produced a study on whether or not observed regional inequality
in real income in Brazil is completely the result of differences in mobile
nongeographic characteristics, or if a "regional" component is also present. We applied different decomposition techniques to assess the role of
demographic and geographical variables in explaining income inequality
in Brazil, following Ravallion and Wodon (1999). Since we have a larger
number of observations, we were able to estimate regressions for each state,
improving on the results of previous studies.

It is clear from the results that it is very important to differentiate urban
and rural situations in studying regional inequality in Brazil. By applying
adequate regional sector-specific deflators, the relative position of different
states in relation to the national income average changes significantly, as
compared to the relative position in terms of nominal (non-region-specifi-
cally deflated) income. The estimated income equations indicate that urban
and rural coefficients are quite different, and that the state dummies are all
significant, indicating that geography matters.

The decomposition of income differences between urban and rural areas
indicates that education variables are the most important factor, followed
by demographic characteristics, but that geographical differences also play
a role. The influence of all explanatory variables was broken down into
returns to the variables and characteristics, and the relative importance of

these components varies across characteristics. In the case of demographic variables, 58 percent of the importance results from the set of characteristics, and the remaining 42 to returns to demographic characteristics. For education, a larger share of the influence comes from characteristics: 72 percent. The urban-rural differentiation in returns to characteristics in large economy states tends to favor these states, where the highest share in the explanation comes from differences in characteristics of rural households. The comparison of observed (unconditional) real income levels with estimated levels, based on national sets of characteristics, indicate that rich states tend to experience higher returns to characteristics than poor states, in both sectors.

This set of results indicates that, although personal characteristics do play an important role in explaining rural-urban regional differences in real income in Brazil, there is still room for regional differentiation. In other words, even after controlling for all types of household characteristics, geography still matters in explaining real income inequality.

Notes

1. In July 2000, US$1.00 = R$ 1.80.
2. Since our sample sizes are large enough, we have assumed that errors are independent, identically distributed (i.i.d). We ran a version correcting for heteroscedasticity and the results are practically the same.
3. Exp (-1.0006) = 0.37.
4. The results for household characteristics are similar to the ones observed in Azzoni and Servo (2002) and to other studies in the same subject in the country, such as Arbache (1998), Reis and Barros (1991).
5. Pension payments to rural elderly people are a very important source of income for rural communities, especially in poor regions.
6. This is obtained by adding and subtracting $\beta_U X^*$ and $\beta_U X^*$ to equation (1) for each type of area, and rearranging the terms.

References

Arbache, J.S. (1998) "How Do Economic Reforms Affect the Structure of Wages? The Case of Brazilian Manufacturing, 1984–1996," *Studies in Economics*, No. 98/17, University of Kent at Canterbury.

Azzoni, C.R. (2001) "Economic Growth and Regional Income Inequality in Brazil," *Annals of Regional Science*, 35, 133–152.

Azzoni, C.R. and L.M. Servo (2002) "Education, Cost of Living and Regional Wage Inequality in Brazil," *Papers in Regional Science*, 81, 157–175.

Baer, W. (2001) *The Brazilian Economy: Growth and Development*, 5th ed., New York: Praeger.

Bird, K., and A. Shepherd (2003) "Livelihoods and Chronic Poverty in Semi-Arid Zimbabwe," *World Development*, 31, 591–610.

Haddad, E.A. (1999) *Regional Inequality and Structural Changes: Lessons from the Brazilian Economy*, Aldershot: Ashgate.

Park, A., S.G. Wang, and G.B. Wu (2002) "Regional Poverty Targeting in China," *Journal of Public Economics*, 86, 123–153.

Ravallion, M. (1993) "Poverty Alleviation through Regional Targeting: A Case Study for Indonesia," in K. Hoff, A. Braverman, and J. Stiglitz (eds.) *The Economics of Rural Organization*, Oxford: Oxford University Press.

Ravallion, M. and Q. Wodon (1999) "Poor Areas, or Only Poor People?" *Journal of Regional Science*, 39, 689–711.

Rocha, S. (1997) "Do consumo observado à linha de pobreza," *Pesquisa e Planejamento Econômico*, 27, 1–15.

Reis, J.G., and R. Paes de Barros (1991) "Wage Inequality and the Distribution of Education: A Study of the Evolution of Regional Differences in Inequality in Metropolitan Brazil," *Journal of Development Economics*, 36, 117–143.

Part IV
New Challenges

15

The Political Economy of the New Left in Latin America: Does the Bell Toll for Neoliberalism?

Edmund Amann

It was with distinct pleasure that I received an invitation to contribute this chapter to help celebrate Werner Baer's seventy-fifth birthday. Werner has played a critical and unique role in the evolution of development economics and the study of the economies of Latin America. In a career spanning six decades, he has been instrumental in producing research that has succeeded in being of the highest quality while also managing to be engaging and accessible. From his base in Vanderbilt University and then the University of Illinois, Werner has fostered the careers of generations of economists. His influence has been especially marked in Latin America where economics departments and finance ministries across the region are replete with his former students. He has also been extraordinarily energetic in fostering ongoing academic ties between the U.S. and Latin America. In this sense, it is no exaggeration to say that Werner has made a significant contribution to hemispheric relations.

Adopting a career as a policy-focused economist working on Latin America is (as Werner would be the first to testify) an occasionally rewarding but invariably challenging path. The 1980s and 1990s were not kind to those academic economists whose research emphasized the importance of institutions, the centrality of country knowledge and a sense of history. At the time, so it seemed, Fukayama's "End of History" was at hand. The world, it appeared, had emerged finally into the sunlit uplands of globalization and orthodox macroeconomic policy. Analyzing the events at hand, best practice in development economics more often than not meant folding up "institutional variables" (most usually a corruption or rule of law variable) into one or two dummies inserted in elaborate cross-country regressions. Those interested in popping open the institutional hood and getting their hands dirty, were viewed as increasingly divorced from the mainstream.

Since the turn of the new millennium, though, the pendulum has begun to reverse direction. The sense that globalization may be stuttering, the unraveling of Western policy in the Middle East, the post-Seattle rise of the anticapitalist movement, and ideological shifts within the multilateral institutions are among the factors propelling a new interest in institutions and country specificities. Both the World Bank and the IMF are now ever more reluctant to advocate one-size-fits-all models. Simultaneously, economists have become much more interested in the institutional and historical intricacies of the development process.

Against this background, Werner's intellectual contributions seem now, in his seventy-fifth year, more timely than ever. It is significant that many of the important "facts on the ground" driving this renewed interest in institutions have originated in Werner's own research bailiwick, Latin America. Within this region, the past five years or so have witnessed the emergence of left-leaning governments whose common theme has been their ostensible opposition to globalization and their commitment to deep-rooted structural reform.

With the rise of Chavez in Venezuela, the recent election of Morales in Bolivia, or even the accession to power of Lula in Brazil, Kirchner in Argentina, Vasquez in Uruguay and Bachelet in Chile, it is now tempting to talk of a decisive shift away from global economic integration and a collective junking of neoliberalism. This, certainly, is the message that has given the academic proponents of globalization pause for thought. But what, if any, is the difference between rhetoric and reality? Do these new governments of the left represent a genuine break with market economics or is the reality more subtle? Is the bell really tolling for neoliberalism in Latin America? Proudly following the tradition of Werner Baer, it will not do to generalize. Instead, the purpose of this chapter is to move beyond the hype and to descend into the often surprising reality, investigating the real political economy of the New Left in Latin America. The discussion begins with a brief background section dealing with the legacy of the Washington Consensus and the market liberalization agenda. Next, the experiences of Brazil, Argentina, Venezuela, and Bolivia are reviewed. Finally, the conclusion draws together the threads of the argument.

Latin America, the "Washington Consensus" and the rise of the new left

At the beginning of the twentieth century, the political economy of Latin America was still rooted in the liberal free trade model which had slowly emerged following independence some eight decades previously. Within 40 years, however, catastrophic external events allied to growing nationalism had entirely altered the political and economic landscape. Eschewing the liberal free trade order of the nineteenth century, the region systematically disengaged itself from the global economy, raising tariff barriers and substituting domestic for foreign investment. Following World War II, the raw nationalism and corporatism that had been the hallmark of the immediate prewar years were progressively discarded in place of a technocratic attempt to engage selectively with the international economy (Bulmer-Thomas, 2003). This process found its outlet in formal import substitution industrialization (ISI) and, later on, in post import substitution industrialization (Post ISI).

Though ISI and Post ISI involved substantial doses of state intervention and dallied with notions of economic autarchy, they were not, in any real sense, the product of a left-wing populism. Instead, at least so far as Argentina, Brazil, and Mexico were concerned, import substitution strategies represented a form of pragmatic economic nationalism. Far from squeezing out the private sector, the postwar industrialization project in Latin America afforded unprecedented opportunities for multinational corporations and domestic enterprises alike. Indeed, the governments remained explicitly committed to the ongoing viability of the private sector and resisted any notion of a move towards state socialism. Looking back at the first three decades following World War II, one could characterize governments (military or civilian) throughout the region as trying to harness the power of the private sector in the interests of national development. In this endeavour, they were not without the support of the United States, which, as in the case of South Korea, saw the state-driven industrialization project as a bulwark against communist encroachment.

For a while the industrialization policies followed across the region proved remarkably successful in delivering accelerated growth, structural transformation, and, up to a point, export diversification (Thorp, 1998). However, as early as the 1960s it had become clear that they were not necessarily consistent with the maintenance of external equilibrium. By the late 1970s and early 1980s, the situation had become still more critical as a result of the impact of recurrent external deficits on the accumulation of foreign debt. With the Mexican default in 1983 and that of Brazil in 1987, the era of the debt crisis had well and truly arrived. Countries were forced to reappraise fundamentally their development strategies.

The policy set that emerged during this period has interchangeably been termed "The Washington Consensus" or, simply, "Neoliberalism." Whichever name one adopts, it is clear that the political economy of the region changed markedly from the mid-1980s onwards. Gone was the view that national development was best pursued at one remove from the global economy. Gone also was the consensus that the state should play an overriding role in the development process whether through direct participation in productive enterprises or through the hands-on formulation of industrial policies. Instead, drawing on the free market experiments of 1970s Chile and the radicalism of the Thatcher and Reagan governments, administrations across the region embraced globalization, reducing barriers to trade and investment, privatizing state-owned enterprises, and deregulating domestic markets.

By the mid-1990s these policies had assumed the status of a new orthodoxy. In Cardoso's Brazil, the early reforms of President Collor de Melo were cast into the shadows by the advent of the world's largest privatization program. In Menem's Argentina, if anything, the reform process was still more radical with extensive market deregulation and an active courting of foreign, especially U.S., investors. In the case of Bolivia and Venezuela, attempts were made to attract more foreign participation into the hydrocarbons sector while in Mexico market reform accompanied the end of the Institutional Revolutionary Party (PRI)'s decades long monopoly in power. In other economies, from Uruguay, to Chile, to Colombia market reform and an embrace of globalization became the order of the day.

Looking back at this period – which is only a decade behind us – one is struck with the comparative ease with which it was possible to reach a political consensus strong enough to overthrow the long-held shibboleths of state-driven development. An important explanation here must lie in the denouement of import substitution and its macroeconomic fallout. By the mid-1980s, as already indicated, countries across the region were battling with the long-term consequences of ISI. Debt servicing costs had become insupportable and now posed a real obstacle to GDP expansion. Perhaps more seriously still, hyperinflation had become a reality. As the real incomes of the middle and working classes eroded, so too did the political bedrock upon which the nationalist/populist industrialization project was built. Under these circumstances, the commitment to price stability – which formed the core of the new orthodoxy – must have seemed a very attractive proposition.

For a while it seemed as if the new wave of policies were indeed delivering the macroeconomic goods and, by extension, dampening any lingering ideological nostalgia for the days of import substitution and quasiautarchy. Central to the assault on inflation – at least in Argentina and Brazil – was the jettisoning of a heterodox approach in favor of rules-based monetary targeting. From the beginning of the 1990s, in the case of Argentina and from 1993 in the case of Brazil, the setting of interest rates was guided by the need to peg the national currency to the U.S. dollar (Amann and Baer, 2003). For Argentina, this policy amounted to a convertibility plan with the peso exchangeable for the dollar on a one-for-one basis. In the case of Brazil's Real Plan an exchange rate targeting system was introduced which allowed a marginally greater degree of freedom in the formulation of monetary policy. The impacts of these policies in inflationary terms could only be described as dramatic. Both in Argentina and Brazil, hyperinflationary conditions rapidly gave way to single-digit price stability.

By the mid-1990s, so impressive did Argentina's counterinflationary achievement appear that, with only a degree of irony, it was pointed out that, unlike many of its transatlantic counterparts Argentina would meet all the key Maastricht criteria for entry into the European Monetary Union!

Unlike Brazil, Argentina's newfound price stability was also associated with a substantial upturn in economic growth. Although Venezuela (unlike Bolivia) failed to register the same spectacular counterinflationary achievements as its Southern Cone counterparts, both governments nevertheless espoused a commitment to orthodox macroeconomic policy. For Bolivia, the need to pursue such a path was bolstered as a result of its agreements with the World Bank and the IMF.

By the start of 1997 the dual commitment to free markets and price stability seemed as firmly anchored in place throughout the region as in any period since the outbreak of World War I. Yet, in retrospect it is evident that this newfound "Washington Consensus" rested on unstable structural foundations. Of course, the fragility, consistency, and friability of this shaky economic bedrock varied from place to place. In the case of Bolivia and Venezuela, as elsewhere in Latin America, the economies had been unable to escape from an overwhelming dependency on commodity exports. For both metals and fossil fuels, the most important of such exports, prices had been relatively depressed throughout the 1990s. This placed a brake on growth and severely limited the fiscal resources of an often-dysfunctional state. At the same time, thanks to a concentrated pattern of asset ownership, the fruits of whatever growth was realized were highly unevenly dispersed both among regions and population groups. Not surprisingly this created a sense of lingering political grievance which was to find its voice very effectively in the years that followed.

In the case of Argentina and especially Brazil, reliance on a narrow spectrum of commodity exports was far less marked than elsewhere in the region. Still, many structural problems remained unresolved. Not the least of these was the fact that the state, despite the ministrations of multilateral institutions, remained overextended and prone to structural deficits. Such deficits made excessive demands on limited domestic savings, intensifying demands on foreign capital markets. Fiscally, the problem was made worse by the fact that the tight monetary policies pursued made the financing and refinancing of debt a very costly process. For both countries, too, the high external value of their currencies imposed a competitive disadvantage, placed pressure on their current account balances, and thereby created another source of potential instability.

Structural weaknesses such as those just described do not necessarily bring an economy to its knees. Rather like a house built on loose shale, all may be well until some external shock – an earthquake – intervenes. The shock, when it arrived in the form of the 1997–1998 emerging markets financial crisis, traced its origins to Asia and then Russia. As investors took fright at events in Asia, they began to look nervously at Latin American assets and the fundamentals underpinning their value. The first major casualty of this crisis was Brazil which, up until 1999, had managed with varying degrees of difficulty to maintain the real within a narrow band against the dollar.

Following the outbreak of the Asian financial crisis in 1997 investors had begun to regard Brazil's large fiscal and trade deficits with growing alarm. The authorities were forced to raise interest rates to maintain vital capital inflows, but the fiscal situation only deteriorated through 1998 and they were eventually forced to reach an interim standby agreement with the IMF (ibid.). Even this, though, proved to be insufficient to support the real and the Central Bank gave in to the inevitable in early 1999, allowing the currency float significantly downward. The fact that inflation failed to return with a vengeance is a significant tribute to the skill of the policymakers. Nevertheless, the reputation for economic competence of the centrist Cardoso administration was holed below the waterline. Brazil then entered a period of stagnant growth and rising unemployment. Not surprisingly, the electorate was influenced by these events and the generally tarnished economic legacy of the mainstream center. In October 2002 Luiz Inácio Lula da Silva (Lula) of the ostensibly left-wing PT (Workers' Party) finally achieved victory, erasing the memory of unsuccessful campaigns in 1989, 1994, and 1998.

President Lula was not the only, and not even the first, left-leaning leader to benefit from the economic malaise engulfing Latin America. In the case of Venezuela, Hugo Chavez Frías came to power in 1999 on the back of a series of recent economic failures engineered by his predecessors, Carlos Andres Perez and Rafael Caldera. President Perez, elected in 1988, had adopted an orthodox macroeconomic policy as part of an agreement with the IMF. However, unlike Bolivia, Brazil, or Argentina, Venezuela's counterinflationary strategy proved largely ineffective in generating price stability. By 1996, under President Caldera (the immediate predecessor of President Chavez) inflation had reached 100 percent per year. Although another deal with the IMF provided a lifeline, by 1999 the damage had been done. Breaking with the establishment center-right traditions of the past, the Venezuelan electorate opted for an ostensibly radical alternative. Explicitly targeting the economic neoliberalism he deemed responsible for Venezuela's (and indeed the region's) plight, Hugo Chavez benefited from a groundswell of support, especially among disadvantaged groups and the urban poor.

The endgame for the center-right in Argentina proved to be a more prolonged affair. This perhaps reflected the superior durability of the macroeconomic framework that had been put in place. Between 1989 and 1999 under President Carlos Menem, the convertibility regime had managed to combine price stability with impressive growth. Yet, as with all currency pegs a successful convertibility regime requires healthy inflows of foreign capital. While investors proved happy to hold Argentinean financial instruments in the initial years of the plan, following the Asian financial crisis of 1997 their outlook became increasingly nervous. As in the case of Brazil, there was considerable concern surrounding the sustainability of fiscal policy. In particular, investors became preoccupied with the deteriorating financial position of regional governments and municipalities. Also, it had become clear that the pegging the Argentine peso to a strengthening dollar was delivering a competitive body blow to the export sector, contributing to the opening up of substantial trade deficits at the end of the 1990s.

By 1999, it was clear that, unless urgent corrective action was taken, Argentina could well end up following the Brazilian example. The government of Radical Party candidate Fernando de la Rua, which came to power in 1999, drew on a weak coalition and proved unable to take the tough measures necessary to preserve convertibility. In particular, too little was done to restore fiscal stability or improve the performance of the trade balance. With regard to the latter, the challenge facing Argentina had only intensified following the decision of Brazil to devalue in early 1999.

At the beginning of 2001, foreign and domestic investors could see that the end of the convertibility regime was only a matter of time. As political and economic confidence ebbed away, Argentina entered its third successive year of recession. By the end of 2001 economic and political crises had well and truly set in. President de la Rua resigned in December to be followed by three stand-in successors in the course of a week (*The Economist*, June 3, 2004). Finally, Eduardo Duhalde – chosen by Congress to see out his predecessor's term – opted for the inevitable, discarding the convertibility plan and allowing the peso to float. The subsequent devaluation and associated debt default were associated with a near-catastrophic decline in GDP in 2002. With the free market sound money legacy of the 1990s in tatters, in April 2003 the electorate opted for the avowedly left-wing Peronist, Nestor Kirchner.

In the case of Bolivia, the recent movement to the left had also been presaged by the adoption of orthodox macroeconomic stabilization policies. By comparison with Argentina, Brazil, and Venezuela, though, Bolivia's macroeconomic record is surprisingly favorable. In the mid-1980s hyperinflation had reached unmanageable levels, rising to over 20,000 percent a year in 1985. However, the late 1980s and 1990s saw IMF-backed fiscal reforms and the adoption of a relatively orthodox approach to monetary policy. These policies proved relatively successful in that they had succeeded in lowering inflation to single-digit levels by the end of the 1990s. In 2005, the year in which President Morales was elected, inflation on an annualized basis stood at just 6 percent. The growth performance of the economy has also been reasonable over the past decade, oscillating between about 0.2 and 5 percent (IDB, 2006). Unlike Argentina, Brazil, and Venezuela Bolivia has not experienced a recession in the past ten years. Against this background, the macroeconomic case for a political rejection of neoliberal precepts seems weak. Nevertheless on December 18, 2005, Evo Morales – a figure matched in his radical credentials only by Hugo Chavez – was elected President.

To understand the economic realities underpinning the recent political trajectory of Bolivia, it is necessary to look beyond the familiar territory of failed stabilization plans. Whereas Bolivia presents a comparatively favorable macroeconomic face, the fact remains that large sectors of the population failed to benefit from the prosperity generated under Presidents Suarez, Sánchez de Lozada, Mesa, and Rodríguez. Economic disadvantage in Bolivia has a strong regional dimension with those inhabiting the Western uplands significantly worse off than those living in the resource rich East. Seeking to improve their situation, indigenous groups in the West had since at least the middle of the 1980s been launching protests against the policies of successive governments in La Paz. In the 1990s, as governments sought to liberalize the hydrocarbons sector, the locus of protest became policies related to oil and gas (Petras, 2006).

One policy in particular, a plan to export gas through a trans-Andean pipeline through Chile, drew unprecedented on the ground resistance. With large parts of the country's infrastructure paralyzed, President Sánchez de Lozada resigned from office in October 2003. The end of the de Sánchez de Lozada administration emboldened a left-wing grass roots indigenous movement that had already been growing in strength. Although oil and gas-related protests have drawn the greatest international attention, other facets of the market liberalization agenda have generated violent protests. Among the most noteworthy examples of this was the nationwide rioting which ensued in 2000 after the announcement of plans to privatize the city of Cochabamba's water utility.

The Bolivian experience is, of course, distinct from that elsewhere in the region in that the rise of the left has drawn succor mainly from perceptions of microeconomic rather than macroeconomic failings. However, it is also distinguished by the fact that political change has been propelled by a sense of oppression of one population group by another. Whatever the particularism of the Bolivian case, there is no doubt – if the rhetoric of Morales is to be taken at face value – that the government sees its ascendancy (and its mission) in terms of a region-wide struggle against neoliberalism and economic orthodoxy. Yet, in truth, does the policy agenda of the new left really represent a break with the recent past? To paraphrase one of my joint papers with Werner, is the gap between the rhetoric and the reality more apparent than real? These questions form the subject matter for the next section.

The left in government: a real break with the past?

Brazil – pragmatic globalization

Of all the manifestations of the new left in Latin America, the most internationally acclaimed is the government of Luiz Inácio Lula da Silva. President Lula, elected in October 2002, has remained an eloquent exponent of progressive/left-wing values and has certainly been keen to build bridges with likeminded leaders around the region and beyond. However, what strikes one most sharply about the Lula administration is the sense of continuity rather than change in relation to the social democratic Cardoso years. Prior to his accession to office in January 2003, domestic but especially foreign investors had expressed profound concern that a Lula government would preside over a wild expansion in the ambit of the state, an unsustainable fiscal loosening, and, worst of all, selective reappropriation of foreign assets. As a result of these fears, the real experienced a dramatic weakening in mid-2002. Currency fears then presented an immediate challenge for the incoming administration.

On coming to office at the start of 2003 President Lula took immediate steps to calm the nerves of the markets, setting out his commitment to the enhancement of macroeconomic stability and the openness of the economy to international investment. The most immediate manifestation of this commitment consisted of the administration's endorsement of the IMF agreement initiated back in 1998 (Amann and Baer, 2006). Central to this agreement were attempts to reduce the operational fiscal deficit (the balance of debt and nondebt related transactions) through the pursuit of ever-higher primary surpluses. Between 2002 and 2003 the primary surplus rose from 3.75 percent of GDP to 4.25. By late 2004 the surplus had risen still further to 4.7 percent.

The improvements in fiscal performance were achieved through highly orthodox means, predominantly through tight expenditure controls. These were especially concentrated in the field of discretionary capital expenditures. Deliberate attempts to improve the flow of revenues through taxation reform proved more frustrating. In particular the Lula administration struggled (and is still struggling) to push through systemic reform of the labyrinthine indirect taxation system. The latter, with its myriad taxes, is both expensive to enforce and, through its cascading effects, unfavorable in its impact on competitiveness. Despite difficulties here, revenues held up reasonably well, especially once growth began to recover in 2004.

The second key plank of the Lula administration's macroeconomic policy was, like the IMF fiscal targets, also inherited from the Cardoso administration. Since the end of the exchange rate anchor in early 1999, the authorities had not by any means abandoned rules based monetary policy. Instead, a program of inflation targeting was introduced along similar lines to that eventually pursued by the U.K. The U.K. had adopted inflation targeting once it fell out of the European Exchange Range Mechanism (ERM) in 1992. The Brazilian inflation-targeting regime, like its fiscal counterpart, set severe self-imposed limits on the authorities' macroeconomic room for maneuver. With markets still nervous and the real under pressure during the early days of the administration, the authorities were understandably reluctant to initiate substantial monetary loosening lest currency depreciation were to introduce imported inflation. Still, once the markets began to take on board the sincerity of the Lula administration in its pursuit of macroeconomic orthodoxy, the Brazilian economy began to reap the benefits (ibid.). During the first half of 2004, base interest rates began to decline quite rapidly, dipping below 20 percent for the first time in three years. The interest rate reductions were reversed in early 2005 but have since resumed. As monetary policy loosened, economic growth accelerated from 0.5 percent in 2003 to 4.94 in 2004, before tailing off somewhat to 2.28 in 2005.

Examining the macroeconomic record of the Lula administration during its first term, one is immediately struck with a profound sense of continuity and, what is more, the impression that the new government even wished to outflank its predecessor as a paragon of macroeconomic virtue. To the traditional supporters of the PT, these developments must have come of as much as a surprise as they did to the international investor community. From a political economy perspective, the interesting question concerns not so much the effectiveness of the government's macroeconomic stance so much as how it was popularly sustained in an ostensibly radical party. The answer to this question has much to do with the recently departed finance minister, Antônio Palocci and the coalition he managed to secure within the upper echelons of the PT machine and within Congress.

Mr. Palocci proved singleminded in his determination that the new administration was not going to be undone by allegations of economic ineptitude. This was a fate which had befallen successive governments up until the 1990s. It appears that Mr. Palocci and his advisors took the view that his party's much- vaunted social reform agenda could not fulfilled without the government establishing its economic credibility in international markets. While this "jam tomorrow" perspective might not have found favor with the PT's traditional support base, this was not necessarily true among the government's coalition partners (notably some PMDB and PFL congressmen). Nor was it true within more pragmatic segments of the PT itself. As a result of this, Mr. Palocci proved remarkably effective in preserving an exacting macroeconomic policy framework.

As should now be clear, in the macroeconomic sphere at least, it would be hard to characterize the Lula administration as a staunch opponent of the "Neoliberal" agenda. Could the same be said of its stance on social policy or of its microeconomic reform agenda? Among the most publicized claims surrounding the new government was that relating to its commitments to poverty alleviation. During the election campaign of 2002, the PT made much of its desire to target poverty directly. It also criticized the Cardoso administration for its supposed failure to elevate social policy above its desire for market liberalization and price stability. The centerpiece of the Lula government's poverty alleviation agenda was the *Fome Zero* (Zero Hunger) package. This consisted of a range of measures including food handouts, "popular restaurants," and support for subsistence farmers (ibid.).

Well intentioned as the program may have been, it was rapidly undone by a combination of poor design and lack of resources. The resource issue is, of course, directly related to the fiscal stringency dominating the government's agenda. Perhaps more successful has been a second initiative, the *Bolsa Familiar* (Family Grant). The latter has set out to capacitate poorer families financially through direct financial assistance, with a particular emphasis being placed on encouraging children to stay in school. There is no doubt that this measure has had positive impacts. However, it needs to be seen in a context of endemic poverty and a failure for substantial rises in formal employment to materialize. Had the latter occurred, then many low-income families could have been hoovered out of poverty without the need for direct government assistance. Unfortunately, the pursuit of tight macroeconomic policy allied to a fumbling of labor market reform ensured that unemployment and underemployment remained stubbornly high.

Besides the Real Plan, the most noteworthy accomplishments of the Cardoso administration centered on the market reform agenda. Accelerating progress begun under the Collor administration, President Cardoso's government instituted constitutional reforms, opening up the energy and telecommunications markets. The Cardoso period was also notable for its privatization program. At the time, this was the world's largest and involved the sale of enterprises in the public utilities sector. In the runup to October 2002's elections there was a real fear among foreign and domestic investors that the future President Lula would rapidly reverse the drift to market liberalization, perhaps even taking back selected enterprises into public sector ownership. As in the macroeconomic sphere, however, these fears soon proved unfounded. While it is true to say that privatization has not surged forward under Lula, this has much to do with the now depleted range of privatizable assets. Only in the case of the electricity generation sector could it be said that the government has stood firm against privatization. Even here, seeking to overcome supply constraints, the government has not been averse to inviting private sector bids for electricity generation contracts. In the telecommunications sector – the filet mignon of the Cardoso privatization program – there has been no serious attempt to roll back the years and institute stronger state control. In the oil exploration and production sector, the administration has continued to conduct auctions, encouraging international bids.

The sense that the current administration is comfortable with low-profile market liberalization finds its response in foreign direct investment data. Although foreign direct investment (FDI) receipts have tailed off compared to the late 1990s (they were US$15.2 billion in 2005 compared with 28.9 billion in 1998), this has to be seen in the context of the conclusion of the privatization program. The fact that FDI has continued to pour in on a substantial scale illustrates a sense of confidence in the administration's economic policy agenda.

Whereas the first half of the previous decade was an active period for trade reform, momentum stalled during the Cardoso years. Under President Lula, enthusiasm for progress on the trade agenda appears to have returned quite forcefully. Far from wishing to retreat to the *status quo ante* of import substitution, the administration is trying to pursue its quest for multilateral trade liberalization both regionally and extraregionally. Dialogue has continued between Brasília and the Bush administration over the possibilities for the eventual creation of a Free Trade Area of the Americas. Brazil has become a key player in the Doha round of WTO negotiations. Brazilian negotiators are very heavily pushing a reciprocal market access agenda. This would see other countries open their markets to commodity-based exports in return for concessions on trade in manufactures and services.

The sense that the Lula administration is committed to cautious market liberalization finds a telling exemplar in the travails of Varig (Brazil's largest international airline). Varig, a lossmaker for years, had been hobbled by a high cost base allied to a dysfunctional corporate governance regime. By the middle of 2006, the airline had been put into judicial administration under the terms of a new bankruptcy law. Despite pleas for BNDES (National Development Bank) or other direct public sector assistance, the government stood firm, apparently prepared to see Varig liquidated unless a financially capable buyer was secured. Eventually the enterprise was taken over by a group of private sector investors who proceeded to slash employee numbers and routes. Such a brazenly promarket stance would have been unthinkable under the rightist military governments of the 1960s and 1970s. Yet, under the administration of their staunch left-wing trade union opponent, the primacy of the market appears to be receiving fulsome endorsement.

From the discussion so far it should be abundantly clear that the Lula administration, while by no means buccaneering free marketeers in the Collor de Melo mould, has nonetheless remained remarkably faithful to the tenets of market liberalization. Above all, the government appears willing to embrace globalization, hoping that selective interventions can mitigate its worst effects. While genuine attempts have been made to tackle poverty and social exclusion, the effectiveness of these has been limited by the constraints imposed by tight fiscal and monetary policy.

The administration is now well into its second term. Having established hard-won market credibility, will the administration veer in a more radical direction? So far the evidence here is limited. However, it is worth noting that with the departure of Antônio Palocci amid a corruption scandal, there has been some loosening of fiscal policy. As part of this process, the quantity of resources destined for social programs has increased. A limited program of raised infrastructure spending, the Growth Acceleration Program (PAC – *Programa de Acceleração de Crescimento*) has been announced. This envisages a slight easing of the primary surplus target. The campaign funding scandals which plagued the government in 2004 and 2005 have also served to diminish the prestige of its more technocratic figures, possibly opening the way for a more radical clique. More radical figures within the

PT are, without doubt, drawing inspiration from their counterparts elsewhere in the region, notably in Venezuela, Argentina, and Bolivia. But how much of a genuinely radical inspiration does the experience of these countries provide? Venezuela, for a start, offers some interesting conclusions.

Venezuela: the Bolivarian market alternative

The government of Hugo Chavez Frías has become, without question, the highest profile exponent of the leftward shift in Latin American politics. As already indicated, Colonel Chavez' arrival in office in 1999 could not be described as an unexpected event. Despite Venezuela's undoubted oil wealth and a geographically advantageous location relative to the U.S. markets, successive administrations had proved unable to secure macroeconomic stability. Nor had they been able to ensure an equitable distribution of the fruits of progress. Coming to power, the Chavez administration drew explicit connections between the plight of Venezuela and the pursuit of a market friendly, pro-U.S. economic policy agenda. Mixing elements of Yugoslav style socialism with a political philosophy drawn from a semimythologized past, Hugo Chavez advanced a "Bolivarian alternative." This would alter the relationship between Venezuela and the global economy, generating prosperity and ensuring that the poor were not left behind.

Taken at face value, the results of this experiment appear reasonable. In 2004 and 2005 Venezuelan GDP grew by 12.1 and 8 percent respectively having contracted in 2002 and 2003. Inflation in 2005 stood at 17 percent, higher than the regional average but a considerable improvement compared with the 100 percent reached in 1996 (IDB, 2006). According to surveys, the relatively benign recent performance of the economy, in combination with increasing social spending, is beginning to have a real impact on poverty. So far, so good but to what extent has the Chavez administration been able to drive real structural reform and change? More pertinently, could what has been accomplished really be described as anti-Neoliberal?

Regarding the latter question, one should be careful not to misinterpret the tenets of the so-called Bolivarian revolution. In economic terms, Bolivarianism is not an explicitly antimarket ideology. Rather, it seeks to reorder what are perceived to be destructive international economic relationships (in particular contracts with multinational corporations) while fortifying domestic entrepreneurs, especially in small and microenterprises (Pandya and Podur, 2003). In its advocacy of "the little guy," the Bolivarian movement has much in common with common-or-garden populist anti-big-business sentiment. To this extent, parallels can be drawn between Bolivarianism and the populist underpinnings of antitrust legislation in early twentieth-century America. The Chavez administration has been keen to promote small businesses and has been encouraging them to compete with imports. This is being attempted through edicts that oblige banks to lend to such enterprises at below market rates (Bamrud, 2005). In addition, small and medium enterprises have been favored with tax breaks to encourage employment generation in economically depressed regions of the country (DFAT, 2007). The attention of the administration may now be turning to the needs of larger businesses. In June 2008, seeking to tackle supply bottlenecks, President Chavez convened a meeting of senior business leaders and announced a program of "cheap credit and joint ventures to 'reactivate' production" (*The Economist*, June 21, 2008).

Perhaps the greatest international attention has centered on the relationship between Venezuela's government and foreign investors. Three examples in particular drew headlines in 2005. During that year the government seized a Heinz tomato processing plant, a Parmalat milk facility, and a 32,000 acre ranch owned by the British-based Vestey group. However, it is worth noting that the seizures involved allegedly idle rather than actively productive assets. In late 2006, the government took a still bolder step, announcing its intention to assert majority control of foreign-owned oil production facilities in the Orinoco basin. However, it is worth stressing that the government does not appear to want to expel foreign oil companies altogether. Rather, the intention seems to be to purchase majority stakes off them and, where appropriate, to secure enhanced royalties. Uncomfortable as these measures might be for the oil majors, they do not necessarily spell the end for foreign enterprises in the Venezuelan hydrocarbons sector. Perhaps more radically, in early 2007 President Chavez announced plans to nationalize components of the electricity sector. The first step in this process has been the takeover of Caracas' electrical utility, the U.S.-owned EDC. Eschewing outright expropriation, the Chavez administration has agreed to pay EDC's owner, AES, US$740M for an 82 percent stake in the enterprise. Seeking to increase the degree of state control over "strategic" industries the government has also moved to nationalize the cement and steel industries.

Perhaps more even than in terms of its relationship with foreign capital, the real radicalism of the Chavez administration appears to be rest on its social agenda. Buoyed by substantially increased oil revenues, social expenditures – especially on health and education – have risen far beyond that of the previous government. However, to characterize this reorientation of spending as "anti-NeoLiberal" does not seem especially meaningful when one considers that the Blair government in the UK undertook similar measures on inheriting power from the Conservatives in 1997. Clearer examples of an explicit attack on the tenets of Neoliberalism tend to be confined to the strategic "commanding heights" of industry and high profile service providers. In addition to the nationalization of steel and cement, Mr. Chavez has established state-owned enterprises in the airlines and telecommunications sectors while a new state-run TV network has been launched (*The Economist*, October 9, 2004).

As already indicated, the Venezuelan economy has been performing quite favorably over the past couple of years. Still, the fact remains that

Venezuelan economic performance is intimately bound up in the fortunes of the oil sector. Following an attempted coup in 2002, strikes at PDVSA, the state-owned oil company, badly impacted production. This directly contributed to GDP contractions of 8.9 and 7.7 percent in 2002 and 2003, respectively. In response to a mounting sense of crisis the government was obliged to introduce emergency measures, among which was an imposition of tight exchange controls. Moving into 2007–2008 growth in the Venezuelan economy had picked up, yet serious macroeconomic difficulties continued to be experienced. Whereas in 2007 annual inflation was running at around 20 percent, in 2008 the indications are that it will hit 30 percent (*Washington Post*, June 8, 2008). This is forcing the authorities to increase interest rates and reduce the rate of increase of public spending.

Events such as this raise the issue of whether recent reforms are proving effective. In particular, doubts must remain as to whether they will prove sufficient to ensure sustained development in the event that oil prices (or production) eventually fall. The Chavez administration hopes that a domestic entrepreneurial renaissance will eventually take up the slack from the foreign dominated traditional lead sectors. The jury is still out.

Argentina: the political economy of crisis management

In many ways the reversal of political polarity has been most dramatic in Argentina. In per capita income terms, long the region's most developed economy, Argentina has nevertheless endured frequent bouts of instability. Indeed, much of the postwar period has been punctuated by fiscal, balance of payments, or currency crises. As a consequence of this, improvements in living standards tended to outpaced by those in neighboring countries. Not surprisingly, this resulted in a collective sense of being under siege and helps explain periodic deviations from democratic rule. Under the government of Carlos Menem (1989–1999), however, Argentina seemed embarked on a new course. Embracing privatization, trade reform, and a restructuring of the public sector, Argentina appeared to be turning its back on the failed recipes of the past and confronting the challenge of globalization head on. The jewel in the crown of the new policy set consisted of the convertibility plan which, as has been noted, pegged the peso to the U.S. dollar on a one-for-one basis. For a while, the plan proved extraordinarily successful. However, it was eventually pulled down by a failure to address underlying structural disequilibria, not least the fiscal imbalances affecting provincial governments.

After a traumatic period of instability and four interim presidents, President Nestor Kirchner was elected to power in April 2003. Although he hailed from the same Peronist party as Mr. Menem, Mr. Kirchner's political and economic outlook was markedly different. Drawing on a power base in a peripheral part of the country (Santa Cruz province in Patagonia), Mr. Kirchner views himself as something of an outsider. Whereas

Mr. Menem made much of his faith in the market mechanism as a solution to Argentina's deep-rooted problems, Mr. Kirchner's faith, such as it is, was initially much more qualified. Perhaps the biggest acid test of the new administration's attitude concerns its handling of Argentina's international debt obligations. Following the departure of Mr. De La Rua in late 2001, Argentina defaulted on its US$80 billion debt, the largest sovereign default in history (*The Economist*, June 3, 2004). Initially hemmed in by an inability to pay, the Kirchner government proved unwilling to accelerate progress toward resuming debt repayments or making an interim arrangement with creditors. As a result, Argentina's status in the international financial markets sank still further.

Three years after its election, the position of the Kirchner administration appeared to have undergone something of a transformation. Rather than continuing to launch populist assaults at the international capital markets, the government has taken quite serious steps towards mending fences with its creditors. Although Mr. Kirchner announced in August 2004 that Argentina was to suspend its agreements with the IMF, subsequently payments have resumed (*The Economist*, December 20, 2005). In December 2005, the government moved further with the announcement that US$9.8 billion would immediately be repaid to the IMF. The Kirchner administration's newfound commitment to economic responsibility is not confined to its policies on debt management. As in the case of Brazil, Argentina has begun to set great store by its pursuit of sound fiscal policy. Reversing the fiscal profligacy which contributed to the undoing of the convertibility plan, stringent primary surplus targets have been set. The objective here has been to chisel away at the operational deficit and so eventually at Argentina's mountain of outstanding debt. In 2004 the primary surplus reached 3.2 percent of GDP with a target of 4.1 set for 2006 (ibid.).

Taken as a whole, the government's stance on fiscal policy is not indicative of a return to the lax practices of the past. Rather, the administration appears to be attempting to emulate the experience of Brazil, combining fiscal prudence with an avowed commitment to securing social justice and raising the rate of growth. In the realm of monetary policy, however, the stance of the Argentinean administration differs markedly from its Brazilian counterpart. Whereas the centerpiece of Brazil's macroeconomic strategy has consisted of the maintenance of high real interest rates as an antiinflationary bulwark, in the case of Argentina monetary policy has proved far looser. By mid-2006 Argentine real interest rates were actually negative. Partially as a result of the accommodative nature of monetary policy, inflation has begun to spike upward, reaching 10.9 percent in 2006 though dipping to 8.5 in 2007.

The approach of Mr. Kirchner's team appears to be driven by a desire to realize higher growth despite the risk to price stability. That the strategy has been successful in delivering higher growth seems beyond question. Following the end of convertibility in early 2002, Argentine GDP has expanded by an annual average rate of about 9 percent. This impressive performance has been driven not only by the looseness of monetary policy but also by the impacts of the peso's dramatic slide against the U.S. dollar and other major currencies. This has helped Argentina to deliver impressive export performance and, to some extent, to contain the flow of imports. The government's reluctance to raise interest rates probably stems from the belief that the ensuing appreciation of the peso would choke off the impressive export-led boom. Still, having made choice, the authorities must realize they are taking a gamble with price stability.

In the microeconomic sphere, the Kirchner administration has not, to any real extent, attempted to undo the legacy of Carlos Menem. Under Menem, as in Brazil, large swathes of the public utilities sector were privatized while through regional and unilateral trade liberalization, the Argentine economy was opened up to imports. Suspicious though elements of the Peronist party might be toward multinational corporations, there have been no moves to appropriate assets. Indeed, the government remains keen to draw in inward investment as part of its attempts to reduce lingering unemployment. Turning to trade, unenthusiastic though the administration is about the FTAA, there is little sign of a return to the protectionist policies of the past. This probably has much to do with the highly competitive valuation of the peso, a factor which has driven a remarkable turnaround in the trade account.

Possibly the most serious bone of contention between the Kirchner administration and the international investment community concerns the setting of utility tariffs. As part of its attempts to curb inflation, Argentina's government has, on occasion, frozen gas and electricity prices. For foreign investors this has turned out to have especially serious implications since they have been unable to compensate partially for the impact on earnings (in foreign currency terms) of peso devaluation. In the case of Metrogas (a subsidiary of the U.K.-based BG, plc.) plans for network expansion have suffered and a legal dispute has erupted. Still, set beside events in Bolivia, foreign enterprises in Argentina have continued to enjoy relatively settled conditions.

Elections at the end of 2007 saw the election of Mr. Kirchner's wife, Cristina, as President. Early in its term, the administration of Mrs. Kirchner has had to confront one of the more unwelcome legacies of her predecessor: rising inflation. This has triggered popular discontent as has – among farmers – a plan to impose windfall taxes on agricultural exports. Both these events may call into question the macroeconomic stance of the government, forcing it to tackle inflation more effectively and refocus the authorities' tax raising efforts.

Bolivia: radicalism in the Andes?

Chile aside, the most recent manifestation of the revival of fortunes of the left in Latin America has occurred in Bolivia. Long one of the region's least developed countries, Bolivia has recently undergone something of a reversal of fortune. Following exploration in the 1980s and 1990s, Bolivia has emerged as one of the world's most important producers of natural gas. During the late 1990s agreements were signed to supply huge quantities of gas along a pipeline linking production fields to Southeastern Brazil, the continent's most urbanized, industrialized region. In addition to hydrocarbons production the Bolivian economy has continued to benefit from its substantial deposits of metallic minerals. As commodity prices have risen, so the Bolivian economy has performed reasonably well, at least in raw GDP terms. However, growth in per capita GDP has lagged behind the overall increase in national output (IDB, 2006). Moreover, Bolivia has remained constrained by a highly uneven distribution of income. This and marked regional and ethnic rivalries provide the background against which Evo Morales, an indigenous leader, surged to electoral victory in December 2005.

Unlike Presidents Lula and Kirchner, President Morales appears to have hitched his political star to Hugo Chavez' Bolivarian revolution. In similar vein to his Venezuelan counterpart, Mr. Morales has been forthright in issuing anti-Neoliberal rhetoric. Ideologically, Mr. Morales's platform has much in common with that of Mr. Chavez. In economic policy terms, the core principles appear to be a reordering of relationships with multinational corporations alongside attempts to reinvigorate small and micro-enterprises. Once again, therefore, Mr. Morales is not attempting to roll back the market so much as draw previously excluded groups into it. The sense that Mr. Morales may be less assiduous in breaking with established forms of economic organization is only accentuated when one examines the composition of his cabinet. For example, the new Minister of Public Works is Salvador Ric Riera a conservative rich Santa Cruz businessman (Petras, 2006). The Ministries of Mines and Defence – both key portfolios – have also been placed in the hands of conservative figures (ibid.). In an indication of the surprisingly moderate inclination of elements of the new administration, the new Minister of Finance, Luis Arce, has pledged his commitment to macroeconomic stability and seems likely to follow the main tenets of Bolivia's existing arrangements with the IMF.

So what, therefore, of the much vaunted radicalness of the Morales administration? In answer to this it is necessary to look at the evolution of policy directed at the hydrocarbons sector. Without question, unlike some of his ostensibly left-wing counterparts elsewhere in the region, Mr. Morales has adopted a very tough stance. Under the terms of a new decree, majority control of oil and gas production assets must pass into the hands of the state-owned oil company, YPFB. At the same time, royalty agreements with foreign oil companies are to be renegotiated in favor of the Bolivian authorities. Demonstrating the seriousness of the government's intent, there have been instances of troop occupation of oil and gas fields along with popular demonstrations against foreign enterprises. The majority state-owned Brazilian enterprise, Petrobrás, which had invested heavily in Bolivian gas, has been badly hit by the new legislation as have such enterprises as BG, Total, and BP (*The Economist*, May 6, 2006). In the case of Petrobrás, the stance of the Morales administration has deeply soured relationships with Brazil, creating tension with a hitherto friendly neighbor. However, it is important to note that the new legislation does not involve the ejection of international oil companies from Bolivia. Rather, the intention is to reduce their participation to minority stakes in national hydrocarbons production. The hope must be here that the enterprises in question find it worth their while to stay on and continue to inject much-needed capital and technology.

At the time of writing the Morales administration was only halfway into its first term and its policy platform was still emerging. Could the future herald more radical gestures such as that visited on the hydrocarbons sector? Perhaps the answer here is yes: in February 2007 Bolivian troops seized a tin smelter owned by the Swiss-based mining enterprise Glencore. This followed the issuing of a decree by Mr. Morales nationalizing the facilities. So far there appear to be no plans to compensate Glencore for the seizure. Still, Mr. Morales' radical instincts are likely to meet with some opposition. In addition to conservative elements within the cabinet Mr. Morales will have to deal with the results of a constitutional assembly election held at the beginning of July 2006. This delivered a less than ringing endorsement for the new government and also indicated the desire of four of Bolivia's nine provinces to pursue their quest for autonomy (*The Seattle Times*, July 4, 2006). Against this background, Mr. Morales will probably have to temper his policy agenda to keep dissident factions on board and prevent more conservative regions – especially Santa Cruz – from breaking away. Having offered up an important populist gesture in "renationalizing" hydrocarbons and elements of the mining sector, the new administration may well be reluctant to seek more confrontation.

Conclusions

This chapter has reviewed a broad canvas on which the paint has yet to dry. Latin America is only five or six years into an experiment whose results are just beginning to trickle in. Judging from the experiences of Argentina, Bolivia, Brazil, and Venezuela, the evidence so far is that the left has been more tentative than might be imagined in its attempts to break with the past and engineer a comprehensive overturning of Neoliberalism. Rather than abandon macroeconomic orthodoxy, governments throughout the region have maintained in place tough primary fiscal targets (although these have struggled to contain high levels of public debt). Neither has there been any serious attempt to return to the *status quo ante* of ISI. Instead, the emphasis seems to be being placed on making markets work in the interests of those previously marginalized. In this sense, the agenda of the Latin American

New Left appears to fit curiously comfortably with that now being developed in multilateral institutions and government aid agencies around the world.

Only in the case of mining and energy sectors has there been substantial evidence of a real desire to displace the private sector and assert state control. It is possible to argue that the experiences of these sectors have less to do with a regional left-wing shift than with a sort of global resurgence in resources nationalism. With commodity prices being driven ever higher, gaining greater control over hydrocarbons and minerals production can be an effective way of fiscally strengthening the state. Such policies also offer a convenient means of pandering to nationalist sentiment. In this sense, the recent experience of Venezuela and Bolivia, in particular, has much in common with that of Russia. There, nationalist resurgence and a reassertion of state control over resources have gone hand in hand.

Turning to the future, is the onward drift to the left in Latin America inevitable? Reviewing the evidence to hand, the answer is not unambiguous. On the one hand, as this chapter has demonstrated, it is necessary to distinguish between the rhetoric and reality: experience seems to demonstrate that once in power, Latin America's new leftist administrations are remarkably reluctant to dispense with the fundamental planks of the Washington Consensus. On the other hand, in the case of Venezuela, at least, growing presidential authoritarianism suggests the stage might be set for a more radical shift than hitherto experienced. The erosion of democracy in Venezuela and in Argentina too (where Néstor Kirchner ruled extensively by decree) is deeply troubling. In regard to the long-run economic development of these countries, the arbitrary use of executive power, the recourse to populism, and the short-circuiting of democratic institutions seems unlikely to be consistent with a healthy climate for the pursuit of long-run efficient and equitable economic development. Still, it would be a mistake to suppose that all countries in the region are keen to opt for a radical, left-wing alternative. One has only to look as far as Colombia and Mexico, for example, to note the enduring popularity of the center and center-right.

References

Amann, E., and W. Baer (2003) "Anchors Away: The Costs and Benefits of Brazil's Devaluation," *World Development*, 31, 1033–1046.

Amann, E., and W. Baer (2006) "Economic Orthodoxy versus Social Development? The Dilemmas Facing Brazil's Labor Government", *Oxford Development Studies*, 34, 21941.

Bamrud, J. (2005) "Chaveznomics: Venezuela's Private Sector under Siege," *Latin Business Chronicle*, September 12.

Bulmer-Thomas, V. (2003) *An Economic History of Latin America Since Independence*, Cambridge: Cambridge University Press.

DFAT (Australian Government Department of Foreign Affairs and Trade) (2007) *Venezuela Country Brief*, December.

The Economist (February 23, 2006) "The Price is Wrong."

The Economist (December 20, 2005) "Kirchner and Lula: Different Ways to Give the Fund the Kiss Off."

The Economist (June 3, 2004) "Becoming a Serious Country."

Inter-American Development Bank (IDB) (2006) Country Indicators – Argentina, Bolivia, and Venezuela.

Pandya, C., and J. Podur (2003) *The Chavez Government's Economic Policies*, Z Net Activism (www.zmag.org).

Petras, J. (2006) "A bizarre beginning in Bolivia," *Counterpunch*, February 4–5.

The Seattle Times, July 4, 2006.

Thorp, R. (1998) *Progress, Poverty and Exclusion: An Economic History of Latin America*, Washington D.C.: Inter-American Development Bank.

16
Deficit Targeting: An Incentive Mechanism for Subnational Fiscal Deficit Reduction in Brazil

Mauricio S. Bugarin, Mirta N.S. Bugarin, and Henrique A. Pires

Introduction

The traditional debate on fiscal federalism focuses on the trade-off between allocative efficiency and distributive concerns. From the point of view of the *allocation* of public resources, it is well known that local governments are better suited to accommodate in an efficient way differing preferences among agents. This view suggests that the best fiscal policies are decided at a decentralized local government level. However, from the point of view of the *distribution* of wealth, the central government has a clear role in designing revenue-sharing rules to achieve a more equitable redistribution of income among different regions of a country with heterogeneous levels of development. This second view suggests a higher level of centralization in a government's fiscal policy decisions.[1] Therefore, the optimal level of decentralization in a federation must reflect the right balance between those two opposing views.[2]

A study of the recent experience of selected developing countries shows a somehow erratic process in the level of centralization of the fiscal federalist system. The case of Brazil, for example, is noteworthy: since 1965 the share of the federal government in terms of total revenue increased from 54.9 percent to 61.3 in 1988 and then decreased again to 51.4 in 1991.[3] As was the case with Brazil, when democracy takes root in a country, there is a natural movement toward fiscal decentralization.[4] A consequence of this trend is the emergence of a third important issue in determining the optimal level of fiscal decentralization: subnational governments' expenditure levels may come to play a significant role in the *macroeconomic management* of the country. Indeed, as a higher proportion of total expenditure is made at the decentralized level, a serious effort to control the federal fiscal deficit may be partially offset by a less disciplined fiscal policy at the lower levels of government. Due to a *free rider* type of problem, local governments may not make macroeconomic management as one of their priorities; in fact they may even find it in their best interest to accumulate important deficits, which will generate a Pareto suboptimal equilibrium for the entire economy.[5]

The present article analyzes the incentives faced by local governments[6] with respect to fiscal discipline in a federalist system where revenue-sharing transfers are important sources of income. The study is based on a model of state fiscal policy under market discipline first introduced in Werneck (1995). Following that model, we show that the central government can use the transfers as a powerful mechanism to induce the states into choosing lower levels of fiscal deficit. This is accomplished by making the transfers contingent on an optimally chosen "deficit targeting" rule, in such a way that the farther the state's realized deficit from the targeted level, the lower the transfers from the central government.

Although desirable, such a contingency may be difficult to implement, as unconditional transfers are often seen as a necessary condition for state autonomy. In the case of Brazil, for example, there is a constitutional requirement that the transfers of the "States Participation Fund" (Fundo de Participação dos Estados, FPE, the most important source of transfers to the states) must be unconditional. In order to study the central government's options when this type of contingency cannot be imposed upon the states, we analyze a fundamental friction of the federative system in many developing countries. The friction is that less financially responsible subnational governments usually have to pay higher interest on their debt than a sounder central government. Therefore, the states have an incentive to renegotiate their debt stocks toward the private sector into debt towards the central government. As the state's interest rate becomes significantly higher than the federal government's one, a strong political pressure ensues, compelling the central government into a costly renegotiation process.

The present study shows that, when the renegotiation is done in a careless manner, it can generate very adverse behavior from the state: facing a looser budget constraint, because of the lower interest payments, a typical state will want indeed to increase its deficit. However, if the federal government implements a proper renegotiation procedure, it will create incentives for the states to accept a special type of transfer contract in order to obtain a lower interest rate. As a result, the expenditure level of the state will be significantly reduced.

The rest of the paper is organized as follows. The second section develops a simple econometric study showing that the Brazilian states' aggregate revenue time series present a clear stationary behavior, whereas their aggregate debt time series present strong evidence of explosive behavior. This empirical evidence points to the need for reform to slow down the states' debt accumulation process.

The following section introduces the basic Werneck (1995) market-discipline model and derives the optimal expenditure rule for a typical state in the presence of unconditional transfers from the central government.

In the next section, it will be shown that the state's deficit will be considerably reduced when the federal government is able to condition the transfers on a measure of fiscal responsibility by the state. The structure introduced is called here a "deficit-targeting" model because of its resemblance to the traditional "inflation-targeting" models used in the monetary policy literature.

The next section shows that, when transfers are unconditional and the state renegotiates with the federal government in order to obtain lower interest rates on the stock of its debt, then the state will choose a higher deficit level than before renegotiation. Thereafter, the next section shows that a well chosen renegotiation process may be devised so that the state will find it in its best interest to sign a deficit-targeting contract in order to obtain the lower interest rate after renegotiation. In that case a lower deficit level will be the solution to the state expenditure problem.

The following section discusses Brazil's recent Fiscal Responsibility Law in the light of the theory developed here and then the next section argues that there is empirical evidence that credit constraints do not play an important role in the states' fiscal policy choices and, therefore, should not be considered as an alternative to the deficit-targeting approach.

The final section concludes the paper with a discussion of possible extensions of the present model.

Empirical evidence for Brazilian subnational governments

In this section we present the main econometric results that characterize the properties of the revenues and debt time series of the Brazilian local governments. We opted to choose the larger of the available time-series datasets, which gave us the period from January 1991 to December 2006.[7] Therefore, we tried to cover the impacts of both the Brazilian National Constitution's postreform (1989) period and the Real Inflation Stabilization Program (1994), as well as the structural reforms undertaken since the beginning of the 1990s, in such a way that we could study as complete a cycle as possible for the country's local government performance.[8]

Revenue

Brazil's local governments[9] have mainly three sources of revenue. The first is the States' Participation Fund (Fundo de Participação dos Estados, FPE). The fund is formed with 21.5 percent of the net revenue of the three main federal taxes: corporate and personal income taxes (IRPJ, IRPF) and the VAT-type industrialized products tax (IPI). The second source is the Municipalities' Participation Fund (Fundo de Participação dos Municípios, FPM), which corresponds to 22.5 percent of the sum of income taxes (IRPJ, IRPF) and the IPI, net of fiscal incentives and tax credits. The third source is the broad-based locally collected VAT-type tax, ICMS.[10]

This paper takes the sum of the FPE, the FPM, and the ICMS as a proxy for aggregate subnational governments' revenue. Figure 16.1 presents that variable, in a monthly time series from January 1991 to December 2006. The ICMS series was collected from the states' Treasury Departments (Secretarias Estaduais de Fazenda), whereas the FPE and FPM series were obtained from the National Treasury Secretariat. The series were deflated with the aggregate price index, IPCA, calculated by the Brazilian Institute of Geography and Statistics, IBGE, taking 1994 as the base year.

Figure 16.1 suggests a rather stable behavior of the aggregate revenue series. In order to investigate the stationarity of the series statistically, we performed the Augmented Dickey-Fuller (ADF) Unit Root test. The specification of the time-series model was based on the Schwarz Information Criterion (SIC),[11] which resulted in a lag length of $p=2$. The null hypothesis is that the series presents a unit root. Table 16.1 presents the ADF statistic and the corresponding 1, 5 and 10 percent critical values. The null hypothesis is rejected at all reported levels of significance, suggesting a stationary behavior of the subnational revenue series.

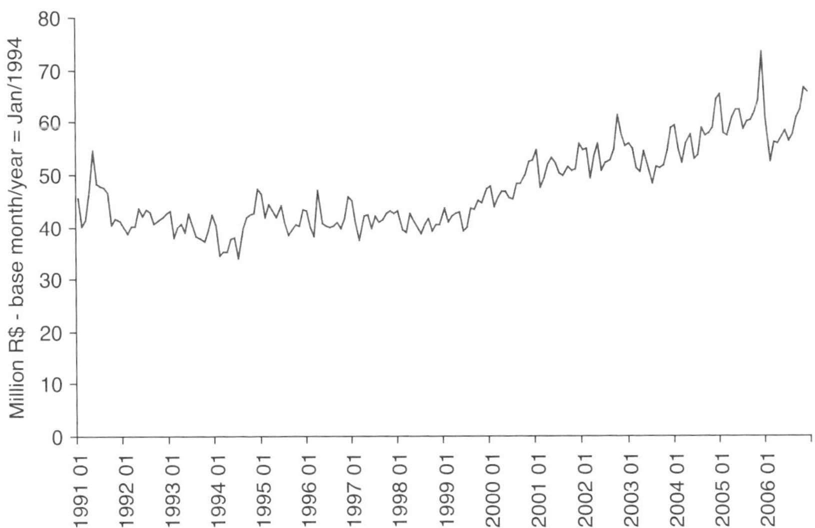

Figure 16.1   Subnational governments' aggregate FPE, FPM, and ICMS revenue January 1991–December 2006

Source: National Treasury Secretariat, States Treasury Departments and IBGE.

Table 16.1   ADF test for the aggregate revenue series

ADF statistic	−4.545736	1% critical value	−3.4650
		5% critical value	−2.8767
		10% critical value	−2.5749

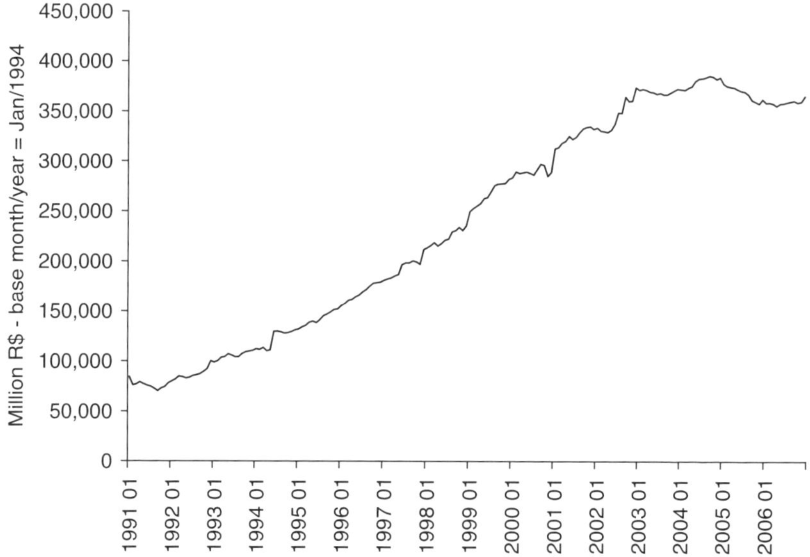

Figure 16.2   Subnational governments' aggregate public debt January 1991–December 2006

Source: Brazilian Central Bank and IBGE.

Public debt

Brazilian subnational governments' aggregate debt monthly series from January 1991 to December 2006 was obtained from the Brazilian Central Bank (BCB, Boletim de Finanças Públicas) and is shown in Figure 16.2. This series was also deflated with the aggregate price index, IPCA, calculated by the Brazilian Institute of Geography and Statistics, IBGE, taking 1994 as the base year.

In opposition to the revenue series, Figure 16.2 suggests a nonstationary behavior of the public debt series. The Augmented Dickey-Fuller Unit Root test is again performed using this time series to test statistically for the presence of unit root(s) in the data. According to the Schwarz Information Criterion, the best fit was obtained with one lag, $p=1$, including a constant term as well as a trend in the model. According to the obtained statistics shown in Table 16.2, we can assess that, since the ADF statistic is greater

Table 16.2   ADF test statistic for the aggregate public debt series

ADF statistic	−0.307025	1% critical value	−4.0068
		5% critical value	−3.4335
		10% critical value	−3.1406

than the reported critical values, the test fails to reject the (unit root) null hypothesis. Therefore, the subnational aggregate debt series is nonstationary and has one unit root, for it is integrated of order one, $I(1)$.

Therefore, the econometric tests above suggest, on one hand, a stationary behavior of states' revenues and, on the other hand, an explosive behavior of states' debt. These results point out that the observed subnational debt accumulation may become a real concern in Brazil in the long run. The rest of the paper analyzes how the design of intergovernmental transfers may be changed in order to create new incentives for reducing subnational debt accumulation.

Local governments' expenditure under market discipline

A typical state's expenditure decision is modeled after Werneck (1995). The state is assumed to solve the following maximization problem.

$$\underset{D_S}{Max}\, U_S(E_S)$$
$$\text{s.t. } E_S + r_S B_S = D_S + T_S \tag{16.1}$$

In (16.1), U_S is the state utility, a continuously differentiable, strictly increasing function. The restriction is the usual budget constraint, which establishes that total expenditure must be equal to total revenue. The elements of expenditure and revenue are detailed below. All variables refer to a typical state S. On the expenditure side, E_S denotes the fiscal expenditure of the state. The total payment of interest on the stock of debt, B_S, is $r_S B_S$, where it is assumed that each state faces its own interest rate r_S. On the revenue side, D_S is the state's deficit and T_S is its total tax revenue.

Therefore, the model assumes that a typical state derives utility from increasing its expenditure levels, constrained by the accounting restriction (16.1). The variables above are interdependent and related to their federal level counterpart as follows.

A typical state's interest rate r_S is given by:

$$r_S = r_F + r\left(D_S, \frac{T_S}{B_S}\right) \tag{16.2}$$

Here r_F is the interest rate the federal government pays on its own debt and r is a *spread* the state has to endure given its own fiscal structure.[12] The spread r is assumed to be increasing on the state's deficit D_S and decreasing on the traditional measure of solvency, the total revenue over debt ratio $T_S / B_S : (\partial r / \partial D_S) > 0; \partial r / \partial [T_S / B_S] < 0.$

Finally, the state's revenue T_S has two components: the revenue obtained by its own tax effort, T_O, and the amount of transfers obtained from the central government, δT_F, a fixed proportion δ of the federal tax effort.[13]

$$T_S = T_O + \delta T_F \tag{16.3}$$

Plugging expressions (16.2) and (16.3) into the budget constraint (16.1) and then substituting the resulting expression for E_S into the utility function of the state yields the following unrestricted maximization problem.

$$\underset{D_S}{Max} \, U_S \left(D_S - r_F B_S - r \left(D_S, \frac{T_O + \delta T_F}{B_S} \right) B_S + T_O + \delta T_F \right)$$

The solution to the above problem is the unique value of D_S that satisfies the identity below.

$$\frac{\partial r}{\partial D_S} \left(D_S, \frac{T_O + \delta T_F}{B_S} \right) B_S = 1 \tag{16.4}$$

Condition , first presented in Werneck (1995), establishes the optimal deficit level of the local government, D_S^w. The left-hand side represents the additional cost to the state when it increases its deficit by one unit: the corresponding additional increase in the spread of the state interest rate r, which applies to the stock of the debt B_S. The right-hand side represents the extra benefit of an increase of one unit of deficit.[14]

The optimal deficit level D_S^w of a typical state does not take into consideration the effect of its expenditure on the overall macroeconomic management of the country. In fact, the free rider problem suggests that the socially optimal deficit level, when the whole country is taken into account, may require a much lower deficit level (Werlang and Fraga-Neto, 1995). The next section shows that a new transfer rule may be used in order to induce the state to choose a lower level of deficit.

Deficit targeting: A second best approach

The budget constraint (16.1) and the discussion on the trend towards decentralization suggest that revenue sharing may be an important source of income for local governments, and this affects the state's optimal fiscal policy. Several articles show that the natural consequence of revenue-sharing rules is that the state chooses a looser fiscal policy. Ribeiro (1998), for example, shows that revenue sharing in Brazil tends to reduce the states' own tax efforts. Moreover, Werneck (1995) shows that an increase in the federal government tax effort T_F may stimulate the states to choose higher level of expenditure.

Revenue sharing may, however, become a strong source of control on local government deficits if a rule of transfers contingent on certain goals is introduced. Suppose, then, that the federal government wishes to create incentives for the state to choose a deficit level D_S^*. This optimal level of deficit typically depends on the overall state of the economy; here it is taken as an exogenous decision of the federal government that could be zero or even negative, that is, the federal government seeks to induce a fiscal surplus in the local accounts. For the sake of simplicity and realism the present article assumes that the optimal deficit level is lower than the deficit that would be chosen in the original model of Werneck: $DS^* < D_S^W$, so the federal government would like to create an incentive for the state to reduce its deficit.[15]

Suppose now the old sharing rule δT_F is replaced by the new rule $f(D_S) T_F$, where f is a single peaked, continuously differentiable concave function defined on the real line, attaining its maximum at $D_S = D_S^*$. To illustrate, a possible choice of f could be:

$$f(D_S) = \gamma - \frac{(D_S^* - D_S)^2}{K} \tag{16.5}$$

In (16.5), the state will be able to receive its total expected transfer only if it chooses $D_S = D_S^*$. Otherwise the state will be "punished" by receiving lower transfers. The farther D_S is from D_S^*, the lower the transfer the state will receive. The parameter K determines the power of the punishment: the smaller K, the more severe is the punishment for deviation from the target D_S^*. The parameter γ represents the opportunity cost of not complying with the targeted deficit and could be set equal to δ, for example.

The revenue-sharing rule f is called here a "deficit-targeting" rule and it has some resemblance to the traditional "inflation-targeting" rule.[16] However, whereas the literature on inflation targeting generally assumes the existence of a Phillips curve, all that is assumed here is that the state has control over its deficit level.

Under the above condition, a typical state's maximization problem becomes:

$$\operatorname*{Max}_{D_S} U_S(E_S)$$

$$\text{s.t. } E_S = D_S - r_F B_S - r\left(D_S, \frac{T_O + f(D_S)T_F}{B_S}\right) B_S + T_O + f(D_S)T_S \tag{16.6}$$

Plugging the new budget constraint into the objective function and calculating the first order condition one obtains the following equality for the optimal deficit level of the local government under the *deficit-targeting* rule *f*.

$$\frac{\partial r}{\partial D_S}\left(D_S, \frac{T_O + \delta T_F}{B_S}\right) B_S = 1 - \alpha \tag{16.7}$$

where,

$$\alpha = \left[-f'(D_S)T_F\right]\left[1 - \frac{\partial r}{\partial \frac{T_S}{B_S}}\left(D_S, \frac{T_O + \delta T_F}{B_S}\right)\right] > 0$$

Expression (16.7) determines the new optimal deficit policy for the state. Compared to expression (16.4), it reduces by α the marginal benefit of increasing the deficit. The term α has a very simple interpretation: on the one hand, by increasing the deficit by one unit, the total transfer to the state is reduced by $-f'(D_S)T_F$; on the other hand, the transfer reduction affects the solvency of the state (T_S/B_S) which, in turns, induces an increase in the spread of the interest rate, r, of $\partial r/\partial(T_S/B_S)$, and further reduces the amount of the transfer available for expenditure.

Note that the reduction in the left-hand side of (16.7) compared to (16.4) implies a choice of a lower level of deficit D_S. Therefore, the *deficit-targeting* rule stimulates the state to adopt a more responsible fiscal policy. The actual effect of this constraint depends on several exogenous and endogenous variables. First, the more the state depends on the central government's transfers, the more effective the rule; indeed, if the transfers when the state chooses $D_S = D_S^*$ are too low compared to the state's own tax effort T_O, then the *power* of the incentive scheme will be very limited. Second, the effectiveness of the rule depends crucially on the choice of the function *f* and, more particularly, on the absolute value of the derivative $f'(D_S)$: the higher that absolute value, the more powerful the incentives.

It is noteworthy that, although such rule will prompt a reduction in a state's deficit, in general it may not actually induce the desired deficit level D_S^*. In that sense the *deficit-targeting* rule may be viewed as a *second best* mechanism.

The approach presented here, however limited, requires a strong central government, which has to be able to impose a change of transfer rules that may not be in the best interest of local governments. Therefore, the political challenges involved may be considerable. In the case of Brazil, for example, the Federal Constitution requires the *States Participation Fund* (Fundo de

Participação dos Estados) to be a direct and unconditional transfer to the states, in the form of the revenue-sharing rule δT_F in (16.3).

In fact, history seems to move in an opposite direction. Indeed, it has often been the case in developing countries that a local government, when faced with an extremely high interest rate, asks for the central government's financial support. The usual procedure is for the central government to bail out the state's debt, becoming the state's new creditor. The interest rate the state will pay to the central government on the transferred debt is decided during the debt renegotiation process and this decision typically has a strong political bias. Usually the renegotiation concludes with an indirect subsidy from the central to the local government: the central government pays the state's debt according to the state's market interest rate r_S, whereas the state pays the federal government back according to the lower interest rate r_F. The next section analyzes the effect on the local government's expenditure decision when, as a result of the renegotiation process, the state has to pay the same interest rate as the central government, r_F.

Unconstrained renegotiation

Suppose that a state faces a high spread r in its own interest rates, due to the application of fiscal rule (16.4). In that case, the state would have a significant gain if it could switch from the high r_F+r interest rate to the lower r_F rate paid by the federal government. Therefore, the incentives are set for debt renegotiation between the local and the federal governments.

This section studies the case where the renegotiation is such that the federal government bails out the local government's debt and becomes the state's creditor. Moreover, the state now has access to the subsidized interest rate r_F, the one faced by the central government.

In this case, the state government fiscal problem becomes:

$$\underset{D_S}{Max}\, U_S \left(D_S - r_F B_S + T_O + \delta T_F \right)$$

Observe that now the interest rate faced by the state does not depend on its own fiscal policy. Therefore, the above problem has no solution: since there is no cost associated with increasing expenditure, the state wants to spend as much as possible and accumulate an infinite amount of debt.[17] That is, the renegotiation process generates an *adverse incentive* (moral hazard), stimulating the state to increase its expenditure above the level selected before renegotiation, which is exactly what the central government would like to avoid. Unfortunately, there seems to be evidence that this very behavior has occurred in Brazilian states' debt renegotiation processes.[18]

However, this type of inefficient renegotiation process does not have to be the institution chosen by the federal government. Indeed, as it has been shown above, central government transfers constitute a powerful instrument that can be used in order to discipline a state's fiscal behavior. The following section analyzes what can be done by the federal government when the institutional framework of the country does not allow for as a radical change in the transfer rule as that proposed in the previous section, but the states still need financial support from the federal government.

Individually rational renegotiation contracts: A third best approach

Suppose now that a state cannot be forced into a contract of the *deficit-targeting* type, so it can always choose to keep the legal fixed transfers δT_F. What can the federal government do in order to encourage the local government to reduce its deficit level? Because the renegotiation of a state debt, with the resulting reduction in its interest rate, implies a softer state budget constraint, the federal government can take advantage of the process to create the conditions for a reduction of the subnational government's fiscal deficit.

The argument is as follow. A typical state can choose not to sign a renegotiation contract with the central government. In that case the state keeps its unconditional transfers δT_F, but faces its own high interest rate $r_S=r_F+r$. On the other hand, the state may choose to renegotiate its debt in order to have access to the lower interest rate r_F, but has to accept the *deficit-targeting* transfer rule f.

Since the state may choose not to renegotiate with the central government, if renegotiation occurs the state must be at least as well off as without negotiation. Recall that D_S^w denotes the optimal deficit level when the state faces its own interest rate, and let $D_S^w = D_S^w - r_S B_S + T_S$ be the corresponding total expenditure. Then the central government's problem can be described as:

$$\underset{f,D_S}{Min\ U_F(D_S,D_S^*)}$$

$$E_S = D_S - r_F B_S + T_O + f(D_S)T_F \tag{16.8}$$

$$E_S \geq E_S^W \tag{16.9}$$

The federal government's objective function, $U_F(D_S,D_S^*)$, is assumed to be decreasing with the distance between D_S and D_S^*. Note that the function need not be symmetric with respect to that distance, that is, it might be the case that the cost of a higher-than-targeted deficit is greater than the cost of a lower-than-targeted deficit.[19] However, the very concept of a deficit target requires below-the-target deficits to be undesirable. This may be justified by the fact that the main goal of governments is to offer public goods, so that a very low level of deficit (or possibly a high level of surplus) may significantly reduce public good production. Given the assumption that $D_S^w > D_S^*$, it will become clear in what follows that the federal government will not need to be concerned with lower-than-targeted deficit in equilibrium.

Equation (16.8) is the budget constraint, when the state accepts the *deficit-targeting* contract, as before. The novelty here is equation (16.9), the *individual rationality* or *participation constraint*, which requires that the state receive at least as much utility when it accepts the new contract as it would have gotten, had it chosen not to renegotiate its debt.

Since the federal government wants to induce the state to choose a deficit level lower than, the optimal contract will be designed in such a way that the additional income available to the state through the reduction in its interest rate payment will be directed entirely toward a reduction of its deficit. This can be obtained by heavily penalizing the state when $D_S > D_S^w$

Therefore, the optimal choice of f will be such that equation (16.9) is met with equality: $E_S = E_S^w$ Composing (16.9) with (16.8), it follows that:

$$D_S^W - D_S = r\left(D_S, \frac{T_O + \delta T_F}{B_S}\right)B_S - (\delta - f(D_S))T_F \tag{16.10}$$

Expression (16.10) shows the maximum gain for the central government in terms of the reduction of the state's fiscal deficit, $D_S^w - D_S$, in an institutional framework where the state is able to choose not to renegotiate. The first term on the right-hand side corresponds to the resources the state obtains given the reduction in the interest payment on the stock of its debt. The second term corresponds to the reduction in transfers from the federal government when the contract is signed. Therefore, the right-hand side corresponds to the net revenue the state receives when signing the *deficit-targeting* contract. The left-hand side shows that all the net gains the state obtains from this new arrangement are directed toward the reduction of its deficit.

To conclude, note that the participation constraint (16.9) puts a limit on the ability of the central government to control the state's fiscal deficit, since the state must be assured an expenditure level at least as high as it would choose without renegotiation. For that reason, this mechanism could be classified as a *third best* approach to the deficit control problem. However, equation (16.10) shows that there is still a potential gain for the federal government if it chooses a suitable renegotiation mechanism. It is important to mention that, because of political pressures or other considerations, the federal government may be forced to renegotiate states' debts anyway.[20] The main point of the present study is to show that debt renegotiation, instead of being a burden to the nation, can be used by the central government as a tool to induce a more responsible fiscal behavior on the part of the subnational governments.

The Brazilian Fiscal Responsibility Law and the deficit-targeting mechanism

Intergovernmental relations in Brazil during the second half of the twentieth century have been characterized by successive bailouts of subnational debt by the federal government. These bailouts created an adverse incentive for responsible local fiscal policy, which contributed to the macroeconomic instability observed in Brazil until recently.[21]

After the "miracle" of the 1970s, the consequent depression of the 1980s forced Brazilian society to accept the fact that macroeconomic stability requires fiscal responsibility. The new 1988 Federal Constitution already included in its Article 169 the requirement for a ceiling for personnel expenditure to be defined by law. In 1995 Law 82/1995, also known as the Camata Law, established a limit of 60 percent of net current revenue, valid for all levels of government.

A stronger control on subnational fiscal policy started with Law 9396/1997, also known as the Fiscal Adjustment and Refinancing Law of 1997, which established a series of mechanisms aimed at assuring that subnational debt would be reduced over time. That control was reinforced in May 2000 when the Fiscal Responsibility Law (LRF, Law 101/2000) was signed.

The Fiscal Responsibility Law is a broad and detailed piece of legislation aimed at disciplining public finances at all levels of government in Brazil. It includes several innovations, among which one should stress the "Golden Rule," which establishes that credit operations may not exceed capital expenditure. In what concerns subnational debt, it requires (by means of a subsequent Senate law) that states consolidated debt should not exceed twice the net current revenue.[22] It also introduces the concept of fiscal targets to be followed by local governments and establishes clear measures to be imposed in cases where the targets are not met. These include institutional penalties, such as blocking voluntary transfers, but also personal penalties (by means of a separate fiscal responsibility crime law) such as the imprisonment of mayors and state governors.

In comparison, the LRF appears not only broader, but also more restrictive than the deficit-targeting mechanism. Indeed, the LRF bases its incentives on penalties to be imposed if the target is not reached, whereas the deficit-targeting mechanism allows for deviations from the target. This distinction suggests that the deficit-targeting approach decentralizes the deficit choice and allows the subnational government to choose a higher deficit if it believes it is worth the corresponding cost. On the other hand, the LRF approach centralizes the deficit choice by establishing very tough penalties if the target is not attained.

One may argue that the LRF needs to be tough in order to induce the subnational governments to really adopt a sound fiscal policy. This is particularly important given the history of irresponsible local debt management in

Brazil. However, economic theory clearly suggests that a more flexible fiscal policy may be optimal in order to deal with the stochastic component of policy management. In that case, a less rigid policy of the deficit-targeting type may be suitable in the long run, after more responsible local policy management has been incorporated in subnational practices thanks to the LRF.

Credit constraints and subnational debt dynamics

The main methodological assumption of the present model is that the market imposes higher interest rates on the states as the levels of debt-to-revenue ratio and deficit increase. An alternative approach would be to let the market impose credit constraints on fiscally unsound states, rather than charging higher interest rates on their debt. This would constrain the fiscal choices of the states and there might be no need for the federal government to intervene with a deficit-targeting mechanism.

We believe there are two possible justifications for the deficit-targeting approach as compared to the credit constraint argument, one theoretical and one empirical. On the theoretical point of view, suppose financial markets work that way, so that credit constraints limit states' ability to issue debt above a certain level; yet, this limit may materialize at too high a debt level from the point of view of the federal government. In that case, the federal government may prefer to create incentives for adequate fiscal behavior by means of the deficit-targeting mechanism, rather than settling with the higher-debt market equilibrium.

The empirical analysis consists of collecting recent data on the debt accumulation process in Brazilian states'. Figure 16.3 presents a monthly series of the aggregate bonds issued by states and municipalities in the Brazilian internal market from January 1980 to January 2005. The series was obtained from IPEADATA, based on the Brazilian Central Bank's data (Boletim de Finanças Públicas) and is deflated with the aggregate price index, IPCA, calculated by the IBGE, taking January 2007 as the base month.

Figure 16.3 clearly suggests an explosive behavior for bonds issuing. The Augmented Dickey-Fuller Unit Root test is again performed using this time series to statistically test for the presence of unit roots in this data. According to the Schwarz Information Criterion, the best fit was obtained with 15 lags, $p=15$, including a constant term as well as a trend in the model. According to the obtained statistics shown in Table 16.3, we can assess that, since the ADF statistic is greater than the reported critical values, the test fails to reject the (unit root) null hypothesis. Therefore, the states' debt series is nonstationary and has one unit root.

Therefore, the empirical evidence suggests that credit rationing has not been a significant factor in reducing subnational debt accumulation. NB, if we divide the sample into two subperiods, then the explosive behavior remains

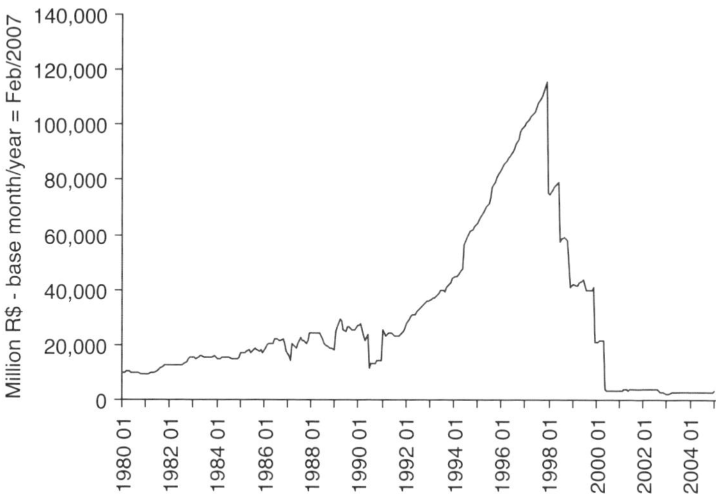

Figure 16.3   Subnational government bonds issued on the Brazilian market January 1980–January 2005

Source: Brazilian Central Bank and IBGE.

Table 16.3   ADF test statistic for the issued bonds series

ADF statistic	−2.643846	1% critical value	−3.990585
		5% critical value	−3.425671
		10% critical value	−3.135994

in the subsample including January 1980–November 1998,[23] whereas a stationary behavior is reached in the subsample including December 1998–January 2005.[24] However, this is most clearly a consequence of the 1997 Fiscal Adjustment and Refinancing Law and the 2000 Fiscal Responsibility Law discussed in the previous section, which imposed strong restrictions on debt issue to the states and municipalities. Therefore, federal government regulations, rather than market credit rationing, appear to be the mechanisms that stimulated debt reduction in Brazil's recent history.

Conclusion

The present chapter considers the fiscal federalist relationship between a higher-level central government and a local-level state government, from the point of view of the control of the state's fiscal deficits. The first result proven here is that the usual revenue-sharing rules between federal and local levels of government are powerful instruments that can be used by the central authority in order to induce the local decisionmakers to reduce their deficit levels. The sharing rules that implement such a responsible fiscal policy at the state level were called *deficit-targeting* rules, because of their resemblance to the traditional *inflation-targeting* rules in the monetary policy literature.

The second main result concerns the case when a deficit-targeting rule cannot be imposed upon a state against its will. In this situation, the federal government can still devise an individually rational deficit-targeting contract that will be accepted by the state when it faces a higher interest rate than the federal government, and needs the central government's financial support in order to reduce interest payments. This approach seems to have been used in the latest rounds of subnational debt renegotiation during the Fernando Henrique Cardoso's presidential terms (1994–2002).

The models developed here are based on a market-discipline framework first introduced in Werneck (1995) in order to study the effect of an increase in the tax effort of the central government on the spending policies of local governments. Those models constitute a first attempt at using a mechanism to deal with the issue of disciplining the fiscal behavior of local governments. They can be extended in many different ways in order to better reflect some aspects of reality, without changing its essence. For instance, it is assumed here that after renegotiation the state faces the federal government interest rate r_F. In fact, recent Brazilian history has shown that it is often the case that the renegotiation contracts establish lower interest rates – an extra subsidy to the local governments. The introduction of such lower interest rate, say r_A (for "after" renegotiation) would only increase the control of the federal government over the state government deficits or, equivalently, loosen the individual rationality constraint (16.9).

Other more fundamental extensions are also of interest. First, although the choice of the optimum fiscal policy of a state is essentially a dynamic issue, it is modeled here in a static framework. A more complete model must incorporate the effects of accumulation of debt in the future decisions of a state. That approach has been followed in Bugarin (2006). Although that paper does not analyze deficit-targeting mechanisms, it presents a dynamic model of debt accumulation where states face increasing interest rates as debt levels raise, and concludes that, in the long run, market discipline is a strong enough incentive for subnational deficit control. However, in the long run equilibrium debt level may be too high and the deficit-reduction process too slow from the point of view of the federal government, so a deficit-targeting mechanism may still be desirable.

Second, still based on a fully dynamic approach, a less smooth version of the deficit-targeting approach may be used based on a "folk theorem" rationale. It would work basically in the following way: a deficit target is agreed with the subnational government and, if the realized deficit is within an acceptable distance of the target, the usual (constitutional) transfers are made; if, however, the realized deficit in one period is outside the acceptable range, then, there will follow a previously defined period of lowered transfers. If the long-run losses resulting from the lowered transfers are costly enough, then an equilibrium is reached where the subnational government finds it optimal to keep the deficit within the "no-punishment" range.[25]

Third, although the renegotiation of a state's debt is essentially a political issue, no model of the political bargaining process is included in this model. Some concepts of positive political economy might greatly enrich the appeal of those models. In particular, the subsidy cost to the nation of this renegotiation process is not taken into consideration in the federal government's minimization problem studied earlier.

Finally, this chapter takes parametrically the optimal state deficit level D_S^*; a more comprehensive model would also take into account how the federal government determines this optimal level of deficit. The extension of the basic models to include the above frictions is left as a suggestion for further research.

Notes

The authors are grateful to Marcelle Chauvet, Hadi Esfahani, Gazi Islam, Fábio Kanczuk, and Flávio Versiani for helpful comments on an earlier version of this article. That version won the "IV Brazilian Federal Treasure Monograph Award" (First prize in the Public Deficit category). The opinions expressed and the remaining mistakes are the authors' sole responsibility.

1. See, for example, Wagner (1983).
2. For very good reviews on the main incentive issues of fiscal federalism see the seminal work of Musgrave (1969) or the more recent Oates (1999).
3. Net of transfers to local governments; see Afonso (1994).
4. In Argentina during the 1980s the federal government's expenditure corresponded on average, to 68 percent of total public expenditure. In 1991 this decreased to 60 percent and in 1996 was 55. The corresponding numbers for the "provincias" (states) are 27, 33, and 38 percent, respectively, according to Murphy and Moskovits (1997).
5. See, for example, Werlang and Fraga-Neto (1995).
6. This article uses the expressions "state," "local government," and "subnational government" for the lower level of government and the expressions "nation," "central government," and "federal government" for the higher level of government in the federation.
7. The period under study begins with the Cruzeiro (Cr$). Then, in August 1993 the nominal unit was transformed into the Cruzeiro Real (CR$=Cr$/1000), which in turn was transformed into the Real (R$=CR$/2,750,00) in July 1994. The corresponding transformation of the series was performed following www:Portal Brasil.net/economia.
8. The authors would like to thank the referee for pointing this out to us.
9. For this empirical study we defined the local governments as the states and municipalities because of the availability of a larger set of time-series data.
10. See, for example, the chapter on Brazil in Ter-Minassian (1997).

11. For details, please refer to Enders (1995), chapter 4.
12. In theory it could be the case that r takes negative values. This would happen if the state is fiscally more sound than the federal government. However, it seems to have been the case in developing countries that local governments tend to act less responsibly than central governments. See Saiegh and Tommasi (1999) on this regard.
13. In Brazil, for instance, the National Congress defines explicitly the coefficient $\delta=\delta_S$ for each state S.
14. The marginal costs and benefits above have to be multiplied by $U'_S (E_S)$ in order to obtain this interpretation in terms of the state's utility. The marginal utility term is not used here to avoid the unnecessary heavy notation.
15. However, there would be no significant change in the model had the goal been to induce the state into increasing expenditure.
16. See, for example, Walsh (1995) and Svensson (1997) for a discussion on inflation-targeting rules.
17. This conclusion is not complete in the sense that it does not take into account the dynamic aspect of the debt accumulation process. Indeed, after renegotiation, the state will have an incentive to accumulate new debt through the market, so that the spread rate r will reappear on the stock of the new debt. As a consequence, the state's deficit will have a new upper bound, similar to the one obtained in the previous model, but higher, given the reduction obtained in the payment of the debt existing before the renegotiation. This new fiscal policy will then remain stable until a new renegotiation takes place. For a more careful analysis of the dynamic debt accumulation process, see Bugarin (2006).
18. See, for example, Santos (1999).
19. The authors are grateful to the referee for this comment.
20. During the period 1987–1997 there were state debt renegotiations in Brazil every other year (Santos 1999).
21. See a discussion on this issue in Barroso and Rocha (2004).
22. The limit is 1.2 times net current revenue for municipalities and the Federal District. For a detailed discussion about the LRF see Rocha and Giuberti (2005).
23. The ADF Test Statistic critical values are −4.0081, −3.4339, −3.1406 respectively for 1, 5, and 10 percent, respectively, and the ADF Test Statistic is −2.2842, thus not rejecting the null hypothesis of unit root.
24. The ADF Test Statistic critical values are −4.0673, −3.4620, −3.1570 respectively for 1, 5, and 10 percent, respectively, and the ADF Test Statistic is −5.4949, rejecting the null hypothesis of unit root.
25. The authors are grateful to the referee for this suggestion.

References

Afonso, J.R.R. (1994) *Descentralização na América Latina: Estudo de Caso para o Brasil* (Decentralization in Latin America: A Case Study for Brazil), Série Política Fiscal, 61, Santiago: CEPAL.

Barroso, R., and R. Rocha (2004) "Is the Brazilian Fiscal Responsibility Law (LRF) Really Binding? Evidence from State-Level Government," *Anais do XXII Encontro Nacional de Economia*, João Pessoa: ANPECwww.anpec.org.br/encontro2004/artigos/A04A024.pdf

Bugarin. M. (2006) "Subnational Debt Renegotiation and Elections: Experimentation and Reputation in the Brazilian Fiscal Federalism," *Brazilian Review of Econometrics*, 26, 67–104.

Enders, W. (1995) *Applied Econometric Time Series*, New York: John Wiley and Sons.

Murphy, R.L., and C. Moskovits (1997) "Descentralização, Relações Fiscais Intergovernamentais e Governança Macroeconômica: O Caso da Argentina," (Decentralization, Inter-government Fiscal Relations and Macroeconomic Governance: The Case of Argentina), Presented at the International Conference on Decentralization, Fiscal Relations and Macroeconomic Governance, Brasilia: ESAF/OECD.

Musgrave, R. (1969) "Theories of Fiscal Federalism," *Public Finance*, 24, 521–532.

Oates, W.E. (1999) "An Essay on Fiscal Federalism," *Journal of Economic Litterature*, 37, 1120–1149.

Ribeiro, E.P. (1998) "Transferências Intergovernamentais e Esforço Fiscal dos Estados Brasileiros," (Intergovernment Transfers and Tax Effort of Brazilian States), *Anais do XX Encontro Brasileiro de Econometria*, 423–444, Vitória: SBE.

Rocha, F., and A. Giuberti (2005) "Consenso Político com Relação à Necessidade de Disciplina Fiscal dos Estados: Um Estudo da Lei de Responsabilidade Fiscal," in *IX Prêmio Tesouro Nacional,* Brasília: ESAF, 801–837.

Saiegh, S.M., and M. Tommasi (1999) "Why is Argentina's Fiscal Federalism so Inefficient? Entering the Labyrinth," *Journal of Applied Economics*, 2, 169–209.

Santos, G.C. (1999) "A dívida dos estados: Composição, evolução e concentração," (Brazilian states debt: Composition, evolution and concentration), in *III Prêmio de Monografia do Tesouro Nacional*, Brasília: ESAF, 177–205.

Svensson, Lars E.O. (1997) "Optimal Inflation Targets, 'Conservative' Central Banks, and Linear Inflation Contracts," *American Economic Review*, 87, 98–114.

Ter-Minassian, T. (1997) *Fiscal Federalism in Theory and Practice*, Washington: IMF.

Wagner, R. (1983) *Public Finance: Revenues and Expenditures in a Democratic Society* Boston, CO: Little, Brown and Co.

Walsh, Carl (1995) "Optimal Contracts for Central Bankers," *American Economic Review*, 85, 150–167.

Werlang, S.R.C., and A. Fraga-Neto (1995) "Os Bancos Estaduais e o Descontrole Fiscal: Alguns Aspectos," (State Banks and Fiscal Unbalance: Some Aspects), *Revista Brasileira de Economia*, 49, 375–390.

Werneck, R.L.F. (1995) "Federalismo Fiscal e a Política de Estabilização no Brasil," (Fiscal Federalism and the Stabilization Policy in Brazil), *Revista Brasileira de Economia*, 49, 375–390.

17
Is there any Difference in Well-being between American and Brazilian College Students?

Tiago V. de V. Cavalcanti, Juliana Ferraz Guimarães, and José Ricardo Nogueira

Introduction

According to large surveys with tourist and travel agencies abroad, Brazil has an image associated with joyfulness and seems to be eternally celebrating. Such surveys indicate that happiness is one of the main characteristic of the Brazilian people.[1] The Brazilian Tourism Institute (EMBRATUR) names the Brazilian Northeast State Bahia as the land of happiness. After a visit to Brazil, moviemaker Fellini once said that he was convinced that Brazilians were the happiest people in the World. Brazilian anthropologist, Darcy Ribeiro (1996), argued that Brazilians have a unique joyfulness for life that is hard to find in other parts of the world.[2] In this article we study happiness in Brazil from a comparative perspective. We study whether there are any differences in the overall reported life satisfaction among Brazilian and American college students. We use two samples collected through direct surveys with college students at Purdue University in Indiana, United States, and at Universidade Federal de Pernambuco (UFPE), Brazil.[3] We asked about their overall life satisfaction (see the two questionnaires in the appendix). We think that it is important to compare two similar groups in two different societies. On the one hand, they share similar aspirations and preoccupations, such as their academic grades, future career, and romance, to any college student around the world. On the other hand, socioeconomic conditions and social norms are very different in the two societies.

Figure 17.1 reports the self-reported level of happiness against per capita GDP in 2002 U.S. dollars for a selected sample of countries. It shows that indeed the level of happiness in Brazil is among the highest, given its level of economic development. However, it is far from being the topmost. Notice also that although per capita income in the United States is about six times higher than in Brazil, the level of self-reported happiness is only slightly

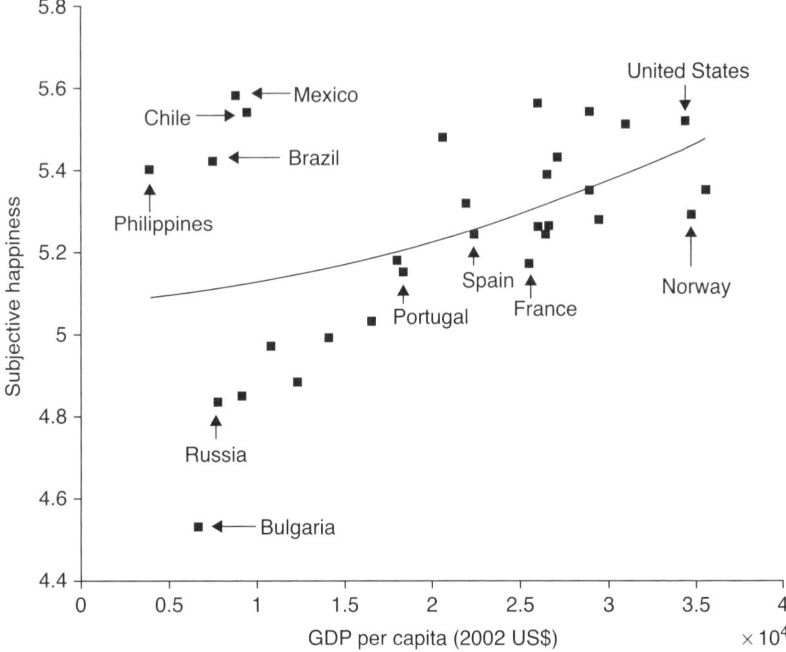

Figure 17.1   Subjective happiness and GDP per capita – Selected counties

Source: Happiness: 2002 International Social Survey Programme (ISSP). GDP per capita: World Development Indicators. The solid line is the best second-order polynomial fit.

higher in the former than in latter. Observers have noticed that there is a threshold level of income per capita (about US\$ 15,000), such that for income above this value there is no correlation between income per capita and self-reported happiness:[4] "In a country where people are starving, economic growth is viewed as the key objective… As economies get richer, however, they can afford to question the need for further riches" (Blanchflower and Oswald, 2004, p. 2). In the United States the level of happiness has not changed in the last 50 years despite an approximately threefold increase in the level of income per head.[5] The percentage of overall life satisfaction also decreased in China in the last decade despite the strong economic growth of this period (see figure 4 in Kahneman and Krueger, 2006).

Our results show that a higher fraction (about two times higher) of students at Purdue than at UFPE who report themselves to be very happy. This result is robust to the introduction of individual control variables, such as age, gender, family income, and working status. Therefore, at least in our sample, college students at Purdue have a higher probability of reporting themselves very happy than those at UFPE. We also show that there are some interesting differences. Women report to be happier (this is a statistically significant effect) than men at Purdue, but men are happier than women at UFPE (this is not statistically significant). This might be related to the socioeconomic conditions of women in these two different societies. We also show that family wealth does seem to buy extra happiness in Brazil, but not in the United States. This might be related to the fact that poor families in Brazil cannot afford tradable consumption goods, and are weakly protected by the state.[6]

It is important to highlight that psychologists find significant validations in such well-being surveys. As reported by Layard (2003), most people find easy to say how good they are feeling and although people's feelings fluctuate from day to day, there is a huge difference in the general level of happiness between different people. "The idiosyncratic effects of recent, irrelevant events are likely to average out in representative population samples" (Kahneman and Krueger (2006, 7)). Moreover, individuals who report higher levels of happiness smile more and meet other psychological measures of well-being (see Davidson et al. 2000; Kahneman and Krueger, 2006).

Besides this introduction, this paper has three more sections. The next section describes the data and summarizes some statistics of the two samples. The third section investigates whether or not there are any differences in self-reported happiness. We first analyze the distribution of overall life satisfaction in the two samples, and then use standard ordered regression analysis to study the probability of individuals to report themselves not happy, pretty happy, and very happy. The last section concludes this paper.

Data

This chapter uses data from two samples collected by the authors using direct surveys with college students at Purdue University in Indiana, United States, and at Universidade Federal de Pernambuco (UFPE), Brazil. We distributed 91 and 96 questionnaires among students at Purdue and at UFPE, respectively (see a sample of the two questionnaires in the appendix). The students at Purdue University were taking an intermediate macroeconomics class in the fall and spring of the 2005/06 academic year.[7] The students at UFPE were taking an intermediate class in public finance in the same academic year.[8]

Our main variable, self-reported happiness is constructed from a question with three possible answers: I am not happy, I am pretty happy, or I am very happy.[9] Using this question,we compared how students at Purdue and UFPE reported themselves happy, controlling for some individual and socioeconomic conditions. The four last questions collected some socioeconomic conditions of the individuals, such as age, gender, parents' income, and working status.

Table 17.1 summarizes the frequency of individuals in the two samples by gender, parents' income, and working status. The gender division in the two samples was almost the same with about 30 percent of women in each group. Regarding parents' income, we observe that the proportion of students coming from a low income family is roughly the same in the two samples; however, a higher frequency of students at Purdue than at UFPE report to coming from a high income family.[10] Table 17.1 also shows that the frequency of students working full-time is higher at UFPE than at Purdue. Conversely, there is a higher frequency of students working part-time at Purdue than at UFPE.

Table 17.2 reports the age of individuals in the two samples. Although on average students in the two samples have almost the same age (the students at UFPE are on average about ten months older than students at Purdue), the standard deviation of age among UFPE students is about 2.7 times higher than is observed among Purdue students. Notice that at UFPE the oldest student in the sample is 51 years old while at Purdue the oldest student in the sample is 27 years old.

Table 17.1 The proportion of individuals by gender, income, and working status

	Purdue students	UFPE students
Male	0.71	0.68
Female	0.29	0.32
Low income	0.05	0.07
Middle income	0.62	0.81
High income	0.33	0.12
Not working	0.42	0.50
Working part-time	0.52	0.38
Working full-time	0.06	0.12

Source: Authors' survey

Table 17.2 Students' age

	Purdue students	UFPE students
Mean	21.95	22.77
Standard deviation	1.57	4.86
Maximum	27	51
Minimum	19	18
Number of observation	91	94

Source: Authors' survey

Differences in self-reported happiness

Now, we investigate whether there is any difference in subjective reported happiness among students at Purdue University and at UFPE. Table 17.3 reports the mean and standard deviation value of subjective happiness by students at both universities. They are produced using 1 for not happy, 2 for pretty happy, and 3 for very happy. Notice that the arithmetic in Table 17.3 assumes cardinality, while reported subjective happiness is an ordered number. Later on, we will report the ordered estimations using standard regression procedures. With this caveat in mind, we observe that the mean reported happiness was smaller among UFPE students than is observed among Purdue students. We also test, using the Mann-Whitney two-sample statistic, the hypothesis that the two independent samples are from populations with the same distribution. Table 17.3 reports the p-value of this test, which rejects this hypothesis with a 99 percent level of confidence. Therefore there is not only a difference in the first moment of the two distributions but also differences in high-ordered moments.

Figure 17.2 shows the histograms of self-reported happiness in the two samples. Notice that the two empirical distributions do not look alike, corroborating the Mann-Whitney test which rejected the hypothesis of equality of distributions. The difference is concentrated in the upper tail of the distribution. Observe that the fraction of not happy individuals is roughly the same among Purdue (4.4 percent) and UFPE students (5.3 percent). However, the fraction of very happy students is two times higher among Purdue students (40 percent) than at UFPE (20 percent). Consequently, the fraction of pretty happy students is higher at UFPE (74 percent) than at Purdue (55 percent).

Next, we estimate the probability of students reporting themselves happy by allowing for a set of individual controls. We take advantage of individual variations and follow many authors, see for instance, Blanchflower and Oswald (2004) to run an ordered logit regression of the form:

$$happy_i = \alpha + \beta X_i + \gamma Purdue_i + \varepsilon_i. \tag{17.1}$$

Table 17.3 Descriptive statistics – self-reported happiness

	Purdue students	UFPE students
Mean	2.36	2.15
Standard deviation	0.58	0.48
Number of observation	91	94
Mann-Whitney rank test (p-value)		0.005

Source: Authors' survey

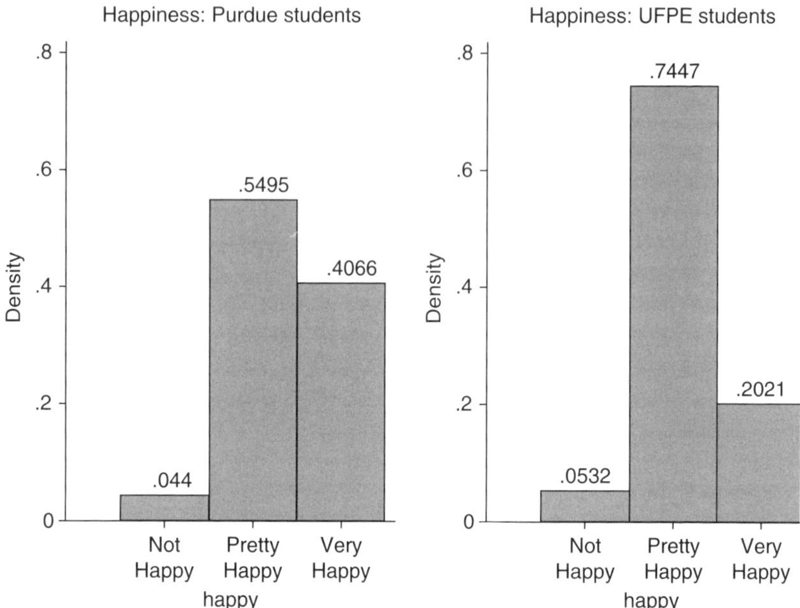

Figure 17.2 Distribution of self-reported happiness
Source: Authors' survey.

The dependent variable *happy*$_i$ is the self-reported happiness, which can take three values (as discussed before, 1 corresponds to the lowest reported happiness level). The description of the independent variables in (17.1) is: X_i a column vector[11] with individual characteristics such as age, age squared, gender (male=1), dummy variable if the student comes from a low income family, dummy variable if the student comes from a middle income family, dummy variable if the student is not working, and another dummy variable if the student is a part-time worker. The variable *Purdue*$_i$ is an indicator variable that takes value 1 if student *i* is at Purdue and 0 if he/she is at UFPE.

From Table 17.4, we observe that the coefficient on the dummy variable *Purdue* is positive and significant in all regressions. This is true when we use Purdue as the only independent variable (Table 17.4, column 1), but also when we add other controls in the regression (Table 17.4 columns 2–6). Therefore, we can conclude that students at Purdue University have a higher probability of reporting themselves happier than do students at UFPE after controlling for a set of individual characteristics. This is consistent to the distribution of self-reported happiness described in Figure 17.2.[12]

When we run the regression with the whole sample the coefficient on gender is negative in all regressions (Table 17.4 columns 3–5),[13] but it is

Table 17.4 Determinants of happiness (ordered logits)

	(1)	(2)	Whole (3)	Sample (4)	(5)	(6)	Purdue (7)	UFPE (8)
Purdue	0.884***	0.832***	0.848***	0.670**	0.599*	1.501**	–	–
	(0.320)	(0.323)	(0.325)	(0.347)	(0.351)	(0.600)		
Age	–	0.077	0.076	0.098	0.041	−0.013	1.798	0.045
		(0.222)	(0.222)	(0.224)	(0.229)	(0.224)	(2.619)	(0.279)
Age^2	–	−0.002	−0.002	−0.002	−0.001	−0.001	−0.041	−0.001
		(0.003)	(0.003)	(0.003)	(0.003)	(0.002)	(0.057)	(0.004)
Gender (male=1)	–	–	−0.247	−0.408	−0.381	0.267	−1.031**	0.228
			(−0.75)	(0.339)	(0.342)	(0.486)	(0.520)	(0.549)
Gender purdue	–	–	–	–	–	−1.304*	–	–
						(0.726)		
Low income	–	–	–	−2.316***	−2.422***	−2.383***	−1.896*	−3.757***
				(0.788)	(0.784)	(0.776)	(1.072)	(1.247)
Middle income	–	–	–	−0.808**	−0.832**	−0.866**	−0.340	−2.074***
				(0.384)	(0.380)	(0.390)	(0.465)	(0.690)
Not working	–	–	–	–	0.427	0.405	0.043	1.026
					(0.582)	(0.405)	(0.898)	(0.861)
Working part-time	–	–	–	–	0.728	0.616	0.263	0.927
	–	–	–	–	(0.589)	(0.616)	(0.898)	(0.873)
Pseudo R^2	0.027	0.034	0.036	0.071	0.078	0.089	0.049	0.126
N	185	185	185	185	185	185	91	94

Note: *, **, *** Statistically significant at 99%, 95%, and 90% confidence level. Robust standard errors are in parentheses.

Source: Authors' survey.

not statistically different from zero. Notice, however, that when we run a regression for each sample separately, the results are quite different. Women are happier than men at Purdue University and the coefficient of this variable is statistically different from zero at a 95 percent level of confidence (Table 17.4, column 7). This result is consistent with other studies which show that women are in fact happier than men in the United States.[14] Among UFPE students, we observe that the sign is positive, which suggests that men are happier than women at UFPE.[15] However, this coefficient is not statistically different from zero. When we multiply the dummy for gender with the dummy for Purdue, the sign of the coefficient of this variable is negative and statistically different from zero (Table 17.4, column 6). Therefore, regarding differences in happiness by gender there is no gender division in overall reported life satisfaction among UFPE students but women report themselves to be happier than do men in the Purdue sample. This might be related to differences in the gender role in the two societies.[16]

Our estimates using the whole sample also show that compared to students from high income families, those who come from low- and middle income families have a lower probability of reporting themselves happier (Table 17.4, columns 4 and 6). These two dummy variables have a negative coefficient and are statistically different from zero at a 99 percent level of confidence for those students from a low income family and at a 95 percent level of confidence for those who come from a middle income family. Therefore, income matters for happiness. Notice that the income dummy variables are constructed by asking students whether they come from low, middle, or high income family within their own societies. We should highlight two important problems here: first, this implicitly takes onto account the issue about relative income. We are not comparing the level of income of families in the United States with the level of income of families in Brazil. We instead are observing the perception of each student about the level of income from her/his family compared to the level of income in the society they belong to. This is important, since as argued by Easterlin (1974, 1995) people compare themselves with others to report their overall level of life satisfaction. Another important issue is that family income might be correlated to other omitted variables that affect happiness, such as family background, parents' education, and family stability. Therefore, the positive effect of parents' income with happiness might be spurious and driven by these other omitted factors.

Observe, however, that these results on happiness and income are not robust when we consider each sample separately.[17] Among Purdue students (Table 17.4, column 7), parents' level of income does not have a strong effect on self-reported happiness. Only the low family income variable is statistically different from zero at a 90 level of percent confidence. There is no statistical difference in self-reported happiness among Purdue students who come from middle and high income families. Studies have shown that inequality does not affect the happiness of the poor in the United States, while it affects the poor in Europe. Alesina et al. (2004) argue that inequality affects the poor in Europe but not in the United States, because Americans have a perception that they live in a mobile society, where individual effort can move people up and down the income ladder, while Europeans believe that they live in a less mobile society. Among students at UFPE (Table 17.4 column 8), we observe that the parents' income dummies have a negative sign and are statistically different from zero at a 99 percent level of confidence. Therefore, UFPE students who come from high income families have a higher probability of reporting themselves happier than those who come from low and middle income families. With respect to overall life satisfaction, income matters more among UFPE students than among Purdue students. Following the analysis from Alesina et al. (2004), this might be because of the perception of low social mobility in the Pernambuco State in Brazil. This might also reflect differences in patterns of consumption, leisure, and job opportunities among the income classes in Brazilian society.

Finally, when we consider the whole sample, full-time working students have a lower probability of reporting themselves happier than students who do not work or who work part-time (Table 17.4 columns 5 and 6). However, the signs of these coefficients are not statistically different from zero. For Purdue students the same pattern is observed and the magnitude of the sign is smaller. For UFPE students these two variables have larger coefficients, but they are still statistically not different from zero. The results show that there is only weak evidence on differences in subjective perception towards working (work-ethic) status among the two samples of students. This result suggest that: either (i) additional leisure time is not an important determinant of happiness among Purdue and UFPE students, or (ii) working full-time does not affect students' perception of their future income and career opportunities.

An interesting hypothetical exercise is to study the possible consequences of moving a randomly chosen student from UFPE to Purdue and vice versa. For instance, assume that a male student in UFPE belongs to the middle income group. Such a student is likely to become a low income student at Purdue, which reduces his happiness, but he will get the benefit of the fixed effect of being at Purdue net of the effect of being male at Purdue. Using equation (17.1), we can observe that the overall well-being of this student will either decrease or increase depending on whether he uses as his reference income group the one in the United States (low income) or the one in Brazil (middle income), respectively. Now, consider a female middle income class student from UFPE and move this student to Purdue. Such a student is likely to become a low income student at Purdue, which reduces her happiness, but she will get the benefit of the fixed effect of being a female at Purdue. Her self-reported happiness will remain the same if she uses the reference income group in the United States, but will increase if her reference income group is the one in Brazil.[18]

Concluding remarks

In this chapter, we investigate differences in overall life satisfaction among Brazilian and American college students. We find that American college students have a higher probability of reporting themselves very happy and happy than Brazilian students. This effect is statistically significant and it is also robust to a set of control variables characterizing individual and socio-economic conditions. We conjecture that the poor life conditions, violence, and youth insecurity have degraded well-being in Brazil compared to what is observed in the United States.

We also found some interesting differences between the two groups of students. Women are happier than men at Purdue, but men are happier than women at UFPE. Moreover, wealth does not seem to have a clear impact on happiness among Purdue students, but it certainly buys some extra happiness among UFPE students. Regarding the effect of wealth on well-being, we believe that not only, on average, the gap between the elite and the other classes is higher in Brazil than in the United States,[19] but also social mobility is lower in the former than in the latter. Therefore, growth in Brazil might increase overall life satisfaction, as well as policies to improve social mobility.

We also plan to investigate what factors would make students happier in these two different universities. What are the barriers for happiness in each society? Such evidence would be related to the students' socioeconomic conditions and social norms. We believe that direct measures of well-being might help public policies to identify their social goals. As argued by Di Tella and MacCulloch (2006), economists usually have a different approach to studying the effects of policies. They look first at how policies affect people's behavior. Then, through a theoretical model and welfare function, they analyze the effects on people's welfare. However, two different models might have two different social functions[20] and depending on the model used welfare might increase or decrease.

Appendix

Questionnaire: Subjective Happiness	Questionário: Felicidade Subjetiva
Are you Happy? 1__ I am not happy 2__ I am pretty happy 3__ I am very happy	Você se sente feliz? 1__ Eu não me sinto feliz 2__ Eu me sinto feliz 3__ Eu me sinto muito feliz

What would make you happier?
(Please, rank you answer.
Use 1, 2, 3, 4, 5, 6, 7, and 8 to describe
which factor makes you happier;
1 being the most important.)
__ More money
__ More friends
__ Live closer to my parents or/and
   friends
__ A love story
__ A Job
__ More leisure
__ Less violence
__ Others
	O que faria você mais feliz?
	(você pode ordenar sua resposta.
	Use 1, 2, ... para descrever que fator
	o faria mais feliz, 1 sendo o mais
	importante)
	__ Mais dinheiro
	__ Mais amigos
	__ Viver mais perto de meus pais e/ou
	   amigos
	__ Uma história de amor
	__ Um trabalho
	__ Mais lazer
	__ Menos violência
	__ Outros

Age: Gender: Male † Female †	Idade: Sexo: Masculino † Feminino †

Continued

Appendix   Continued

Do you come from a?	Que tipo de família é a sua?
1__ Low income family	1__ Família de renda baixa
2__ Middle income family	2__ Família de renda média
3__ High income family	3__ Família de renda alta

Do you work?	Você trabalha?
1__ No, I do not work	1__ Não, eu não trabalho
2__ Yes, I work part-time	2__ Sim, eu trabalho 1 expediente
3__ Yes, I work full-time	3__ Sim, eu trabalho em tempo integral

Notes

We are indebt to Werner Baer for helpful conversations and also to Hadi Esfahani and Donald Pianto for insightful comments. We are responsible for any errors. Cavalcanti and Nogueira are also thankful to Conselho Nacional de Desenvolvimento Científico e Tecnológico (CNPq) for financial support. Part of this paper was written while Tiago Cavalcanti was visiting the department of economics at Purdue University. He is thankful to the people at Purdue University, especially Gabriele Camera, for their hospitality.

1. See the official website of EMBRATUR (www.braziltour.com).
2. *"Isso é o Brasil, uma Roma melhor porque mestiça, lavada em sangue negro, em sangue índio, sofrida e tropical. Com as vantagens imensas de um mundo enorme que não tem inverno e onde tudo é verde e lindo, e a vida é mais bela…E é uma gente que acompanha esse ambiente com uma alegria de viver que não se vê em outra parte."* (Darcy Ribeiro speech to TV Cultura, 1995)
3. UFPE is the leading Northeast Brazilian University in research. It has about 35,000 students. Purdue University in West Lafayette has about 38,000 students. Both universities are public schools, but while there are no tuition fees at UFPE, the estimated annual expenses at Purdue University are about US$17,000. Of course, the infrastructure and the quality of installations are quite different in the two universities.
4. See the Lionel Robbins Memorial Lectures 2002/03 by Richard Layard at the London School of Economics (http://cep.lse.uk/events/lectures/layard/RL030303.pdf).
5. See Carroll et al. (2000) for a model where income per capita increases over time but overall life satisfaction remains constant.
6. Since relative differences matter more than absolutes ones, this might be also related to the perception of the gap in income in the two countries.
7. One of the authors was teaching this course at Purdue University in this academic year.
8. We believe that the courses taken by students do not affect their self-reported happiness. Notice that students at UFPE, who are usually taking intermediate public finance, already took or are taking an intermediate course in macroeconomics. The questionnaires were answered in 2005 Fall and 2006 Spring at Purdue University. Ordered regression analysis shows that there is no statistical difference

in well-being between students in the Fall and in the Spring. At UFPE the questionnaires were answered in February 2006.

 9. Notice that this is similar to the question from the General Social Survey (GSS) in the United States and used by many authors, such as Alesina et al. (2004) and Blanchflower and Oswald (2004).

10. It is important to highlight that low, middle, or high income families are based on income in each country separately. In the questionnaire, we do not ask what their parents' annual income is, but whether they come from a low, middle, or high income family.

11. Therefore, β is a row vector with the number of rows as the number of columns of vector X_i.

12. We find that the coefficients on age and age squared are not statistically different from zero (Table 17.4 columns 2–8). There is not much variation on age in our dataset. We also run a regression with individuals younger than 30. Coefficients on the age variables are almost unchanged.

13. Since this variable takes value 1 for men and 0 for women, this means that women have a higher probability of reporting themselves happier than men do.

14. See, for instance, Blanchflower and Oswald (2004).

15. A recent study by Graham and Felton (2006) shows that, in Latin America, men are happier than women. See also Graham and Pettinato (2001).

16. Data from the World Development Indicators show that in the United States the female unemployment rate is similar to the total unemployment rate (the female unemployment rate is about 5.4 percent, while the total unemployment rate is roughly 5.5 percent). In Brazil, the data show that the female unemployment rate is about 12.3 percent while the total unemployment rate is about 7.8 percent. In 2000 about 26 percent of the total ministerial level positions in the United States were occupied by women. This number is only 4 percent in Brazil.

17. An important caveat is needed here. According to a *Time* magazine survey about 19 percent of Americans say they are in the richest 1 percent. In Brazil, we believe, from informal conversations and simple analysis from the household survey PNAD, that most people who report themselves as being in the middle class are indeed in the top 1 percent of income.

18. Of course, this is a static exercise. The move from UFPE to Purdue might have a strong impact on career opportunities for a student at UFPE and the overall long run impact on well-being might be very different.

19. This does not suggest that there is no inequality among income classes in the United States. However, we believe that life conditions, such access to education and public infrastructure, are on average more unequal between rich and poor income families in Brazil than in the United States.

20. A cigarette tax hike might decrease welfare in a rational addiction model à la Becker and Murphy (1988), but might increase welfare if we assume that people have some self-control problem, such as in Laibson (1997). Using happiness data, Gruber and Mullainathan (2002) find some support in Laibson's model.

References

Alesina, A., R. Di Tella, and R. MacCulloch (2004) "Inequality and Happiness: Are Europeans and Americans Different?" *Journal of Public Economics*, 88, 2009–2042.

Becker, G., and K. Murphy (1988) "A Theory of Rational Addiction," *Journal of Political Economy*, 96, 675–700.

Blanchflower, D.G. and A.J. Oswald (2004) "Well-Being Over Time in Britain and the USA," *Journal of Public Economics*, 88, 1359–1386.

Blanchflower, D.G. and A.J. Oswald (2004) "Happiness and the Human Development Index: The Paradox of Australia," NBER Working Paper 11416.

Carroll, C.D., J. Overland, and D.N. Weil (2000) "Saving and Growth with Habit Formation," *American Economic Review*, 90, 341–355.

Davidson, R.J., D.C. Jackson, and N.H. Kalin (2000) "Emotion, Plasticity, Context and Regulation: Perspective from Affective Neuroscience," *Psychological Bulletin*, 126, 890–906.

Di Tella, R., and R. MacCulloch (2006) "Some Uses of Happiness Data in Economics," *Journal of Economic Perspectives*, 20, 25–46.

Easterlin, R.A. (1974) "Does Economic Growth Improve the Human Lot? Some Empirical Evidence," in P. David and M. Reader (eds.) *Nations and Households in Economic Growth: Essays in Honor of Moses Abramowitz*, New York: Academic Press.

Easterlin, R.A. (1995) "Will Raising the Incomes of All Increase the Happiness of All?" *Journal of Economic Behavior and Organization*, 27, 35–47.

Graham, C., and A. Felton (2006) "Inequality and Happiness: Insights from Latin America," *Journal of Income Inequality*, 4, 107–122.

Graham, C., and S. Pettinato (2001) "Happiness, Markets, and Democracy: Latin America in Comparative Perspective," *Journal of Happiness Studies*, 2, 237–268.

Gruber, J., and S. Mullainathan (2002) "Do Cigarette Taxes Make Smokers Happier?" NBER Working Paper 8872.

Kahneman, D., and A. Krueger (2006) "Developments in the Measurement of Subjective Well-Being," *Journal of Economic Perspectives*, 20, 3–24.

Laibson, D. (1997) "Golden Eggs and Hyperbolic Discounting," *Quarterly Journal of Economics*, 112, 443–477.

Layard, R. (2003) "Happiness: Has Social Science a Clue?" *Lionel Robbins Memorial Lectures*, London School of Economics.

Ribeiro, D. (1996) O Povo Brasileiro: A formação e o sentido do Brasil, 2nd ed.

Part V

A Retrospective on Werner Baer

18
Economics the Werner Baer Way

Larry Samuelson

Introduction

I arrived as a new graduate student at the University of Illinois some few years ago, not long after Werner Baer had joined the faculty. I was fairly quickly to become one of Werner's great failures, and have only gradually developed into what I hope is one of his modest successes.

My first-year classes at Illinois included Werner's course in International Finance. Werner at that time was passionate about his work, a passion that readily crossed into the evangelical and that the years have done nothing to diminish. Werner was happy to explain, to anyone who would listen, why it was exciting to study development economics in general and Latin American development in particular. At the same time, Werner was always willing to let his actions speak louder than his words. In my case, his actions culminated in my spending a summer traveling in South America, with particular emphasis on Brazil. I visited universities and research institutes, government agencies, and the odd tourist attraction. I talked to professors and policymakers, students, and bureaucrats, all with an eye toward generating an enthusiasm for development economics. It was a tremendous experience. I went from struggling to name the countries and capitals of South America to talking about nuances of Brazilian industrial policy or Latin American inflation. Alas, however, we are faced with a vast array of interesting things to study and all too little time. I have spent the intervening years doing primarily economic theory rather than development economics. It is in this sense that I am one of Werner's failures.

Although I did not follow in his footsteps in terms of *what* has been the focus of my work in economics, I did learn a great deal from Werner about *how* to do economics. This is the sense in which I hope to be one of his modest successes. My remarks here will review three rules for doing economics that I learned from Werner Baer.

Study the world

When I arrived as a graduate student at Illinois, general equilibrium theory filled the air. In the view of many, this was the crowning achievement of economics. It was beautiful in its mathematics and profound in its insights. But what were its implications? This was less clear. Indeed, newly breaking contributions to general equilibrium theory, the Debreu/Mantel/Sonnenschein theorems (Debreu, 1974; Mantel, 1974; 1976; and Sonnenschein, 1973), suggested it had no implications at all. General equilibrium theory provides a precise statement of what it means for a profile of prices and attendant excess demands to simultaneously clear all of an economy's markets, and shows that such prices and excess demands exist. The Debreu/Mantel/Sonnenschein theorems show that essentially *any* budget-balancing collection of prices and excess demands is compatible with competitive equilibrium. As a result, any behavioral configuration we could observe is consistent with equilibrium. Unfortunately, a theory compatible with anything predicts nothing.

More generally, economists have been periodically criticized for producing research and filling graduate programs with material that has all sorts of virtues *except* a connection with the economy around us. Werner Baer, in contrast, has been committed throughout his career to the proposition that economics should be about the world. We are not mathematicians, we are not simply creating and solving puzzles, we are not logicians or philosophers – our purpose is to study the world.

This is not a contention that we should all do empirical work. In the course of inventing modern economics, Adam Smith identified the division of labor as a central feature of modern economies. Economists similarly recognize that the division of labor has a place in our profession. Allowing some people to study economic theory while trusting others to do more applied and empirical work makes good use of our profession's resources. However, work in economics should be collectively guided by a goal of directly or indirectly contributing to our understanding of economic behavior. Economics has a place for the abstract as well as the applied, for those who study upper-hemicontinuity, and those who study unemployment, but the combination should be designed to push us closer to understanding behavior.

How do we make this interest in the world operational? My suggestion is that economists should regularly accompany any piece of economic theory with an indication of what conceivably observable behavior would reinforce their belief that the proposed model was on the right track in terms of understanding behavior, and what they could observe that would call the model into question (Samuelson, 1975). As indicated in the previous paragraph, I am not suggesting that theorists need make these observations personally. Having predicted that the Sun's gravity would bend passing light waves, Einstein was not required himself to stand with a telescope in the path of an eclipse and collect the relevant measurements. But he was required to tell others what to do and what to expect. Nor would I insist that the requisite data be readily available. A contribution to particle physics is not considered a failure just because its predictions can only be tested at energy levels not yet attainable. However, I would insist that at least the potential behavioral content of the theory be explored by identifying observations that would fall into the pro and con camps.

In some cases, there may be no such observations. General equilibrium theory is one likely such case.[1] This alone does not doom it to irrelevance. General equilibrium theory is important because it provides a language for talking about the efficiency properties of markets and for evaluating market interventions. Utility maximization is similarly useful not because it has empirical content but because it gives us a language for talking about individual behavior.[2] But we cannot build a discipline solely around creating language, and we should be clear as to when we are creating language and when we think our models have substantive content. When we do make claims for substantive content, we should be willing to take the first simple steps toward identifying that content. It is not enough to simply say that a model is more realistic or more general – we work with models precisely because they are *not* perfectly realistic or completely general. A model has content only if there are observations consistent with the model and observations inconsistent with the model. Making it clear what these observations are is an important step in ensuring that economics actually does study the world.

Look out the window

Early in our study of international finance, Werner Baer directed the class's attention to balance of payments problems. He explained how a payments imbalance tended to put pressure on the exchange rate, and how the adjusting exchange rate tended to push payments back into balance. Werner mentioned that some elasticity conditions needed to be met in order for this to work. My classmates and I leaned forward in anticipation. It seemed as if now we were going to learn some real economics. To our surprise, Werner then remarked that the derivation of such conditions was a straightforward exercise, one that we could perform on our own if we wanted, while he went on to other considerations.

At the time, I had a mild feeling of having been swindled out of something important. Looking back, I see that a fundamental distinction was at work. There are two aspects to doing effective economics. One is to do the right thing once one has a model. This is what we spend most of our time teaching in the first-year core of our graduate programs. Students learn to take first-order conditions, take implicit derivatives and solve for comparative statics, check equilibrium conditions, prove existence, and take all sorts of other technical steps, even sometimes computing the Marshall-Lerner conditions. Another aspect of doing economics effectively is to construct the right model for the purpose at hand. This is a much more difficult task, one we would like to teach in our graduate classes, but one we typically have no real idea how to teach. Model construction is as much art as science and defies reduction to a recipe. One can point to examples, but this all too often becomes the economics equivalent of telling aspiring athletes that they need only play basketball like Michael Jordan to be a success.

It was a concern with finding the right model that prompted Werner Baer to skip past the algebra others might have pursued, in favor of a discussion of the balance of payments problems facing various countries, primarily Latin American, while emphasizing the extent to which their particular circumstances made the model useful or irrelevant. We see here his basic prescription for seeking the right model: start by learning about the economic behavior one would like to explain. What form does the behavior take? What are the constraints and institutional considerations that shape it? How has it changed? How were the data describing this behavior collected? Do they measure what one claims to measure, and do they allow the interpretation one would like to attach to them? A host of similar questions are important. Spurred on by such questions, it is no surprise that Werner Baer has spent a great deal of time in Brazil. Indeed, Werner would wonder how one could study Latin American development without doing so, and more generally how one could study economics without an abiding interest in economic behavior.

I often startle graduate students in my attempts to put this rule into practice. I can recall a student interested in evolutionary models of segregation expecting to hear questions about dynamic processes, being surprised when asked to identify the most segregated American cities and explain how their residential composition had changed over the last 50 years. A student interested in the effects of competition in markets for expert services was surprised when asked for examples of such markets that are relatively concentrated and others that are relatively competitive, and to explain how their performance differed. More generally, if economists have succeeded in nothing else, we have made it abundantly clear that we can construct models to rationalize virtually any behavior one can imagine. There are many questions that remain open in economics, but we need never wonder for long whether we can find a model. How do we know when our models tell us something useful? I can think of no better prescription than to start with a look at behavior the model is designed to explain.

Do some good

A fellow graduate student and I once walked into the office of one of Werner's colleagues, finding him gleaming over a stack of newly arrived reprints. Holding up one of them, he exclaimed, "Now this is a good paper." Sensing a lesson to be learned, I asked why. Pointing his finger at the name on the paper, the author replied, "Because it gets this name in front of lots of eyes."

Werner's take on what makes a good piece of economics is somewhat different. He has been concerned not so much with where his work shows up in print, but where his work shows up in practice. In his view, economics is not something to be done for other economists, binding us together in an academic world disconnected from society outside. Instead, the goal of economics is to have an effect on the world beyond – to do some good. Once one takes this perspective, the distinction between teaching and research fades. Rather than doing research for its prestige and enduring teaching because it pays the bills, the two blend together. Rather than doing research simply to publish, one does research to teach others, inside and outside academics, how to think usefully about the economy.

This concern with doing something good has long shown itself in Werner's research and his teaching. He has tirelessly recruited students both for Illinois' Ph.D. program and for the MSPE (Master of Science in Policy Economics) program that he was instrumental in creating, recognizing that both programs have a role to play in advancing the understanding and practice of economics. His teaching of graduate students and younger colleagues has regularly spilled over into joint research. Perhaps the most striking measure of his success can be read in the fact that throughout Latin America and beyond, one finds his students in universities, finance ministries, central banks, governors' mansions, and presidential palaces. What better indication of an impact on the world could one ask for?

Conclusion

These three simple rules have characterized Werner Baer's work in economics. His career provides an example that makes these rules available to all who would take notice of them. I believe we would do well to follow them, and that we would be much more effective as a profession for doing so.

Notes

1. Interestingly, recent work shows that general equilibrium theory may not be devoid of empirical content after all (cf. Brown and Matzkin, 1996, and the subsequent literature).
2. It is common to identify the generalized axiom of revealed preference (Varian, 1982) as the empirical content of utility maximization. Even this content is an illusion. Revealed preference theory imposes consistency conditions across choices made from different feasible sets according to the same preferences. In practice, we either observe choices made by different people or by the same person in different circumstances – one choice is invariably made at a different time, with a slightly

different history of past consumption. This allows enough leeway to rationalize any seeming failure of the revealed preference axioms. It is only with the addition of further assumptions, albeit often very palatable ones (such as an assumption that these slightly different histories should not affect preferences over current consumption) that utility maximization attains empirical content.

References

Brown, D., and R. Matzkin (1996) "Testable Restrictions on the Equilibrium Manifold," *Econometrica*, 64, 1249–1262.

Debreu, G. (1974) "Excess Demand Functions," *Journal of Mathematical Economics*, 1, 15–21.

Mantel, R. (1974) "On the Characterization of Aggregate Excess Demand," *Journal of Economic Theory*, 7, 348–353.

Mantel, R. (1976) "Homothetic Preferences and Community Excess Demand Functions," *Journal of Economic Theory*, 12, 197–201.

Samuelson, L. (1975) "Economic Theory and Experimental Economics," *Journal of Economic Literature*, 43, 65–107.

Sonnenschein, H. (1973) "Do Walras' Identity and Continuity Characterize the Class of Community Excess Demand Functions?" *Journal of Economic Theory*, 6, 345–354.

Varian, H. (1982) "The Nonparametric Approach to Demand Analysis," *Econometrica*, 50, 945–974.

19

Making a Great Difference: The Influence of Professor Werner Baer on the Economic Literature in Brazil, and on Brazil

Carlos R. Azzoni

Introduction

The contribution of Professor Werner Baer to Economics in Brazil is enormous. His contribution was, and of course still is, multidimensional, and it is very difficult to tell which aspect is the most important. His influence in the shaping up of graduate studies in the country is recognized by all the Brazilian pioneers. He was instrumental in developing institutions, organizing courses, identifying young professors to be trained abroad, arranging scholarships for them in the U.S., and helping them to be accepted in American universities, introducing academic standards in the selection of graduate students in the country, forming an association of graduate programs, etc. His permanent residence in Brazil in the fledgling years of the organization of the Brazilian graduate programs in Economics was very important. Not only did he teach courses but he also advised students, invited visiting professors, and managed to lead the newborn system to safe grounds.

After he went back to the U.S., he continued to do a great job in accepting students from Brazil to graduate programs in the U.S., providing recommendation letters to students applying to a multitude of schools in the U.S. and Europe. More recently, he managed to obtain funds for a Chair at the University of Illinois, in which he receives Brazilian candidates for the Ph.D. Program in Economics. Considering the recent shortage of scholarships in Brazil, and the large number of students he has received in the past, he must be responsible for at least 20 percent of all Ph.D. degrees in Economics among Brazilians, at U of I and at other universities.

In partnership with Professor Joseph Lowe, a renowned historian from U of I, he has obtained funding from The Hewlett Foundation for the University of Illinois Brazil Project. Funds from this project allowed the organization of several academic conferences in the U.S. and Brazil, involving a dozen Brazilian departments, and producing three important publications. Many scholars from U of I visited Brazil, and many scholars from Brazil visited U of I for sabbatical periods with funding from this project and from the Chair he holds.

Considering the manifold nature of his contribution, I would need many more pages than those on offer here to make a more thorough assessment of the fundamental role Prof. Baer played in the shaping, developing, and, even today, updating of Economics in Brazil. In this modest piece, I will focus on only one aspect of Werner's influence on Brazilian economic profession, that is, his importance as a researcher, as it is measured by the long list of his publications, and the strong impact his works had on many generations of Brazilian scholars, as well as on all students of Brazilian society.

The chapter is organized into four sections, plus this introduction. The next section presents a very brief overview of his publications. This is followed by an assessment of the impact of his publications as measured by citations of his work in papers and books published by scholars working in non-Brazilian institutions. The following section presents the same sort of information regarding scholars working in Brazilian institutions. The last section presents the final comments.

Publications

A first look at the importance of Prof. Werner Baer for Brazilian studies has to start with his many publications. Always interested in Development Economics, his concerns cover many different areas, such as regional policy (neoliberalism, federalism, and regional policy in Brazil); sources of funds for financing development (credit and banks in the development of the São Paulo state economy, 1850–1930); health (health conditions and health policy in Brazil: an assessment of recent decades); and privatization of banks, the steel industry, etc. A search on internet databases reveals a total of 80 works cited. A list of these articles and books is presented in Appendix 1.

His textbook on the Brazilian economy is now in its fifth international edition and has many editions and reprints in Brazil. His study of industrialization is a classic in the Brazilian literature. Therefore, his importance as an author and as an analyst of Brazilian society, mainly focusing on its economic foundations, is overwhelming. He was a pioneer in applying economic tools to the study of Brazilian problems, setting the pace for future studies, and challenging the narrative and discursive analysis traditionally present in the country. He has shown that the use of economic theory and the analysis of empirical data are crucial for any sound analysis of economic and social issues.

He applied theoretical analysis to empirical data with great intellectual rigor, and in doing so changed the way social analysts in Brazil tackled economic problems, teaching them to become real economists. This has produced a whole series of pioneering empirical studies testing some of the hypotheses formulated qualitatively by many important authors, such as Celso Furtado. Depth of analysis, sound theoretical basis, and a profound respect for history and institutional background conditions within which relevant phenomena take place are key features of all his studies.

International citations

One way of assessing the importance of one author is to look at the number of citations he/she receives. An important piece will be read by many, and probably cited by them. In many fields the number of citations has been used as a performance measure (Azzoni, 1998 and 2000; Durden and Ellis, 1993; Faria, 2000; Issler and Ferreira, 2004; Laband, 1990; Moed et al., 1998; Nederhof and Van Vijk, 1999; Nisonger, 1999; Ratnatunga and Romano, 1997; Stegmann, 1999). Of course, such a procedure is not perfect and is subject to much criticism. Macroberts and Macroberts (1987) argue that advances in science are also obtained by average, or mediocre, people. Considering the other end of the quality spectrum, Lederberg (1972) points out that some very important works become so popular that no one would care to cite them. It may also be that introducing a citation of an important work into a paper could be used as a sign of erudition, or to upscale the citing work. Self-citation is also a problem, especially in the case of papers with several authors, a common case in natural sciences. Kostoff (1998) and Phelan (1999) provide a detailed analysis of the subject; Osareh (1996) offers a review of literature, provides a historical overview of the subject, and discusses the arguments for and against.

In this study, we use citations to assess the importance of different authors, mainly concerned with that of Prof. Werner Baer. In this section we deal with citations outside Brazil, based on information collected from Google Scholar[1] and on the ISI Web of Science.[2] In the next section we analyze citations by authors publishing in Brazilian journals. We have listed both the work citing and the study cited, so that we can have a broader view of Prof. Baer's importance. To begin with, his textbook *The Brazilian Economy* received 64 international citations, an impressive number for a textbook. He was cited, for his several works, by other 460 different studies, involving 368 sources (papers, books, and sites). A list of all sources citing Prof. Baer is presented in Table 19A.1.

Citations in Brazil

For citations within Brazil we have updated a series of studies by Azzoni (1998; 2000; and 2001). All articles ever published in the most important Brazilian academic journals in Economics were considered. The Ministry of Education (Capes) ranks Brazilian journals on an A–C scale, and the following receive grade A: *Revista Brasileira de Economia*, *Estudos Econômicos*, *Pesquisa e Planejamento Econômico*, *Revista de Economia Política*, and *Revista Brasileira de Econometria*. We have also added two B-rated journals: *Economia Aplicada* and *Revista Econômica do Nordeste*. Azzoni (1998) included 1931 articles published by 1998; another 596 were added, bridging the period to reach 2005. Thus, we deal with a total of 2527 articles.

One could argue the need to include more journals, since alternatives for publishing academic work in Economics have increased dramatically in Brazil in the last two decades, as the Brazilian academy develops and becomes more and more professional. Today, at least 36 academic journals are available. However, if a paper published in these journals is important enough, it would end up being cited in the more traditional and respected journals we have considered. The set of papers involved represents a large enough sample to give a consistent view of the Brazilian economic scene. In the previous work, a total of 8147 studies were cited; more than 5000 have been included since 1999. For each citing article, basic information was collected and coded, such as name of author, title, institution of author, area of expertise, name of journal, number, date, etc.

Part of the results is displayed in Table 19.1. As can be seen, Prof. Werner Baer is ranked twenty-second, well above any other economist working in non-Brazilian institutions. The list includes authors who have already ended their academic careers, for various reasons. Considering only authors still working in Brazilian universities, Prof. Baer is in fifth place. This gives an idea of his long-lasting influence in Brazilian academia. Naturally, given the fast-growing number of new journals and authors, his influence is decreasing proportionally, in terms of citations of all his works. But if we consider individual works, the Portuguese version of his *Brazilian Economy* textbook ranks fourteenth among all studies published up to 2005.

Conclusions

This chapter presented a very brief analysis of Prof. Werner Baer´s influence in Brazil and on Brazilian studies in general. As shown in the lists of publications and citations, his influence in Latin America is also noteworthy. Although only citations were considered in this study as an indicator of his huge and positive influence, they give an idea of his importance for this field of study. But, as mentioned in the introduction, his positive influence extends to many other initiatives and has to be acknowledged.

Table 19.1   Number of citations received in Brazilian journals through 2005

Ranking	Author	Number of citations received
1	Simonsen, M H	324
2	Bacha, E L	274
3	Furtado, C	237
4	Barros, R P	195
5	Pastore, A C	177
6	Melo, F B H	175
7	Bonelli, R	171
8	Hoffmann, R	169
9	Lopes, F L P	145
10	Langoni, C G	130
11	Tavares, M C	129
12	Suzigan, W	126
13	Bresser-Pereira, L C	126
14	Resende, A L	110
15	Cardoso, E A	110
16	Costa, I N	101
17	Barros, J R M	94
18	Arida, P	93
19	Malan, P S	89
20	Macedo, R B M	89
21	Camargo, J M	79
22	Baer, W	78
23	Mata, M	77
24	Modiano, E M	77
25	Contador, C R	76

Appendix 1

Table 19 A.1   Source of Professor Baer´s publications

A Economia Brasileira
A Industrialização e o Desenvolvimento Econômico Do Brasil
A Retomada Da Inflação No Brasil: 1974–1986
A Return to the Past? Brazil's Privatization of Public Utilities
Anchors Away: The Cost and Benefits of Brazil's Devaluation
As Modificações No Papel Do Estado Na Economia Brasileira
Brasiliens Inflationäre Erblast Und Der Plano Real
Brazil – Inflation and Economic-efficiency
Brazil's Drifting Economy. Stagnation and Inflation during 1987–1996
Changing Paradigms: Changing Interpretations of the Public Sector in Latin
    America's Economies
Economic Integration without Policy Coordination: The Case of Mercosur
Employment and Industrialization in Developing Countries

Continued

Table 19 A.1   Continued

Environmental Aspects of Brazil's Economic Development
Expansion of the Economic Frontier – Paraguayan Growth in the 1970S
Foreign Direct Investment in Latin America: Its Changing Nature at the Turn of the
  Century
From Inward to Outward-Oriented Growth: PARAGUAY in the 1980s
From Technology Absorption to Tecnology Production
Furtado on Development: A Review Essay
Growth with Inequality: The Cases of Brazil and Mexico
Health in the Development Process: The Case OF Brazil
Import Substitution and Industrialization in Brazil
Import Substitution and Industrialization in Latin-America – Experiences and
Interpretations
Import-Substitution, Stagnation, and Structural Change – Interpretation of
  Brazilian Case
Indexing in Brazil
Industrial Growth and Industrialization – Revisions in Stages of Brazils Economic
  Development
Industrialization and Economic Development in Brazil
Industrialization in Latin America: Successes and Failures
Inflation and Growth in Latin America
Inflation Controversy in Latin-America – Survey
Latin America: Privatization, Property Rights, and Deregulation
Latin-America in Post-Import-Substitution Era – Introduction
Liberalization and Its Consequences: A Comparative Perspective on Latin America
  and Eastern Europe
Mudanças Estruturais Na Economia Industrial Brasileira, 1960–1980
Neoliberalism and Income Distribution in Latin America
Neoliberalism and Its Consequences in Brazil
Neoliberalismo e Distribuição De Renda Na América Latina
O Brasil Dos Brasilianistas: Um Guia Dos Estudos Sobre o Brasil Nos Estados Unidos,
  1945–2000
On State Capitalism in Brazil: Some New Issues and Questions
Paraguayan Economic Condition – Past and Current Obstacles to Economic
  Modernization
Paying the Costs of Austerity in Latin America
Privatization and Equity in Brazil and Russia
Privatization and Restructuring of Banks in Brazil
Privatization and the Changing Role of the State in Brazil
Privatization and the Changing Role of the State in Latin America
Privatization in Latin America: New Roles for the Public and Private Sectors
Privatization in Latin-America
Regional Inequality and Economic-Growth in Brazil
Social Aspects of Latin American Inflations
State Capitalism in Brazil – Some New Issues and Questions
Structural Changes in Brazil's Economy, 1960–1980
Substituição Das Importações, Estagnação e Mudança Estrutural
Technology, Employment and Development – Empirical Findings
The Achievements and Failures of Argentina's Neo-Liberal Economic Policies

Continued

Table 19 A.1   Continued

The Brazilian Economy
The Brazilian Economy: Growth and Development
The Changing Nature of Development Banking in Brazil
The Changing Nature of Technological Dependence: Brazil's Public Utilities Before
  and After Privatization
The Changing Role of the State in the Brazilian Economy
The Decline and Fall of Brazils Cruzado
The Development of Brazilian Steel Industry
The Economics of Prebisch and Ecla
The Economy of Portugal Within the European Union: 1990–2002
The End of the Asian Myth: Why Were the Experts Fooled?
The Illusion of Stability: The Brazilian Economy Under Cardoso
The Inflation Controversy in Latin America: A Survey
The International Economic-Relations of a Small Country – The Case of Paraguay
The Privatization Experience of Brazil
The Regional Impact of Neo-Liberal Policies in Brazil
The Resurgence of Inflation in Brazil, 1974–1986
The Resurgence of Inflation in Latin-America – Introduction
The Role of Government Enterprises in Latin America's Industrialization
The Role of the United States Regional Development
The State and the Private-Sector in Latin-America – Reflections on the Past, the
  Present and the Future
The Trouble With Index-Linking – Reflections on the Recent Brazilian Experience
Toward a Service-Oriented Growth Strategy
Transportation and Inflation – A Study of Irrational Policy Making in Brazil
Um Retorno Ao Passado? A Privatização De Empresas De Serviços Públicos No Brasil
United States Policies and the Latin American Economies

Table 19 A.2   List of journals citing Professor Baer's works

Agricultural Systems
Agroforestry Systems
Ambiente & sociedade
American Journal of Economics and Sociology
Annals of Regional Science
Annual Review of Sociology
Antipode
Applied Economics
Bahia Análise & Dados
Bulletin for International Fiscal Documentation
Bulletin of Latin American Research
Bulletin of the Oxford University Institute of Economic and Statistics
Business History Review
Columbia Journal of World Business
Comparative Education Review
Comparative Politics

Continued

Table 19 A.2   Continued

Comparative Studies in Society and History
Comparative Studies in Society and History
Cornell International Law Journal
Crime, Law and Social Change
Current Sociology
Dados
Defence and Peace Economics
Demography
Desarrollo Economico-Revista De Ciencias Sociales
Development and Change
Econometrica
Economia
Economic Development and Cultural Change
Economic Geography
Economic Journal
Ekistics
Emerging Markets Finance and Trade
Empirical Economics
Ensaios Econòmicos
Environment and Planning
Environmental and Resource Economics
Estudios de Economía Aplicada
Geografiska Annaler Series B-Human Geography
Geographical Analysis
Growth and Change
Health Care Management Science
Historical Materialism
Human Organization
Informações Econômicas
International Criminal Justice Review
International Economic Journal
International Journal
International Journal of Health Services
International Journal of Middle East Studies
International Journal of Public Sector Management
International Journal of Urban and Regional Research
International Labour Review
International Migration Review
International Monetary Fund Staff Papers
International Organization
International Regional Science Review
International Studies Quarterly
Journal of Comparative Economics
Journal of Contemporary Asia
Journal of Contemporary Religion
Journal of Democracy
Journal of Developing Areas
Journal of Development Economics

Continued

Table 19 A.2   Continued

Journal of Development Studies
Journal of Economic Issues
Journal of Economic Studies
Journal of Environmental Management
Journal of Financial Economics
Journal of Interamerican Studies and World Affairs
Journal of Interdisciplinary History
Journal of International Business Studies
Journal of International Money and Finance
Journal of Latin American Studies
Journal of Media Economics
Journal of Money Credit and Banking
Journal of Nutrition
Journal of Policy Modeling
Journal of Political Economy
Journal of Regional Science
Journal of Rural Studies
Journal of Southeast Asian Studies
Journal of the History of Economic Thought
Kyklos
Latin American Economics Abstracts
Latin American Politics and Society
Latin American Research Review
Malayan Economic Review
Middle East Journal
Millennium-Journal of International Studies
National Geographic Research
NBER Working Paper Series
New England Economic Review
Nova Economia
Open Economies Review
Oxford Bulletin of Economics and Statistics
Oxford Economic Papers-New Series
Political Research Quarterly
Political Studies
Proceedings of the Academy of Political Science
Public Finance-Finances Publiques
Public Policy
Quarterly Review of Economics and Business
Quarterly Review of Economics and Finance
Revista de Econonomia Contemporânea
Rationality and Society
Regional Science and Urban Economics
Regional Studies
Revista Brasileira de Economia
Review of Development Economics
Review of Economics and Statistics
Review of International Political Economy

Continued

Table 19 A.2   Continued

Review of Social Economy
Revista Adusp
Revista Brasileira de Economia
Revista de Economía del Rosario
Revista de la CEPAL
Revista Portuguesa de Educação
Revue Canadienne d Etudes du Developpement
São Paulo Perspec
Science & Society
Scientia Agricola
Serie Ensayos
Social and Economic Studies
Social Indicators Research
Social Science History
Society & Natural Resources
South African Journal of Economics
Southern Economic Journal
Stanford Journal of International Law
Stanford Law Review
Studies in Comparative International Development
Studies in Comparative International Development (SCID)
Systems Analysis Modelling Simulation
Tempo Social
The Academy of Management Review
The Annals of Regional Science
The Developing Economies
The Quarterly Review of Economics and Finance
Third World Quarterly
Thunderbird International Business Review
Transactions of the American Philosophical Society
Transactions of the Institute Of British Geographers
Transportation
Trimestre Economico
Urban Studies
Weltwirtschaftliches Archiv-Review of World Economics
Western Economic Journal
World Development
World Politics
Zeitschrift Fur Nationalokonomie-Journal of Economics

Notes

I would like to acknowledge the skillful help of Patricia Morales, undergraduate student of Economics at FEA/USP, in organizing the data on citations.

1. http://scholar.google.com.br/
2. http://www.thomsonisi.com/, accessed from http://www.capes.gov.br/capes/portal/

References

Azzoni, C.R. (1998) "Clássicos da literatura econômica brasileira," *Economia Aplicada*, 2, 771–780.

Azzoni, C.R. (2000) "Desempenho das revistas e dos departamentos de economia brasileiros segundo publicações e citações recebidas no Brasil," *Economia Aplicada*, 4, 787–822.

Azzoni, C.R. (2001) "Onde Vender o Peixe? Repercussão das Principais Revistas Brasileiras de Economia na Virada do Século," *Economia Aplicada*, 5, 885–894.

Durden, G.C., and L.V. Ellis (1993) "A Method for Identifying the Most Influential Articles in an Academic Discipline," *Atlantic Economic Journal*, 21, 1–10.

Faria, J.R. (2000) "The Research Output of Academic Economists in Brazil," *Economia Aplicada*, 4, 95–113.

Issler, J.V., and Ferreira, R.C. (2004) "Avaliando pesquisadores e departamentos de economia no Brasil a partir de citações internacionais," *Pesquisa e Planejamento Econômico*, 34, 491–538.

Kostoff, R.N. (1998) "The Use and Misuse of Citation Analysis in Research Evaluation – Comments on Theories of Citation," *Scientometrics*, 43, 27–43.

Laband, D.N. (1990) "Measuring the Relative Impact of Economics Book Publishers and Economics Journals," *Journal of Economic Literature*, 28, 237–253.

Lederberg, J. (1972) "Reply to H. V. Wyant," *Nature*, 239, 5369, 234.

Macroberts, M.H., and B.R. Macroberts (1987) "Testing the Ortega Hypothesis: Facts and Artifacts," *Scientometrics*, 12, 293–295.

Moed, H.F., T.N. Van Leeuwen, and J. Reedijk (1998) "A New Classification System to Describe the Ageing of Scientific Journals and Their Impact Factors," *Journal of Documentation*, 54, 387–419.

Nederhof, A.J., and E. Van Vijk (1999) "Profiling Institutes: Identifying High Research Performance and Social Relevance in the Social and Behavioral Sciences," *Scientometrics*, 44, 487–506.

Nisonger, T.E. (1999) "JASIS and Library and Information Science Journal Rankings: A Review and Analysis of the Last Half-Century," *Journal of the American Society for Information Science*, 50, 1004–1019.

Osareh, F. (1996) "Bibliometrics, Citation Analysis and Co-Citation Analysis: A Review of the Literature," *Libri*, 46, 149–158.

Phelan, T. J. (1999) "A Compendium of Issues for Citation Analysis," *Scientometrics*, 45, 117–136.

Ratnatunga, J., and C. Romano (1997) "A 'Citation Classics' Analysis of Articles in Contemporary Small Enterprise Research," *Journal of Business Venturing*, 12, 197–212.

Stegmann, J. (1999) "Building a List of Journals with Constructed Impact Factors," *Journal of Documentation*, 55, 310–324.

Index